Artificial Life Models in Software

Andrew Adamatzky and
Maciej Komosinski (Eds)

Artificial Life Models in Software

With 189 Figures

 Springer

Andrew Adamatzky, DSc, MSc
Faculty of Computing,
Engineering and Maths Sciences
University of the West of England
Bristol, UK

Maciej Komosinski, PhD
Institute of Computing Science
Poznan University of Technology
Poznan, Poland

British Library Cataloguing in Publication Data
A catalogue record for this book is available from the British Library

Library of Congress Control Number: 2005926657

ISBN-10: 1-85233-945-4   Printed on acid-free paper.
ISBN-13: 978-1-85233-945-6

© Springer-Verlag London Limited 2005
Apart from any fair dealing for the purposes of research or private study, or criticism or review, as permitted under the Copyright, Designs and Patents Act 1988, this publication may only be reproduced, stored or transmitted, in any form or by any means, with the prior permission in writing of the publishers, or in the case of reprographic reproduction in accordance with the terms of licences issued by the Copyright Licensing Agency. Enquiries concerning reproduction outside those terms should be sent to the publishers.

The use of registered names, trademarks, etc. in this publication does not imply, even in the absence of a specific statement, that such names are exempt from the relevant laws and regulations and therefore free for general use.

The publisher makes no representation, express or implied, with regard to the accuracy of the information contained in this book and cannot accept any legal responsibility or liability for any errors or omissions that may be made.

Printed in the United States of America.   (EB)

9 8 7 6 5 4 3 2 1

Springer Science+Business Media
springeronline.com

Preface

Artificial life is an interdisciplinary field of science, hosting experts from computer science, biology, physics, chemistry, and mathematics, as well as philosophers and artists. It focuses on studying the phenomena of life on all levels of complexity and organization — molecular, cellular, organismic, and population. These studies not only employ conventional computers (using both software and hardware), but also take place in wetware, using techniques of biochemical laboratory. Artificial life research is not limited to life forms existing on the Earth. It rather attempts to study the general principles of life which are common to all instances of life, both already recognized and yet unknown.

This book is dedicated to the software medium, the most popular and widely employed in the artificial life research. The software medium offers almost unlimited abilities for experiments, which are cheap, easily arranged, and modified. Additionally, such experiments can be repeated under the same conditions, and large amounts of data (unavailable in biological studies) can be collected for analysis. To begin experimentation, a model of life is required. Such models are built in software for all organizational levels of life. Most of the models described in this book are very general and therefore allow for a wide range of experiments.

Researchers, academicians and students in artificial life use specialized software to verify their ideas related to evolution dynamics, self-organization, origins of life, multicellular development, natural and artificial morphogenesis, intelligent autonomous robotics, evolutionary robotics, evolvable hardware, emergent collective behaviors, swarm intelligence, evolution of communication and evolution of social behaviors. Artificial life software systems are also essential tools in practical demonstrations in undergraduate and postgraduate courses in adaptive systems, evolutionary biology, collective robotics, and nature-inspired computing.

This monograph provides an introduction and guidance in modern, attractive software tools for modeling and simulation of life-like phenomena. Software projects covered here are still actively developed and supported by the developers, who create their programs with both professional and amateur users in mind. In most cases, the simulators are employed in research, and results are published. Each chapter describes a single — usually free-to-use — software model, but references to other similar software packages and related scientific works are included as well. The origins of software packages, milestones in their development, and the most important or interesting experiments are also reported.

Every chapter is self-consistent and can be read independently. The compendium of chapters is split into four parts. The first part — Virtual Living Worlds, focuses on individual creatures and their populations. It includes discussions of *Avida*: a digital laboratory for studying populations of evolving programs; *Framsticks*: a model of three-dimensional creatures, their simulation, evolution, and experimentation with would-be animals and prototypes of bio-inspired robots; *Nerve Garden*: an Internet-based virtual terrarium reminiscent of a simple ecosystem; *GenePool*: an interactive software for experimenting with aesthetics-based sexual selection and evolution of swimming organisms; and *Sodarace*: an online-based interface, learning support and environment for construction, experimenting and competition between virtual two-dimensional mobile robots.

Dynamics of collectives of simple locally interacting entities is dealt with in the second part — Collective Artificial Life. There, we find discussion of several unique software (and also hardware) platforms — *Repast*: an advanced agent-based simulation toolkit for studying development of natural and artificial social structures; *EINSTein*: a multiagent-based simulator of land combat modeling individual behaviors and personalities of combatants; *StarLogo*: an educational programming language for simulation of life-like phenomena — from population dynamics to emergent behavior of complex systems; and *Eden*: an interactive artwork, including hardware implementation of cellular automata and agents, allowing observers to interact with the installation and influence the development of the artificial ecosystem.

Already mentioned in previous chapters, cellular automata — arrays of locally interacting finite automata, which update their states depending on the states of their neighbors, get a proper treatment in the third part — Magic of Discrete Worlds. Two remarkable software tools for studies of discrete universes are introduced here. *MCell* is a powerful explorer of cellular automata, which supports almost all known nontrivial cellular automaton rules and has a regularly updated database of old and newly discovered patterns. *Discrete Dynamics Lab (DDLab)* is an interactive tool for designing and investigating dynamics of discrete dynamical networks, including simulation of decision networks, generating attraction basins, and searching for mobile patterns.

The book completes — the fourth part — Artificial Life Arts, with two chapters raising aesthetical issues of would-be worlds. The first chapter of this part reveals ways to breed images and sounds using *SBEAT* (for graphics) and *SBART* (for music). These computer programs are designed to select and breed genotypes that represent graphical and musical pieces. The last chapter of the book searches for a phenomenological understanding of what makes artificial life appealing to scientists, artists and laymen, and why people become attracted to certain forms of creative computer art.

The Appendix contains a table that summarizes software systems described in this book. For each program, the table includes a short description, information about availability on various platforms and operating systems, software requirements, license type, and the Internet web site address.

The book covers hot topics related to computer science, evolutionary and computational biology, simulation, robotics, cognitive science, cybernetics, artificial intelligence, multiagent societies, virtual worlds, computer graphics and animation, neuroscience, and philosophy. We hope that academics, researchers, graduate students, and amateurs interested in these fields will find this monograph a valuable guide to artificial life and an excellent supplementary reading.

April 2005

Andrew Adamatzky
Maciej Komosinski

Contents

Part I Virtual Living Worlds

1 Avida: Evolution Experiments with Self-Replicating Computer Programs
Charles Ofria, Claus O. Wilke 3

2 Framsticks: A Platform for Modeling, Simulating, and Evolving 3D Creatures
Maciej Komosinski 37

3 Nerve Garden: Germinating Biological Metaphors in Net-based Virtual Worlds
Bruce Damer, Karen Marcelo, Frank Revi, Todd Furmanski, Chris Laurel 67

4 GenePool: Exploring the Interaction Between Natural Selection and Sexual Selection
Jeffrey Ventrella 81

5 Sodarace: Adventures in Artificial Life
Peter W. McOwan, Edward J. Burton 97

Part II Collective Artificial Life

6 Escaping the Accidents of History: An Overview of Artificial Life Modeling with Repast
Michael J. North, Charles M. Macal 115

7 EINSTein: A Multiagent-based Model of Combat
Andrew Ilachinski 143

8 StarLogo: A Programmable Complex Systems Modeling Environment for Students and Teachers
Andrew Begel, Eric Klopfer 187

9 On the Evolution of Sonic Ecosystems
Jon McCormack 211

Part III Magic of Discrete Worlds

10 Exploring Cellular Automata with MCell
Mirek Wojtowicz 233

11 Discrete Dynamics Lab: Tools for Investigating Cellular Automata and Discrete Dynamical Networks
Andrew Wuensche 263

Part IV Artificial Life Arts

12 Simulated Breeding — A Framework of Breeding Artifacts on the Computer
Tatsuo Unemi 301

13 Enriching Aesthetics with Artificial Life
Alan Dorin 323

A Appendix: Artificial Life Software
.... 337

Index 343

List of Contributors

Andrew Adamatzky
Faculty of Computing, Engineering
and Mathematical Sciences
University of the West of England
Bristol BS16 1QY UK
andrew.adamatzky@uwe.ac.uk

Andrew Begel
University of California
Berkeley, CA USA
abegel@cs.berkeley.edu

Edward J. Burton
Soda Creative Ltd.
London E2 8HD UK
ed@soda.co.uk

Bruce Damer
Biota.org Special Interest Group
P.O. Box 66866, Scotts Valley, CA
95067-6866 USA
bdamer@ccon.org

Alan Dorin
Center for Electronic Media Art,
School of Computer Science and
Software Engineering
Monash University
3800 Australia
aland@csse.monash.edu.au

Todd Furmanski
School of Cinema-Television
University of Southern California
LUC-310B Los Angeles, CA
90089-2211 USA
revontuli@aol.com

Andrew Ilachinski
The Center for Naval Analyses
Corporation, Virginia, USA
ilachina@cna.org

Eric Klopfer
Massachusetts Institute of Technology, Cambridge, MA, USA
kloper@mit.edu

Maciej Komosinski
Institute of Computing Science
Poznan University of Technology
Piotrowo 3A, 60-965 Poznan, Poland
maciej.komosinski@cs.put.poznan.pl

Chris Laurel
Contact Consortium, P.O. Box 66866
Scotts Valley, CA 95067-6866 USA

Charles Macal
Argonne National Laboratory, 9700
S. Cass Avenue, Argonne, IL, USA
macal@anl.gov

Karen Marcelo
Biota.org Special Interest Group
P.O. Box 66866, Scotts Valley, CA
95067-6866 USA

Jon McCormack
Centre for Electronic Media Art,
School of Computer Science and
Software Engineering
Monash University, Victoria, 3800
Australia
jonmc@csse.monash.edu.au

Peter W. McOwan
Computer Science, Queen Mary,
University of London, E1 4NS UK
pmco@dcs.qmul.ac.uk

Michael J. North
Argonne National Laboratory, 9700
S. Cass Avenue, Argonne, IL, USA
north@anl.gov

Charles Ofria
Department of Computer Science
and Engineering, Michigan State
University, East Lansing
MI 48840 USA
ofria@msu.edu

Frank Revi
Biota.org Special Interest Group
P.O. Box 66866, Scotts Valley, CA
95067-6866 USA

Tatsuo Unemi
Department of Information Systems
Science, Soka University
1-236 Tangi-machi, Hachiōji, Tokyo,
192-8577 Japan
unemi@iss.soka.ac.jp

Jeffrey Ventrella
Adobe Systems Incorporated
345 Park Avenue
San Jose, CA, 95110-2704 USA
jeffrey@ventrella.com

Claus O. Wilke
Keck Graduate Institute, 535 Watson
Drive, Claremont, CA 91711 USA
wilke@kgi.edu

Mirek Wojtowicz
wellCAM CCS s.c.
ul. B. Smialego 3-1
20-611 Lublin
Poland
info@mirekw.com

Andrew Wuensche
Faculty of Computing, Engineering
and Mathematical Sciences
University of the West of England
Bristol BS16 1QY UK
andy@ddlab.org

Part I

Virtual Living Worlds

1

Avida: Evolution Experiments with Self-Replicating Computer Programs

Charles Ofria and Claus O. Wilke

Avida* is a software platform for experiments with self-replicating and evolving computer programs. It provides detailed control over experimental settings and protocols, a large array of measurement tools, and sophisticated methods to analyze and postprocess experimental data. This chapter explains the general principles on which Avida is built, its main components and their interactions, and gives an overview of some prior research with Avida.

1.1 Introduction to Avida

When studying biological evolution, we have to overcome a large obstacle: Evolution happens extremely slowly. Traditionally, evolution has therefore been a field dominated by observation and theory, even though some regard the domestication of plants and animals as early, unwitting evolution experiments. Realistically, we can carry out controlled evolution experiments only with organisms that have very short generation times, so that populations can undergo hundreds of generations within a timeframe of months to a few years. With the advances in microbiology, such experiments in evolution have become feasible with bacteria and viruses [14, 39]. However, even with microorganisms, evolution experiments still take a lot of time to complete and are often cumbersome to carry out. In particular, certain data can be difficult or impossible to obtain, and it is often impractical to carry out enough replicas for high statistical accuracy.

According to Daniel Dennett, "evolution will occur whenever and wherever three conditions are met: replication, variation (mutation), and differential fitness (competition)" [9]. It seems to be an obvious idea to set up these conditions in a computer and to study evolution *in silico* rather than *in vitro*.

---

* Parts of the material in this chapter previously appeared in Artificial Life 10:191-229 (2004) by the chapter authors, and in the Avida documentation, whose coauthors also include C. Adami, R. Lenski and K. Nanlohy.

In a computer, it is easy to measure any quantity of interest with arbitrary precision, and the time it takes to propagate organisms for several hundred generations is only limited by the processing power available. In fact, population geneticists have long been carrying out computer simulations of evolving loci, in order to test or augment their mathematical theories (see [17,23,31] for some recent examples). However, the assumptions put into these simulations typically mirror exactly the assumptions of the analytical calculations. Therefore, the simulations can be used only to test whether the analytic calculations are error-free, or whether stochastic effects cause a system to deviate from its deterministic description, but they cannot test the model assumptions on a more basic level.

An approach to studying evolution that lies somewhere in between evolution experiments with biochemical organisms and standard Monte Carlo simulations is the study of self-replicating and evolving computer programs (digital organisms). These digital organisms can be quite complex and interact in a multitude of different ways with their environment or each other, so that their study is not a simulation of a particular evolutionary theory but becomes an experimental study in its own right. In recent years, research with digital organisms has grown substantially ([2,13,21,43,45,46]; see [41] for a recent review), and is being increasingly accepted by evolutionary biologists [30]. (However, as Barton and Zuidema [3] note, general acceptance will ultimately hinge on whether artificial life researchers embrace or ignore the large body of population-genetics literature.) Avida is arguably the most advanced software platform to study digital organisms to date and is certainly the one that has had the biggest impact in the biological literature so far. Having reached version 2.0, it now supports detailed control over experimental settings, a sophisticated system to design and execute experimental protocols, a multitude of possibilities for organisms to interact with their environment, including depletable resources and conversion from one resource into another, and a module to postprocess data from evolution experiments, including tools to find the line of descent from final organisms to their ultimate ancestor, to carry out knock-out studies with organisms, and to align and compare organisms' genomes.

1.1.1 History of Digital Life

The most well-known intersection of evolutionary biology with computer science is the genetic algorithm or its many variants (genetic programming, evolutionary strategies, and so on). All these variants boil down to the same basic recipe: (1) Create random potential solutions; (2) evaluate each solution assigning it a fitness value to represent its quality; (3) select a subset of solutions using fitness as a key criterion; (4) vary these solutions by making random changes or recombining portions of them; (5) repeat from step 2 until you find a solution that is sufficiently good.

This technique turns out to be an excellent method for solving problems, but it ignores many aspects of natural living systems. Most notably, natural organisms must replicate themselves, as there is no external force to do so; therefore, their ability to pass their genetic information on to the next generation is the final arbiter of their fitness. Furthermore, organisms in a natural system have the ability to interact with their environment and with each other in ways that are excluded from most algorithmic applications of evolution.

Work on more naturally evolving computational systems began in 1990, when Steen Rasmussen was inspired by the computer game "Core War" [10]. In this game, programs are written in a simplified assembly language and made to compete in the simulated core memory of a computer. The winning program is the one that manages to shut down all processes associated with its competitors. Rasmussen observed that the most successful of these programs were the ones that replicated themselves, so that if one copy were destroyed, others would still persist. In the original Core War game, the diversity of organisms could not increase, and hence no evolution was possible. Rasmussen then designed a system similar to Core War in which the command that copied instructions was flawed and would sometimes write a random instruction instead on the one intended [33]. This flawed copy command introduced *mutations* into the system, and thus the potential for evolution. Rasmussen dubbed his new program "Core World," created a simple self-replicating ancestor, and let it run.

Unfortunately, this first experiment failed. While the programs seemed to evolve initially, they soon started to copy code into each other, to the point where no proper self-replicators survived — the system collapsed into a nonliving state. Nevertheless, the dynamics of this system turned out to be intriguing, displaying the partial replication of fragments of code, and repeated occurrences of simple patterns.

The first successful experiment with evolving populations of self-replicating computer programs was performed the following year. Thomas Ray at the University of Delaware designed a program of his own with significant, biologically inspired modifications. The result was the Tierra system [34]. In Tierra, digital organisms must allocate memory before they have permission to write to it, which prevents stray copy commands from killing other organisms. Death only occurs when memory fills up, at which point the oldest programs are removed to make room for new ones to be born.

The first Tierra experiment was initialized with an ancestral program that was 80 lines long. It filled up the available memory with copies of itself, many of which had mutations that caused a loss of functionality. Yet other mutations were actually neutral and did not affect the organism's ability to replicate — and a few were even beneficial. In this initial experiment, the only selective pressure on the population was for the organisms to increase their rate of replication. Indeed, Ray witnessed that the organisms were slowly shrinking the length of their genomes, since a shorter genome meant that there was less genetic material to copy, and thus it could be copied more rapidly.

This result was interesting enough on its own. However, other forms of adaptation, some quite surprising, occurred as well. For example, some organisms were able to shrink further by removing critical portions of their genome and then use those same portions from more complete competitors, in a technique that Ray noted was a form of parasitism. Arms races transpired where hosts evolved methods of eluding the parasites, and they, in turn, evolved to get around these new defenses. Some would-be hosts, known as hyperparasites, even evolved mechanisms for tricking the parasites into aiding them in the copying of their own genomes. Evolution continued in all sorts of interesting manner, making Tierra seem like a choice system for experimental evolution work.

In 1992, Chris Adami began research on evolutionary adaptation with Ray's Tierra system. His intent was to get these digital organisms to evolve solutions to specific mathematical problems, without forcing them use a predefined approach. His core idea was the following: If he wanted a population of organisms to evolve, for example, the ability to add two numbers together, he would monitor organisms' input and output numbers. If an output ever was the sum of two inputs, the successful organisms would receive extra CPU cycles as a bonus. As long as the number of extra cycles was greater than the time it took the organism to perform the computation, the leftover cycles could be applied toward the replication process, providing a competitive advantage to the organism. Sure enough, Adami was able to get the organisms to evolve some simple tasks, but he faced many limitations in trying to use Tierra to study the evolutionary process.

In the summer of 1993, Charles Ofria and C. Titus Brown joined Adami to develop a new digital life software platform, the Avida system. Avida was designed to have detailed and versatile configuration capabilities, along with high-precision measurements to record all aspects of a population. Furthermore, whereas organisms are executed sequentially in Tierra, the Avida system simulates a parallel computer, wherein all organisms are executed effectively simultaneously. Since its inception, Avida has had many new features added to it, including a sophisticated environment with localized resources, an events system to schedule actions to occur over the course of an experiment, multiple types of CPUs to form the bodies of the digital organisms, and a sophisticated analysis mode to postprocess data from an Avida experiment. Avida is still under active development at both Michigan State University, led by Charles Ofria, and at the California Institute of Technology, led by Claus Wilke.

1.1.2 The Scientific Motivation for Avida

Intuitively, it seems that natural systems should be used to best understand how evolution produces complexity in nature, but this can be prohibitively difficult for many questions and does not provide enough detail. Using digital organisms in a system such as Avida can be justified on five grounds:

1. *Artificial life forms provide an opportunity to seek generalizations about self-replicating systems* beyond the organic forms that biologists have studied to date, all of which share a common ancestor and essentially the same chemistry of DNA, RNA, and proteins. As John Maynard Smith [22] made the case: "So far, we have been able to study only one evolving system and we cannot wait for interstellar flight to provide us with a second. If we want to discover generalizations about evolving systems, we will have to look at artificial ones." Of course, digital systems should always be studied in parallel with natural ones, but any differences we find between their evolutionary dynamics open up what is perhaps an even more interesting set of questions.

2. *Digital organisms enable us to address questions that are impossible to study with organic life forms.* For example, in one of our current experiments we are investigating the importance of genetic drift to the evolution of complexity by explicitly reverting all neutral mutations while leaving both beneficial and deleterious mutations unaffected. Such invasive micromanaging of a population is not possible in a natural system, especially without disturbing other aspects of the evolutionary process. In a digital evolving system, every bit of memory can be viewed without disrupting the system, and changes can be made at the precise points desired.

3. *Other questions can be addressed on a scale that is unattainable with natural organisms.* In an earlier experiment with digital organisms [20], we examined billions of genotypes to quantify the effects of mutations as well as the form and extent of their interactions. By contrast, an experiment with *E. coli* was necessarily confined to one level of genomic complexity. Digital organisms also have a speed advantage: A population with 10,000 organisms can have 20,000 generations processed per day on a modern desktop computer. A similar experiment with bacteria took over a decade [19].

4. *Digital organisms possess the ability to truly evolve, unlike mere numerical simulations.* Evolution is open-ended and the design of the evolved solutions is unpredictable. These properties arise because selection in digital organisms (as in real ones) occurs at the level of the whole-organism's phenotype; it depends on the rates at which organisms perform tasks that enable them to metabolize resources to convert them to energy, and the efficiency with which they use that energy for reproduction. Genome sizes are sufficiently large that evolving populations cannot test every possible genotype, so replicate populations always find different local optima. A genome typically consists of 50 to 1000 sequential instructions. With 26 possible instructions at each position, there are many more potential genome states than there are atoms in the universe.

5. *Digital organisms can be used to design solutions to computational problems* where it is difficult to write explicit programs that produce the desired behavior [15, 18]. Current evolutionary algorithm approaches are based on a simplistic view of evolution, leaving out many of the factors that are believed to make it such a powerful force. Thus there are new opportunities for biological concepts to have a large impact outside of biology, just as principles

of physics and mathematics are often used throughout other fields, including biology.

1.2 The Avida Software

The Avida software is composed of three main modules: The first is the *Avida core*, which maintains all of the key components needed for an experiment to run without user interaction, including a population of digital organisms (each with their own genomes, virtual hardware, etc.), an environment that determines the reactions and resources with which the organisms interact, a scheduler to allocate CPU cycles to the organisms, and various data collection objects. The second module is the *graphical user interface* (GUI) that the researcher can use to observe and interact with the rest of the Avida software, including a population monitor, graphing utilities, and other tools to measure or alter quantities in a population. The final component is a collection of *analysis and statistics* tools, including a test environment to study organisms outside the population, data manipulation tools to rebuild phylogenies and examine lines of descent, mutation and local fitness analysis tools, and many others, all bound together in a simple scripting language. A fourth module, an interactive help and documentation system, is currently under development.

In this section, we will discuss the core module of Avida, which is the only one needed to perform experiments with digital organisms. In the next section, we will go into the user tools to interact with an Avida population (the user interface) and postprocess the data that comes out of an experiment (the analyze mode).

1.2.1 Avida Organisms

In Avida, each digital organism is a self-contained computing automaton that has the ability to construct new automata. The organism is responsible for building the genome (computer program) that will control the offspring automaton and for transferring that genome to the Avida world. Avida will then construct virtual hardware for the genome to be run on, and determine how this new organism should be placed into the population. In a typical Avida experiment, a successful organism attempts to make an identical copy of its own genome, and Avida randomly places that copy into the population, typically by replacing another member of the population.

In principle, the only assumption made about these self-replicating automata in the core Avida software is that their initial state can be described by a string of symbols (their genome) and that it is possible through processing these symbols to autonomously produce offspring organisms. However, in practice, our work has focused on automata with a simple von Neumann architecture that operate on an assembly-like language inspired by the Tierra system. Future research projects will likely have us implement additional organism instantiations to allow us to explore additional biological questions.

In the following sections, we describe the default hardware of our virtual computers and explain the principles of the language these machines work on.

Virtual Hardware

The structure of a virtual machine in Avida is depicted in Fig. 1.1. The core of the machine is the central processing unit (CPU), which processes each instruction in the genome and modifies the states of its components appropriately. Mathematical operations, comparisons, and so on can be done on three registers: `AX`, `BX`, and `CX`. These registers each store and manipulate data in in the form of a single, 32-bit number. The registers behave identically, but different instructions may act on different registers by default (see below). The CPU also has the ability to store data in two stacks. Only one of the two stacks is active at a time, but it is possible to switch the active stack, so that both stacks are accessible.

The program memory is initialized with the genome of the organism. Execution begins with the first instruction in memory and proceeds sequentially: Instructions are executed one after the other, unless an instruction (such as a jump) explicitly interrupts sequential execution. Technically, the memory space is organized in a circular fashion, such that after the CPU executes the last instruction in memory, it will loop back and continue execution with the first instruction again. However, at the same time the memory has a well-defined starting point, important for the creation and activation of offspring organisms.

Somewhat out of the ordinary in comparison to standard von Neumann architectures are the four CPU components labeled *heads*. Heads are essentially pointers to locations in the memory. They remove the need of absolute addressing of memory positions, which makes the evolution of programs more robust to size changes that would otherwise alter these absolute positions. Among the four heads, only one, the instruction head, has a counterpart in standard computer architectures. The instruction head corresponds to the instruction pointer in standard architectures and identifies the instruction currently being executed by the CPU. It moves one instruction forward whenever the execution of the previous instruction has been completed, unless that instruction specifically moved the instruction head elsewhere.

The other three heads (the read head, the write head, and the flow control head) are unique to the Avida virtual hardware. The read and write heads are used in the self-replication process. In order to generate a copy of its genome, an organism must have a means of reading instructions from memory and writing them back to a different location. The read head indicates the position in memory from which instructions are currently being read, and the write head likewise indicates the position to which instructions are currently being written. The positions of all four heads can be manipulated with special

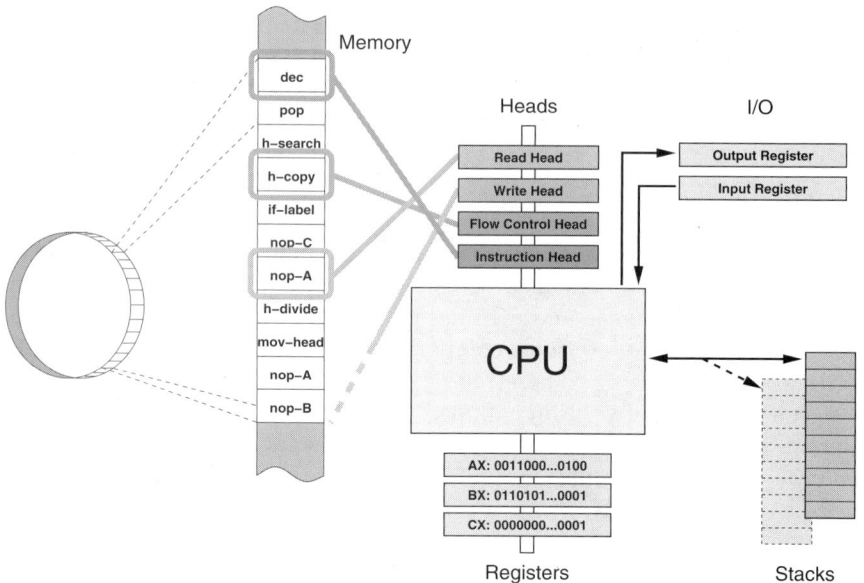

Fig. 1.1. The standard virtual hardware in Avida: CPU, registers, stacks, heads, memory, and I/O functionality.

commands. In that way a program can position the read and write heads appropriately in order to self-replicate.

The flow control head is used for jumps and loops. Several commands will reposition the flow control head, and other commands will move specific heads to the same position in memory as the flow control head.

Finally, the virtual machines have an input buffer and an output buffer, which they use to interact with their environment. The way in which this communication works is that the machines can read in one or several numbers from the input buffer, perform computations on these numbers with the help of the internal registers AX, BX, CX, and the stacks, and then write the results to the output buffer. This interaction with the environment plays a crucial role in the evolution of Avida organisms and will be explained in detail in Sec. 1.2.2.

Genetic Language

It is important to understand that there is not a single language that controls the virtual hardware of an Avida organism. Instead, we have a collection of different languages. The virtual hardware in its current form can execute hundreds of different instructions, but only a small fraction of them are used in a typical experiment. The instructions are organized into subsets of the full range of implemented instructions. We call these subsets *instruction sets*.

Each instruction set forms a logical unit and can be considered a complete genetic programming language.

Each instruction has a well-defined function in any context, that is, there are no syntactically incorrect programs. Instructions do not have arguments per se, but the behavior of certain instructions can be modified by succeeding instructions in memory. A genome is therefore nothing more than a sequence of symbols in an alphabet composed of the instruction set, similar to how DNA is a sequence made up of 4 nucleotides or proteins are sequences with an alphabet of 20 amino acids.

Here, we will give an overview of the default instruction set, which contains 26 instructions. This set is explained in greater detail in the Avida documentation, for those who wish to work with it.

Template Matching and Heads: One important ingredient of most Avida instruction sets is the concept of template matching. Template matching is a method of indirectly addressing a position in memory. This method is similar to the use of labels in many programming languages: Labels tag a position in the program, so that jumps and function calls always go to the correct place, even when other portions of the source code are edited. The same reasoning applies to Avida genomes, because mutations may cause insertions or deletions of instructions that shift the position of code segments and would otherwise jeopardize the positions referred to. Since there are no arguments to instructions, positions in memory are determined by series of subsequent instructions. We refer to a series of instructions that indicates a position in the genome as a *template*.

Template-based addressing works as follows. When an instruction is executed that must reference another position in memory, subsequent *nop* instructions (described ahead) are read in as the template. The CPU then searches linearly through the genome for the first occurrence of the complement to this template and uses the end of the complement as the position needed by the instruction. Both the direction of the search (forward or backward from the current instruction) and the behavior of the instruction if no complement is found are defined specifically for each instruction.

Avida templates are constructed out of no-operation (nop) instructions; that is, instructions that do not alter the state of either CPU or memory when they are directly executed. There are three template-forming NOPs, nop-A, nop-B, and nop-C. They are circularly complementary, i.e., the complement of nop-A is nop-B, the complement of nop-B is nop-C, and the complement of nop-C is nop-A. A template is composed of consecutive nops only. A template will end with the first non-nop instruction.

Nonlinear execution of code ("jumps") has to be implemented through clever manipulation of the different heads. This happens in two stages. First, the instruction h-search is used to position the flow control head at the desired position in memory. Then, the instruction head is moved to that position with the command mov-head. Figure 1.2 shows an example of this.

⋮		Some code.
10	h-search	Prepare the jump by placing the flow control head at the end of the complement template in forward direction.
11	nop-A	This is the template. Let's call it α.
12	nop-B	
13	mov-head	The actual jump. Move the flow control head to the position of the instruction head.
14	pop	Some other code that is skipped.
⋮		
18	nop-B	The complement template $\bar{\alpha}$.
19	nop-C	
⋮		The program continues ...

Fig. 1.2. Example code demonstrating flow control with heads-based instruction set.

Although this example looks somewhat awkward on first glance, evolution of control structures such as loops are actually facilitated by this mechanism. In order to loop over some piece of code, it is only necessary to position the flow control head correctly once and to have the command mov-head at the end of the block of code that should be looped over. Since there are several ways in which the flow control head can be positioned correctly, of which the above example is only a single one, there are many ways in which loops can be generated.

Nop's as Modifiers: The instructions in the Avida programming language do not have arguments in the usual sense. However, as we have seen above for the case of template matching, the effect of certain instructions can be modified if they are immediately followed by nop instructions. A similar concept exists for operations that access registers. The inc instruction, for example, increments a register by one. If inc is not followed by any nop, then by default it acts on the BX register. However, if a nop is present immediately after the inc, then the register on which inc acts is specified by the type of the nop. For example, inc nop-A increments the AX register and inc nop-C the CX register. Of course, inc nop-B increments the BX register, and hence works identical to a single inc command. Similar nop modifications exist for a range of instructions, such as those that perform arithmetic like inc or dec, stack operations such as push or pop, and comparisons such as if-n-equ. The details for specific instructions can be found in [29] or in the Avida documentation. For some instructions that work on two registers, in particular comparisons, the concept of the complement nop is important, because the two registers are specified in this way. Similarly to the nops in the template matching, registers are cyclically complementary to each other, i.e., BX is the complement to AX,

CX to BX, and AX to CX. The instruction if-n-equ, for example, acts on a register and its complement register. By default, if-n-equ compares whether the contents of the BX and CX registers are identical. However, if if-n-equ is followed by a nop-A, then it will compare AX and BX. Figure 1.3 shows a piece of example code that demonstrates the principles of nop modification and complement registers.

01	pop	We assume the stack is empty. In that case, the pop returns 0, which is stored in BX.
02	pop	Write 0 into the register AX as well.
03	nop-A	
04	inc	Increment BX.
05	inc	Increment AX.
06	nop-A	
07	inc	Increment AX a second time.
08	nop-A	
09	swap	The swap command exchanges the contents of a register with that of its complement register. Followed by a nop-C, it exchanges the contents of AX and CX. Now, BX= 1, CX= 2, and AX is undefined.
10	nop-C	
11	add	Now add BX and CX and store the result in AX.
12	nop-A	The program continues with BX= 1, CX= 2, and AX= 3.
⋮		

Fig. 1.3. Example code demonstrating the principle of nop modification.

Nop modification is also necessary for the manipulation of heads. The instruction mov-head, for example, by default moves the instruction head to the position of the flow control head. However, if it is followed by either a nop-B or a nop-C, it moves the read head or the write head, respectively. A nop-A following a mov-head leaves the default behavior unaltered.

Memory Allocation and Division: When a new Avida organism is created, the CPUs memory is exactly the size of its genome, i.e., there is no additional space that the organism could use to store its offspring-to-be as it makes a copy of its program. Therefore, the first thing an organism has to do at the start of self-replication is to allocate new memory. In the default instruction set, memory allocation is done with the command h-alloc. This command extends the memory by the maximal size that a child organism is allowed to have. As we will discuss later, there are some restrictions on how large or small a child organism is allowed to be in comparison to the parent organism, and the restriction on the maximum size of a child organism determines the amount of memory that `h-alloc` adds. The allocation happens always at a well-defined position in the memory. Although the memory is considered to be circular in the sense that the CPU will continue with the first instruction of the program once it has executed the last one, the virtual machine nevertheless keeps track of which instruction is the beginning of the program, and which is the end. By default, `h-alloc` (as well as all alternative memory allocation instructions, such as the old `allocate`) insert the new memory between the end and the beginning of the program. After the insertion, the new end is at the end of the inserted memory. The newly inserted memory is either initialized to a default instruction, typically `nop-A`, or to random code, depending on the choice of the experimenter.

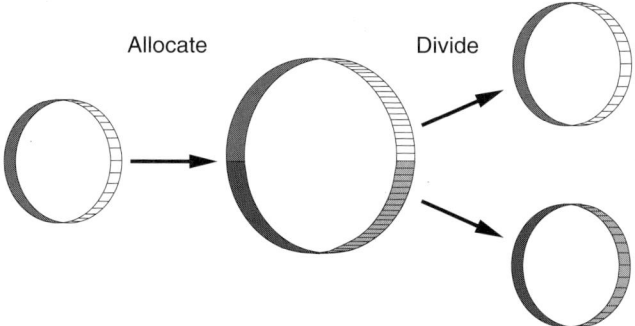

Fig. 1.4. The `h-alloc` command extends the memory, so that the program of the child organism can be stored. Later, on `h-divide`, the program is split into two parts, one of which turns into the child organism.

Once an organism has allocated memory, it can start to copy its program code into the newly available memory block. This copying is done with the help of the control structures we have already described, in conjunction with the instruction `h-copy`. This instruction copies the instruction at the position of the read head to the position of the write head and advances both heads. Therefore, for successful self-replication an organism mainly has to assure that initially, the read head is at the beginning of the memory, and the write head is at the beginning of the newly allocated memory, and then it has to call `h-copy` for the correct number of times.

After the self-replication has been completed, an organism issues the `h-divide` command, which splits off the instructions between the read head and the write head, and uses them as the genome of a new organism. The new organism is handed to the Avida world, which takes care of placing it into a suitable environment and so on. If there are instructions left between the write head and the end of the memory, these instructions are discarded, so that only the part of the memory from the beginning to the position of the read head remains after the divide.

In most natural asexual organisms, the process of division results in organisms literally splitting in half, effectively creating two offspring. As such, the default behavior of Avida is to reset the state of the parent's CPU after the divide, turning it back into the state it was in when it was first born. In other words, all registers and stacks are cleared, and all heads are positioned at the beginning of the memory. The allocation and division cycle is illustrated in Fig. 1.4.

Not all h-divide commands that an organism issues lead necessarily to the creation of an offspring organism. There are a number of conditions that have to be satisfied; otherwise the command will fail. Failure of a command means essentially that the command is ignored, while a counter keeping track of the number of failed commands in an organism is increased. It is possible to configure Avida to punish organisms with failed commands. The following conditions are in place: An h-divide fails if either the parent or the offspring would have less than 10 instructions, the parent has not allocated memory, less than half of the parent was executed, less than half of the offspring's memory was copied into, or the offspring would be too small or to large (as defined by the experimenter).

Mutations

So far, we have described all the elements that are necessary for self-replication. However, self-replication alone is not sufficient for evolution. There must be a source of variation in the population, which comes from random *mutations*.

The main form of mutations in Avida are so-called copy mutations, which arise through erroneously copied instructions. Such miscopies are a built-in property of the instruction h-copy. With a certain probability, chosen by the experimenter, the command h-copy does not properly copy the instruction at the location of the read head to the location of the write head, but instead writes a random instruction to the position of the write head. It is important to note that the instruction written will always be a legal one, in the sense that the CPU can execute it. However, the instruction may not be meaningful in the context in which it is placed in the genome, which in the worst case can render the offspring organism nonfunctional.

Another commonly used source of mutations are insertion and deletion mutations. These mutations are applied on h-divide. After an organism has successfully divided off a child organism, an instruction in the child's memory may by chance be deleted, or a random instruction may be inserted. The probabilities with which these events occur are again determined by the experimenter. Insertion and deletion mutations are useful in experiments in which frequent changes in genome size are desired. Two types of insertion/deletion mutations are available in the configuration files; they differ in that one is a genome-level rate and the other is a per-site rate.

Next, there are point (or cosmic ray) mutations. These mutations affect not only organisms as they are being created (like the other types described above), but all living organisms. Point mutations are random changes in the memory of the virtual machines. One of the consequences of point mutations is that a program may change while it is being executed. In particular, the longer a program runs, the larger target it is for point mutations. This is in contrast to copy or insertion and deletion mutations, whose impact depends only on the length of the program, but not on the execution time.

Finally, it is important to note that organisms in Avida can also have *implicit* mutations. Implicit mutations are modifications in a child's program that are not directly caused by any of the external mutation mechanisms described above, but rather by an incorrect copy algorithm of the parent organism. For example, the copy algorithm might skip some instructions of the parent program, or copy a section of the program twice (effectively a gene duplication event). Another example is an incorrectly placed read head or write head on divide. Implicit mutations are the only ones that cannot easily be controlled by the experimenter. They can, however, be turned off completely by using the FAIL_IMPLICIT option in the configuration files, which gets rid of any offspring that will always contain a deterministic difference from its parent, as opposed to one that is associated with an explicit mutation.

Phenotype

Each organism in an Avida population has a phenotype associated with it. Phenotypes of Avida organisms are defined in the same way as they are defined for organisms in the natural world: The phenotype of an organism comprises all observable characteristics of that organism. As an organism in Avida goes through its life cycle, it will self-replicate and, at the same time, interact with the environment. The primary mode of environmental interaction is by inputting numbers from the environment, performing computations on those numbers, and outputting the results. The organisms receive a benefit for performing specific computations associated with resources as determined by the experimenter.

In addition to tracking computations, the phenotype also monitors several other aspects of the organism's behavior, such as the organism's gestation length (the number of instructions the organism executes to produce an offspring, often also called *gestation time*), its age, if it has been affected by any mutations, how it interacts with other organisms, and its overall fitness. These data are used to determine how many CPU cycles should be allocated to the organism and also for various statistical purposes.

Genotypes

In Avida, organisms can be classified into several taxonomic levels. The lowest, but most important taxonomic level is called *genotype*. All organisms that have exactly the same initial genomes are considered to have the same genotype. Certain statistical data are collected only at the genotype level. We pay special attention to the most abundant genotype in the population — the *dominant* genotype — as a method of determining what the most successful organisms in the population are capable of. If a new genotype is truly more fit than than the dominant one, organisms with this higher fitness will rapidly take over the population.

We classify a genotype as *threshold* if there are three or more organisms that have ever existed of that genotype (again, the value 3 is not hard-coded, but configurable by the experimenter). Often, deleterious mutants appear in the population. These mutants are effectively dead and disappear again in short order. Since these mutants are not able to successfully self-replicate (or at least not well), there is a low probability of them reaching an abundance of three. As such, for any statistics we want to collect about the *living* portion of the population, we focus on those organisms whose genotype has the threshold characteristic.

1.2.2 The Avida World

In general, the Avida world has a fixed number N of positions or *cells*. Each cell can be occupied by exactly one organism, such that the maximum population size at any given time is N. Each of these organisms is being run on a virtual CPU, and some of them may be running faster than others. Avida has a scheduler (see below) that divides up time from the real CPU such that these virtual CPUs execute in a simulated parallel fashion.

While an Avida organism runs, it may interact with the environment or other organisms. When it finally reproduces, it hands its offspring organism to the Avida world, which places the newborn organism into either an empty or an occupied cell, according to rules we describe ahead. If the offspring organism is placed into an already occupied cell, the organism currently occupying that cell is killed and removed, irrespective of whether it has already reproduced or not.

Scheduling

In the simplest of Avida experiments, all virtual CPUs run at the same speed. This method of time sharing is simulated by executing one instruction on each of the N virtual CPUs in order, then starting over to execute a second instruction on each one, and so on. An *update* in Avida is defined as the point where the average organism has executed k instructions (where $k = 30$ by default). In this simple case, for one update we carry out k rounds of execution.

In more complex environments, however, the situation is not so trivial. Different organisms will have their virtual CPUs running at different speeds, and the scheduler must portion out cycles appropriately to simulate that all CPUs are running in parallel. Each organism has associated with it a value called *merit*. The merit indicates how fast the CPU should run. Merit is a unitless quantity and is only meaningful when compared to the merits of other organisms. Thus, if organism A has twice the merit of organism B, then A should execute twice as many instructions in any given timeframe as B.

Avida handles this with two different schedulers. The first one is a perfectly integrated scheduler, which comes as close as possible to portioning out CPU cycles proportional to merit. Obviously, only whole time steps can be used; therefore, perfect proportionality is not possible in general for small timeframes. For timeframes long enough such that the granularity of individual time steps can be neglected, the difference between the number of cycles given to an organism and the number of cycles the organism should receive according to its merit is negligible.

The second scheduler is probabilistic. At each point in time, the next organism to be selected is chosen at random, with a probability of being chosen proportional to its merit. Thus, *on average* this scheduler is perfect, but there are no guarantees.

In practice, the perfectly integrated scheduler is faster, but occasionally can cause odd effects, because it is possible for the organisms to become synchronized, particularly at low mutation rates where a single genotype can represent a large portion of the population. The stochastic scheduler may be preferred for projects where this effect might be a problem. By default, Avida uses the perfectly integrated scheduler.

World Topologies and Birth Methods

The N cells of the Avida world can be assembled into different topologies that affect how offspring organisms are placed and how organisms interact (as described ahead). Currently, there are two world topologies: a 2D grid with Moore neighborhood (each cell has 8 neighbors) and a fully connected (sometimes called *well-stirred* or *mass action*) topology. In the latter, fully connected topology, each cell is a neighbor to every other cell. New topologies can easily be implemented by listing the neighbors associated with each cell (though more work might need to be done in the user interface to properly visualize the new topology).

When a new organism is about to be born, it will replace either the parent cell or another cell from the neighborhood. The specifics of this placement are set up by the experimenter. The two most commonly used methods are *replace random*, which chooses randomly from the neighborhood, or *replace oldest*, which picks the oldest organism from the neighborhood to replace (with a preference for empty cells if any exist).

Fully connected topologies are used in analogy to experiments with microbes in well-stirred flasks or chemostats. These setups allow for exponential growth of new genotypes with a competitive advantage, so that transitions in the state of the population can happen rapidly. Local neighborhoods, on the other hand, are more akin to a Petri dish, and the spatial separation between different organisms puts limits on growth rates and allows for a slightly more diverse population [5].

In choosing which organism in a neighborhood to replace, a random placement matches up well with the behavior of a chemostat, where a random portion of the population is continuously drawn out to keep population size constant. Experiments have shown [1], however, that evolution occurs more rapidly when the oldest organism in a neighborhood is the first to be killed off. In such cases, all organisms are given approximately the same chance to prove their worth, whereas in random replacement, about half the organisms are killed before they have the opportunity to produce a single offspring. Interestingly, when replace oldest is used in 2D neighborhoods, 40% of the time it is the parent that is killed off. This observation makes sense, because the parent is definitely old enough to have produced at least one offspring.

Note that in the default setup of Avida, the only way for an organism to die is for it to be replaced by another organism being born. It is also possible to enable an independent death method that will kill off an organism after it has executed a specified number of instructions, which can be either a constant or proportional to the organism's genome length. In some cases a population without any form of death turned on can lose all ability to self-replicate, but persist since organisms have no way of being purged. This situation can lead to confusing results for the research if the cause is not identified.

Environment and Resources

All organisms in Avida are provided with the ability to absorb a default resource that gives them their base merit. An Avida environment can, however, contain other resources that the organisms can absorb to modify their merit. The organisms absorb a resource by carrying out the corresponding computation or *task*.

An Avida environment is described by a set of resources and a set of reactions that can be triggered to interact with those resources. A reaction is defined by a computation that the organism must perform to trigger it, a resource that is consumed by it, a merit effect on the organism (which can be proportional to the amount of resource absorbed or available), and a byproduct resource if one should be produced. Reactions can also have restrictions associated with them that limit when a trigger will be successful. For example, another reaction can be required to have been triggered first, or a limit can be placed on the number of times an organism can trigger a certain reaction.

A resource is described by an initial quantity (which can be infinite if a resource should not be depletable), an inflow rate (the amount of that resource that should come into the population per update), and an outflow rate (the fraction of the resource that should be removed each update). If resources are made to be depletable, then the more organisms trigger a reaction, the less of that resource is available for each of them. This setup allows multiple, diverse subpopulations to stably coexist in an Avida world [4, 6].

The default Avida environment rewards nine boolean logic operations, each associated with a nondepletable resource, but organisms can receive only one reward per computation. Other prebuilt environments that come with Avida include one with 78 different logic operations rewarded, one similar to the default nine-resource environment, but with the resources set up to be depletable, with fixed inflow and outflow rates, and one with nine computations rewarded, and where only the resources associated with the simplest computations have an inflow into the system, and those for more complex operations are produced as byproducts, in sequence, from the reactions using up resources associated to simpler computations.

An important aspect of Avida is that the environment does not care *how* a computation is performed, only that the output of the organism being tested is correct given the inputs it took in. As a consequence, the organisms find a wide variety of ways of computing their outputs, some of which can be surprising to a human observer, seeming to be almost inspired.

Even though organisms can carry out tasks and collect rewards at any time in their gestation cycle, these rewards do not immediately affect the speed at which their CPU runs. The CPU speed (merit) is set only once, at the beginning of the gestation cycle, and then held constant until the organism divides. At that point, both the organism and its offspring get a new merit, which reflects the bonuses the organism collected during the gestation cycle it just completed. In a sense, the organisms collect rewards that go to their offspring rather than for themselves. The reason why we do not change an organism's merit during its gestation cycle is to level the playing field between old and young organisms. If organisms were always born with a low initial CPU speed, then they might never execute enough instructions to carry out tasks in the first place. At the same time, mutants specialized in carrying out tasks but not dividing could concentrate all CPU time on them, thus effectively shutting down replication in the population. It can be shown that the average fitness of a population in equilibrium is independent of whether organisms get the bonuses directly or collect them for their offspring [40].

Organism Interactions

As explained above, populations in Avida have a firm cap on their size, which makes space the fundamental resource that the organisms must compete for. In the simplest Avida experiments, the only interaction between organisms is that an organism is killed when another gives birth, in order to make room for the offspring. In slightly more complex experiments, the organisms are rewarded with a higher merit and hence a larger share of the CPU cycles for performing tasks. Since only a fixed number of CPU cycles is given out each update, the competition for them becomes a second level of indirect interactions among the organisms. As the environment becomes more complex still, multiple resources take the place of fixed merit bonuses for performing tasks, and the organisms must now compete over each of these resources independently. In the end, however, all these interactions boil down to the indirect competition for space: More resources imply a higher merit, which in turn grants the organisms a larger share of the CPU cycles, allowing them to replicate more rapidly and claim more space for their genotype.

In most Avida experiments, indirect competition for space is the only level of interaction we allow; organisms are not allowed to directly write to or read from each other's genomes, so that Tierra-style parasites cannot form (although the configuration files do allow the experimenter to enable them). The more typical way of allowing parasites in Avida is to enable the `inject` command in the Avida instruction set. This command works similar to divide, except that instead of replacing an organism in a target cell, the would-be offspring is inserted into the memory of the organism occupying the target cell; the specific position in memory to which it is placed is determined by the template that follows the `inject`.

In Tierra, parasites can replicate more rapidly than nonparasites, but an individual parasite poses no direct harm to the host whose code it uses. These organisms could, therefore, be thought of more directly as cheaters in the classic biological sense, as they effectively take advantage of the population as a whole. In Avida, a parasite exists directly inside its host and makes use of the CPU cycles that would otherwise belong to the host, thereby slowing down the host's replication rate. Depending on the type of parasite, it can either take all of the host's CPU cycles (thereby killing the host) and use them for replicating and spreading the infection, or else spread more slowly by using only a portion of the hosts CPU cycles (sickening it), but reducing the probability of driving the hosts — and hence itself — into extinction.

In the future, we plan to implement two other forms of interactions. First, we plan to implement *sensors* with which organisms can detect the presence of resources, which would allow them to exchange chemical signals. Second, we are considering more direct *communication*, whereby the organisms can send numbers to each other, and possibly distribute computations among themselves to solve environmental challenges more rapidly.

1.2.3 Test Environments

Often when examining populations in Avida, the user will need to know the fitness or some other characteristic of an organism that has not yet gone through a full gestation cycle during the course of the experiment. For this reason, we have constructed a *test environment* for the organisms to be run in, without affecting the rest of the population. This test environment will run the organism for at least one generation and can be used either during a run or as part of post-processing.

When an organism is loaded into a test environment, its instructions are executed until it produces a viable offspring or until a timeout is reached.

Unfortunately, it is not possible to guarantee identification of nonreplicative organisms (this is known as the halting problem in computer science), so at some point we must give up on any program we are testing and assume it to be dead. If age-based death is turned on in the actual population, this becomes a good limit for how long a CPU in the test environment should be run.

The fact that we want to determine if an organism is viable can also cause some problems in a test environment. For example, we might determine that an organism does produce an offspring but that this offspring is not identical to itself. In this case, we take the next step of continuing to run the offspring in the test environment, and if necessary its offspring until we find either a self-replicator or a sustainable cycle. By default, we will only test three levels of offspring before we assume the original organism to be nonviable. Such cases happen very rarely, and not at all if implicit mutations are turned on.

Two final problems with the test environments include that they do not properly reflect the levels of limited resources (resource levels can be difficult to estimate, particularly if we are postprocessing) and that they do not handle any special interactions with other organisms since only one is being tested at a time. Both of these issues are currently being examined and we plan to have a much improved test environment in the future. Test environments do, however, work remarkably well in most circumstances.

In addition to reconstructing statistics about organisms as they existed in the population, it is also possible to determine how an organism would have fared in an alternate environment, or even to construct entirely new genomes to determine how they perform. This last approach includes techniques such as performing all single-point mutations on a genome and testing each result to determine what its local fitness landscape looks like, or to artificially crossover pairs of organisms to determine their viability. Test environments are most commonly used in the postprocessing of Avida data, as described in the next section.

1.3 Using Avida

The Avida software currently runs under all three major operating systems: Windows XP, Mac OS X, and Linux. The current version of Avida (including both stable releases and development versions) is available at http://sourceforge.net/projects/avida/.

Avida can be run either in an experimental mode, in which a population evolves under the experimental regimme designed by the user, or in an analyze mode in which the user can postprocess their data to a form more useful for them. Both of these modes are explained ahead.

1.3.1 Performing Avida Experiments

Currently there are two main methods of running Avida — either with the graphical user interface (GUI) or in primitive mode (which is faster, but the user must pre-script the complete experimental protocol). Researchers will often use the GUI to get an intuitive feel of how an experiment works, but then they will shift to the primitive mode when they are ready to perform more exensive data collection.

The configuration of an Avida experiment requires either using the "Configuration Wizard" in the GUI, or manual editing of five different initialization files. The most important of these is the *genesis* file, which contains a list of variables that control all of the basic settings of a run, including the population size, the mutation rates, and the names of all of the other configuration files to use. Next, we have the *instruction set*, which describes the specific genetic language used in the experiment. Third is the *ancestral organism* that the population should be seeded with. Fourth, we have the *environment* file that describes which resources are available to the organisms and defines reactions by the tasks that trigger them, their value, the resource that they use, and any byproducts that they produce. The final configuration file is *events*, which is used to describe specific actions that should occur at designated time points during the experiment, including most data collection and any direct disruptions to the population. Each of these files is described in more detail in the Avida documentation.

Once Avida has been properly installed, and the configuration files set up, it can be started in primitve mode by going into the work/ directory and typing `primitive` on the command line (or else by clicking on the corresponding icon). Some basic information will scroll by on the screen (specifically, current update being processed, number of generations, average fitness, and current population size). When the experiment has completed, the process will terminate automatically, leaving a set of output files that describe the completed experiment. Each output file begins with an index describing the contents of that file.

Running the graphical version of Avida differs by platform but is well described in the documentation that is contained within the appropriate version. When Avida is started, it will give the option to use pre-existing configuration files (which can be set up in the same way as for the primitive mode), or else by running the configuration wizard, which will take the user step-by-step through all of the choices necessary to specifying an experimental protocol. The wizard can operate in two different modes, a basic mode, where only a few simple questions need to be answered, or a more advanced mode that provides access to all settings of Avida.

The first window that opens once Avida has started displays a view of the whole population, as shown in Fig. 1.5. This screen provides a pull-down menu that allows the user to choose what information should be displayed about each organism, such as its genotype, its fitness, or its age. Several other Avida viewers can also be launched from this screen. These viewers include graphs of data being collected, an instruction viewer to demonstrate how individual organisms function (as shown in Fig. 1.6), editors to control events

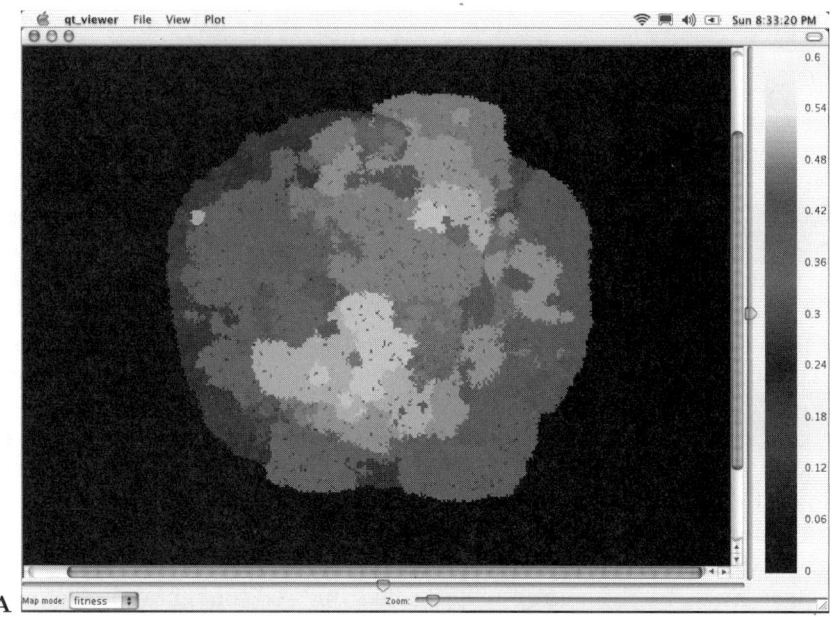

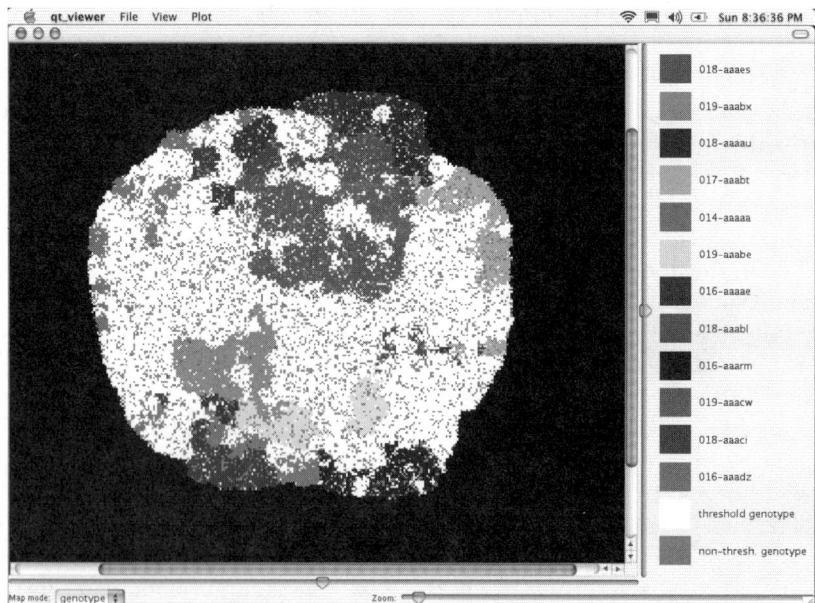

Fig. 1.5. The grid viewer from a typical Avida experiment. (A) Fitness map. (B) Genotype map.

or the environment, or even additonal map viewers (if multiple aspects of the population should be displayed at the same time).

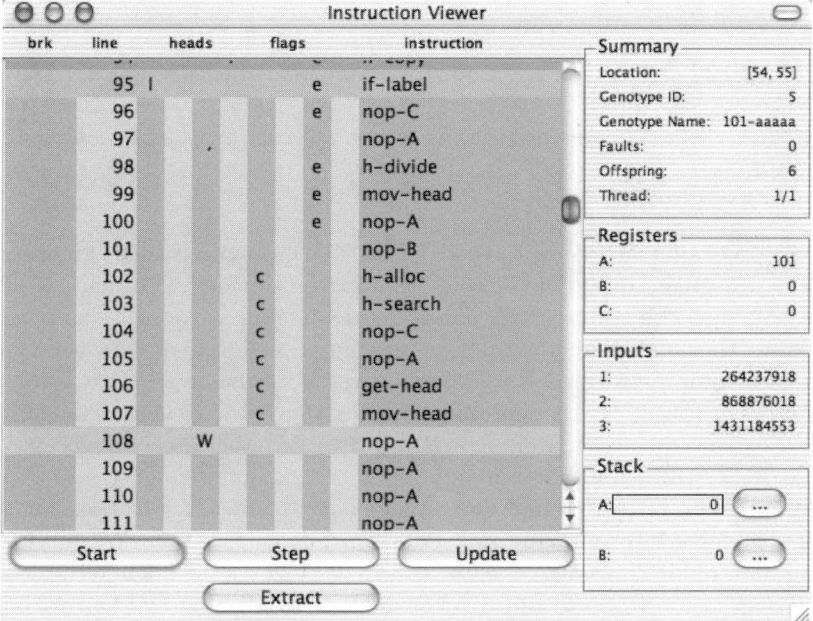

Fig. 1.6. A viewer window that allows the user to focus on a single Avida organism and monitor it as it executes its genome.

The graphical interface to Avida is currently under heavy development, with many new visualization tools expected to be introduced in the near future, as well as an extensive help and tutorial system, and an easy interface to the analysis tools described in the next section.

1.3.2 Analyze Mode

Avida has an analysis-only mode (short *analyze mode*), which allows for powerful postprocessing of data. Avida is brought into the analyze mode by the command-line parameter "-a". In the analyze model, Avida processes the analyze file specified in the genesis file ("analyze.cfg" by default). The analyze file contains a program written in a simple scripting language. The structure of the program involves loading in genotypes in one or more *batches*, and then either manipulating single batches, or doing comparisons between batches.

In the following paragraphs, we present a couple of example programs that will illustrate the basics of the analyze scripting language. A full list of commands available in analysis mode is given in the Avida documentation.

Testing a Genome Sequence

The following program will load in a genome sequence, run it in a test environment, and output the results of the tests in a couple of formats.

```
VERBOSE
LOAD_SEQUENCE rmzavcgmciqqptqpqcpctletncogcbeamqdtqcptipqfpg
RECALCULATE
DETAIL detail_test.dat fitness merit length viable sequence
TRACE
PRINT
```

The program starts off with the VERBOSE command, which causes Avida to print to screen all details of what is going on during the execution of the analyze script; the command is useful for debugging purposes. The program then uses the LOAD_SEQUENCE command to define a specific genome sequence in compressed format. (The compressed format is used by Avida in a number of output files. The mapping from instructions to letters is determined by the instruction set file and may change if the instruction set file is altered.)

The RECALCULATE command places the genome sequence into the test environment and determines the organism's fitness, merit, gestation time, and so on. The DETAIL command that follows prints this information into the file "detail_test.dat". (This filename is specified as the first argument of DETAIL.) The TRACE and PRINT commands will then print individual files with data on this genome, the first tracing the genome's execution line by line, and the second summarizing several test results and printing the genome line by line. Since no directory was specified for these commands, "genebank/" is assumed, and the filenames are "org-S1.trace" and "org-S1.gen". If a genotype has a name when it is loaded, then that name will be kept. Otherwise, it will be assigned a name starting with "org-S1", then "org-S2", and so on. The TRACE and PRINT commands add their own suffixes (".trace" and ".gen") to the genome's name to determine the filenames they will use.

Finding Lineages

The portion of an Avida run that we will often be most interested in is the lineage from a genotype (typically the final dominant genotype) back to the original ancestor. There are tools in the analyze mode to obtain this information, if the necessary population and ancestral dumps have been written out with the events `detail_pop` and `dump_historic_pop`. The following program demonstrates how to make use of these dump files.

```
FORRANGE i 100 199
    SET d /home/charles/dev/Avida/runs/evo-neut/evo_neut_$i
    PURGE_BATCH
    LOAD_DETAIL_DUMP $d/detail_pop.100000
```

```
    LOAD_DETAIL_DUMP $d/historic_dump.100000
    FIND_LINEAGE num_cpus
    RECALCULATE
    DETAIL lineage.$i.html depth parent_dist html.sequence
END
```

The FORRANGE command runs the contents of the loop once for each possible value in the range, setting the variable i to each of these values in turn. Thus the first time through the loop, 'i' will be equal to the value 100, then 101, 102, and so on, all the way up to 199. In this particular case, we have 100 runs (numbered 100 through 199) we want to work with.

The first thing we do once we are inside the loop is to set the value of the variable 'd' to be the name of the directory we are going to be working with. Since this directory name is long, we do not want to have to type it every time we need it. If we set it to the variable 'd', then all we need to do is to type "$d" in the future. Note that in this case we are setting a variable to a string instead of a number; that is fine, and Avida will figure out how to handle the contents of the variable properly. The directory we are working with changes each time the loop is executed, since the variable 'i' is part of the directory name.

We then use the command PURGE_BATCH to get rid of all genotypes from the last execution of the loop (lest we are not accumulating more and more genotypes in the current batch), and refill the batch by using LOAD_DETAIL_DUMP to load in all genotypes saved in the file "detail_pop.100000" within our chosen directory. A detail file contains all of the genotypes that were currently alive in the population at the time the detail file was printed, while a historic file (the next one loaded) contains all of the genotypes that are ancestors of those that are still alive. The combination of these two files gives us the lineages of the entire population back to the original ancestor. Since we are only interested in a single lineage, we next run the FIND_LINEAGE command to pick out a single genotype, and discard everything else except for its lineage. In this case, we pick the genotype with the highest abundance (i.e., the highest number of organisms, or virtual CPUs, associated with it) at the time of output.

As before, the RECALCULATE command gets us any additional information we may need about the genotypes, and then we print that information to a file using the DETAIL command. The filenames that we are using this time have the format "lineage.$i.html", that is, they are all being written to the current directory, with filenames that incorporate the run number. Also, because the filename ends in the suffix ".html", Avida prints the file in html format, rather than in plain text. Note that the specific values that we choose to print take advantage of the fact that we have a lineage (and hence have measured things like the genetic distance to the parent) and are in html mode (and thus can print the sequence using colors to specify where exactly mutations occurred).

These examples are only meant to present the reader with an idea of the types of analyses available in this built-in scripting language. Many more are possible, but a more exhaustive discussion of these possibilities is beyond the scope of this chapter.

1.4 A Summary of Avida Research

Avida has been used in several dozen peer-reviewed scientific publications, including some in *Nature* [20, 21, 43] and *Science* [4]. We describe a few of our more interesting efforts ahead.

1.4.1 The Evolution of Complex Features

When Darwin first proposed his theory of evolution by natural selection, he realized that it had a problem explaining the origins of the vertebrate eye [7]. Darwin noted that "In considering transitions of organs, it is so important to bear in mind the probability of conversion from one function to another." That is, populations do not evolve complex new features *de novo*, but instead modify existing, less complex features for use as building blocks of the new feature. Darwin further hypothesized that "Different kinds of modification would [...] serve for the same general purpose," noting that just because any one particular complex solution may be unlikely, there may be many other possible solutions, and we only witness the single one lying on the path evolution took. As long as the aggregate probability of all solutions is high enough, the individual probabilities of the possible solutions are almost irrelevant.

Substantial evidence now exists that supports Darwin's general model for the evolution of complexity (e.g., [8, 16, 25, 26, 44]), but it is still difficult to provide a complete account of the origin of any complex feature due to the extinction of the intermediate forms, imperfection of the fossil record, and incomplete knowledge of the genetic and developmental mechanisms that produce such features. Digital evolution allowed us to surmount these difficulties and track all genotypic and phenotypic changes during the evolution of a complex trait with enough replication to obtain statistically powerful results [21]. We isolated the computation EQU (logical equals) as a complex trait, and showed that at least 19 coordinated instructions are needed to perform this task. We then performed an experiment that consisted of 100 independent populations of digital organisms being evolved for approximately 17,000 generations. We evolved 50 of these populations in a control environment where EQU was the only task rewarded; we evolved the other 50 in a more complex environment where an assortment of 8 simpler tasks were rewarded as well, to test the importance of intermediates in the evolution of a complex feature.

Results: In 23 of the 50 experiments in the complex environment, the EQU task was evolved, whereas *none* of the 50 control populations evolved

EQU, illustrating the critical importance of features of intermediate complexity ($P \approx 4.3 \times 10^{-9}$, Fisher's exact test). Furthermore, all 23 implementations of the complex trait were unique, with many quite distinct from each other in their approach, indicating that, indeed, this trait had numerous solutions. This observation is not surprising, since even the shortest of the implementations found were extraordinarily unlikely (approximately 1 in 10^{27}). We further analyzed these results by tracing back the line of descent for each population to find the critical mutation that first produced the complex trait. In each case, these random mutations transformed a genotype unable to perform EQU into one that could, and even though these mutations typically affected only 1 to 2 positions in the genome, a median of 28 instructions were required to perform this complex task — a change in any of these instruction would cause the task to be lost, thus it was complex from the moment of its creation. It is noteworthy to mention that in 20 of the 23 cases the critical mutations would have been detrimental if EQU were not rewarded, and in three cases the prior mutation was actively detrimental (causing the replication rate for the organisms to drop by as much as half), yet turned out to be critical for the evolution of EQU; when we reverted these seemingly detrimental mutations, EQU was lost.

1.4.2 Survival of the Flattest

When organisms have to evolve under high mutation pressure, their evolutionary dynamics is substantially different from that of organisms evolving under low mutation pressure, and some of the high-mutation-rate effects can appear paradoxical at first glance. Most of population genetics theory has been developed under the assumption that mutation rates are fairly low, which is justified for the majority of DNA-based organisms. However, RNA viruses, the large class of viruses that cause diseases such as the common cold, influenza, HIV, SARS, or Ebola, tend to suffer high mutation rates, up to 10^{-4} substitutions per nucleotide and generation [12]. The theory describing the evolutionary dynamics at high mutation rates is called quasispecies theory [11].

The main prediction for the evolutionary process at high mutation rates is that selection acts on a cloud of mutants, rather than on individual sequences. We tested this hypothesis in Avida [43]. First, we let strains of digital organisms evolve to both a high-mutation-rate and a low-mutation-rate environment. The rationale behind this initial adaptation was that strains that evolved at a low mutation rate should adapt to ordinary individual-based selection, whereas strains that evolved at a high mutation rate should adapt to selection on mutant clouds, which means that these organisms should maximize the overall replication rate of their mutant clouds, rather than their individual replication rates. This adaptation to maximized overall replication rate under high mutation pressure takes place when organisms trade individual fitness for mutational robustness, so that their individual replication rate is reduced but in return the probability that mutations cause further reduction in the replication rate is also reduced [42]. Specifically, we took 40 strains of already evolved digital organisms, and let each evolve for an additional 1000 generations in both a low-mutation-rate and a high-mutation-rate environment. As result, we ended up with 40 pairs of strains. The two strains of each pair were genetically and phenotypically similar, apart from the fact that one was adapted to a low and one to a high mutation rate. As expected, we found that in the majority of cases the strains evolved at a high mutation rate had a lower replication speed than the ones evolved at a low mutation rate.

Next, we let the two types of strains compete with each other, in a setup where both strains would suffer from the same mutation rate, which was either low, intermediate, or high. Not surprisingly, at a low mutation rate the strains adapted to that mutation rate consistently outcompeted the ones adapted to a high mutation rate, since after all the former ones had the higher replication rate (we excluded those cases in which the strain evolved at a low mutation rate had a lower or almost equal fitness to the strain evolved at a high mutation rate). However, without fail, the strain adapted to a high mutation rate could win the competition if the mutation rate during the competition was sufficiently high [43]. This result may sound surprising at first, but it has a very simple explanation. At a high mutation rate (1 mutation per genome per generation or higher), the majority of an organism's offspring differ genetically from their parent. Therefore, if the parent is genetically very brittle, so that most of these mutants have a low replication rate or are even lethal, then the overall replication rate of all the organism's offspring will be fairly moderate, even though the organism itself may produce offspring at a rapid pace. If a different organism produces offspring at a slower pace, but is more robust towards mutations, so that the majority of this organism's offspring have a replication rate similar to that of their parent, then the overall replication rate of this organism's offspring will be larger than the one of the first organism. Hence, this organism will win the competition, even though it is the slower replicator. We termed this effect the "survival of the flattest," because at a sufficiently high mutation rate a strain that is located on a low but flat fitness peak can outcompete one that is located on a high but steep fitness peak.

1.4.3 Evolution of Digital Ecosystems

The experiments discussed above both used single-niche Avida populations, but evolutionary design is more interesting (and more powerful) when we consider ecosystems. The selective pressures that cause the formation and diversity of ecosystems are still poorly understood [36, 38]. In part, the lack of progress is due to the difficulty of performing precise, replicated, and controlled experiments on whole ecosystems [24]. To study simple ecosystems in a laboratory microcosm (reviewed in [39]), biologists often use a chemostat, which slowly pumps resource rich media into a flask containing bacteria, while simultaneously draining the flask's contents to keep the volume constant. Unfortunately, even in these simple model systems, ecosystems can evolve to be more complex than is experimentally tractable, and understanding their formation remains difficult [27, 28, 32].

We set up Avida experiments based on this chemostat model [6] wherein 9 resources flow into the population, and 1% of unused resources flow out. We used populations with 2500 organisms, each of which absorbed a small portion of an available resource whenever they performed the corresponding task. If too many organisms focus on the same resource, it will no longer be plentiful enough to encourage additional use.

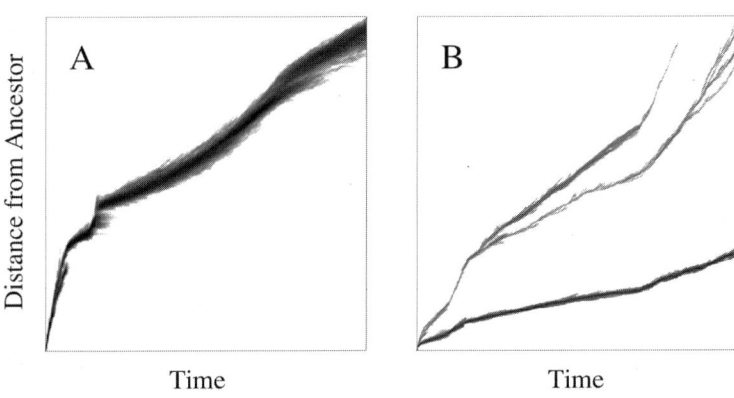

Fig. 1.7. Visualizations of phylogenies from the evolution of (A) a single niche population, and (B) a population with limited resources (and hence multiple niches). The x-axis represents time, while the y-axis is depth in the phylogeny (distance from the original ancestor). Intensity at each position indicates the number of organisms alive at the corresponding point in time and depth in the tree.

Theory predicts that an environment with either a single resource or with resources in unlimited quantities is capable of supporting only one species [37], and this is exactly what we see in the standard Avida experiments. It is the competition over multiple, limited resources that is believed to play a key role in the structuring of communities [35, 39]. In 30 trials under the chemostat regime in Avida, a variety of distinct community structures developed [6]. Some evolved nine stably coexisting specialists, one per resource, while others had just a couple of generalists that divided the resources between them. Others still mixed both generalists and specialists. In all cases, the ecosystems proved to be stable because they persisted after all mutations were shut off in the system, and if any abundant phenotype were removed, it would consistently reinvade.

Phylogeny visualizations provide a striking demonstration of the differences between populations that evolved in a single niche and those from ecosystems, as displayed in Fig. 1.7. Single niche populations can have branching events that persist for a short time, but in the long term one species will out compete the others, or simply drift to dominance if the fitness values are truly identical. By contrast, in ecosystems with multiple resources, the branches that correspond to speciation events persist.

We also studied the number of stably coexisting species as a function of resource availability [4]. We varied the inflow rate of resources over six orders of magnitude and found that multispecies communities evolved at intermediate resource abundance, but not at very high or very low resource abundance. The reason for this observation is that if resources are too scarce, they cannot provide much value to the organisms and base merit dominates, while if resources are too abundant, then they are no longer a limiting factor, which means that space becomes the only limit. In both cases the system reduces down to only a single niche that the organisms can take advantage of.

1.5 Outlook

Digital organisms are a powerful research tool that has opened up methods to experimentally study evolution in ways that have never before been possible. We have explained the capabilities of the Avida system and detailed the methods by which researchers can make use of them. We must be careful, however, not to be lured into the trap of thinking that because these systems can be set up and examined so easily that any experiment will be possible. There are definite limits on the questions that can be answered.

Using digital organisms, we cannot learn anything about physical structures evolved in the natural world, nor the specifics of an evolutionary event in our own history; the questions we ask must be about *how* evolution works in general, and how we can harness it. Even for the latter type of questions, it is sometimes difficult to set up experiments in such a way that they give meaningful results. We must always remember that we are working with an arguably living system that will evolve to survive as best it can, not always in the direction that we intend. Avida has become, in many ways, its own bug tester. If we make a mistake, the organisms will exploit it. For example, we originally had only 16-bit inputs for the organisms to process; they quickly discovered that random guessing often took less time than actually performing the computation. In this case, the organisms indeed found the most efficient way to solve the problem we gave them, only that it wasn't the problem we had thought we were giving. This error happened to be easy to find and easy to fix — now all inputs are 32 bits long — but not all "cheating" will be so simple to identify and prevent. When performing an Avida experiment, it is always important that we step through the population and try to understand how some of the organisms are functioning. More often than not they will surprise us with the cleverness of the survival strategies that they are using. And sometimes they will even make us step back to rethink our experiments.

Many possible future directions exist in the development of Avida. Ongoing efforts include (among others) the implementation of a new CPU model that is more powerful and realistic, an overhaul of the graphical user interface that will include more visualization tools and will be designed so that it can easily be used by those not familiar with the software, an expanded analyze mode based on the scripting language Python, and the move from asexual to sexual organisms. We hope for these additions to expand the user base of the software as well as the range of experiments possible.

Finally, we have an Avida Educational Initiative underway that is focusing on modifying the software so that it will be more conducive for use in a classroom. Our initial goal is for it to be used in introductory college biology courses to help elucidate simple evolutionary concepts. Eventually we plan to both simplify it further for a high school setting and to create a bridge to the research version of Avida so that it will be useful in more specialized biology courses as well.

References

1. Adami C, Brown CT, Haggerty MR (1995) Abundance distributions in artificial life and stochastic models: "Age and Area" revisited. Lect Notes AI 929: 503–514.
2. Adami C, Ofria C, Collier TC (2000) Evolution of biological complexity. Proc. Natl. Acad. Sci. U.S.A. 97:4463–4468.
3. Barton N, Zuidema W (2003) Evolution: The erratic path towards complexity. Curr Biol 13:R649–R651.
4. Chow SS, Wilke CO, Ofria C, Lenski RE, Adami C (2004) Adaptive radiation from resource competition in digital organisms. Science 305:84–86.
5. Chu J, Adami C (1997) Propagation of information in populations of self-replicating code. In: Langton CG, Shimohara T (eds.) Proc. Artificial Life V, pp. 462–469, MIT Press.
6. Cooper T, Ofria C (2002) Evolution of stable ecosystems in populations of digital organisms. In: Standish RK, Bedau MA, Abbass HA (eds.), Proc. Artificial Life VIII, pp. 227–232, MIT Press.
7. Darwin C (1859) On the Origin of Species by Means of Natural Selection. Murray.
8. Dawkins R (1986) The Blind Watchmaker. Norton.
9. Dennett D (2002) The New Replicators. In: Pagel M (ed.) Encyclopedia of Evolution, Oxford Univ. Press.
10. Dewdney AK (1984) In a game called core war hostile programs engage in a battle of bits. Scientific American, May issue, pp. 14–22.

11. Domingo E, Biebricher CK, Eigen M, Holland JJ (2001) Quasispecies and RNA Virus Evolution: Principles and Consequences. Landes Bioscience, Georgetown, TX, USA.
12. Drake JW, Holland JJ (1999) Mutation rates among RNA viruses. Proc Natl Acad Sci 96:13910–13913.
13. Egri-Nagy A, Nehaniv CL (2003) Evolvability of the genotype-phenotype relation in populations of self-replicating digital organisms in a Tierra-like system. Lect Notes Artif Int 2801:238–247.
14. Elena SF, Lenski RE (2003) Evolution experiments with microorganisms: The dynamics and genetic bases of adaptation. Nature Reviews Genetics 4:457–469.
15. Goldberg DE (2002) The Design of Innovation. Kluwer, Dordecht, Netherlands.
16. Jacob F (1977) Evolution and Tinkering. Science, 196:1161–1166.
17. Kim Y, Stephan W (2003) Selective sweeps in the presence of interference among partially linked loci. Genetics 164:389–398.
18. Koza J (ed.) (2003) Genetic Programming IV: Routine Human-Competitive Machine Intelligence. Kluwer, Dordecht, Netherlands.
19. Lenski RE (2004) Phenotypic and genomic evolution during a 20,000-generation experiment with the bacterium, *Escherichia coli*. Plant Breeding Reviews 24:225–265.
20. Lenski RE, Ofria C, Collier TC Adami C (1999) Genome complexity, robustness and genetic interactions in digital organisms. Nature 400:661–664.
21. Lenski RE, Ofria C, Pennock RT, Adami C (2003) The evolutionary origin of complex features. Nature 423:129–144.
22. Maynard Smith J (1992) Byte-sized evolution. Nature 355:772–773.
23. McVean GAT, Charlesworth B (2000) The effects of Hill-Robertson interference between weakly selected mutations on patterns of molecular evolution and variation. Genetics 155:929–944.
24. Morin PJ (2002) Biodiversity's ups and downs, Nature 406:463–464.
25. Newcomb RD, Campbell PM, Ollis DL, Cheah E, Russell RJ, Oakeshott JG (1997) A single amino acid substitution converts a carboxylesterase to an organophosphorus hydrolase and confers insecticide resistance on a blowfly. Proc Natl Acad Sci 94:7464–7468.
26. Nilsson D-E and Pelger SA (1994) A pessimistic estimate of the time required for an eye to evolve. Proc R Soc Lond B 256:53–58.
27. Notley-McRobb L, Ferenci T (1999) Adaptive mgl-regulatory mutations and genetic diversity evolving in glucose limited *Escherichia coli* populations. Env Microbiol 1:33–43.
28. Notley-McRobb L, Ferenci T (1999) The generation of multiple co-existing mal-regulatory mutations through polygenic evolution in glucose-limited populations of *Escherichia coli*. Env Microbiol 1:45–52.
29. Ofria C, Wilke CO (2004) Avida: A software platform for research in computational evolutionary biology. Artificial Life 10:191–229.
30. O'Neill B (2003) Digital evolution. PLoS Biology 1:011–014.
31. Orr HA (2000) The rate of adaptation in asexuals. Genetics 155:961–968.
32. Rainey PB, Travisano M (1998) Adaptive radiation in an heterogeneous environment. Nature 394:69–72.
33. Rasmussen S, Knudsen C, Feldberg R, Hindsholm M (1990) The coreworld — Emergence and evolution of cooperative structures in a computational chemistry. Physica D 75:1–3.

34. Ray TS (1992) An approach to the synthesis of life. In: Langton CG, Taylor C, Farmer JD, Rasmussen S (eds.). Proc. of Artificial Life II, p. 371. Addison-Wesley.
35. Schluter D (1996) Ecological causes of adaptive radiation, Am Nat 148:s40–s64.
36. Schluter D (2001) Ecology and the origin of species, Trends Ecol Evol 16:372–379.
37. Tilman D (1982) Resource Competition and Community Structure, Princeton University Press.
38. Tilman D (2000) Causes, consequences and ethics of biodiversity, Nature 405:208–211.
39. Travisano M, Rainey PB (2000) Studies of adaptive radiation using model microbial systems. Am Nat 156:S35–S44.
40. Wilke CO (2002) Maternal effects in molecular evolution. Phys Rev Lett 88:078–101.
41. Wilke C, Adami C (2002) The biology of digital organisms. Trends Ecol Evol 17:528–532.
42. Wilke CO, Adami C (2003) Evolution of mutational robustness. Mutat Res 522:3–1.
43. Wilke CO, Wang JL, Ofria C, Lenski RE, Adami C (2001) Evolution of digital organisms at high mutation rates leads to survival of the flattest. Nature 412:331–333.
44. Wilkins AS (2002) The Evolution of Developmental Pathways, Sinauer.
45. Yedid G, Bell G (2001) Microevolution in an electronic microcosm. Am Nat 157:465–487.
46. Yedid G, Bell G (2002) Macrocvolution simulated with autonomously replicating computer programs. Nature 420:810–812.

2

Framsticks: A Platform for Modeling, Simulating, and Evolving 3D Creatures

Maciej Komosinski

Life is one of the most complex phenomena known in our world. Researchers construct various models of life, which serve diverse purposes and are applied in a wide range of areas — from medicine to entertainment. A part of artificial life research focuses on designing three-dimensional models of life forms. Obviously, such simulated creatures are appealing to the observers, because the world we live in is three-dimensional. Thus we can easily understand behaviors demonstrated by virtual individuals, study behavior changes during simulated evolution, analyze dependencies between groups of creatures, etc. However, 3D models of life forms are not only attractive because of their resemblance of the real-world organisms. Simulating 3D agents has practical implications: If the simulation is accurate enough, then real robots can be built based on the simulation, as in [14]. Agents can be designed, tested, and optimized in a virtual environment, and the best ones can be constructed as real robots with embedded control systems. This way artificial intelligence algorithms can be "embodied" in the 3D mechanical structures.

Perhaps the first best known simulation of three-dimensional life was 1994's Karl Sims' virtual creatures [17]. Being visually attractive, it demonstrated a successful competitive coevolutionary process, complex control systems, and interesting (evolved) behaviors. However, this work did not become available for users as documented software. A number of 3D simulation packages was developed later (see [18] for their review), but most of them either are used for a specific application or experiment (and are not available as general tools for users), or focus on simulation exclusively (without built-in support of genetic encodings and evolutionary optimization).

Framsticks [10–12], a software platform described in this chapter, does not address a single purpose or a single research problem. On the contrary, it is built to support a wide range of experiments and to provide all of its functionality to users, who can use this system in a variety of ways. The significance of understanding is central for the development of Framsticks. Although the system is a simplified model of reality, it is easily capable of producing phenomena more complex than a human can comprehend [8]. Thus it is essential to provide automatic analysis and support tools. Intelligible visualization is one of the most fundamental means for human understanding of artificial life forms, and this feature is present in the software.

The Framsticks system is designed so that it does not introduce restrictions concerning complexity and size of creatures. Therefore, neural networks can have any topology and dimension, allowing for a range of complex behaviors, some described in Section 4 of [8]. Avoiding limitations is important because Framsticks is ultimately destined to experiments with open-ended evolution, where interactions between creatures and environment are the sources of competition, cooperation, communication, intelligence, etc.

Further sections of this chapter focus on the following issues: 2.1 — available Framsticks software; 2.2 – simulation (morphology, control system, environment); 2.3 — general system framework, genotype-phenotype relationship, simulation architecture and possible usage of the system; 2.4 — some tools that the system provides to support research and education; 2.5 — sample experiments that have already been performed, as well as some new ideas; 2.6 — entertaining Framsticks applications. Section 2.7 summarizes this chapter.

2.1 Available Software and Tools

Framsticks was first released in late 1996, but the first official releases became available on the Internet in June 1997. There is a great difference between versions 1.x and 2.x. Until 2000, the system had a great number of parameters, but the experiment logic, visualization, neurons, etc. were hard-coded. In 2002, starting with version 2.0, the scripting language *FramScript* was introduced, which allows for flexible control of most parts of the software — on both a high level (adjusting parameters) and low level (writing custom procedures). Scripting is addressed in Section 2.3.2.

The first official release of the Framsticks Theater (a simple-interface, attractive graphical application) took place in 2004, with unofficial releases available since 2002. The Framsticks family of programs includes

- Framsticks GUI (Graphical User Interface) — the most popular program, where simulated creatures, genotypes, and the virtual world are presented visually, and allow for user interaction (dragging creatures, online genotype visualization, etc.).
- Framsticks CLI (Command-Line Interface) — a program where commands are issued using text. Useful for long, time-consuming and/or well-defined experiments, which can be performed automatically (batch processing) or remotely. This program has no overheads of the GUI and can be compiled for most operating systems.
- Framsticks Viewer — a simple program that displays creatures built from genotypes that are specified by a user.

- Framsticks Theater — a complete Framsticks simulator with a simple menu and predefined actions ("shows"), described in more detail in Section 2.6.
- Framsticks Editor (FRED) — a simple graphical editor that allows users to easily design creatures without the knowledge of genetic encodings. Described in more detail in Section 2.6.
- Framsticks (network) Server and Framsticks (network) Clients — the server is analogous to the Framsticks CLI, but commands (and their results) are sent through the network.* Two basic roles of clients are (1) the GUI for the server, and (2) visualization of the virtual world simulated on the server, as shown in Fig. 2.1. However, clients can use the server in a number of ways, including distributed evolution, modeling of ecosystems and migration, real-time interaction in mixed realities, and much more. Many clients can connect to the same server at the same time, and clients can exchange some information between themselves.
- Other helper programs, like brain optimizers, analyzers of experiment output data, etc.

The above applications are in continuous development, with new releases coming out periodically. Framsticks genotypes and experiment proposals can be browsed, downloaded, and uploaded using the Internet database, Framsticks Experimentation Center.

Framsticks documentation is available in many forms, including web site information [12], Framsticks Manual contained in a single document, tutorials, and the FramScript reference that describes objects and functions useful when writing scripts.

2.2 Simulation

Simulation in Framsticks concerns the three-dimensional world and creatures. All kinds of interaction between physical objects are considered: static and dynamic friction, damping, action and reaction forces, energy losses after deformations, gravitation, and uplift pressure — buoyancy (in a water environment).

There is always a tradeoff between simulation accuracy and simulation time. Fast simulation is needed to perform evolution; on the other hand, the model should be as realistic (detailed) as possible to display realistic behaviors. As we expect emergence of more and more sophisticated phenomena, the evolution takes more time. Thus simulation needs to be faster, and therefore less accurate. In order to make the simulation fast and to avoid computational

---

* The server(s) and client(s) can also be run on a single computer.

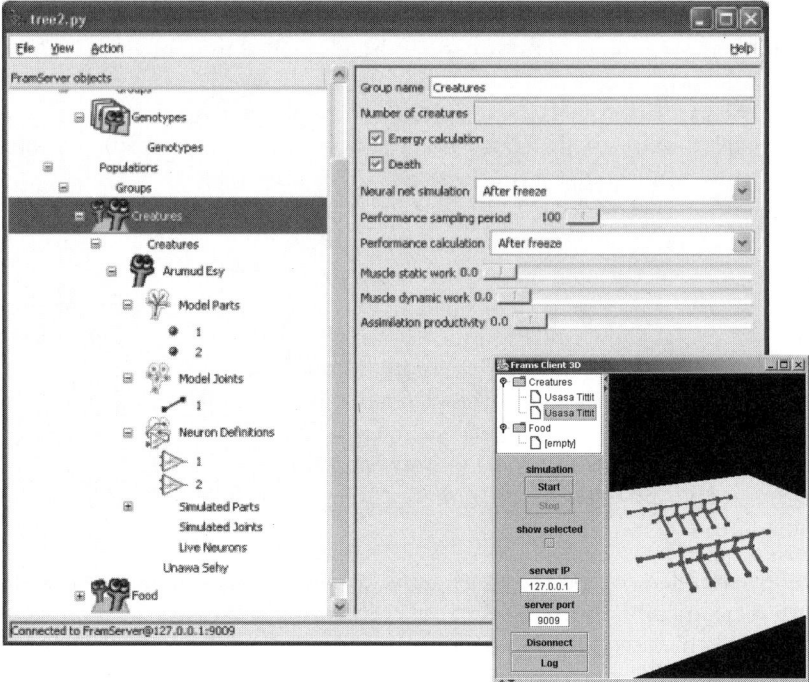

Fig. 2.1. Two sample network clients: the GUI and the virtual world display.

complexity, some less important aspects, like collisions between parts of an organism itself, were discarded in the native Framsticks simulator.**

Artificial creatures in Framsticks are built of body and brain. Body is composed of material points (called parts) connected by elastic joints. Brain is made from neurons (these are signal processing units, receptors, and effectors) and neural connections. For a more detailed description of this model, refer to the GDK at [19].

2.2.1 Body

The basic body element is a stick made of two flexibly joined parts (in the native simulator, finite-element method is used for step-by-step simulation). Parts and joints have some fundamental properties, like position, orientation, weight, and friction, but there may also be other (custom) properties, like the ability to assimilate energy, durability of joints in collisions, etc. Articulations

---

** The power of contemporary computers suffices to use very accurate simulation engines for evolutionary optimization processes [18]. The integration of such an engine is planned for Framsticks version 3.0.

exist between sticks where they share an endpoint; the articulations are unrestricted in all three degrees of freedom (bending in two planes plus twisting). Figure 2.2 shows forces considered in the native Framsticks simulator.

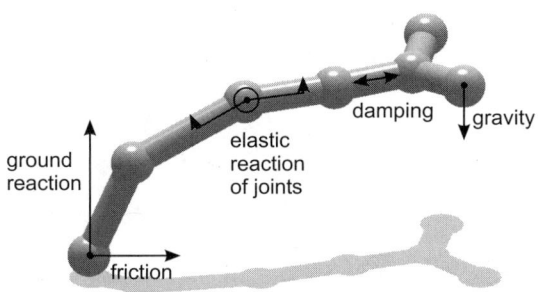

Fig. 2.2. Forces involved in the native Framsticks simulation.

2.2.2 Brain

Brain (the control system) is made of neurons and their connections. A neuron may be a signal processing unit, but it may also interact with body as a receptor (sensor) or effector (actuator). There are some predefined types of neurons, for example:

- "N" — the standard Framsticks neuron, which is a generalized version of the popular weighted-sum sigmoid transfer function neuron used commonly in AI. The three additionally introduced parameters influence speed and tendency of changes of the inner neuron state, and the steepness of the sigmoid transfer function. In a special case, when the three parameters are assigned specific values, the characteristics of the "N" neuron become identical to the popular, reactive AI neuron. In this case, neural output reflects instantly input signals. More information and sample neuronal runs can be found in *simulation details* section at [12].
- "Sin" — a sinusoidal generator with frequency controlled by its inputs.
- "Rnd" — random noise generator.
- "Thr" — thresholding neuron.
- "Delay" — delaying neuron.
- "D" — differentiating neuron.

It is possible to easily add custom, user-designed neurons by using FramScript — an example is shown in Section 2.3.2.

The neural network can have any topology and complexity. Neurons can be connected with each other in any way (some may be unconnected). Inputs can be connected to outputs of another neuron (including sensors), while outputs can be connected to inputs of another neuron (including effectors — muscles). Sample control systems are shown in Fig. 2.3. Note that a single control system may be composed of many unconnected or independent subsystems.

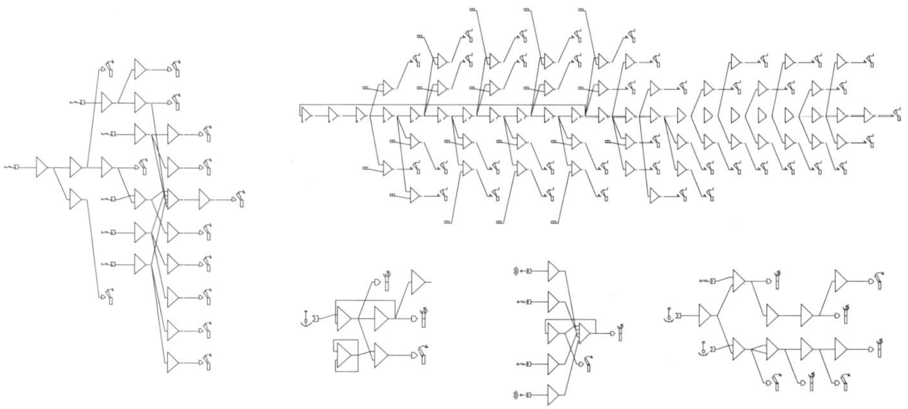

Fig. 2.3. Sample neural networks. Triangles are the standard signal-processing neurons ("N"). Receptors can be seen as inputs (shown usually on the left side: gyroscope, touch, smell, constant signal). Controlled muscles (rotating, bending) are usually on the right side. Note recurrent connections. Parallel connections are also allowed.

2.2.3 Receptors and Effectors

Receptors and effectors are interacting between body and brain. They must be connected to brain in order to be useful, but they also interact with creature's body and the world. The three basic Framsticks receptors (sensors) include "G" for orientation in space (equilibrium sense, gyroscope), "T" for detection of physical contact (touch), and "S" for detection of energy (smell) — see Figs. 2.3 and 2.4.

The two basic Framsticks effectors are muscles: bending and rotating. Positive and negative changes of muscle control signal make the sticks move in either direction, which is analogous to the natural systems of muscles, with flexors and extensors. The strength of a muscle determines its effective ability of movement and speed (acceleration). If energetic issues are considered in an experiment, then a stronger muscle consumes more energy during its work.

A sample framstick equipped with basic receptors and effectors is shown in Fig. 2.4. Other examples of receptors and effectors are energy level tester, water detector, vector eye, length muscle, and thrust.

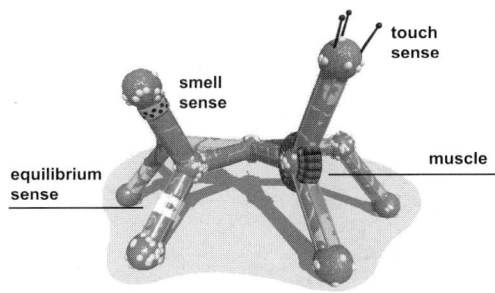

Fig. 2.4. Basic receptors (equilibrium, touch, smell) and effectors (muscles) in Framsticks.

2.2.4 Environment

The world can be flat or built of smooth slopes, or blocks. It is possible to adjust the water level, so that not only walking/running/jumping creatures, but also the swimming ones, are simulated. The boundaries of the virtual world can be one of three types:

- hard (surrounding wall: it is impossible to cross the boundary);
- wrap (crossing the boundary means teleportation to the other world edge);
- no boundaries (the world is infinite).

These options are useful in various kinds of experiments and performance measurements.

2.3 Framework and Evolution

2.3.1 Genetics

The Framsticks system supports multiple genetic encodings (called also representations or "genotype languages") [13]. The system manipulates and transforms genotype strings expressed in various representations and ultimately decodes them into the internal representation used by the simulator to construct a creature (phenotype). It means that one can describe a creature using genomes expressed in different "languages."

Any creature can be completely described using a low-level representation labeled *f0*, by listing all of its components and their properties. Other higher-level encodings convert their representation into the corresponding *f0* version (possibly through another intermediary representation), as shown in Fig. 2.5. The reverse mapping into higher-level encodings is difficult to compute, which is also true for biological phenotype encodings. As a consequence, in the general case it is not possible to convert a lower-level representation into a higher-level one (or a higher-level one into another higher-level one).

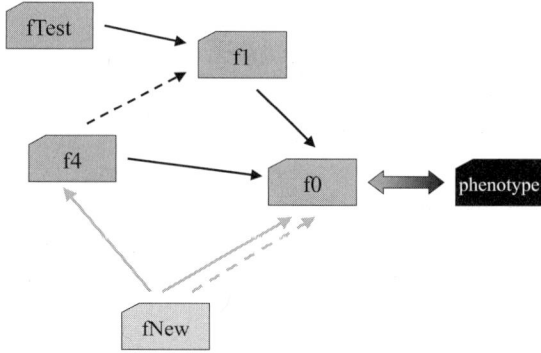

Fig. 2.5. A graph showing genetic encodings (nodes) and their translation procedures (arcs). The dashed arrow depicts an approximate translation. Multiple, alternative translation methods may exist, as shown for the translation from *fNew* to *f0*.

Each encoding has its associated genetic operators (mutation, crossover, and optional repair) and a translation procedure that allows users to compute a phenotype from each genotype expressed in this encoding. A new encoding can be added relatively easily, by implementing these components. The Framsticks system is accompanied by the Genotype Development Kit (GDK), which simplifies this process [19]. The most popular genetic encodings are characterized ahead.

The direct low-level, or *f0*, encoding describes agents exactly as they are represented in the simulator. It does not use any higher-level features to make genotypes more compact or flexible. Its useful characteristics are that it has a minimal decoding cost and that every possible creature can be described using this encoding. Each *f0* genotype consists of a list of descriptions of all the elements a creature is composed of: parts, joints, neurons, and neural connections.

The recurrent direct encoding (labeled *f1*) also describes all the parts of the corresponding phenotype. Body properties are represented locally, so that most of the properties (and neural network connections) are maintained when a genotype section is moved to another place of the genotype. Control elements (neurons, receptors) are described near the elements under their control (muscles, sticks). Only tree-like body structures can be represented in *f1* (no cycles allowed). This encoding is relatively easy for humans to manipulate and manually design creatures by editing their genotypes. For example, the 'X' char means a stick, parentheses are used to branch body structure, 'r' and 'R' letters are used to rotate the branching plane, etc.

The developmental encoding (*f4*) is development-oriented, similar to the encodings applied for evolving neural networks [5]. An interesting merit of developmental encoding is that it can incorporate symmetry and modularity, features commonly found in natural systems, yet difficult to formalize. *f4* is similar to *f1*, but codes are interpreted as commands by cells (sticks, neurons, etc.). Cells can change their properties, and divide. Each cell maintains its own pointer to the current command in the genetic code. After division, cells can execute different codes, and thus differentiate themselves. The final body (phenotype) is the result of a development process: It starts with an undifferentiated ancestor cell and ends with a collection of interconnected differentiated cells (sticks, neurons, and connections).

Each of the three described encodings and the corresponding genetic operators has been carefully designed and tested, and each encoding was based on numerous theoretical considerations. More detailed descriptions can be found in [11]. Examples of simple genotypes and corresponding phenotypes (creatures) are shown in Fig. 2.6.

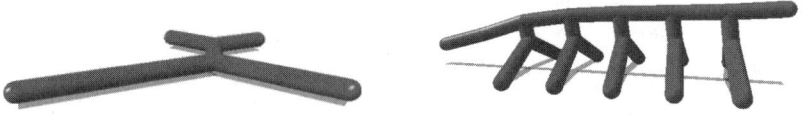

Fig. 2.6. Left: example of the *f1* genotype XXX(XX,X(X,X)). Right: example of the *f4* genotype with the repetition gene: rr<X>#5<,<X>RR<<11X>LX>LX>>X.

The procedure of translation of genotypes may provide additional information regarding the relation of individual genes in the source and target encodings. If this information is available, then it is possible to track the relationship between parts of a genotype (genes) and parts of the corresponding creature (phenes). Details of this process and examples are shown in [13]. Figure 2.7 presents the way this information can be visualized and used both ways.

In the Framsticks software, it is possible to select parts of the phenotype and genotype to get an instant visual feedback and understand their relationship — see Fig. 2.8. A user can move the cursor along the genotype to see which phenotype parts are influenced by the genotype character under cursor. Another option available is to modify the genotype by adding, deleting, or editing its parts while the corresponding phenotype is instantly computed and displayed. Framsticks can be used to illustrate the phenomena of polygeny and pleiotropy and to perform direct experiments with artificial genetic encodings, increasing comprehension of the genotype-to-phenotype translation process and properties of genetic encodings — including modularity, compression, redundancy, and many more.

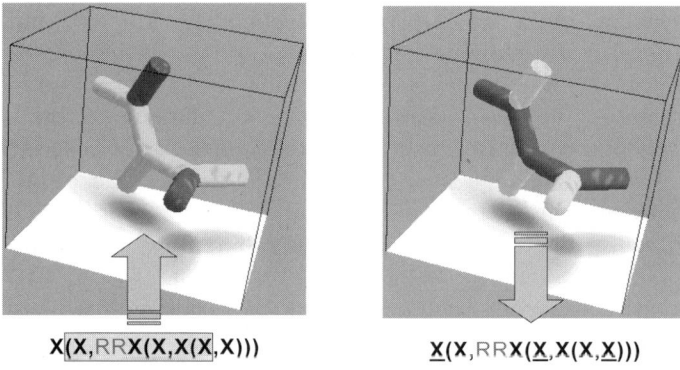

Fig. 2.7. A simple mapping between an *f1* genotype and the corresponding phenotype. Left: user selected a part of the genotype, corresponding phenes are highlighted. Right: user highlighted some parts of the body, corresponding genes are underlined.

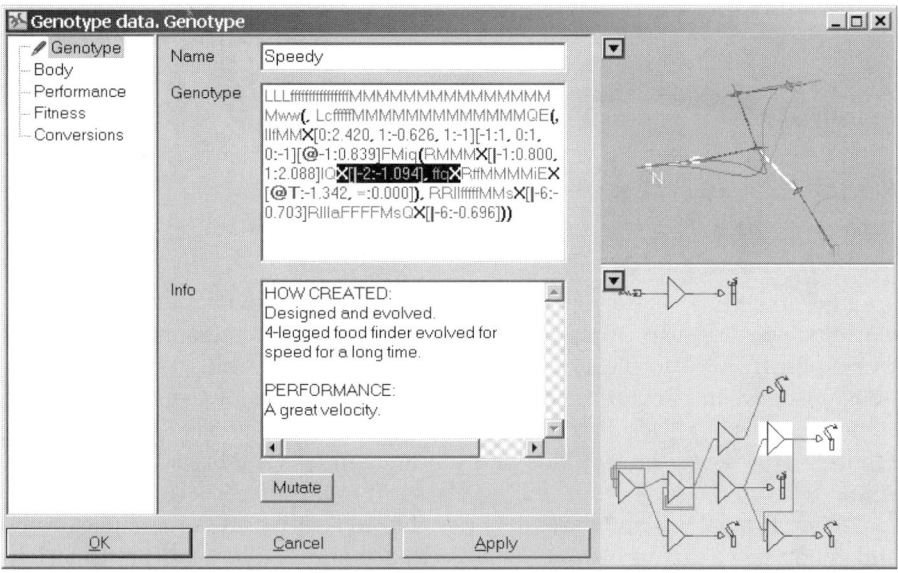

Fig. 2.8. A sample genotype and the corresponding creature (body and brain). Some genes are selected by a user, and the corresponding parts of body and brain are highlighted. See also color plate.

2.3.2 Scripting

The Framsticks system can interpret commands written in a simple language, called *FramScript*. FramScript can be used for a range of tasks, from custom fitness functions, macros, and user-defined neurons, to user-defined experiment definitions, creatures behaviors, events, and even 3D visualization styles. Understanding FramScript allows users to exploit the full potential of Framsticks, because scripts can control the Framsticks system.

The FramScript syntax and semantics are very similar to JAVA, C, C++, PHP, etc. In FramScript,

- all variables are untyped and declared using *var* or *global* statements,
- functions are defined with the *function* statement,
- references can be used for existing objects,
- no structures and no pointers can be declared,
- there is the *Vector* object, which handles dynamic arrays,
- FramScript code can access Framsticks object fields as "Object.field".

To demonstrate how scripting can be used, we will design a "noisy" neuron, which generates occasional noise (random output). Otherwise it will pass the weighted sum of inputs into its output. In neuron definitions, the neural output can be controlled directly. We can read from neuron inputs, define any internal function, and preserve the neural state using "private" neuron properties. "Public" properties can be used to influence the neuron behavior — genetic operators (mutation, crossing over) will by default operate on such properties.

For a neuron, two functions can be defined: the initialization function (*init*) and the working function (*go*), which is executed in each simulation step. For our noisy neuron, we do not need the initialization function — there are no internal properties to initialize. However, the public "error rate" property will be useful to control how much noise is generated. For each neuron, we first have to define its name, long name, description, the number of preferred inputs (any number in this case) and outputs (the noisy neuron provides meaningful output signal):

```
class:
name:Nn
longname:Noisy neuron
description:occassionally generates a random value
prefinputs:-1
prefoutput:1
```

The error rate property ("e") will be a floating-point number within the range of 0.0 and 0.1:

```
prop:
id:e
name:Error rate
type:f 0.0 0.1
```

Finally, we implement the working function, which uses the `rnd01` function of the `Math` object to obtain a random value in the range from 0.0 to 1.0:

```
function go()
{
  if (Math.rnd01 < Fields.e)
    Neuro.state = Neuro.weightedInputSum;
  else
    Neuro.state = (Math.rnd01 * 2) - 1.0;
}
```

We join these three fragments into a single file, name it "noisy.ncuro", place it in the appropriate directory, run Framsticks, build a creature that uses the noisy neuron with the error rate set to 0.1, and start the simulation to see what is shown in Fig. 2.9. Now the FramScript source of the neuron can be easily modified to extend its functionality and to exhibit more complex behavior. The noisy neuron is ready to be used in neural networks, and even in evolution, without any additional work.

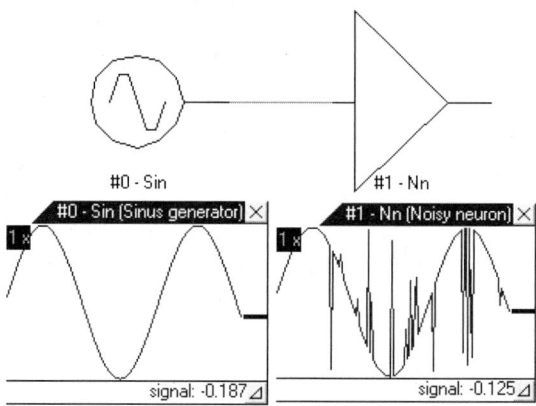

Fig. 2.9. The noisy neuron defined by the script, connected to the sinus generator. Random output values are generated with the rate of 0.1.

2.3.3 Experiment Definitions

A very important feature of Framsticks is that you may define custom rules for the simulator. There are no predetermined laws, but a script called the *experiment definition*. It is analogous to the neuron definition explained in the previous section. The experiment definition script is more complex and defines behavior of the Framsticks system in a few associated areas:

- Creation of objects in the world. The script defines where, when, and how much of which objects will be created. An object is an evolved organism, food particle, or any other element of the world designed by a researcher. Thus, depending on some specific script, food or obstacles might appear, move and disappear, their location might depend on where creatures are, etc.
- Objects interactions. Object collision/contact is an event, which may cause some action defined by the script developer. For example, physical contact may result in energy ingestion, pushing each other, destruction, or reproduction.
- Evolution. A steady-state (one-at-a-time) selection model, where a single genotype is inserted into a gene pool one at a time, can be used. But a standard (i.e., generational replacement) evolutionary algorithm approach is also possible (a new gene pool replaces the whole old gene pool). Another possibility is tournament competition for all pairs of genotypes. The script can define many gene pools and many populations (generally called groups) and perform independent evolutions under different conditions.
- Evaluation criteria. These are flexible and do not have to be as simple as the performances supplied by the simulator. For example, fitness may depend on time or energy required to fulfill some task, or degree of success (distance from target, number of successful actions, etc.).

The script is built of "functions" assigned to system events, which include

- `onExpDefLoad` — occurs after experiment definition was loaded. This procedure should prepare the environment, create necessary gene pools and populations, etc.
- `onExpInit` — occurs at the beginning of the experiment.
- `onExpSave` — occurs on save experiment data request.
- `onExpLoad` — occurs on load experiment data request. The script should restore the system state saved by `onExpSave`.
- `onStep` — occurs in each simulation step.
- `onBorn` — occurs when a new organism is created in the world.
- `onKill` — occurs when a creature is removed from the world.
- `onUpdate` — occurs periodically, which is useful for performance evaluation.
- `on[X]Collision` — occurs when an object of population [X] has touched some other object.

Therefore, a user may define the behavior of the whole system by implementing appropriate actions within these events. A single script (experiment definition) may use parameters, which allows users to perform a whole bunch (class) of diversified experiments. Available experiment definitions include

- standard — can be used to perform a range of common experiments. Provides one gene pool, one population for individuals, one "population" for

food, steady-state evolutionary optimization, fitness as a weighted sum of performance values, custom fitness formulas, fitness scaling, and roulette or tournament selection.
- generational — a simple "genetic algorithm" experiment. Provides two gene pools (previous and current generation), one population for individuals, generational replacement of genotypes, roulette selection, and script-defined fitness formula.
- reproduction — asexual reproduction in the world. Each creature with a sufficient energy level produces an offspring, which is then put close to its parent. Food is created at a constant rate and placed randomly.
- neuroanalysis — simulates all loaded creatures and computes average and standard deviation of the output signal for each neuron in each creature. After evaluation, a simple statistics report is printed. No evolution is performed.
- standard-eval — evaluates loaded genotypes thoroughly one by one, and produces a report of fitness averages, standard deviations, and average evaluation times. No evolution is performed.
- standard-log — logs genetic and evaluation operations, producing a detailed history of evolutionary process. Useful for various analyses.
- standard-tricks — serves as an example of a few advanced techniques: Random force can be applied to parts of a living creature during its life span, neuron property values can be used in the fitness function, and some statistical data can be acquired from coordinates of simulated creature parts.
- deathmatch — an educational tool intended for use in practical courses in evolutionary computing, evolutionary robotics, and artificial life. Using "education by competition," it implements a tournament among teams of creatures, as well as among teams of students. To win, a team has to provide a creature that stays alive longer than creatures submitted by other teams. To stay alive, creatures need energy, which can be collected by touching energy resources, winning fights, avoiding fights, cooperation, etc.

Other experiment definitions are reported in Section 2.5.4.

2.3.4 Illustrative Example ("Standard Experiment" Definition)

The file "standard.expdef" contains the full source for the standard experiment definition script used to optimize creatures on a steady-state basis, with fitness defined as a weighted sum of their performances. This script is quite versatile and complex. Below its general concept is explained, with much simplified actions assigned to events. This digest gives an idea of what components constitute a complete experiment definition.

`onExpDefLoad`:

- create a single gene pool named "Genotypes."
- create two populations: "Creatures" and "Food."

`onExpInit`:

- empty all gene pools and populations.
- place the initial genotype in "Genotypes."

`onStep`:

- if too little food: create a new object in "Food."
- if too few organisms: select a parent from "Genotypes"; mutate, crossover, or copy it. Based on the resulting genotype, create an individual in "Creatures."

`onBorn`:

- move the new object into a randomly chosen place in the world.
- set its starting energy depending on the object's type (creature or food).

`onKill`:

- if "Creatures" object died, save its performance in "Genotypes" (possibly creating a new genotype). If there are too many genotypes in "Genotypes", remove one.

`onFoodCollision`:

- send a piece of energy from the "Food" object to the colliding "Creature" object.

2.4 Advanced Tools for Research and Education

Many research works concern studies of evolutionary processes, their dynamics and efficiency. Various methods and measures have been developed in order to be able to analyze evolution, complexity, and interaction in the observed systems. Other works try to understand behaviors of artificial creatures, regarding them as subjects of survey rather than "black boxes" with assigned performance and fitness.

Artificial life systems, especially those applied to evolutionary robotics and design [2,3,14], are quite complex, and it is difficult to understand behaviors of artificial agents in detail. The only way is to observe them carefully and use human intelligence to draw conclusions. Usually, the behavior of such agents is nondeterministic, and their control systems are sophisticated, often coupled with morphology and very strongly connected functionally [15].

Therefore, for the purposes of studying behaviors and populations of individuals, one needs high-level, intelligent support tools [10]. It is not likely that automatic tools will soon be able to produce understandable, nontrivial explanations of sophisticated artificial agents. Nonetheless, their role and help cannot be ignored. Even simple automatic support is of great relevance to a human, which becomes obvious after spending hours investigating relatively simple artificial creatures. In the future, some advanced analysis methods, developed within artificial life methodology, may become useful for real-life studies, biology, and medicine.

One of the purposes of the Framsticks system is to allow creating and testing such tools and procedures, and to develop methodology needed for their use. Realistic artificial life environments are the right place for such research. On the other hand, education does not require automatic tools for analysis. Rather it calls for techniques that make complex systems attractive and easier to understand. Visualization of relations between genotypes and creatures, as described in Section 2.3.1, is an example of such educational instrument.

2.4.1 Brain Analysis

An (artificial) creature is composed of body and brain. Body can be easily seen, and some statistical information is easy to obtain (the number of parts, body size, weight, degree of consistency, etc.). Brains are much more difficult to present and comprehend. The Framsticks software provides a special algorithm for laying out neural networks so that their structure can be exposed. Without this visualization algorithm, a complex neural network looks chaotic, but after the algorithm is applied, the brain structure is revealed — see Fig. 2.3. Additionally, if a neuron that is embodied (located in body) is selected, it is highlighted in both the body view and the brain view (Fig. 2.8).

To understand how the brain works, charts showing signal flow are helpful. Users can open multiple views of a single brain and connect many "probes" to neurons, as shown in Figs. 2.9 and 2.10. It is also possible to force states of neurons using these probes so that parts of the brain can be turned off, oscillation can be stopped, or the desired signal shape can be interactively "drawn." This way, muscles can be directly controlled while simulation is running.

Some sensors reflect the state of the body. If body is moved, output values of these neurons change (like, for example, equilibrium or touch sensors). This is immediately seen in the neural probes. Figure 2.10 shows a creature under such analysis.

A simple automatic tool for brain analysis is the experiment definition named "neuroanalysis." During simulation, it watches each neuron in each creature and computes averages and standard deviations for all neural output signals. The final report summarizes activity of brains and helps in location

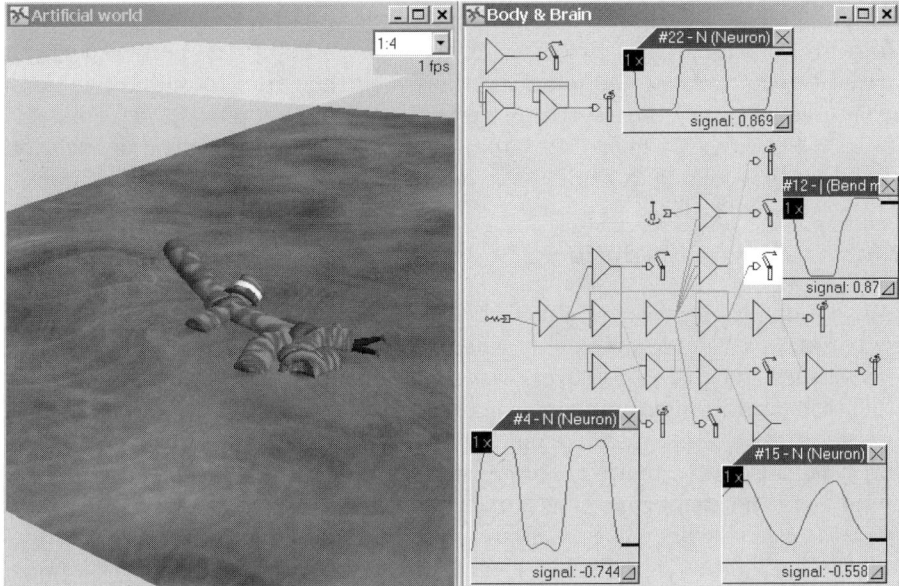

Fig. 2.10. A simulated creature with the control system under investigation. Four neural probes can be seen, showing signals in different locations of the neural network. See also color plate.

of inactive and redundant brain areas. It also gives clues on possible ways of simplification of analyzed neural networks.

2.4.2 Clustering of Similar Individuals

Similarity is usually considered to be a simple property. However, automatic measures of similarity can be extremely helpful in observation of regularities, groups of related individuals, etc. Similarity can be identified in many ways, including aspects of morphology (body), brain, size, function, behavior, performance, fitness, etc. When computed automatically, it can be useful in

- optimization, to introduce artificial niches by modification of fitness values [4],
- studies of evolutionary processes and structures of populations of individuals,
- studies of function/behavior of agents,
- reduction of the number of agents to a small subset of interesting, diverse, unique individuals,
- inferring dendrograms (and hopefully, phylogenetic trees) based on dissimilarities between organisms.

For Framsticks, a heuristic method was constructed that is able to estimate the degree of similarity of two individuals. This method treats body as a graph (with parts as vertices and joints as edges) and then tries to match two body structures based on the degrees of vertices as the main piece of information. It can also take body geometry into account. For a more detailed description of this method see [9]; a sample application is presented in Section 2.5.3.

2.4.3 History of Evolution

In real life, although we are able to trace genetic relationships within existing creatures, we do not know exactly what happens during mutation and crossing over of their genomes. Moreover, we cannot trace genetic relations in a longer time scale and in high numbers of individuals.

In Framsticks, it is possible not only to remember all parent–child relationships, but also to estimate genotype shares of related individuals (how many genes have mutated or have been exchanged). This allows users to derive and draw the real tree of evolution, as shown in Fig. 2.11. The vertical axis is time, and the horizontal one reflects a local degree of genetic dissimilarity (between a pair of individuals). Vertices in the tree are single individuals. This way of visualizing evolution exposes milestones — genotypes with many descendants. The overall characteristics of the evolutionary process (convergence, high pressure, or random drift) can also be seen in such pictures.

2.4.4 Understanding Evolved Behaviors: Fuzzy Control

Traditional neural networks with many neurons and connections are hard to understand. They are often presented as "black boxes," successful but impossible to explain — and therefore not trustworthy for some applications. But there is another paradigm used for control — the *fuzzy* control. It is used in many domains of our life, including washing machines, video cameras, ABS in cars, air condition, etc. It is also applied for controlling nonlinear, fast-changing processes, where quick decisions are more important than exact ones [20]. Fuzzy control is attractive because

- it allows for linguistic variables (like "drive fast," where "fast" is a fuzzy term).
- it is easier to understand by humans. The fuzzy rule "if X is Big and Y is Small then Z is Medium" is much easier to understand than the crisp one "if X is between 32.22 and 43.32 and Y is less than 5.2 then Z is 19.2."

To evolve controllers whose work can be explained, fuzzy control has been developed in Framsticks. Fuzzy control, similarly to neural networks, can also cope with uncertainty of information — when the process is compound, depends on random events or measurements are affected by errors. The fuzzy approach can manage these problems by generalization of information.

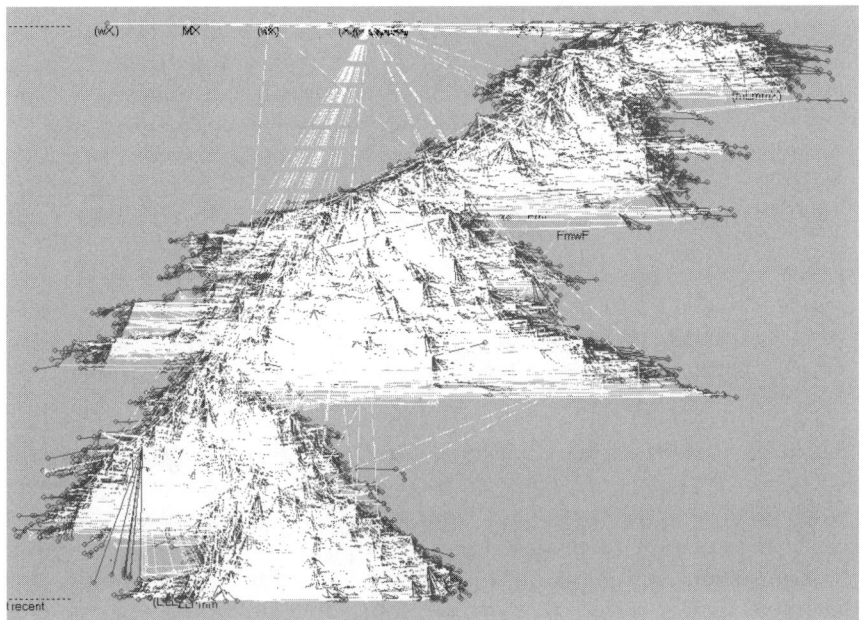

Fig. 2.11. The real tree of simulated evolution. Top: single ancestor and beginning of time. Black lines represent mutations; white ones are crossovers.

Having the fuzzy neuron designed, and mutation and crossing over procedures provided, the "inverted pendulum" experiment was set up with two goals in mind [6]. The first goal was to check the efficiency of evolution in optimizing the desired fuzzy control system. The second goal was to check whether the evolved fuzzy control systems can really explain behaviors in a human-friendly way.

The base of the pendulum was composed of three joints (J_0, J_1, J_2) equipped with two actuators (bottom and top) working in two planes — see Fig. 2.12. The top part of the pendulum was composed of four perpendicular sticks, each equipped with a single equilibrium sensor (G_0, G_1, G_2, G_3). The sensors provided information for the control system, which controlled the actuators. The sensors produced signals from the $[-1, 1]$ range depending on the spatial orientation of the joint they are located in.

The optimization task was to evolve a control system capable of keeping the inverted pendulum from falling down for as long as possible. Evolved fuzzy systems were compared to evolved neural networks in the same experiment, and their quality was similar. Since optimization experiments considered only behaviors, not the complexity of the control systems, the typical evolved fuzzy systems employed many fuzzy sets and fuzzy rules. Before attempting to analyze the control system, it was reasonable to try to simplify it. This was

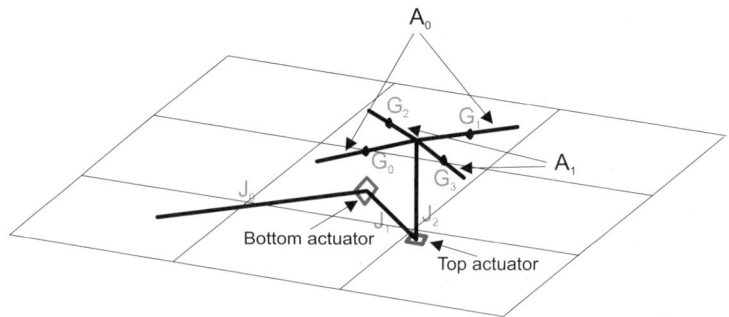

Fig. 2.12. The pendulum body structure (shown in a bent position).

achieved by performing an additional, short optimization process with disabled genetic operators of adding fuzzy sets and fuzzy rules. Modifications and deletions were allowed. Thus the complexity of the control system was radically decreased without deteriorating its fitness.

Fuzzy systems considered in this experiment had four inputs and two outputs. Input signals s_0, s_1, s_2, s_3 come from four equilibrium sensors. Based on their values, the fuzzy system sends two outputs signals for actuators: bend_bottom and bend_top. Linguistic variables for inputs (upright, leveled, and upside_down) and outputs characterizing bending directions (right, none, left) need to be defined to present the fuzzy system in a human-readable form. After they are introduced, the best evolved fuzzy system consisting of five rules can be rendered as

1. **if** (s_2=leveled and s_0=leveled) **then** (bend_bottom=left and bend_top=left)
2. **if** (s_3=leveled and s_1=upside_down) **then** (bend_top=left)
3. **if** (s_1=upright) **then** (bend_bottom=left and bend_top=left)
4. **if** (s_3=upside_down) **then** (bend_bottom=right and bend_top=left)
5. **if** (s_1=upside_down) **then** (bend_bottom=left and bend_top=none)

The behavior of the inverted pendulum follows the above rules. The results of this experiment show that evolution of both neural and fuzzy controllers for active inverted pendulum leads to similar pendulum behaviors. However, careful analysis of the evolved fuzzy knowledge confirms additional, explanatory value of the fuzzy controller. The evolved fuzzy rules, when referenced to the pendulum structure, are plain and easily understandable by a human.

2.5 Research Experiments

2.5.1 Comparison of Genotype Encodings

There are a number of studies on the evolution of simulated creatures with realistic physical behavior. In such systems, the use of a physical simulation layer implements a complex genotype–fitness relationship. Physical interactions between body parts, the coupling between control and physical body, and interactions during body development can all add a level of indirection between the genotype and its fitness. The complexity of the genotype–fitness relationship offers a potential for rich evolutionary dynamics.

The most important element of the genotype-to-fitness relationship is the genotype-to-phenotype mapping, or genotype encoding. There is no obvious simple way to encode a complex phenotype — which consists of a variable-size, structured body and a matching control system — into a simpler genotype. Moreover, an evolutionary algorithm can perform poorly when using a certain genotype encoding, and better when using others, for reasons not yet immediately obvious. The employed genotype encoding can have a significant effect on the performance of the evolution.

The Framsticks system has been used as the context of analysis of various genotype encodings. The performance of the three encodings described in Section 2.3.1 was compared in three optimization tasks: passive and active height, and velocity maximization [11]. The solutions produced by evolution are considered to be successful for the given tasks in all three cases. However, there were some important differences in the degree of success. The *f0* encoding performed worse than the two higher-level encodings. The most important differences between these encodings are that *f0* has a minimal bias and is unrestrictive, while the higher-level encodings (*f1* and *f4*) restrict the search space and introduce a strong bias toward structured phenotypes. These results indicate that a more structured genotype encoding, with genetic operators working on a higher level, is beneficial in the evolution of 3D agents. The existence of a bias toward structured phenotypes can overcome the apparent limitation that entire regions of the search space are not accessible for the optimization search. This bias may be useful in some applications (engineering and robotics, for example). The significant influence of encodings can be clearly seen in the obtained creatures: Those with *f0* encoding displayed neither order nor structure. The two encodings restricting morphology to a tree produced more clear constructions, and for developmental encoding segmentation and modularity can be observed (Fig. 2.13).

2.5.2 Automatic Optimization Versus Human Design

Designing agents by hand is a very complex process. In professional applications, it requires planning and extensive knowledge about how the control system, sensors, and actuators work, as well as knowledge about the simulator. Designing neural networks for control by hand is especially difficult and tedious. For this reason, agents built by humans have usually lower fitness than agents produced by evolution. However, human creations are often interesting qualitatively. Human designs bear such properties as explicit purpose, elegance, simplicity (minimum of means), and often symmetry and modularity. These features are opposed to evolutionary results, which are characterized

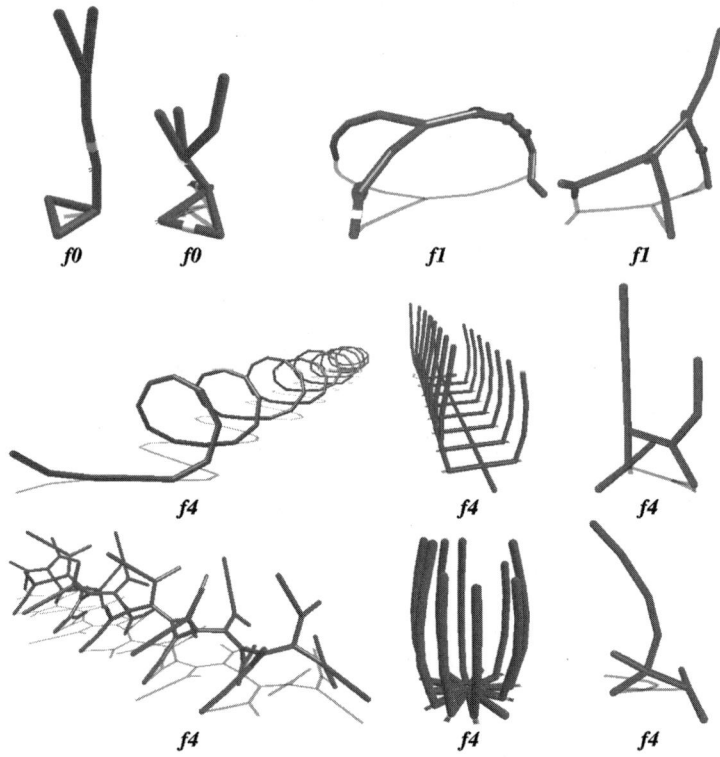

Fig. 2.13. Representative agents for three distinct genetic encodings and height maximization task.

by hidden purpose, complexity, implicit and very strong interdependencies between parts, as well as redundancy and randomness [11].

The difficult process of designing neural networks can be circumvented by a hybrid solution: Bodies can be hand-constructed, and control structures evolved for it. This popular approach can yield interesting creatures [1, 8, 10, 12], often resembling in behavior creatures found in nature [7].

2.5.3 Clustering with Similarity Measure

The similarity measure outlined in Section 2.4.2 allowed users to perform a number of experiments [9]. As stated earlier, the availability of automatic similarity estimation can be very useful. A sample application of similarity measure for clustering is presented here. A specific clustering method (called UPGMA) is applied after similarity is computed for every pair of considered individuals. Figure 2.14 shows the result of clustering of 10 individuals taken from the height maximization experiments. The clustering tree is accompanied by creature morphologies.

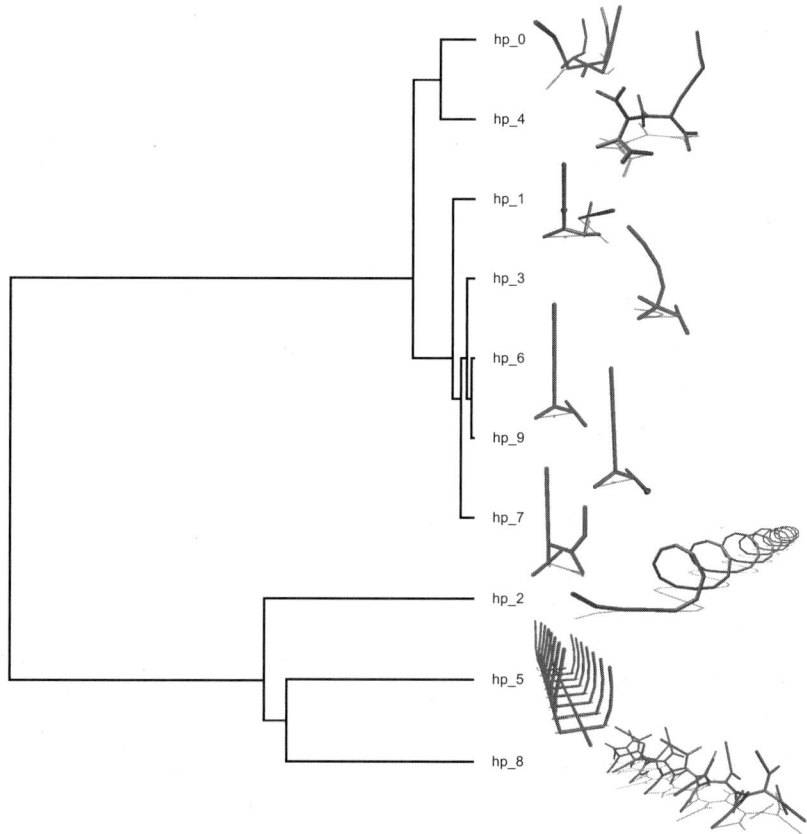

Fig. 2.14. The clustering tree for 10 best individuals in the height maximization task.

It can be seen that the three big organisms are in a single, distinct cluster. They are similar in size, but different in structure, so the distance in-between them is high. Moreover, the measure also captured functional similarity (hp_1, 3, 6, 9, 7) — all these agents have a single stick upwards and a similar base. The agents hp_0 and hp_4 are of medium size, but certainly closer to the small organisms group than to the big ones. They are also similar in structure; that is why they constitute a separate cluster.

The similarity measure is very helpful for study and analysis of groups of individuals. Manual work of classification of the agents shown in Fig. 2.14 yielded similar results, but it was a very mundane and time-consuming process. It also lacked objectivism and accuracy, which are properties of the automatic procedure.

2.5.4 Other Experiments

Considering open architecture of the Framsticks system, many possibilities exist to define diverse genetic representations, experimental setups, interaction rules, and environments (see Sections 2.3.2 and 2.3.3). Most obvious ideas include coevolution of individuals in populations, predator–prey relationships, multiple gene pools and populations, and their specialization. Experiment ideas related to biology include introducing geographical constraints, and then investigating differences in clusters obtained after a period of time, or studying two or more populations of highly different sizes. The latter, under geographical constraints, can be used to simulate and understand speciation.

A number of interesting experiments regarding evolutionary and neurocomputational bases of the emergence of complex cognition forms, and a discussion about semantics of evolved neural networks, perception, and memory is presented in [16]. Other experiments focus on evolution of sensory-motor coordination system. For this purpose, an artificial eye sensor has been developed in Framsticks. The basic experiment concerns evolution of the eye-muscles coordination so that creatures are able to move to a particular location, where a target object is seen in some specific (awarded) way. The decisions about where to move are based solely on what can be perceived by the artificial eye. Other experiments concern maze environments, space exploration and location of targets based on various kinds of available sensory information.

In the virtual life lab at Utrecht University, Framsticks is used for experiments related to evolutionary robotics, animal locomotion, distributed intelligence, artificial ecosystems, biosemiotics, and sexual and natural selection. Some experiments investigate the evolutionary origins and emergence of behavior patterns. In contrast to standard evolutionary computation, in which selection criteria are imposed by the experimenter outside the evolving system ("exogenous" or artificial selection), in these studies, as in nature, selection emerges from within the system ("endogenous" or natural selection). Experiments are designed to include the problems of survival and reproduction in which creatures are born, survive (by eating food), reproduce (by colliding with potential mates), and die (if their energy level is insufficient). Such experimental setup enables the investigation of environmental conditions under which certain behaviors offer reproductive advantages. Natural selection in Framsticks is, among others, used in the following experiments.

Predator–Prey

Coevolutionary processes in predator–prey systems are considered to result in arms races that promote *complexification*. For such complexification to emerge, the system must exhibit (semi)stable population dynamics. The primary goal of this experiment is to establish the conditions in which the simulated ecosystem is stable. Food, prey and predator creatures are modeled in a small food chain and allowed to consume each other and reproduce (see

Fig. 2.15. A snapshot of the predator–prey simulation. The two dark creatures are predators, hunting down the lighter prey. Prey have evolved to smartly flee from their predators.

Fig. 2.15). The resulting population dynamics are analyzed using an extended Lotka–Volterra model. When the relations between the parameters in the biological model and the simulation are established, stable conditions can be predicted which enables studies in long-term coevolutionary complexification.

Semiotics

Semiosis is the establishment of connections between a sign and the signified via a situated interpretant. The segregation of the sign and the signified from the environment is not given a priori to agents. A sign becomes a part of an agent's subjective environment only if it offers benefits in terms of survival and/or reproduction. In this experiment, the evolutionary emergence of the relation between signs and signified is studied by putting a population of creatures into an environment which contains many signs emitted by — for example — toxic and nutritious food resources, or fertile and infertile conspecifics. Through natural selection, the agents that have established behavioral relations between the signs and the signified are promoted. A sample of such a relation is movement toward the sign (*chemotaxis*). In varieties of this experiment, agents can leave trails of signs (e.g., pheromones) in the environment or evolve the ability to signal to each other by using *symbols* so that the relation between the sign and the signified is arbitrary.

Sympatric Speciation

Usually, speciation occurs through geographical isolation, which disables gene flow and promotes genetic drift. This kind of speciation is called *allopatric*.

However, *sympatric* speciation also happens in populations that live in the same geographical area. Reproducing this phenomenon is the goal of this experiment. Sympatric speciation is hypothesized to occur if selection disrupts gene flow, when intraspecific competition drives a part of the population to adapt to another type of food. In the experiment, a single population is modeled in which all agents are generally intermediate in consuming each of the two types of food. Genetic drift to consuming one type of food occurs, since this promotes survival and reproduction. With the population growing, intraspecific competition grows, and a part of the population may adapt to consume the (previously unused) type of food. When sexual preferences are evolved such that agents prefer to mate with agents that feed on the same type of food, gene flow diminishes, which means that two species have evolved from one initial population.

2.6 Education with Entertainment

Simulating evolution of three-dimensional agents is not a trivial task. On the other hand, three-dimensional creatures are very attractive and appealing to both young and older users, who spend much time enjoying the simulation. Many users wish to design their own creatures, simulate them, improve, and evaluate, but designing creatures is not very obvious when it takes place on the genetic level. To simplify this process, the Framsticks graphical editor (FRED) was released. It helps in building creatures similarly as CAD programs help in creating 3D models. The user-friendly graphical interface (shown in Fig. 2.16), drag-and-drop operations, and instant preview allow users to develop structures of their imagination. Designing neural networks lets users understand the basic principles of control systems, their architecture, and applications. The editor can also browse and download existing genotypes from the Internet database.

Framsticks can be used to illustrate some basic phenomena, like genes and genetics, mutation, evolution, user-driven evolution and artificial selection, walking and swimming, artificial life simulation, virtual world interactions, etc. However, the simulator has numerous options and parameters that make it complicated for the first-time users to handle. Thus a predefined set of parameters and program behaviors was created for the purposes of presentation of the aforementioned phenomena.

Most often, users of this demonstration program observe what is happening in the virtual world, so the program was named the *Framsticks Theater*. It is an easy-to-use application that includes a number of "shows," and new shows can be added by advanced users or developers using scripts (Section 2.3.2). The shows already included have their script source files available. Each show available in the theater has a few basic options to select (like the number of running creatures, length, and difficulty for the "Race" show) . The list of shows (see also Fig. 2.17) includes

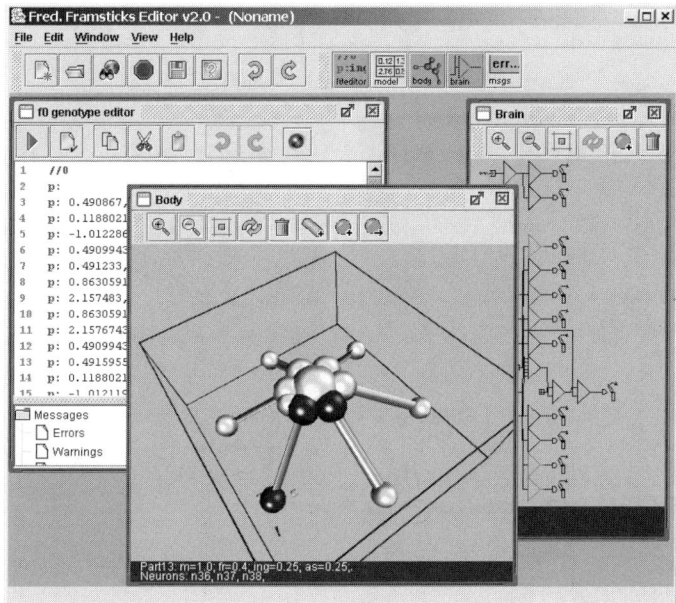

Fig. 2.16. FRED: the user-friendly graphical editor of Framsticks.

- Biomorph — illustrates a user-driven evolution. Users select a creature and double-click it to create its offspring. Eight creatures are mutated from the one in the middle.
- Dance — effectors of all simulated creatures are forced to work synchronously.
- Evolution — shows evolutionary optimization with user-selected fitness criteria, 50 genotypes in the gene pool, and tournament selection.
- Mixed world — no evolution takes place, creatures are just simulated in a mixed land-and-water environment.
- Mutation — presents a chain of subsequent mutants.
- Presentation — shows various walking and swimming methods of creatures evolved or constructed by the Framsticks users.
- Race — creatures compete in a terrain race running to the finish line.
- Reproduction — illustrates spontaneous evolution. Each creature with a sufficient energy level produces an offspring, which is then put close to its parent. Food is created at a constant rate and placed randomly.
- Touch of life — creatures pass life from one to another by touching.

The Framsticks Theater can be run on standalone workstations as a show (artistic installations, shops, fairs), as well as for education (e.g., in biology, evolution, optimization, simulation, robotics), illustration, attractive graphical background for music, advertisement, entertainment, screen-saving mode, etc.

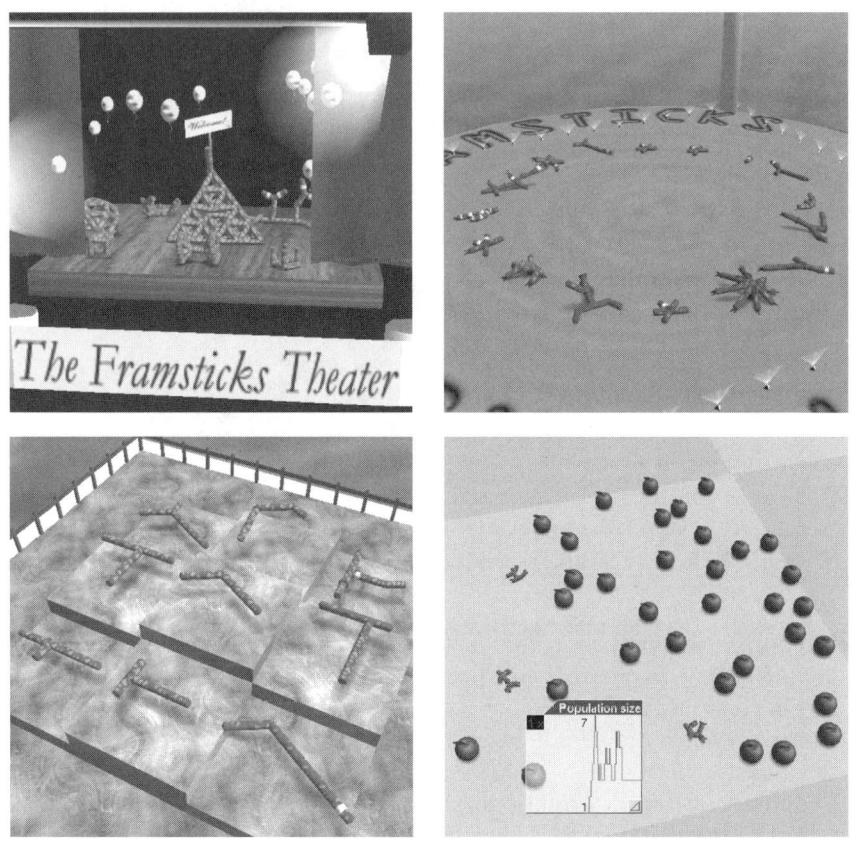

Fig. 2.17. Four Framsticks Theater shows: introduction, dance, biomorph, and reproduction. See also color plate.

2.7 Summary

This chapter presents Framsticks, a general tool for modeling, simulation, optimization, and evolution of three-dimensional creatures. Sections 2.4, 2.5, and 2.6, demonstrate applications for research, education, and entertainment. Framsticks is developed with a vision of combining these three aspects, to make research and education — attractive, playing for fun — educationally involving, and education — a demonstration and introduction to research.

Although the Framsticks system is versatile and complex, it can be simplified when some features are not needed. For example, control systems can be neglected if only static structures are to be considered. Genetic encoding may only allow for two-dimensional structures if 3D is not required. The simulation can be restricted to a specific type of a neuron. A local optimization framework can be used if the task does not require evolutionary algorithms. The experiment definition may be tailored for only one, specific purpose, e.g., to perform evaluation, analysis, or simulation without evolution.

Complexity is useless when it cannot be understood or applied. This is why the Framsticks software tries to present information in a human-friendly and clear way, helping to understand the phenomena of life. Framsticks is employed both in research experiments and in education. It is used by computer scientists, biologists, roboticists, and other scientists, and also by students and laypeople of various ages.

Acknowledgment

This work has been supported by the State Committee for Scientific Research, from KBN research grant no. 3 T11C 050 26, and by the Foundation for Polish Science, from subsidy no. 38/2004.

References

1. Adamatzky A (2000) Software review: Framsticks. Kybernetes 29:1344–1351.
2. Bentley P (1999) Evolutionary design by computers. Morgan Kaufmann.
3. Funes P and Pollack JB (1998) Evolutionary body building: Adaptive physical designs for robots. Artificial Life 4:337–357.
4. Goldberg DE (1989) Genetic Algorithms in Search, Optimization and Machine Learning. Addison-Wesley Publishing Co.
5. Gruau F, Whitley D and Pyeatt L (1996) A comparison between cellular encoding and direct encoding for genetic neural networks. In: Koza JR, Goldberg DE, Fogel DB and Riolo RR (eds.) Proceedings of the First Annual Conference Genetic Programming 1996, MIT Press, Cambridge, MA, pp 81–89.
6. Hapke M, Komosinski M and Waclawski D (2003) Application of evolutionarily optimized fuzzy controllers for virtual robots. In: Proceedings of the 7th Joint Conference on Information Sciences. ACM, North Carolina, USA, pp. 1605–1608.
7. Ijspeert AJ (2000) A 3-D biomechanical model of the salamander. In: Heudin J-C (ed.) Proceedings of 2nd International Conference on Virtual Worlds (VW2000), Paris, France. Lect Notes AI 1834:225–234.
8. Komosinski M (2000) The world of Framsticks: Simulation, evolution, interaction. In: Heudin J-C (ed.) Virtual Worlds. Lect Notes AI 1834:214–224.
9. Komosinski M, Koczyk G and Kubiak M (2001) On estimating similarity of artificial and real organisms. Theory in Biosciences 120:271–286.
10. Komosinski M and Rotaru-Varga A (2000) From directed to open-ended evolution in a complex simulation model. In: Bedau MA, McCaskill JS, Packard NH and Rasmussen S (eds.) Artificial Life VII, MIT Press, pp. 293–299.

11. Komosinski M and Rotaru-Varga A (2001) Comparison of different genotype encodings for simulated 3D agents. Artificial Life Journal 7:395–418.
12. Komosinski M and Ulatowski S (1997) Framsticks web site, http://www.frams.alife.pl.
13. Komosinski M and Ulatowski S (2004) Genetic mappings in artificial genomes. Theory in Biosciences 123:125–137.
14. Lipson H and Pollack JB (2000) Automatic design and manufacture of robotic lifeforms. Nature 406:974–978.
15. Lund H-H, Hallam J and Lee W-P (1997) Evolving robot morphology. In: Proceedings of IEEE 4th International Conference on Evolutionary Computation, IEEE Press, NJ, USA.
16. Mandik P (2002) Synthetic neuroethology. Metaphilosophy, Special Issue on Cyberphilosophy: The Intersection of Philosophy and Computing 33.
17. Sims K (1994) Evolving 3D morphology and behavior by competition. In: Brooks RA and Maes P (eds.) Proceedings of the 4th International Conference on Artificial Life. MIT Press, Cambridge, MA, pp. 28–39
18. Taylor T and Massey C (2001) Recent developments in the evolution of morphologies and controllers for physically simulated creatures. Artificial Life 7:77–88.
19. Ulatowski S (2000) Framsticks GDK (genotype development kit), http://www.frams.alife.pl/dev.
20. Yager RR and Filev DP (1994) Foundations of fuzzy control. Wiley, New York.

3

Nerve Garden: Germinating Biological Metaphors in Net-based Virtual Worlds

Bruce Damer, Karen Marcelo, Frank Revi, Todd Furmanski, Chris Laurel

Nerve Garden is a biologically inspired, multi-user, collaborative 3D virtual world available to a wide Internet audience. The project combines a number of methods and technologies, including L-systems, Java, cellular automata, and VRML. Nerve Garden is a work in progress designed to provide a compelling experience of a virtual terrarium that exhibits properties of growth, decay, and energy transfer reminiscent of a simple ecosystem. The goals of the Nerve Garden project are to create an online "collaborative A-Life laboratory" that can be extended by a large number of users for purposes of education and research.

3.1 History and Background of the Project

3.1.1 Artificial Life Meets the World Wide Web

During the summer of 1994, one of us (Damer) paid a visit to the Santa Fe Institute for discussions with Chris Langton and his student team working on the Swarm project. Two fortuitous things were happening during that visit, SFI was installing the first Mosaic web browsers, and digital movies of Karl Sims' evolving "evolving virtual creatures" [13] were being viewed through the web by amazed students (see Fig. 3.1 and view on the Internet in the reference section at Sims). It was postulated then that the combination of the emerging backbone of the Internet, a distributed simulation environment like Swarm, and the compelling 3D visuals and underlying techniques of Sims' creatures could be combined to produce something very compelling: online virtual worlds in which thousands of users could collaboratively experiment with biological paradigms.

One of the Contact Consortium's special interest groups, called *Biota.org* — *The Digital Biology Project*, was chartered in mid-1996 to develop virtual worlds using techniques from the artificial life (ALife) field. Its first effort was

Fig. 3.1. View of Karl Sims' original evolving block creatures in competition.

Nerve Garden experienced as an art installation at the SIGGRAPH 97 conference and made available online starting in August of 1997. Several hundred visitors to the SIGGRAPH "Electric Garden" Nerve Garden installation used L-systems and Java to germinate plant models into shared VRML (Virtual Reality Modeling Language) island worlds hosted on the Internet. Biota.org is now seeking support to develop a subsequent version of Nerve Garden, which will embody more biological paradigms and, we hope, create an environment capable of supporting education, research, and cross-pollination between traditional artificial life (ALife) subject areas and other fields.

3.1.2 Background: L-Systems

L-systems [10] have become a commonly used tool for many computer applications. Commercial 3D packages like Worldbuilder utilize L-systems to model and simulate vegetation [15]. Instead of hand modeling potentially thousands of trees, procedural generation offers a large amount of data compression and an incredible amount of variance. No two trees in a forest may look alike, but each could be identified as a pine or oak.

While L-systems have classically been used to describe plants, there have been several cases in which the grammars and implementations have been used for other ends. Karl Sims' own virtual creatures used L-system like branching structures. Limbs and sublimbs, much like arms and fingers on a human, determined the basic structure of the evolved animals. One program, LMUSe, converts L-system strings into MIDI format, transforming the systems into musical compositions [14]. Instead of moving in world space and drawing to the screen, the program interprets the grammar as cues to change pitch or transpose. Famous patterns like Koch's Snowflake can not only be seen but also heard.

L-systems have proven useful in modeling virtual cities [9]. Tasks from generating street layouts to house and building appearances have been accomplished using L-systems in one way or another. The advantages of compression and levels of detail apply just as well in a "built" environment as a "grown" one. Buildings can show similarities, but nevertheless possess enough variance to avoid unrealistic repetition. Architectural "styles" offer an analog to biological "species" in this sense. The cities themselves can be seeded like forests, and expand over time, implying a complex history of growth and development. Local and global factors can be incorporated into such growth, further adding to the complexity and believability of the city.

The ability to generate complex geometries from simple rules means that, like Conway's "Game of Life" [4], L-Systems can be manipulated with a few simple parameters and permit children and adults alike to explore forms that with ordinary artistic abilities, they would not be able to express. The motivation for Nerve Garden was to permit ordinary users of the Internet to engage in this exploration using the familiar metaphors of landscapes featuring a range of L-system derived plant forms.

3.2 Nerve Garden I: Inspiration, Architecture, and Experience

3.2.1 Inspiration

Nerve Garden I (interface shown in Fig. 3.2) is a biologically inspired, shared state 3D virtual world available to a wide audience through standard Internet protocols running on all major hardware platforms. Nerve Garden was inspired by the original work on ALife by Chris Langton [7], the digital ecosystem called Tierra by Tom Ray [11], the evolving 3D virtual creatures of Karl Sims [13], and the Telegarden developed at the University of Southern California [5]. Nerve Garden sources its models from the work on L-systems by Aristide Lindenmayer, Przemyslaw Prusinkiewicz, and Radomir Mech [8, 10].

3.2.2 Architectural Elements

Nerve Garden I allowed users to operate a Java-based thin client, the Germinator (see Fig. 3.3), to visually extrude 3D plant models generated from L-systems. The 3D interface in the Java client provided an immediate 3D experience of various L-system plant and even some arthropod forms (see Fig. 3.4). Users employed a slider bar to extrude the models in real time and a mutator to randomize select production rules in the L-systems and generate variants on the plant models. After germinating several plants, the user would

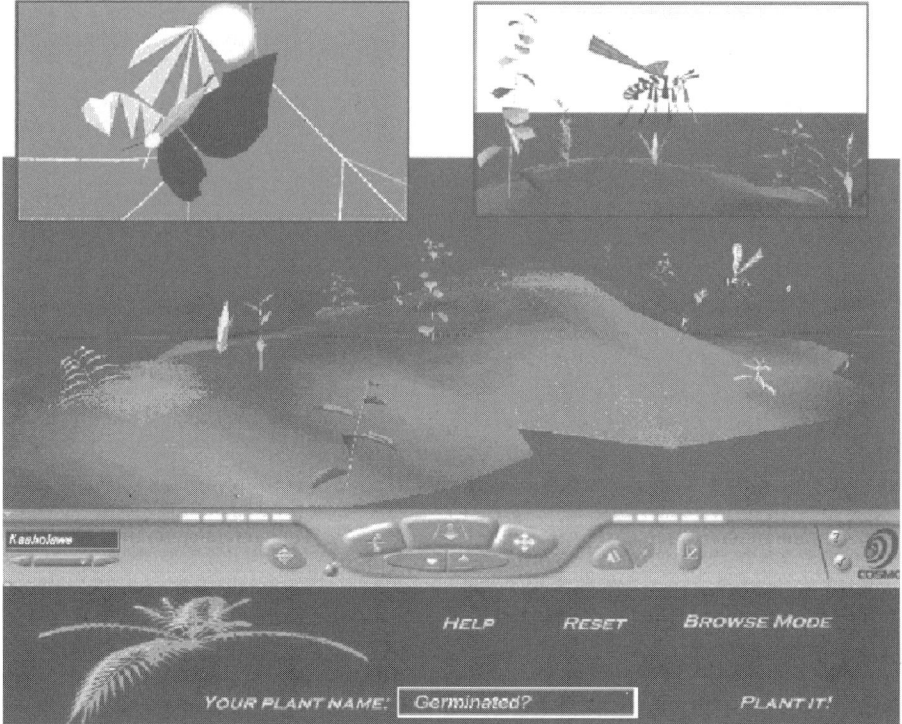

Fig. 3.2. Nerve Garden interface in web browser. See also color plate.

select one, name it, and submit it into a common VRML97 scenegraph called the Seeder Garden.

The object passed to the Seeder Garden contained the VRML export from the Germinator, the plant name, and other data. Another Java application, called NerveServer, received this object and determined a free "plot" on an island model in a VRML scenegraph (shown in Fig. 3.2). Each island had a set number of plots and showed the user where his or her plant was assigned by a red sphere operated through the VRML external authoring interface (EAI). Cybergardeners would open the Seeder Garden, window where they would then move the indicator sphere with their plant attached and place it into the scene. Various scenegraph viewpoints were available to users, including a moving viewpoint on the back of an animated model of a flying insect endlessly touring the island (the bee and butterfly shown in Fig. 3.2). Users would often spot their plant as the bee or butterfly made a close approach over the island. Over 10 MB of sound, some of it also generated algorithmically, emanated from different objects on the island added to the immersion of the experience. For added effect, L-system-based fractal VRML lightening (with generated thunder) occasionally streaked across the sky above the Seeder Garden islands.

Fig. 3.3. Lace Germinator Java client interface.

NerveServer permitted multiple users to update and view the same island. In addition, users could navigate the same space using standard VRML plug-ins to web browsers on SGI workstations, PCs, or Macintosh computers from various parts of the Internet. One problem was that the distributed L-system clients could easily generate scenes with several hundred thousand polygons, rendering them impossible to visit. We used 3D hardware acceleration, including an SGI Onyx II Infinite Reality system and a PC running a 3D Labs Permedia video acceleration card to permit a more complex environment to be experienced by users. In 2004 and beyond, a whole new generation of 3D chip sets on 32- and 64-bit platforms will enable highly complex 3D interactive environments. There is an interesting parallel here to Ray's work on Tierra, where the energy of the system was proportional to the power of the CPU serving the virtual machine inhabited by Tierran organisms. In many artificial life systems, it is not important to have a compelling 3D interface. The benefits to providing one for Nerve Garden are that it encouraged participation and experimentation from a wide group of users.

Fig. 3.4. Plant models generated by the Germinator.

3.2.3 Experience: What Was Learned

As a complex set of parts including a Java client, simple object distribution system, a multi-user server, a rudimentary database, and a shared, persistent VRML scenegraph, Nerve Garden functioned well under the pressures of a diverse range of users on multiple hardware platforms. Users were able to use the Germinator applet without our assistance to generate fairly complex, unique, and aesthetically pleasing models. Users were all familiar with the metaphor of gardens and many were eager to "visit their plant" again from their home computers. Placing their plants in the VRML Seeder Gardens was more challenging due to the difficulty of navigating in 3D using VRML browsers. Younger users tended to be much more adept at using the 3D environment. A photo of a user of the Nerve Garden installation at the Electric Garden emerging technologies pavilion at SIGGRAPH 1997 in Los Angeles is featured in Fig. 3.5.

While it was a successful user experience of a generative environment, Nerve Garden I lacked the sophistication of a "true ALife system" like Tierra [11] in that plant model objects did not reproduce or communicate between virtual machines containing other gardens. In addition, unlike an adaptive

Fig. 3.5. User at SIGGRAPH Nerve Garden Installation, August 1997.

L-system space such as the one described in [8], the plant models did not interact with their neighbors or the environment. Lastly, there was no concept of autonomous, self replicating objects within the environment. Nerve Garden II will address some of these shortcomings and, we hope, contribute a powerful tool for education and research in the ALife community.

Did Nerve Garden attain some of the goals we set for presenting an ALife-inspired virtual world? The environment did provide a compelling space to draw attention while also proving that an abstraction of a world, that of a virtual forest of L-systems, could be transmitted in algorithmic form and then generated on the client computer, achieving great compression and efficiency. When combined with streaming and ecosystem controls, Nerve Garden II could evolve into a powerful virtual world architecture testbed.

Visiting Nerve Garden I

Nerve Garden I can be visited using a suitable VRML97 compatible browser running Java 1.1. Scenes like the ones in Fig. 3.6 can be experienced in real-time rendered virtual islands that may be toured through the traveling "bee" viewpoint. All of the islands and L-Systems made at SIGGRAPH 97 can be viewed on the web (see References). The Biota special interest group and its annual conferences are covered at http://www.biota.org.

Fig. 3.6. Bee flight through a Nerve Garden island populated by user-generated L-System plants. See also color plate.

3.3 A Next Evolutionary Step: Nerve Garden II

The Biota special interest group is seeking support for a subsequent version of Nerve Garden. Our goals for Nerve Garden II are

- to develop a simple functioning ecosystem within the VRML scenegraph to control polygon growth and evolve elements of the world through time as partially described in [8],
- to integrate with a stronger database to permit garden cloning and inter-garden communication permitting cross-pollination between islands,
- to embody a cellular automata engine that will support autonomous growth and replication of plant models and introduce a class of virtual herbivores ("polyvores") that prey on the plants' polygonal energy stores,

- to stream world geometry through the transmission of generative algorithms (such as the L-systems) rather than geometry, achieving great compression, efficient use of bandwidth, and control of polygon explosion and scene evolution on the client side.

Much of the above depends on the availability of a comprehensive scenegraph and behavior control mechanism. In development over the past several years, Nerves™ is a simple but high-performance general-purpose cellular automata engine written as both a C++ and Java kernel. Nerves is modeled on the biological processes seen in animal nervous systems, and plant and animal circulatory systems, vastly simplified into a token passing and storage mechanism. Nerves and its associated language, NerveScript, allows users to define a large number of pathways and collection pools supporting flows of arbitrary tokens, token storage, token correlation, and filtering. Nerves borrows many concepts from neural networks and directed graphs used in concert with genetic and generative algorithms as reported by Ray [12], Sims [13], and others.

Nerves components will underlie the Seeder Gardens providing functions analogous to a drip irrigation system, defining a finite and therefore regulatory resource from which the plant models must draw for continued growth. In addition, Nerves control paths will be generated as L-system models extrude, providing wiring paths connected to the geometry and proximity sensors in the model. This will permit interaction with the plant models. When pruning of plant geometry occurs or growth stimulus becomes scarce, the transformation of the plant models can be triggered. One step beyond this will be the introduction of autonomous entities into the gardens, which we term "polyvores", that will seek to convert the "energy" represented by the polygons in the plant models, into reproductive capacity. Polyvores will provide another source of regulation in this simple ecosystem. Gardens will maintain their interactive capacity, allowing users to enter, germinate plants, introduce polyvores, and prune plants or cull polyvores. Gardens will also run as automatous systems, maintaining polygon complexity within boundaries that allow users to enter the environment.

```
spinalTap.nrv
DEF spinalCordSeg Bundle {
-spinalTapA-Swim-bodyMotion[4]-Complex;
-spinalTapB-Swim-bodyMotion[4]-Complex;
}
```

Fig. 3.7. Sample NerveScript coding language.

We expect to use Nerves to tie much of the preceding processes together. Like VRML, Nerves is described by a set of public domain APIs and a published language, NerveScript [2]. Figure 3.7 lists some typical NerveScript statements, which describe a two-chain neural pathway that might be used as a spinal chord of a simple swimming fish. DEF defines a reusable object spinalCordSeg consisting of input paths spinalTapA and spinalTapB, which will only pass the token Swim into a four-stage filter called bodyMotion. All generated tokens end up in Complex, another Nerve bundle, defined elsewhere.

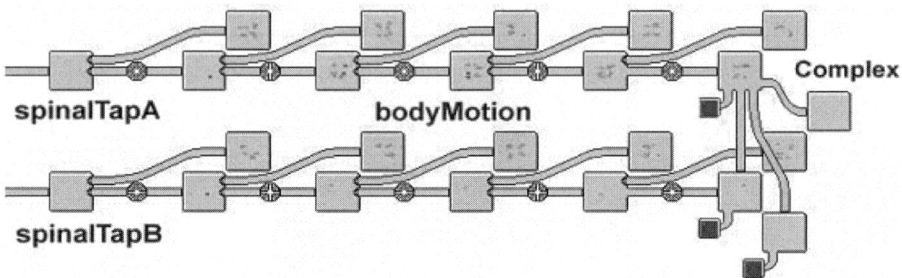

Fig. 3.8. Nerves visualizer running within the NerveScript development environment.

Figure 3.8 shows the visualization of the running NerveScript code in the NerveScript development environment. In the VRML setting, pathways spinalTapA and B are fed by eventOut messages drawn out of the scenegraph while the Nerve bundles generate eventIns back to VRML using the EAI. Nerves is fully described at the web address referenced at the end of this chapter.

3.4 The Role of ALife in Virtual Worlds on the Internet

3.4.1 Multi-User Online Worlds: A Rich Space for Biological Metaphors

Multi-user "avatar"-enabled Internet-based virtual worlds have evolved from relatively simple environments in the mid-1990s to multimillion-dollar massively multiplayer online role-playing games and simulations today [3]. There is a large commercial and research-driven motivation to create richer environments to attract and keep users of these online spaces. Techniques from the artificial life field, such as L-Systems, have become increasingly employed in online virtual worlds in the following roles:

- to provide biologically inspired behaviors, including animated behaviors, growth and decay of the environment, and generation and mutation of nonplayer characters to draw users into these spaces, for purposes of entertainment or learning about the living world,
- to power underlying architectures with biological metaphors.

3.4.2 Using ALife to Draw Attention Span

The commercial success of nonnetworked CD-ROM games such as "Creatures" from Cyberlife of Cambridge, UK, Petz from P.F. Magic of San Francisco, and the ubiquitous Tomogatchi of Japan have been successful in capturing the human imagination, attention span, and the pocketbook. For networked gaming in environments such as EverQuest^{TM}, The Sims^{TM}, AmericasArmy, Neverwinter's Night^{TM}, Second Life^{TM}, and Star Wars Galaxies^{TM}, the drive for more lifelike animation, better nonplayer characters, and more rich and changeable worlds inspires innovative efforts within many projects. The third Biota conference held at San Jose State University in 1999 (see Biota references) focused on the application of ALife to this new world.

3.4.3 Artifical Life Techniques Powering Better Virtual World Architectures

Players soon tire of key-framed repeatable behavior sequences and yearn for objects that seem to learn their moves through stimuli from the human players. Believable physics, noncanned motion, stimulus and response learning drive developers to borrow from biology. Pets and gardens, perhaps our most intimate biological companions in the physical world, would serve to improve the quality of life in the virtual fold.

The key to delivery of better experiences to a variety of user platforms on low-bandwidth connections is to understand that the visual representation of a world and its underlying coding need to be separated. This separation is a fundamental principle of living forms: The abstract coding, the DNA, is vastly different than the resulting body. This phenotype/genotype separation also has another powerful property: compression. The VRML 3D scenegraph language simply defined a file format, a phenotype, which would be delivered to a variety of different client computers (akin to ecosystems) without any consideration of scaling, or adapting to the capabilities of those computers. A biologically inspired virtual world would more effectively package itself in some abstract representation, travel highly compressed along the relatively thin pipes of the Internet, and then generate itself to a complexity appropriate to the compute space in which it finds itself.

As the virtual environment unfolds from its abstraction, it can generate useful controls, or lines of communication, which allow it to talk to processes back on servers or to peers on the network. These lines of control can also create new interfaces to the user, providing unique behaviors. One might imagine users plucking fruit from virtual vines only to have those vines grow new runners with fruit in different places. With nongenerative, or totally phenotypic models, such interaction would be difficult, if not impossible. As we saw from the example of Nerve Garden earlier in this chapter, important scenegraph management techniques such as polygon reduction or level of detail and level of behavior scaling could also be accomplished by the introduction of ecosystem-styled metaphors. If we define the energy state of a virtual world inversely to the computing resources it is consuming, as in a natural habitat, it would be inevitable for any scenegraph or objects in it to evolve more efficient representations.

3.5 Other Examples of L-System-based Virtual World Construction and Considerations for the Future Use of L-Systems

Chojo, depicted in Fig. 3.9, is a current mobile project developed by the Integrated Media Systems Center and the Cinema Television's Interactive Media Department at USC. Chojo makes use of emergent L-system rules, but uses the movements of human participants in the physical world as a primary generative force [1]. Tracking users through GPS, Chojo maps movements, path intersections, and user-defined "traits" and uses these data to generate evolving shapes in a virtual space. A point in this virtual space can be viewed from a corresponding physical space a viewer in front of an undergraduate library might see a series of vine- and crystal-like structures covering the building through his or her PDA.

Fig. 3.9. Visual output from USC's Chojo.

Exterior forces can continue to enhance ALife systems. Tropism, for instance, can alter a branching pattern globally [6]. Forces like wind and gravity change the way a tree grows, for instance. Flowers and leaves move to seek sunlight. L-systems can accommodate such external forces, adding a further life-like quality. Tropism could also be used in a more abstract sense, depending on the context of the L-system. For instance, variables like population density could be integrated into an algorithm describing a city, or various goals and wants of a virtual creature could ripple through its physical structure.

The recursive and parametric nature of L-systems and other emergent algorithms means that a computer and handle and display varying degrees of resolution and detail. Networked applications like Nerve Garden must take into account computers of varying speeds and abilities. The ability to easily generate variable complexity from a fairly simple set of equations or library of shapes means that a world generated through these emergent methods can be as simple or complex as the machine allows.

We hope that the scope of projects like Nerve Garden will continue to expand not just in size but also in relationships. In the physical world, terrain affects how plants grow in a given area, but the terrain itself can change because of the presence of plants: A hillside without trees will be susceptible to landslides and will erode from the wind. Animals migrate when their food supply dwindles, due to either season or overpopulation.

Much of the emergent and complex nature of artificial and real life arises from the interaction of fairly simple rules. The algorithmic principles underlying this complexity are often hard to divine in nature, yet casting biologically suggestive rule-bases (such as L-Systems) in software and observing the results can prove challenging, entertaining, and informative.

References

1. Chojo (2004), University of Southern California, available on the web at http://interactive.usc.edu/chojo.
2. Damer B (1996) Nerves language definition and examples on the web at http://www.digitalspace.com/nerves/.
3. Damer B (1997) Avatars, Exploring and Building Virtual Worlds on the Internet. Peachpit Press, Berkeley.
4. Gardner M (1970) The fantastic combinations of John Conway's new solitaire game "Life." Scientific American 223:120–123.
5. Goldberg K, Mascha M, Gentner S, Rothenberg N, Sutter C, and Wiegley J (1995) Desktop tele-operation via the world wide web. In: Proceedings of the IEEE International Conference on Robotics and Automation.
6. Hart JC (2003) Procedural Synthesis of Geometry. In: David S et al (eds.) Texturing and modeling: A Procedural Approach Ebert. Morgan Kaufman Publishers, Amsterdam.
7. Langton C (1992) Life at the edge of chaos. In: Artificial Life II. Addison-Wesley, Redwood City, CA, pp 41–91.

8. Mech R and Prusinkiewicz P (1996) Visual models of plants interacting with their environment. In: Proc. SIGGRAPH 96. ACM Publications, pp 397–410.
9. Parish YIH and Müller P (2001) Procedural Modeling of Cities, In: SIGGRAPH 2001 Conference Proceedings, SIGGRAPH 2001, Los Angeles, California, USA, pp 301–308. Available on the web at http://graphics.ethz.ch/Downloads/Publications/Papers/2001/p_Par01.pdf.
10. Prusinkiewicz P and Lindenmayer A (eds.) (1990) The Algorithmic Beauty of Plants. Springer-Verlag, New York.
11. Ray TS (1994) Netlife — Creating a jungle on the Internet: Nonlocated online digital territories, incorporations and the matrix. Knowbotic Research 3.
12. Ray TS (1994) Neural networks, genetic algorithms and artificial life: Adaptive computation. In: Proc. 1994 ALife, Genetic Algorithm and Neural Networks Seminar. Institute of Systems, Control and Information Engineers, pp 1–14.
13. Sims K (1994) Evolving virtual creatures. Computer Graphics (Siggraph '94), pp 43–50.
14. Sharp D (2003) LMUSe: L Systems to Music, available on the web at http://www.geocities.com/Athens/Academy/8764/lmuse/lmuse.html.
15. WorldBuilder 4. Digital Element. (2004), available on the web at http://www.digi-element.com/site/index.htm.

Online Resources

- Nerve Garden with SIGGRAPH 1997 samples is available on the web at http://www.biota.org/nervegarden/
- Damer B (1996) Nerves language definition and examples on the web at http://www.digitalspace.com/nerves/
- Biota Special Interest Group of the Contact Consortium is described on the web at
  http://www.biota.org
- The Contact Consortium is described on the web at
  http://www.ccon.org
- The USC Telegarden is documented on the web at
  http://www.usc.edu/dept/garden/
- Recent publications on virtual worlds are available on the web at
  http://www.digitalspace.com/papers/

4

GenePool: Exploring the Interaction Between Natural Selection and Sexual Selection

Jeffrey Ventrella

GenePool is an artificial life simulation designed to bring some basic principles of evolution to light in an entertaining and instructive way. Most significant is the aspect of sexual selection — where mate choice is a factor in the evolution of morphology and motor control in physically based animated organisms. We see in the examples of deer antlers, peacock tails, and fish coloration a magnificent world of variation that makes the study of animals fascinating for us — aesthetically-driven humans that we are. But aesthetics is in the eye of the beholder. And sometimes aesthetics can run counter to the rules of basic survival. GenePool was designed to explore this topic.

4.1 History

In 1996, an animated artificial life simulation, called Darwin Pond, was designed, and a paper was published describing the simulation [13]. In Darwin Pond, hundreds of physically based organisms achieve locomotion via genetically based motor control and morphology. The ability to have more offspring is a direct outcome of two factors: (1) better ability to swim to within a critical distance to a chosen mate, and (2) the ability to attract other organisms who want to mate.

Because Darwin Pond was developed at a computer game company (Rocket Science Games, Inc.), it included a significant interactive component. Rocket Science did not survive as a company, and after much effort, Darwin Pond was released from the corporate and legal complexities of the software games world, and it was published for free at [15], where it has remained.

GenePool was developed as a derivation of Darwin Pond. Although it has fewer interactive aspects, it extends Darwin Pond in terms of the simulation by emphasizing the effects of sexual selection on morphology and behavior. The term "swimbot" was chosen to describe the organisms in GenePool, because of their robot-like mechanical appearance and the fact that they evolve into virtual swimming machines. A subsequent paper [14] discusses this work.

4.2 Background

Chaos theory and fractals popularized the notion that the complexity we appreciate in nature can often be described with a small number of parameters or rules. The key is iteration — the repeated application of those rules over time. The genetic algorithm (GA) [4, 5] mimics an aspect of nature's way through the iterative application of the principles of Darwinism over many populations. The GA has been used for generating adaptive behavior in simulated organisms, such as locomotion [7, 10, 12]. These explorations have shown how artificial evolution can be used to solve certain design problems that are too complex or multidimensional for humans to solve. Animal locomotion is an appropriate problem for this technique — it came about through evolution after all.

4.2.1 Dawkins' Call

The classic GA, however, does not model the asynchronous nature of population evolution. This limitation is what motivated further exploration into building a more realistic Darwinian model for evolving locomotion. Richard Dawkins had expressed a wish for more naturalistic models in artificial life [2], whereby the dynamics of genetic evolution are not constrained to the lock-step generation updating used in the classic GA, but rather are asynchronous and autonomous, and where the definition of "fitness" is not arbitrary. Darwin Pond was an attempt to answer this call.

4.2.2 Physics, in Various Forms

Many artificial life simulations explore the adaptation of organisms or populations within an environment — which can be quite abstract. These simulations are less concerned with the accuracy and verisimilitude of physical modeling as with the nature of the organisms' adaptation that takes place within, and in accordance with, the environment. Tierra [8] is a compelling and life-like artificial life simulation that has no physics — at least not in the Newtonian sense. In contrast, Sims' Blockies [10] uses a sophisticated 3D physical model — but here again, the main emphasis is the way in which the population adapts to accomplish a goal — and in this case the realism of the physical environment allows their adaptive solutions to be appropriately complex, as well as familiar to our own goal-oriented behaviors.

GenePool uses an abbreviated physical model, implemented in 2D. This simplification of mechanics is meant to strike a balance between having realistic enough physics to allow sufficient complexity of morphology and motor control, yet at the same time being computationally lean so it can animate hundreds of organisms in real time on average desktop computers, and thus allow detailed visualization and interaction.

4.2.3 Sexual Selection

Autonomous mating naturally brings us to the question of mate choice, which is what GenePool addresses. Could a simulation be built that demonstrates the effects of sexual selection that run counter to the need for energy efficient locomotion? In other words, can a simulation show an inherent conflict between the forces of natural selection and the forces of sexual selection? If so, what similarities to the natural world might emerge? GenePool implements a number of possible "attractiveness criteria" allowing interactive exploration of sexual selection forces on the evolution of swimbots. Thus, the primary scientific inquiry that GenePool hopes to shed light on is the interactions between natural selection and sexual selection, especially in regards to energy efficiency.

4.3 Description of the Software

GenePool is modeled as a continuous two-dimensional square area constrained by four boundaries. These boundaries do not wrap — as in a torus topology. GenePool uses simulation time rather than clock time. Time cannot be run backwards due to the nature of the forward dynamics affecting the positions and orientations of the swimbots. Within this continuous field are two kinds of entities: swimbots and food bits.

4.3.1 Initialization

At the start of a simulation run, 200 swimbots are initialized with random gene values (these genes are explained ahead). They are accompanied by a number of food bits, which serve as packets of energy for swimbots to consume. The total energy in the environment is stored in swimbots and food bits (the number of food bits being typically over 1000, depending on the total energy setting). Both swimbots and food bits are distributed randomly in a disk region, as shown in Fig. 4.1.

This disk region allows sufficient density of swimbots and food bits to give the few slightly more fit swimbots a chance to get to food and or mates before running out of energy, thus giving evolution a jump-start. Sometimes, as luck would have it, all the swimbots die off after a while. But in most cases, small clusters of swimbots appear in a few locations in the disk region — groups of genetically related swimbots, or "gene pools" — and eventually one gene pool takes over the whole environment.

Figure 4.2 shows a close-up view of a group of swimbots to show variation in an unevolved population. Food bits can be seen scattered around.

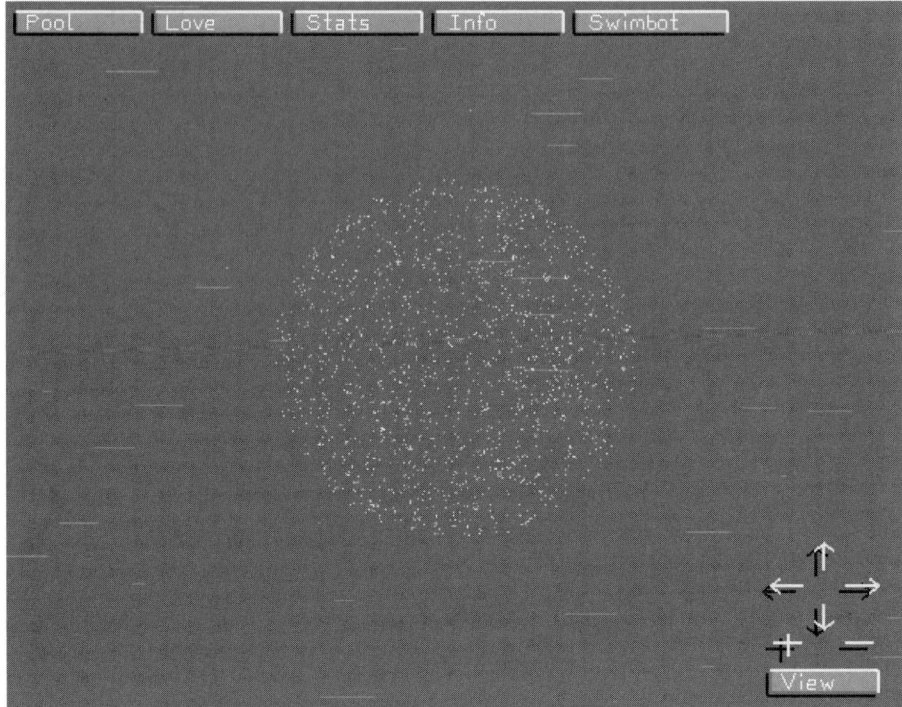

Fig. 4.1. Initial distribution of 200 swimbots and food bits.

4.3.2 Food Bit Behavior

Food bits replicate by periodically sending imaginary spores out, which appear nearby. Thus, the food bits occupying the initial disk region begin to spread, as swimbots consume them.

4.3.3 Swimbots

Swimbots are made of parts, ranging in number from 2 to 10. Parts are rigidly connected from end to end and rotate off each other in pendulum fashion, using sine functions. Parts come in six colors (red, orange, yellow, green, blue, and violet). Figure 4.3 shows a swimbot that has six parts.

Genes for morphology determine the length, thickness, color, and "resting angle" of each part. (The resting angle of a part is relative to the angle of the part to which it is attached.) Genes for motor control determine the phases and amplitudes of the sine functions, per part. Figure 4.4 shows how three unique sine waves, determined by six genes, combine to create a unique periodic swimming motion in the whole body.

Frequency of sine-wave motions is constant among all the parts, but can vary among swimbots according to another gene.

4 GenePool 85

Fig. 4.2. Swimbots.

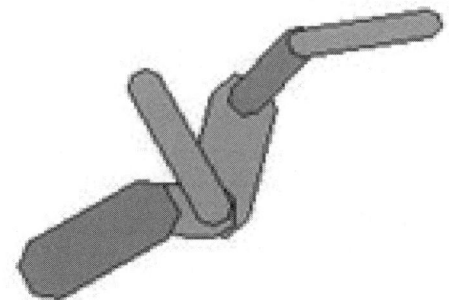

Fig. 4.3. An example swimbot with six parts.

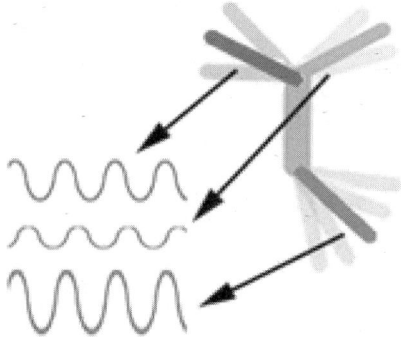

Fig. 4.4. A schematic showing variations in amplitude and phase among body part angular motions.

Within the simulation environment, swimbots have position and orientation, translational velocity, and rotational velocity. They can transform their positions and orientations autonomously by way of the articulated motions of their parts. When a part moves perpendicular to its axis, it has a greater effect on swimbot position and orientation than if the part moves parallel to its axis. Compare to a canoe paddle: Setting the paddle in the water with its plane perpendicular to its motion forces the paddler (and thus the canoe) in the opposite direction of the sweep. Thrusting the paddle in the water in the direction of its axis has little effect.

4.3.4 Locomotion Is Required for Mating

With as many as 10 body parts, each having many possible lengths and widths, attached in many possible ways, and rotating back and forth with various possible phases and amplitudes, the phenotype space is very large. The majority of swimbots at the beginning of a simulation are bound to be poor swimmers and never reach their destinations of food bits or mates before dying. Those few who are lucky enough to be initialized with genes allowing their motions to propel them in the direction of their goal are the ones who will be able to mate and thereby pass on their more fit genetic building blocks into the future.

4.3.5 Special Body Parts

Swimbots have no heads, torsos, or explicitly defined limbs with special functions. There is one special exception to this rule: There is one part (the root part) that has a genital at one end and a mouth at the other end. These two locations correspond to the two goals in a swimbot's life and are used in computing the distance from the genitals of potential mates, and food bits, respectively.

Mouths and genitals are visualized using a vector attached to these locations and aimed in the direction of the swimbot's goal. When a swimbot is pursuing food, the mouth vector is shown and a green dot appears at the end of it. When the swimbot is pursuing a mate, the genital vector is shown and a white dot appears at the end of it. The length of these vectors is important for the detection of swimbots coming to within proximity of a goal — it visualizes the radius of critical contact. Figure 4.5 shows a circle and a white line superimposed on a swimbot pursuing a food bit to emphasize the mouth vector and to indicate the radius.

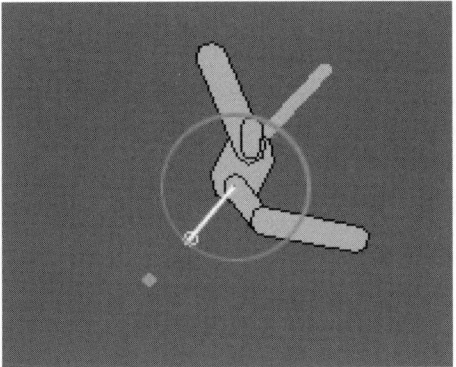

Fig. 4.5. The mouth vector and a circle showing the critical distance for eating a food bit.

4.3.6 Swimbot Mental States

Swimbots have four continuous mental states: (1) looking for a mate; (2) pursuing a chosen mate; (3) looking for a food bit; and (4) pursuing a chosen food bit, as illustrated in Fig. 4.6. The acts of eating and mating are brief — they are instantaneous states.

4.3.7 Energy Flow

Energy is stored in three locations, (1) in swimbots, (2) in food bits, and (3) in the ambient fluid of the pool as a whole. New food bits take energy from the pool and appear randomly in the pool within the vicinity of other food bits. Swimbots get their energy from these food bits. Swimbots expend energy by moving their parts — that energy is dissipated back into the pool (Fig. 4.7).

"Efficient" swimmers expend less energy while covering larger distances and more rapidly converging on a goal. These swimbots spend more time

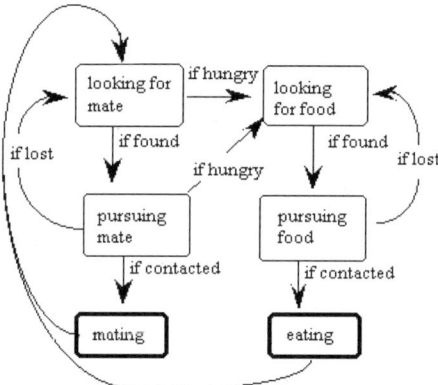

Fig. 4.6. Swimbot mental states.

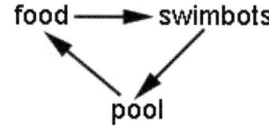

Fig. 4.7. Energy flow in GenePool.

pursuing mates and less time pursuing food. When a swimbot's energy dips below a specific threshold (the hunger level), the swimbot becomes hungry and looks for a food bit to pursue. If the swimbot's energy reaches zero, it dies. If a swimbot has succeeded in reaching a food bit, that swimbot's energy goes up — if its energy level is high enough (above hunger threshold), it begins to look for a mate. A successful that which produces an offspring causes the energy level of each parent swimbot to decrease by 50% — that energy is given to the offspring.

4.3.8 Turning

Each swimbot has an innate orientation, or heading, determined by the axis of its main body part. While pursuing a goal, the direction from the swimbot to its goal is compared to its orientation at every step, as illustrated in Fig. 4.8.

The size and sign of the resulting angle are used to modify the phases and amplitudes of all the part motions. Genetic factors determine the amounts that these phases and amplitudes are modified, per part. No explicit definition of turning is provided — the solutions are those of a blind watchmaker. Turning solutions are among the more complex emergent behaviors in swimbots and are difficult to describe objectively.

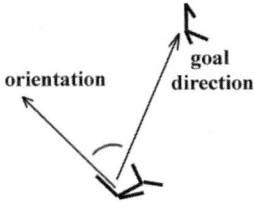

Fig. 4.8. Swimbot orientation compared to goal direction modifies genetically determined turning mechanisms.

4.3.9 Perceiving and Choosing Mates

When a swimbot's mental state switches to looking for a mate, it scans all the swimbots within a specific radius (its "view horizon") at one instant, with a "snapshot." It then chooses the one that most satisfied the attractiveness criterion (see the list of attractiveness criteria ahead). Each attractiveness criterion has an associated algorithm, which is used to measure a particular phenotypic feature in the body of each swimbot scanned. The swimbot with the greatest value is the one chosen. This design was meant to enable the phenomenon of runaway sexual selection, whereby the population will try to maximize its attractiveness, even at the expense of overall efficiency.

As an example, if the attractiveness criterion is "big," then to determine attractiveness in a potential mate, the areas of all its parts are added up to determine the total body area. This is one of the more straightforward algorithms. Attractiveness criteria having to do with motion and body pose (such as "hyper," or "straight") are more involved — they refer to the instantaneous velocities of the parts, or to the pose the body happens to be in during the snapshot. Presumably, a swimbot may appear uncharacteristically attractive during the snapshot only because of the particular configuration or motions of its body parts at that time. But these misinterpretations of attractiveness would be rare and small, due to the fact that many swimbots are evaluated per snapshot — the attractiveness gradient is fairly robust, especially over evolutionary time.

4.3.10 Pseudo-FlatLand

Although swimbots occupy a 2D plane, perception is not modeled as occurring in this imaginary space, as in the entities of Flatland [1]. This kind of visual modeling would be ambiguous at any rate. Instead, swimbots are assumed to have the ability to perceive the body structures of other swimbots as if looking down upon the picture-plane. This is admittedly an abstraction. A true 3D simulation would allow more realistic visual modeling and consequently more interesting emergent behaviors in terms of range of mate selection criteria. But for the purposes of the basic experiment in GenePool, this is sufficient.

4.3.11 Mating and Birth

When two swimbots mate (i.e., at least one of them is pursuing the other, and the distance between their genitals is less than the length of the genital vector), one offspring appears in between them, which inherits genetic building blocks from both parents. Crossover and mutation operators are used.

4.4 Usage

Although the animated computer graphics aspect of GenePool is not critical to the simulation, it is always running, so that the user can explore various aspects of the simulation at any time. Overlaid on top of the animated simulation view are various menu options. These include the following.

4.4.1 Pool Menu

The Pool menu allows the user to save and load pool files, or start a new "Primordial Pool" from scratch.

4.4.2 Love Menu

The Love menu allows the user to set the attractiveness criteria. For instance, if the user sets the attractiveness criteria to "long," then from that point forth all swimbots will tend to choose swimbots as mates which have longer bodies (at the point in time in which the swimbot scans for attractive swimbots). There are 10 attractiveness criteria: 5 primary attributes, each with an opposing attribute, as shown:

Similar Color	Opposite Color
Big	Small
Hyper	Still
Long	Short
Straight	Crooked

4.4.3 Stats Menu

The Stats menu brings up a graph that shows food population vs. swimbot population in a time-series graph. In mature populations, familiar oscillations of predator-prey populations can be observed.

4.4.4 Info Menu

This is the help page for GenePool.

4.4.5 Affecting Views

An important aspect of GenePool is the Microscope, a tool for controlling the view, as seen in Fig. 4.1 at the lower right. The microscope has left, right, up, and down translation controls, and zoom in/out. In addition to this, it has the following special settings:

- Whole Pool: The microscope backs up to view the entire pool.
- Auto-tracking: In auto-tracking mode, the view shifts around according to the positions of swimbots, so as always to keep some kind of activity in view.
- View Selected Swimbot: When the user selects a swimbot with the mouse cursor, that swimbot becomes the selected swimbot. This microscope setting keeps the selected swimbot within view at all times.

4.4.6 Ways to Use GenePool

GenePool can be used in three ways:

1. As reference material for continuing artificial life research: Some references of GenePool in artificial life research include [9].
2. As a children's software toy: GenePool/Darwin Pond can captivate youngsters. Children have been observed exploring and manipulating swimbots from many minutes to nearly an hour. This is an indication that young children have an opportunity to catch a glimpse of the complex world of evolutionary dynamics, while at the same time having some fun. An ultimate goal in developing entertaining artificial life simulations is that it will help prepare children's minds for the kinds of environmental, ecological, and social problems we face today — understanding complex dynamical systems is important to the future stewards of the Earth.
3. As an introduction to evolution for science students: A handful of high school and college teachers have expressed interest in GenePool and Darwin Pond as tools for learning about evolution, and have included them in their courses.

4.4.7 A Sample User Session

This is what is recommended as a suggested user session, in the INFO page of GenePool:

How to use GenePool:

1. Start up a primordial pool from the "Pool" menu.
2. Select the attractiveness criterion from the "Love" menu.
3. Explore mate choice behavior by using the microscope (controls at lower right).
4. Go away.

5. Come back after a while and notice what has evolved.
6. If you like what you see, save the pool in one of four files, as specified in the "Pool" menu.

4.4.8 Mini-Dramas

While global dynamics are going on, one can witness on local scales events such as two swimbots racing to reach a common food bit, a swimbot dying from starvation, or a swimbot chasing another swimbot it has chosen as a mate, who is chasing yet another swimbot that it has chosen as a mate. Emergent behavior occurs on the local scale as well as the global scale. One can choose among the following Mini-Dramas:

- Most Loved: shows the swimbot who has produced the most offspring (as pursued)
- Best at Mating: shows the swimbot who has produced the most offspring (as pursuer)
- Biggest Eater: shows the swimbot who has eaten the most food bits
- Mutual Love: shows two swimbots pursuing each other as mates (if found)
- Love Triangle: shows three swimbots in a circular loop of mate pursuit (if found)
- Competition for food: shows group of swimbots pursuing a common food bit (if found).

4.4.9 Anthropomorphizing

A special setting of the simulation can be run in which all the swimbots are initialized with genes for morphology set to roughly resemble human forms. Motor control, however, is randomized, to allow differential swimming ability at the start of the simulation. Watching these anthropomorphized figures struggle to swim can be amusing, as we project our own bodies onto them. Figure 4.9 shows a screenshot of two such swimbots immediately after they have mated (offspring appear small and white between the parents and grow to full size within a few seconds). Both swimbots are pursuing the food bit at top right.

These human-like forms generally do not persist over evolutionary time, usually giving way to simpler body types. Often, the vestiges of a human-like ancestor can be detected.

4.5 Discoveries

4.5.1 Polymorphism?

In specific simulation runs, an attraction criterion was chosen which was intentionally in conflict with normal pressures for efficient swimming: attraction

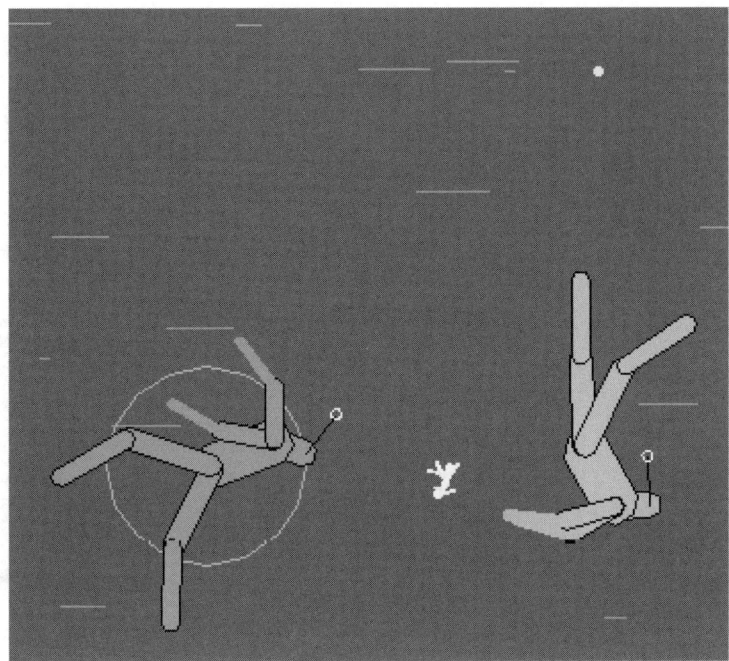

Fig. 4.9. Swimbots with morphological genes initialized to resemble a human-like figure.

was set to "still" (i.e., swimbots exhibiting the least amount of motion become the most attractive). The prediction was that this would cause mass extinction. But many populations actually thrived, converging on a distinct bifurcation among body types, with the majority being small and nearly motionless, and a small minority being similar with the exception of having whip-like tails enabling them to swim rapidly. These rapid swimbots (the "breeders") are largely responsible for propagating the genes throughout the population, while the majority of swimbots simply lie around being attractive (the "sitters"). The breeders expend more energy and eat more food bits, while the sitters eat very little and expend very little energy.

A number of simulation runs with the same attractiveness criterion have converged on similar results. Figure 4.10 shows one of the breeders (top center) among some sitters.

An hypothesis is as follows: These populations had discovered a way to take advantage of a mutation at a specific locus of the genotype that accounts for this phenotypic difference — possibly a few genes are involved. This bifurcation of the phenotype may be an expression of the inherent conflict between swimming efficiency and attractiveness, which, in this case, are at odds. Natural selection pressures exploit this mutation for the sake of propagation, while

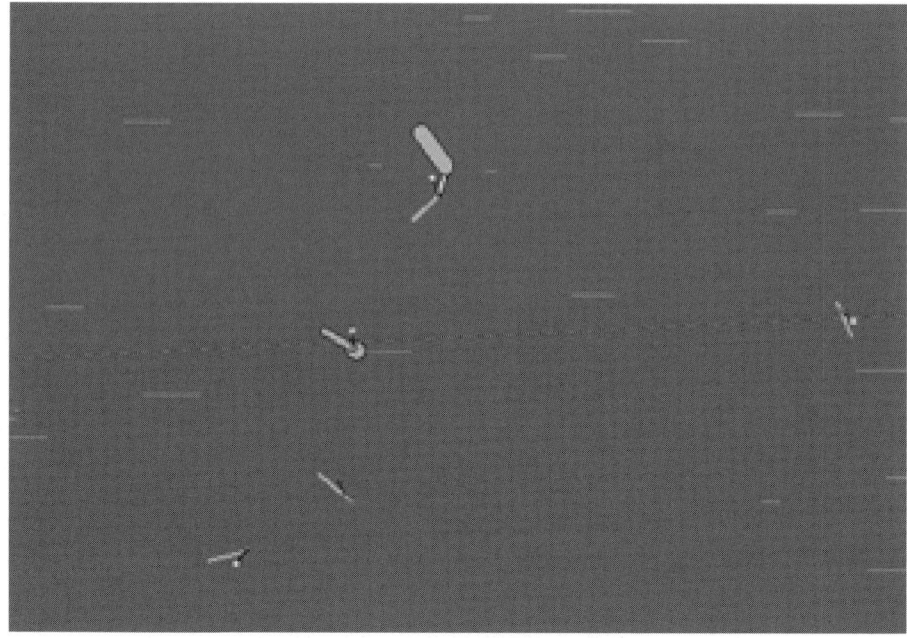

Fig. 4.10. A "breeder" (top center) among a majority of "sitters."

sexual selection keeps the majority of the population in a generally stable state of motionlessness.

4.5.2 Celebrating Diversity

One of the attractiveness criteria is "similar color." When this is turned on, swimbots will choose mates whose bodies contain the closest spectrum of colors to their own. One experiment was to encourage interracial mating by adding a new attractiveness criterion called "opposite color" — as shown above. Not surprisingly, when this is turned on, the population converges on a perpetual state of psychedelic diversity.

4.6 Future Development

Three main enhancements to GenePool are planned, as described here.

4.6.1 Recursive Embryology

The current mapping of genotype to phenotype is without structure in terms of topological arrangement of parts, part proportions, and motor control among parts. Thus, there is no innate tendency toward segmentation, symmetry, or regular limb-branching. This was intentional in the original scheme, so as to remove any bias and to focus only on emergent behaviors. But this lack of structure may inhibit certain creative solutions. In the works is a new recursive scheme for embryology such that fewer genes are required to determine morphology and motor control, and forms of symmetry and segmentation can emerge.

4.6.2 Parental Investment and Gender

The polymorphism-like behavior described above suggests further exploration. Females typically invest more energy and/or time toward birthing and raising offspring, most specifically in terms of investment in gametes. Without specifying gender difference explicitly, new attributes could be added to the swimbot genotype/phenotype causing them to have differences in parental investment (i.e., fraction of energy given to offspring in the event of mating — currently it is set to 50% per parent — an arbitrary ratio indeed). This gene might evolve in correlation with emergent behaviors such as rate of energy burn, attractiveness, and perhaps other, unforeseen behaviors.

4.6.3 Environmental Variation

One reason GenePool converges so quickly is that the environment is simple and undifferentiated. Having the food bits move according to fluid flows, or according to their own evolvable traits, would make for a more dynamic fitness landscape. Also, more complex barriers to genetic flow would help (besides the "Great Wall" tool — a line the user can place as a barrier to encourage localized isolated gene populations).

4.7 Similar Simulations

A number of Alife software simulations share common features with GenePool:

- Framsticks [3]: far exceeds GenePool in functionality and physical simulation, including features for many variations of 3D simulation and user-manipulation. Like GenePool, Framsticks creatures consist of jointed body parts which rotate against each other.
- SodaPlay [11]: demonstrates great variety of form and motion using 2D graphics, in an entertaining format. SodaPlay uses a more "molecular" style of physics modeling, base on spring forces, to affect the positions and orientations of potentially large-scale spring structures having semi-coherent positions and orientations.
- LifeDrop [6]: shows intriguing biomorphs breeding in an ethereal setting, with ways to interactively change the view. Like GenePool, LifeDrop shows multiple biomorphs interacting at once.

References

1. Abbot E (1963) Flatland, A Romance of Many Dimensions. Barnes and Noble.
2. Dawkins R (1996) Climbing Mount Improbable. W. W. Norton & Company.
3. The Framsticks system, http://www.frams.alife.pl/.
4. Goldberg D (1989) Genetic Algorithms in Search, Optimization, and Machine Learning. Addison-Wesley.
5. Holland J (1975) Adaptation in Natural and Artificial Systems. University of Michigan Press, Ann Arbor.
6. LifeDrop, http://www.virtual-worlds.net/lifedrop/.
7. Ngo T and Marks J (1993) Spacetime Constraints Revisited. Computer Graphics. pp. 343–350.
8. Ray T (1991) An Approach to the Synthesis of Life. In: Artificial Life II Proceedings, Addison-Wesley.
9. References to ALife applications of GenePool
   http://www.cs.vu.nl/~wai/Papers/deliberate_evolution_agents.pdf
   http://homepages.inf.ed.ac.uk/timt/papers/recent_developments/Taylor-RecentDevelopments.html
   http://citeseer.ist.psu.edu/watson99embodied.html
   http://www.cogs.susx.ac.uk/users/inmanh/easy/alife04/Seminar%20reading/bongardsymmetry3.pdf
10. Sims K (1994) Evolving 3D Morphology and Behavior by Competition. In: Artificial Life IV Proceedings. MIT Press.
11. Sodaplay, http://www.sodaplay.com/.
12. Ventrella J (1994) Explorations in the Emergence of Morphology and Motion Behavior in Animated Characters. Artificial Life IV Proceedings, MIT Press.
13. Ventrella J (1996) Sexual Swimmers, Emergent Morphology and Locomotion Without a Fitness Function. From Animals to Animats, MIT Press.
14. Ventrella J (1998) Attractiveness vs. Efficiency (How Mate Preference Affects Locomotion in the Evolution of Artificial Swimming Organisms). Artificial Life Vi Proceedings. MIT Press.
15. Ventrella J. (2004) http://www.ventrella.com/.

5
Sodarace: Adventures in Artificial Life

Peter W. McOwan and Edward J. Burton

Much like life, the Sodarace project (www.sodarace.net) defies easy description [1]. Originally developed as an online Olympics pitching human against machine intelligence, the project has flourished to incorporate an impressive range of science- and arts-based activities. Sodarace uses creative play as a bridge to foster dialogue and shared awareness between two very different audiences: a broad public of learners, both in and out of school, and the artificial intelligence and artificial life research communities. The Sodarace project is an extension of the Sodaconstructor software, an online construction kit comprising masses, springs, and muscles, providing tools for open-ended discovery and exploration. Though the mechanics are simple, the forms created often have a very life-like appearance and gait, and as such are frequently anthropomorphized by users.

5.1 Introduction: The Sodarace Project

Sodarace comprises a flexible asynchronous environment for races between virtual robots, either built by the public with the Sodaconstructor interface and learning support from the Sodarace community forums, or created by artificial intelligences using an equivalent Sodarace Application Programming Interface (API) developed specifically for Sodarace; see Fig. 5.1. These intuitive tools combined with an active user forum and the provocative Humans vs. Machines narrative have proved to be both popular, educational, and fun [1].

Sodarace: The Beginnings

Officially, the Sodaconstructor was released in March of 2000. It started 10 years earlier with a simple version, programmed in Basic, and developed by Burton, which was later updated to Java when he joined the team of digital artists at Soda Creative Ltd. in London. The applet was placed online as an element of the Play section content on Soda web site, where over a

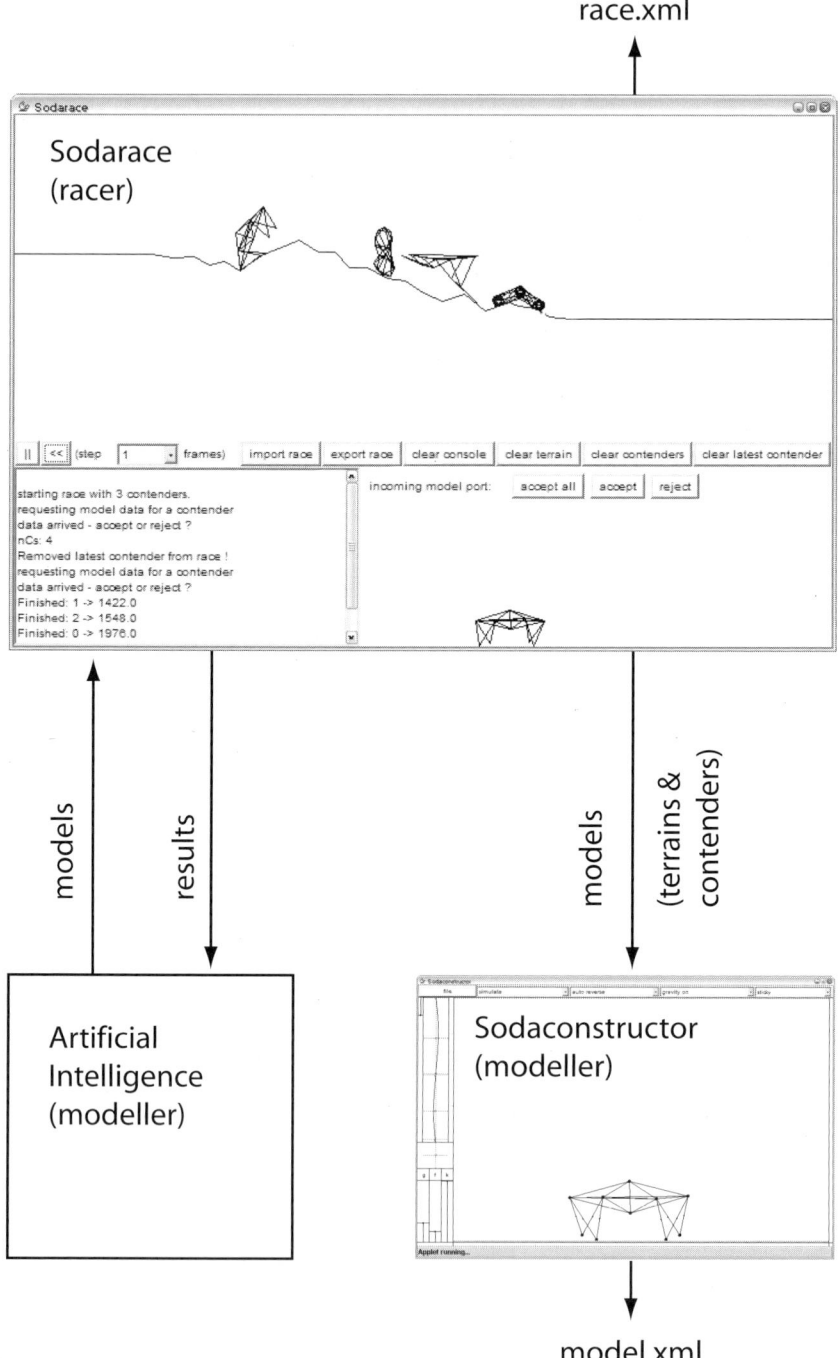

Fig. 5.1. The Sodarace software architecture.

short period of time its clear design, high-quality interactivity, and addictive open-ended problem-solving play made it extremely popular. Sodaconstructor exploded across the Internet through e-mails, newsgroup postings, and other such informal "word-of-mouth" advertising. By the end of the month there were one million constructors using the applet each week.

In September of 2000, the applet was redeveloped in order to allow Sodaconstructions to be saved, and from this the Sodazoo was developed, where creations could be sent and the best archived for all to see and learn from. It was at this stage that the educational merit of the project and its natural symbiosis with artificial life research began to crystallize, as a number of research groups around the world contacted Soda interested in exploring this application of the software.

In April 2002 the Sodarace project was launched, supported by funds from the UK Engineering and Physical Sciences Research Council (EPSRC). Core to Sodarace's construction, and subsequent development were the Sodarace community forums, where constructors and artificial intelligence researchers could interact and get involved in developing the specifications for the new software. This proved an extremely worthwhile experience for those involved, as it gave a transparent view into the development of a major software project while also ensuring that user requirements were met. The first human vs. machine races occurred in December 2003. It took the form of a race over flat terrain with simple wheel-like creations, named amoebas by the community. The artificial intelligence technique of genetic algorithms was used to optimize the parameters of the wheel to cover the racetrack in a competitive time. For the record, the humans won the first race, but only just!

5.2 Scientific Background

5.2.1 Sodaconstructor: The Physics Engine of Sodarace

Sodarace is based on the popular Sodaconstructor software [1], which allows the simulation of structures comprised of a linked set of node masses and interconnecting springs, simulated using a simple implementation of Newtonian and Hook's law mechanics. To provide movement constructors may select springs to drive in simple harmonic motion (SHM); these are called "muscles." The interface also provides an intuitive graphical representation of the phase relations of the driven muscle elements through a moving sine wave. The muscles are mapped to appropriate positions on the wave generator to fix their relative oscillation phases; see Fig. 5.2. By connecting both static and appropriately phased SHM driven elements together, it is possible to create a whole menagerie of lively perambulating creations. The amplitude, initial wave phase offset, and speed of the driving sinusoidal wave may also be controlled.

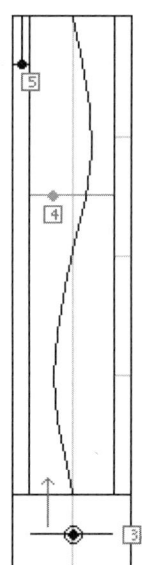

Fig. 5.2. The "muscle" wave generator.

```
<?xml version="1.0" encoding="ISO-8859-1" standalone="no"?>
<!DOCTYPE sodaconstructor>
<model>
 <comment></comment>
 <container width="651" height="422"/>
 <environment gravity="0.3" friction="0.05" springyness="0.2"/>
 <collisions surface_friction="0.1" surface_reflection="-0.75"/>
 <wave amplitude="0.5" phase="0.0" speed="0.001"/>
 <settings gravitydirection="down" wavedirection="forward"
   autoreverse="on"/>
<nodes>
 <mass id="m0" x="254.0" y="291.0" vx="0.0" vy="0.0"/>
 <mass id="m1" x="332.0" y="194.0" vx="0.0" vy="0.0"/>
 <mass id="m2" x="259.0" y="157.0" vx="0.0" vy="0.0"/>
</nodes>
<links>
 <spring a="m0" b="m1" restlength="124.0"/>
 <muscle a="m1" b="m2" restlength="82.0" amplitude="0.5"
   phase="0.5"/>
</links>
</model>
```

Fig. 5.3. An example of the structure of an XML file.

5.2.2 Sodarace Environmental Variables

To enable terrain construction, Sodarace includes elements inspired by the PIVOT (Proximity Information from VOronoi Techniques) collision detection algorithm [2]. In effect, these Sodarace 'bar springs' do not allow other structures to pass through them. They can be used to construct terrain that models can walk over; by default, these collisions are "sticky," meaning they lose energy to friction, this can be changed to "slippery" for friction-free collisions. The racers and terrain data are held in the form of XML files (Fig. 5.3) which allows the manual editing of components but also allows the computer generation of these files. This is the essential element to allow artificial intelligence to enter the races.

The environmental variables that can be set globally are length and height of the environment, gravity (both strength and direction up/down), spring damping friction, and spring constant. For the terrain there are two parameters, the surface friction and the surface reflectance, which are related to the portion of velocity parallel to the surface, and perpendicular to the surface, respectively, which is lost in a collision.

The Sodarace application (Fig. 5.1), receives terrains and contestants from a "modeller," which could be either the Sodaconstructor application or an artificial intelligence. The Sodarace application adjudicates the race and can export the results, including terrain and contestant(s) as an XML file, which you may upload to the Sodarace League Forum for others to download and add their contestants to. The software also provides timing information to allow adjudication of the races, but also acts as feedback for fitness functions for the artificial intelligence-based racers.

5.2.3 Previous Work

Sodarace makes no attempt to simulate more than 2D physical interactions between the mass, spring, and muscle racers and the terrain. It is within this world that both artificial intelligence and humans compete and evolve. However, as will be discussed later, these constraints do not significantly hinder user creativity. An obvious related artificial life project is Framsticks [3], which allows the study of evolution capabilities of three-dimensional creatures in simplified Earth-like conditions. The creatures in this case also have in addition to genotype representations of their physical body, sensory, neural network, and effectors.

Karl Sims' earlier work in visualising simulated block creatures performing evolved behaviors was also an inspiration for the Sodarace project [4,5]. Sims' research project involving simulated Darwinian evolutions, using genetic algorithms, to develop again 3D virtual block creatures. An initial random population of several hundred creatures is created, and each creature is then tested for its ability to perform a given task, such the ability to swim in a simulated water environment. The fittest creatures for the task are then passed into the next generation and mutations applied to produce a new population. The new creatures are again tested, and through the mutation process some may be conferred with improvements on their parents' abilities. As this iterative cycle of variation and selection continues, creatures with more and more successful niche behaviors can emerge.

Sodarace builds on these previous works but reduces the dimensionality and complexity of the simulation in an effort to increase interaction. In addition, the central driving presence of the discussion forums provides both an evolving archive of human and artificial intelligence design activity and educational support. Interestingly we also see the evolution of specialist descriptive vocabulary within the community, for example, the "Pandora's" structures discussed in Sec. 5.4.6.

5.3 Software for Artificial Life in Sodarace

There have been to date a number of approaches to developing artificial creatures to compete in the Sodaraces. The accessibility of the XML import/export format, plus timing information from the race itself naturally allows the application of optimization algorithms such as genetic algorithms [6,7] and simulated annealing [8] to the task of building better racers.

5.3.1 Approaches to Optimization

There have been two approaches so far exploited in the races; the first is to use a previously human designed racer, and to apply an optimization algorithm to improve on human design. The second approach is the more traditional breeding from scratch." In keeping with the educational remit of the project, both approaches have been discussed in the forums, and the software used made available. It is interesting to note how the audience reacted to the issues raised by simply using an algorithm to optimize a previous human-designed racer, that we specifically chose Daintywalker, a well-beloved early creation of Burton that had in effect become the Sodarace mascot. The initial feeling in the forum was that this was somehow "cheating." However, on later reflection the general consensus was that nature and human creativity frequently work by modifying and improving on earlier designs, which in turn led to some deep discussions on evolution.

Fig. 5.4. An optimized racer beats the original human engineered version.

5.3.2 Simulated Annealing and Daintywalker

Using Daintywalker the method of optimization by simulated annealing [8] was explored; see Fig. 5.4. Daintywalker was randomly modified, then raced and the new version retained if it improves performance, but we also allow non-improving modification to survive with a probability that decreases over time. The rate of this decrease is determined by the cooling schedule, a term in keeping with the thermodynamic metaphor on which this heuristic optimization algorithm is based. With some appropriate assumptions about the cooling schedule, this algorithm will converge in probability to a global optimum. This was not, however, necessary in our application; we just wanted a racer to beat the competition.

5.3.3 Genetic Algorithms and the Amoeba

A similar modification to a previous design, this time an 'amoeba', was undertaken early on in the project to introduce the community to genetic algorithm (GA) optimization. An amoeba is a term coined by the forum for a wheel-like structure that is easy to build and races well over many types of terrain as featured in Fig. 5.1. Using a simple generic GA approach random amoebas, constrained using a basic template design, were created and raced. The fittest then bred forward with parents to the next generation. Using this method we could in effect breed amoebas to the required performance level. The intuitive nature of the GA approach, combined with the freely available source code, facilitated a number of community members developing their own genetically enhanced amoeba racers.

5.3.4 Genetic Algorithms from Scratch; the Wodka Way

Wodka, an Austrian AI group, has created a program that generates robots from scratch instead of optimizing existing robots. Wodka uses a genetic algorithm that generates a random set of muscles, masses, and springs, forming multiple Sodarace creatures. These creatures are then loaded and raced, and those that finish quickest breed, and their fastest offspring breed, and so on. Initially they started off as simple segmented sticks that bounced across the screen (Fig. 5.5). However, later the best creatures start to develop structure and look as if they have powered 'flippers' in the front. This software was made open source and has been used by others in the community to experiment with digital evolution.

5.4 Usage

5.4.1 Interactions in Sodarace: The Evolution of the Forums

It's fair to say that there is no typical usage or user for Sodarace; the range and diversity of usage are among the great strengths of the 'tools not rules'

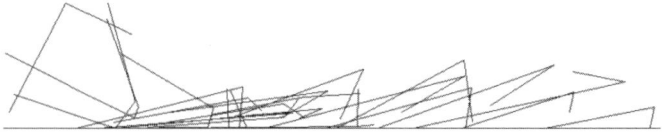

Fig. 5.5. Optimization of racers from "scratch."

philosophy. The following section highlights some of the fascinating stories that have evolved through the project. The Sodarace forums realize the audience's own potential to create, contribute, and share significant ideas and to interact with the artificial intelligence and artificial life research communities. To date, highlights have included the spontaneous emergence among users of peer-to-peer learning, mentoring, an embryonic scientific research process of hypothesis, experiment, theory development and subsequent racers' exploitation of developed technologies, and a surprisingly seamless integration of creative and technical dialogues. There has also been a spontaneous expansion of community learning on the subject of artificial intelligence programming, with tutorial web sites and open source code to allow interested users to construct and experiment with their own AI systems. The distinctions between AI researcher and community members are blurring.

5.4.2 Forum Involvement in Scientific Research Projects

Karl Sims' work on evolved virtual creatures [4, 5] was identified as one of the main inspirations behind Sodarace. Karl Sims studied computer graphics at the MIT Media Lab, and Life Sciences as an undergraduate at MIT. He currently leads GenArts, Inc. in Cambridge, Massachusetts, which creates special effects software for the motion picture industry. The forum raised questions put to Karl in the first Sodarace interview. The interview was wide ranging, discussing his career and inspirations, technical issues in the development of artificial intelligence, and possible future applications of AI. See http://sodarace.net/sims/index.jsp. It is expected that a number of subsequent interviews with notable researchers will be undertaken, particularly in response to community demands.

5.4.3 Community Development of Peer-to-Peer Learning Web Sites

Independent superuser sites have been created by model-making masters within the community. With step-by-step tutorials for beginners and expert engineering tips, they prove an invaluable resource for the model-making community and support peer-to-peer learning. Of particular interest was the spontaneous emergence of peer review of tutorials and other learning materials by accepted 'Sodarace experts' to merit inclusion on these sites. A links page was developed on the main Sodarace site to catalogue these valuable resources.

5.4.4 Programming Support Web Sites

The XML model format enabled computer programs to generate models using algorithms instead of using manual construction. Programs written by community members include AmoebaMatic, which its creator claims "takes the strain out of making amoebas," while the Sodagenerator web site includes a suite of web applications that create turbines, worms, and flexloops, a range of engineering structures devised and defined by the forum and used in developing racing creatures, see Fig. 5.6. Web sites with learning resources and the source code for developing artificial intelligence have also started to appear to promulgate a much wider appreciation understanding and take-up of these key research methodologies.

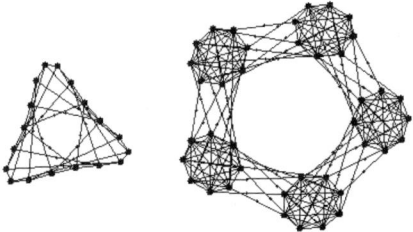

Fig. 5.6. A flex loop and a worm creature algorithmically designed.

5.4.5 Experimental Investigation into the Physics of Sodarace

One of the community members undertook a detailed study of the physical principles behind the Sodaconstructor environment simulation. The user called Jeckyll, collaborating with Lectvay, one of the forum's most respected members, applied mathematical analysis supported with an extensive set of constructed experiments to hypothesize and prove the physics of Sodaconstructor in remarkable detail. This thesis was then published along with the supporting experiments in an online "digital laboratory," which can be accessed at one of the most impressive fan web sites, sodaplaycentral.com. The paper and the experimental approach are widely cited; for example, a new user asks in regard to the Sodaconstructor interface

> "What does it actually do when you move the dots onto either side of the centre line? Sorry I'm a noob" [Note: a noob is a new user]. A mentor in the forum swiftly responds, "A great way to figure this kind of stuff out is to do little "experiments" — that's a trick I learned

from Jeckyll's paper on www.sodaplaycentral.com. Go to the "soda Math" section and look at the Laboratory."

5.4.6 The Pandora's Box: An Example of the Spontaneous Development of Scientific Method

A deceptively simple yet mind-bending model was created. As community members collaborated to study its mysterious properties, hypothesize about how it works, and construct experiments to prove their theories, we witnessed a remarkable and spontaneous microcosm of scientific method emerge.

- **The Initial Discovery**— A user in the forum writes
  Have you ever made something and then just sat and stared at the screen and said "Hummmm..." Just mess with it for a little bit.
- **The Experiments** — A short time later another user posts
  Think I figured out this phenomena. Step1: in Sodaconstructor, value of spring force has relation with only extension of the spring proportional maybe, and does not have any relation with the length at rest. See this these are a variety length of springs. left-side one is a zero-length spring, 2nd one is 1-pixel-length, 3rd is 2-pixel, and so on. Besides, they are located as the free masses line up horizontally, try drag G value up slowly. Then, you will see all of them are elongated similarly, and not related to their length at rest. Step2: think about a rectangular with diagonal lines. as we see in step1, the pulling force of spring is related to its extension. Now, let's assume that the force is proportional to extension. so, for example, if the ratio of two side lines = 2 : 3, the forces acting on the springs = 2 : 3 also. so, the direction of the resultant of these two vectors overlaps the diagonal line. the resultant of these two vectors and the expanding force acting on the diagonal line are completely on a straight line and the direction of the force is opposite. So, the length of these lines come to settle in a fixed value. This happens only the shape is rectangle and the side springs are zero-length.
- **The Pandora's Calculus: Engineering Formalism and Commercial Exploitation** — The development of an empirical understanding and experimental validation of the by then named "Pandora" effect was followed by a formalization into the Pandora's Calculus,
  I wanted to share something I figured out in case people wanted to learn a new technique. Basically I came up with a Pandora Calculus that is similar to the way Tension Spring Calculus works. It allows you to: 1. Create Pandoras to fit any specific size you need. 2. Create multiple Pandoras on the same base. 3. Embed any Pandora on a tension spring. This means that Pandoras can be used like hubless bearings to mount rotors or turbines on, and who knows what else.

This technique is now widely used in the community to develop numerous virtual motors to drive Sodaracers. Another user develops "motors" for use in others racers and writes

> So far i found out that motor 4 is just 2 RAM's connected in the middle with some crossbeams..but because of the fact that the crossbeams get compressed they make the 2 RAM's much sturdier..and better..1 and 3 look mesmerizing. but aren't really stable...but ill work on that.. PLZ DONT JUST READ OVER THIS.... I WOULD REALLY LIKE TO WORK WITH SOME OF THE GREAT CONSTRUCTORS...TO IMPROVE MOTORS

5.4.7 Interdisciplinary Interaction: Art & Music Meet Science and Engineering in Sodarace

Sodarace also raises awareness of the important interactions between science, design and engineering, and the arts. Using Sodasound, an option that attaches sounds to the motion of masses and springs, members of the forum created creature motion to produce specific sound patterns, musical art pieces, and their own virtual musical instruments. Members of this specialist community invented ingenious ways to tune the mechanical structures; for example, the "bell-gate" system shown in Fig. 5.7, where the wave generator is now used to drive musical "muscles" to produce a predefined tune. For over 10 years artist Theo Jansen has been building incredibly engineered walking constructions on the beaches of Holland that feed on the wind [9]. It looks uncannily as if some of the most complex Sodaconstructor models have left the screen and become real. In the forum the artist agreed to discuss his work and explain the mechanisms by which his creations move. A teacher commented in the forum, "I am also an art teacher who tries to convince colleagues of the cross-curricular potential of sodaplay. I really want to bring interactive media into the art-classroom — even if only to showcase it as an example of emergent creative culture."

5.4.8 Sodarace in Schools

The Sodarace project is widely used in schools around the world. Forum users often mention the education benefit that they find over a number of science and technology curricula. Here are some representative samples taken from the forums; there are many more:

> One 15-year-old student wrote, "I presented Sodaconstructor to my class today, my intentions to give them enough skill to make a daintywalker [Note: this is a type of racer]. It was extremely difficult to keep everyone focused on creating and not playing around with the sample model, which is very entertaining, I have to admit. I actually

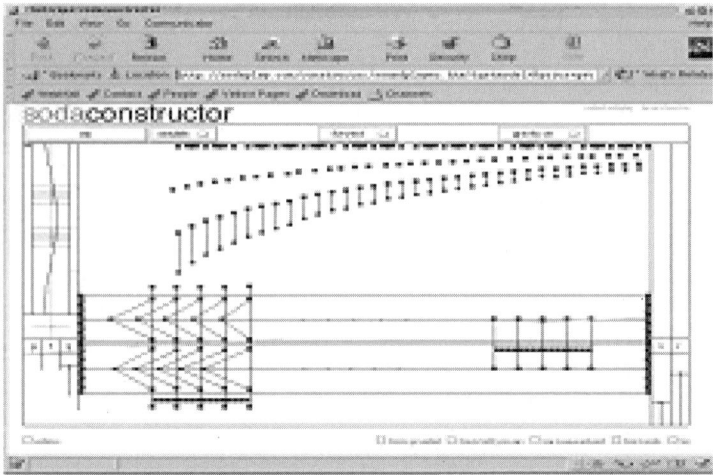

Fig. 5.7. A musical structure.

started teaching them on a blackboard first, not with how the concepts are put into action but the basic concepts themselves — like how an amoeba [Note: another type of racer] shifts its weight forward, or how a leg requires elliptical motion. Some of these aren't so obvious, I soon found out. PS: So hats off to all the teachers. Now that I know what it feels like to be one you guys have my utmost respect."

"I found out about sodaplay at school, from a friend. At the moment, I am using it to help me survive Physics, particularly waves."

"I am a High School student. I use sodaplay for geometry classes. It is easier to understand the properties of shapes and how different support loads can be dispersed. I enjoy working with the program and it helped me achieve an above average grade for the class."

"My whole 8th grade class has been using sodaplay. They all love it. We have learned ton of physics, I did a project for my physics class on your Sodaconstructor. I recreated Galileo's "Leaning Tower of Pisa" experiment and made a simple pendulum."

The discussion forums is also supporting a growing teachers' user community to develop allowing a peer-to-peer interchange of teaching ideas and materials. Younger users not yet competent or confident enough to develop racers themselves still have an active voice in the community, often creating animated artworks or cartoons, designing terrain racetrack as challenges to others, or undertaking to build interactive 'games'. All these projects require the user to covertly develop an understanding of simple physical processes and principles of the Sodarace world.

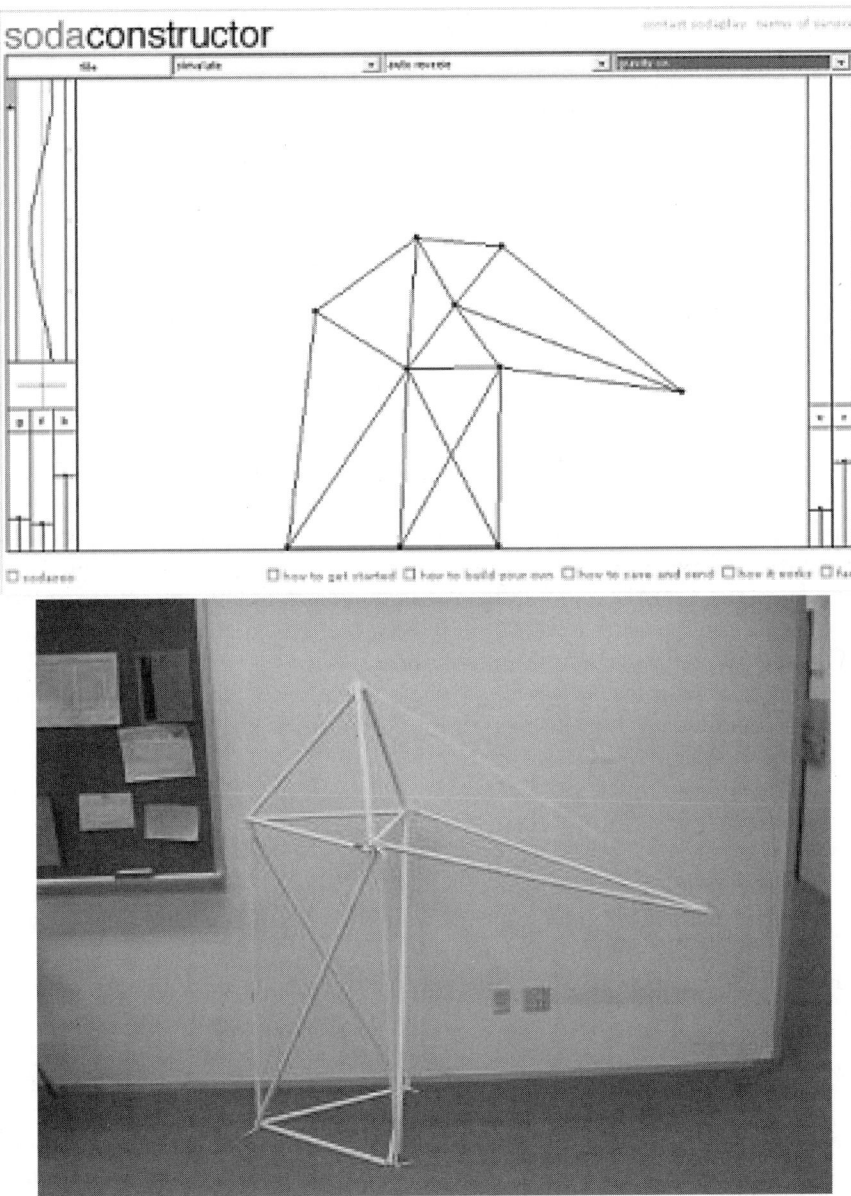

Fig. 5.8. Experiments with Sodaconstructor. A virtual structure and its real-world counterpart.

5.5 Experiments with Sodarace

One of the significant findings during both human- and machine-generated racer construction is the ability to effectively exploit the limitations of the simulator physics to solve particular problems. Examples abound of creatures exploiting so-called 'holes' in the simulation to allow creations to fly or crawl along the underside of surfaces. This ability to capitalize on particular simulation-world niches has produced a rich range of unexpected behaviors.

Another study of particular interest was the Berta's Tower [10], see Fig. 5.8, conducted at the University of Wisconsin–Madison Center for Education. Using the theory of pedagogical praxis [11], which argues that professional practices are useful models for technology-supported school learning environments, the researchers designed and implemented workshops for middle school students based on the professional practices of engineers. During the experiment, the participants engaged in a series of engineering design challenges on Sodarace as a pathway for learning concepts in physics. The students demonstrated a statistically significant gain in understanding about the concept of center of mass and a high level of interest and engagement when using the tool [12]. The data further suggest that the short, rapid iterations of the engineering design-build-test cycle on Sodarace simultaneously increased their motivation and understanding. The study offers an example of how the use of Sodarace in a rich activity system promotes scientific learning, and thus provides a potential new vision for physics education.

5.6 Summary: The Future of Sodarace

The vibrant community forums of Sodarace, central to its creation and success, show no signs of running out of new and creative ideas, and new software specifically aimed at engaging younger constructors, called Moovl, in is development. Sodarace has proved a very successful collaboration between science and design and has allowed access for many into the world of artificial life research. The introduction and evolution of the forums, providing the educational backbone and knowledge archive of the venture, guarantee the project will continue to grow in popularity over the years as the interplay between learning communities of human and artificial intelligence users mature. The tools Sodarace provides mean races and racers will evolve, the forums expand, and we can expect many more surprises from this powerful combination of science, peer-to-peer learning, and creative interactive play.

Acknowledgments

The authors are grateful to EPSRC for funding support for the Sodarace project, Gina Svarovsvky for her work on Berta's Tower, and Adam Sherwood for assistance in preparation of this manuscript. And most of all, thanks go to the community of model makers, mentors, and programmers who contribute to the forum and whose creativity never ceases to amaze us.

References

1. Voth D and Deuel RL (2004) When Virtual Robots Race, Science Wins. IEEE Intelligent Systems: March/April.
2. Kenneth E, Hoff KE, Zaferakis A, Lin M, and Manocha D (2001) Fast and Simple 2D Geometric Proximity Queries Using Graphics Hardware, Symposium on Interactive 3D Graphics (I3D).
3. Komosinski M (2003) The Framsticks system: Versatile simulator of 3D agents and their evolution. Kybernetes 32:156–173, available at http://www.frams.alife.pl/.
4. Sims K (1994) Evolving Virtual Creatures Computer Graphics, Siggraph'94 Proceedings, pp. 15–22.
5. Sims K (1994) Evolving 3D Morphology and Behavior by Competition in Artificial Life IV Proceedings, Brooks & Maes Editors, MIT Press, pp. 28–39.
6. Holland JH (1975) Adaptation in natural and artificial system. The University of Michigan Press, Ann Arbor.
7. Goldberg D (1988) Genetic Algorithms. Addison-Wesley, New York.
8. Kirkpatrick S, Gelatt Jr. CD, Vecchi MP (1983) Optimization by Simulated Annealing. Science 220:671–680.
9. Walking constructions, see http://www.strandbeest.com/.
10. Svarovsvky GN (2003) Berta's Tower: Understanding physics through virtual engineering. MA Thesis, University of Wisconsin–Madison.
11. Shaffer DW (2004) Pedagogical praxis: The professions as models for post-industrial education. Teachers' College Record. 106:1401–1421.
12. Svarovsky GN and Shaffer DW (2004) Sodaconstructing knowledge through exploratoids. Manuscript submitted for publication Journal of Research in Science Teaching.

Part II

Collective Artificial Life

6

Escaping the Accidents of History: An Overview of Artificial Life Modeling with Repast

Michael J. North and Charles M. Macal

Artificial life focuses on synthesizing forms and functions that appear alive. Artificial life allows scientific studies of biological systems outside the currently observable accidents of history. Agent-based modeling and simulation are used to create computational laboratories that replicate real or potential behaviors of actual or possible complex adaptive systems. Agent-based modeling thus provides a natural framework in which to perform artificial life experiments. The free and open source Recursive Porous Agent Simulation Toolkit (Repast) is one of several advanced agent-based modeling toolkits currently available. Repast seeks to support the development of extremely flexible models of living social agents, but is not limited to modeling living social entities alone. The Repast system is described in detail, and artificial life software models constructed with Repast are reviewed.

6.1 Introduction

Artificial life focuses on synthesizing "life-like behaviors from scratch in computers, machines, molecules, and other alternative media" [29]. Artificial life expands the "horizons of empirical research in biology beyond the territory currently circumscribed by life-as-we-know-it" to provide "access to the domain of life-as-it-could-be" [29]. Agent-based modeling and simulation (ABMS) are used to create computational laboratories that replicate real or potential behaviors of actual or possible complex adaptive systems (CAS). The goal of agent modeling is to allow experimentation with simulated complex systems. To achieve this, agent-based modeling uses sets of agents and frameworks for simulating the agents' decisions and interactions. Agent models can show how complex adaptive systems can evolve through time in a way that is difficult to predict from knowledge of the behaviors of the individual agents alone. Agent-based modeling thus provides a natural framework in which to perform artificial life experiments. The free and open source Recursive Porous Agent Simulation Toolkit (Repast) is one of several advanced agent-based modeling toolkits that are currently available.

6.1.1 Artificial Life

The discipline of artificial life studies the synthesis of forms and functions that appear alive. Artificial life allows scientific studies of biological systems outside the currently observable accidents of history. According to Langton [29]:

> Biology is the scientific study of life — in principle, anyway. In practice, biology is the scientific study of life on Earth based on carbon-chain chemistry. There is nothing in its charter that restricts biology to carbon-based life; it is simply that this is the only kind of life that has been available to study. Thus, theoretical biology has long faced the fundamental obstacle that it is impossible to derive general principles from single examples.
>
> Without other examples, it is difficult to distinguish essential properties of life — properties that would be shared by any living system — from properties that may be incidental to life in principle, but which happen to be universal to life on Earth due solely to a combination of local historical accident and common genetic descent.
>
> In order to derive general theories about life, we need an ensemble of instances to generalize over. Since it is quite unlikely that alien life forms will present themselves to us for study in the near future, our only option is to try to create alternative life-forms ourselves — artificial life — literally "life made by Man rather than by Nature."

Langton's description of artificial life indicates the depth but belies the age of the disciple. According to Di Paolo [12]:

> To say that artificial life is a young discipline in name only is to exaggerate, but it would be mistaken to think that its goals are new. The marriage of synthetic scientific aims with computational techniques makes artificial life a product of the last fifteen years, but its motivations have much deeper roots in cybernetics, theoretical biology, and the age-old drive to comprehend the mysteries of life and mind. Little wonder that a good part of the work in this field has been one of rediscovery and renewal of hard questions. Other disciplines have sidestepped such questions, often for very valid reasons, or have put them out of the focus of everyday research; yet these questions are particularly amenable to be treated with novel techniques such as computational modeling and other synthetic methodologies. What is an organism? What is cognition? Where do purposes come from?

6.1.2 Agent-based Modeling for Artificial Life

Agent-based modeling and simulation are used to create computational laboratories that replicate selected real or potential behaviors of actual or possible complex adaptive systems. A complex adaptive system is made up of agents that interact, mutate, replicate and die while adapting to a changing environment. Holland has identified the three properties and four mechanisms that are common to all complex adaptive systems [22]:

1. The nonlinearity property occurs when components or agents exchange resources or information in ways that are not simply additive. An example is a photosynthetic cell agent that returns one calorie of energy when one calorie is requested, two calories of energy when two calories are requested, and three calories of energy when ten calories are requested.
2. The diversity property is observed when agents or groups of agents differentiate from one another over time. An example is the evolutionary emergence of new species.
3. The aggregation property occurs when a group of agents is treated as a single agent at a higher level. An example is the ants in an ant colony.
4. The flows mechanism involves exchange of resources or information between agents such that the resources or information can be repeatedly forwarded from agent to agent. An example is the flow of energy between agents in an ecosystem.
5. The tagging mechanism involves the presence of identifiable flags that let agents identify the traits of other agents. An example is the use of formal titles such as "Dr." in a social system.
6. The internal models mechanism involves formal, informal, or implicit representations of the world embedded within agents. An example is a predator's evolving view of the directions prey are likely to flee during pursuit.
7. The building blocks mechanism is used when an agent participates in more than one kind of interaction. An example is a predator agent that can also be prey for larger predators.

Of course, these properties and mechanisms are interrelated. For example, with aggregation, many agents can act as one. With building blocks, one agent in some sense can act as many. Agent-based models normally incorporate some or all of the properties and mechanisms of complex adaptive systems.

The goal of agent modeling is to allow experimentation with simulated complex systems. To achieve this, agent-based modeling uses sets of agents and frameworks for simulating the agent's decisions and interactions. Agent models can show how complex adaptive systems can evolve through time in a way that is difficult to predict from knowledge of the behaviors of the individual agents alone. Agent modeling focuses on individual behavior. The agent rules are often based on theories of the individual such as Rational Individual Behavior, Bounded Rationality, or Satisficing [42]. Based on these simple types of rules, agent models can be used to study how patterns emerge.

Agent modeling may reveal behavioral patterns at the macro or system level that are not obvious from an examination of the underlying agent rules alone — these patterns are called emergent behavior. Agent-based modeling and simulation thus provide a natural framework in which to perform artificial life experiments.*

Agent-based modeling and simulation are closely related to the field of Multi-agent Systems (MAS). Both fields concentrate on the creation of computational complex adaptive systems. However, agent simulation models the real or potential behaviors of complex adaptive systems while MAS often focuses on applications of artificial intelligence to robotic systems, interactive systems, and proxy systems.

6.1.3 Chapter Organization

This chapter provides an overview of the Repast agent modeling toolkit from the perspective of artificial life. This chapter is organized into four parts. The introduction describes artificial life and agent-based modeling and simulation. The second section discusses the Repast agent modeling toolkit's development ecosystem and underlying concepts. The third section reviews a series of Repast artificial life models of artificial evolution and ecosystems; artificial societies; and artificial biological systems. The final section presents a summary and conclusions.

6.2 REPAST

The Recursive Porous Agent Simulation Toolkit (Repast) is one of several agent modeling toolkits available. Repast borrows many concepts from the Swarm agent-based modeling toolkit [44]. Repast is differentiated from Swarm in several respects. First, Repast is available in pure Java and pure Mcirosoft.Net forms, while Swarm is a mixture of Objective-C and Java. Second, Swarm is distributed under the GNU General Public License (GPL), which requires developers to make the source code for their entire model available to anyone who obtains a legitimate copy of the model's binary code. Repast is distributed under a variation of the Berkeley Software Distribution (BSD) license that does not require model source code to be released. Third, Repast provides an integrated set of libraries for neural networks, genetic algorithms, social network modeling, and other topics. For reviews of Swarm, Repast, and other agent-modeling toolkits, see the survey by Serenko and Detlor, the survey by Gilbert and Bankes, and the toolkit review by Tobias

---

* ABMS, agent-based modeling (ABM), agent-based simulation (ABS), and individual modeling (IBM) are all synonymous. ABMS is used here since ABM can be confused with antiballistic missile, ABS can be confused with antilock brakes, and IBM can be confused with International Business Machines Corporation.

and Hofmann [20,43,45]. In particular, Tobias and Hofmann performed a review of 16 agent modeling toolkits and found that "we can conclude with great certainty that according to the available information, Repast is at the moment the most suitable simulation framework for the applied modeling of social interventions based on theories and data" [45].

Repast is a free open source toolkit that was originally developed by Sallach, Collier, Howe, North, and others [10]. Repast was created at the University of Chicago. Subsequently, it has been maintained by organizations such as Argonne National Laboratory. Repast is now managed by the nonprofit volunteer Repast Organization for Architecture and Design (ROAD). ROAD is lead by a board of directors that includes members from a wide range of government, academic, and industrial organizations. The Repast system, including the source code, is available directly from the web [41].

Repast seeks to support the development of extremely flexible models of living social agents, but is not limited to modeling living social entities alone. From the ROAD home page [41]:

> Our goal with Repast is to move beyond the representation of agents as discrete, self-contained entities in favor of a view of social actors as permeable, interleaved, and mutually defining; with cascading and recombinant motives... We intend to support the modeling of belief systems, agents, organizations, and institutions as recursive social constructions.

6.2.1 The Repast Development Ecosystem

At its heart, Repast toolkit version 3.0 can be thought of as a specification for agent-based modeling services or functions. There are three concrete implementations of this conceptual specification. Naturally, all of these versions have the same core services that constitute the Repast system. The implementations differ in their underlying platform and model development languages. The three implementations are Repast for Java (RepastJ), Repast for the Microsoft.Net framework (Repast.Net), and Repast for Python Scripting (RepastPy). RepastJ is the reference implementation that defines the core services. The fourth version of Repast, namely Repast for Oz/Mozart (RepastOz), is an experimental system that partially implements the Repast conceptual specification while adding advanced new features [33,47]. In general, it is recommended that basic models be written in Python using RepastPy due to its visual interface and that advanced models be written in Java with RepastJ or in C# with Repast.Net. An example Repast model user interface is shown in Fig. 6.1.

Repast 3.0 has a variety of features, including the following:

- Repast includes a variety of agent templates and examples. However, the toolkit gives users complete flexibility as to how they specify the properties and behaviors of agents.

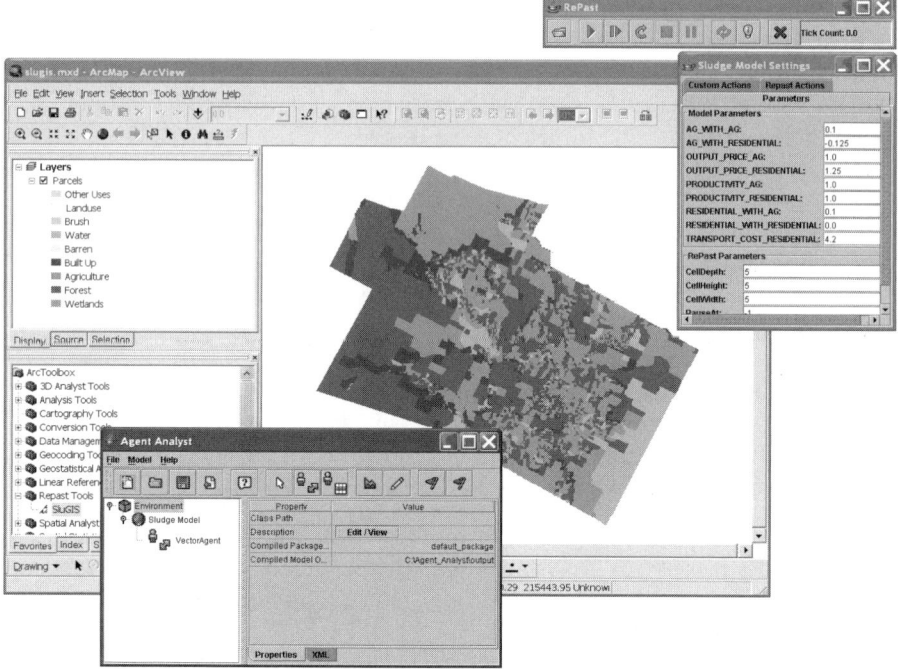

Fig. 6.1. A Repast model user interface. See also color plate.

- Repast is fully object-oriented.
- Repast includes a fully concurrent discrete event scheduler. This scheduler supports both sequential and parallel discrete event operations.
- Repast offers built-in simulation results logging and graphing tools.
- Repast has an automated Monte Carlo simulation framework.
- Repast provides a range of two-dimensional agent environments and visualizations.
- Repast allows users to dynamically access and modify agent properties, agent behavioral equations, and model properties at run time.
- Repast includes libraries for genetic algorithms, neural networks, random number generation, and specialized mathematics.
- Repast includes built-in systems dynamics modeling.
- Repast has social network modeling support tools.
- Repast has integrated geographical information systems (GIS) support.
- Repast is fully implemented in a variety of languages, including Java and C#.
- Repast models can be developed in many languages including Java, C#, Managed C++, Visual Basic.Net, Managed Lisp, Managed Prolog, and Python scripting.

- Repast is available on virtually all modern computing platforms, including Windows, Mac OS, and Linux. The platform support includes both personal computers and large-scale scientific computing clusters.

Repast's features directly support the implementation of models with Holland's three properties and four mechanisms [22]:

1. Repast allows nonlinearity in agents since their behaviors are completely designed by users. Repast's systems dynamics, genetic algorithms, neural networks, random number generation, and social networks libraries make this process easy.
2. Repast supports diversity by giving users complete control over the way their agents are defined and initialized. Again, the Repast libraries simplify the specification of diversity.
3. Repast allows the aggregation property by allowing users to specify and maintain groups of agents.
4. Repast supports the flows mechanism with features such as its systems dynamics tools and social network library.
5. Repast provides for the tagging mechanism by allowing agents to present arbitrary markers.
6. Repast makes the internal models mechanism available through both its flexible definition of agents and its many behavioral libraries.
7. Repast supports the building blocks mechanism through its object-oriented polymorphism.

Repast for Python Scripting (RepastPy) enables visual model construction with agent behaviors defined in Python [31]. RepastPy models can be automatically converted to RepastJ models using RepastPy's export option.

RepastPy users work with the interface shown in upper left-hand window of Fig. 6.2 to add the components to their models. RepastPy users then employ Python to script the behaviors of their agents, as shown in lower right-hand window of Fig. 6.2.

The components in the example model are shown on the left-hand side of the upper window of Fig. 6.2. These components include the simulation environment specification, the model specification ("Schelling GIS"), the ZIP code region agent specification ("ZipRegion"), and the residential agent specification ("Resident"). Properties for the model specification such as the "Actions," "Display Name," and "Master Schedule" are shown on the right-hand side of the upper window in the figure. The Actions "Edit" button is used to access the Python scripting for the agent behaviors.

The Python scripting window for the example model is shown in the lower window of Fig. 6.2. The agent properties ("Variables"), the agent behavior libraries ("Java Imports"), and behavior code ("Source") can be seen in this window.

There is a special version of RepastPy known as the Agent Analyst that is an extension to the ESRI ArcGIS geographical information systems platform.

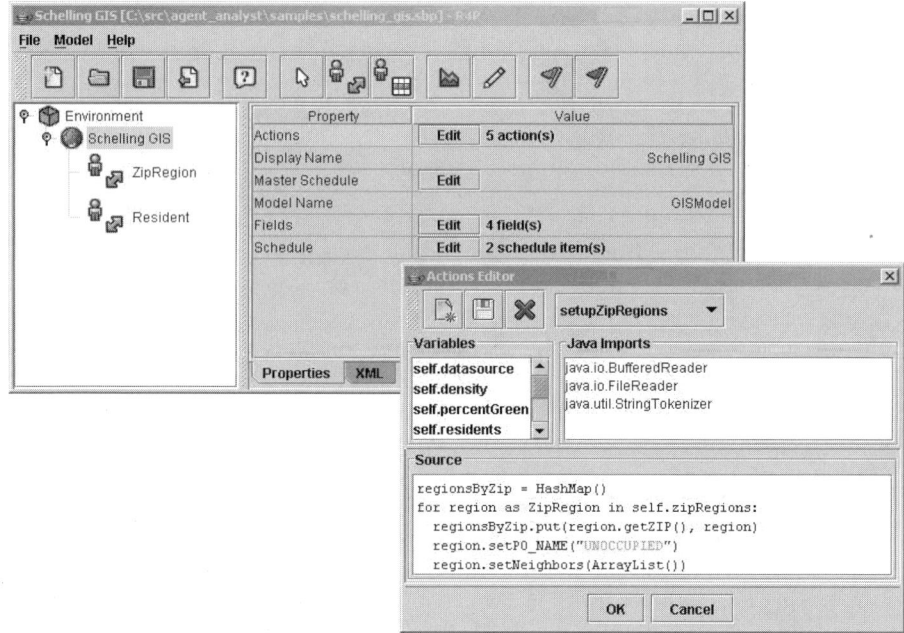

Fig. 6.2. The RepastPy interface.

ESRI ArcGIS is the leading commercial geographical information system, with well over one million users. Agent Analyst is a fully integrated ArcGIS Model Tool. This means that Agent Analyst has drag-and-drop integration with ArcGIS. Agent Analyst users can create RepastPy models from within ArcGIS with a few mouse clicks. Figure 6.1 shows the SLUDGE Geographical Information System (SluGIS) Agent Analyst model running within ArcGIS. SluGIS is described in the section on artificial societies.

RepastJ is written entirely in Java [18]. An example RepastJ model, Hexabugs, is shown in Fig. 6.3. The Hexabugs model is discussed in the section on artificial biological systems. Since RepastJ is pure Java, any development environment that supports Java can be used. The free and open source Eclipse development environment is recommended [13]. Eclipse provides a variety of powerful editing and development features, including code authoring wizards, automatic code restructuring tools, design analysis tools, Unified Modeling Language (UML) tools, extensible markup language (XML) tools, and integration with version control systems. Figure 6.4 shows part of the RepastJ AgentCell model in Eclipse. The AgentCell modules are shown in the upper left "Package Explorer" tab. The cell agent component is highlighted in this tab. Part of the cell agent code is shown in the upper middle "Cell.java" tab. Some of the cell agent properties and methods can be seen in the "Outline" tab on the far right. Part of the cell agent documentation is shown in the button right tab. Additionally, a code module dependency graph can be seen

6 Repast   123

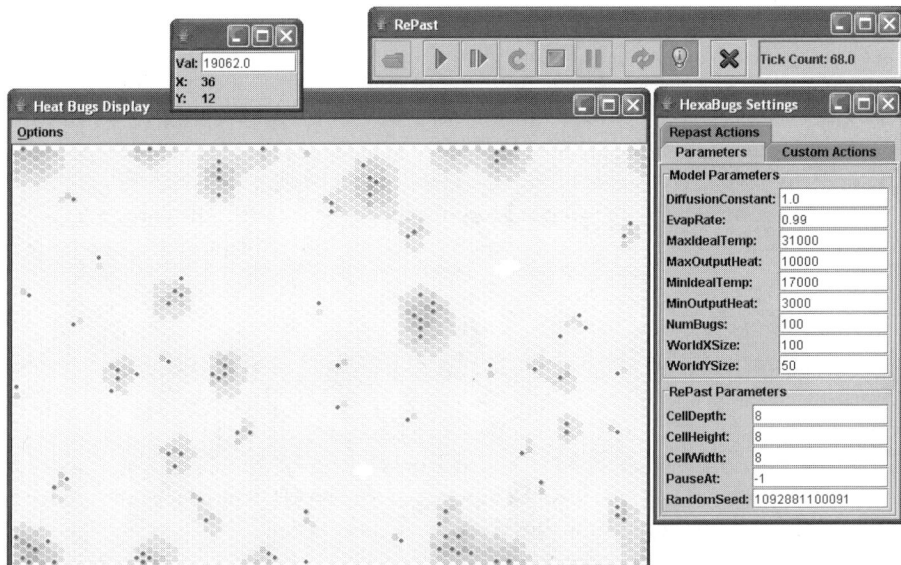

Fig. 6.3. The RepastJ Hexabugs Model.

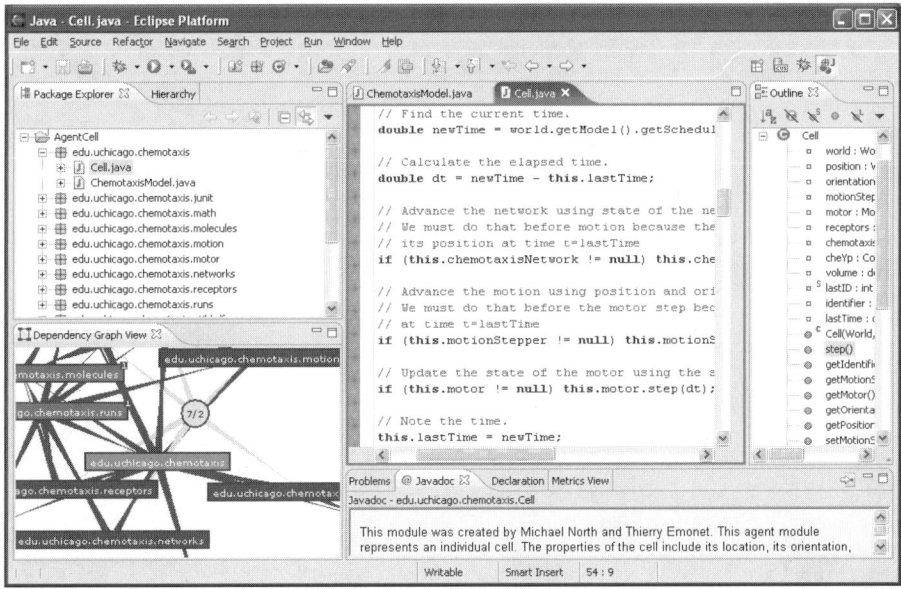

Fig. 6.4. RepastJ in the Eclipse Development Environment. See also color plate.

in the lower left "Dependency Graph View" tab. This graph shows the connections between some of the main Agent Cell modules. The AgentCell model is detailed in the section on artificial biological systems.

Both RepastJ and RepastPy models can be developed and executed on nearly any modern computing platform. This is particularly beneficial for artificial life researchers since models can be constructed on readily available workstations and then executed on large-scale clusters without changing code. An example of this will be provided along with the description of the AgentCell model.

6.3 RepastJ in the Eclipse Development Environment

Repast for the Microsoft.Net framework (Repast.Net) is written entirely in C# [1]. An example Repast.Net named Rocket Bugs is shown in Fig. 6.5. The Rocket Bugs model is a Cartesian elaboration of the Hexabugs model in which some of the agents herd the other agents in the system.

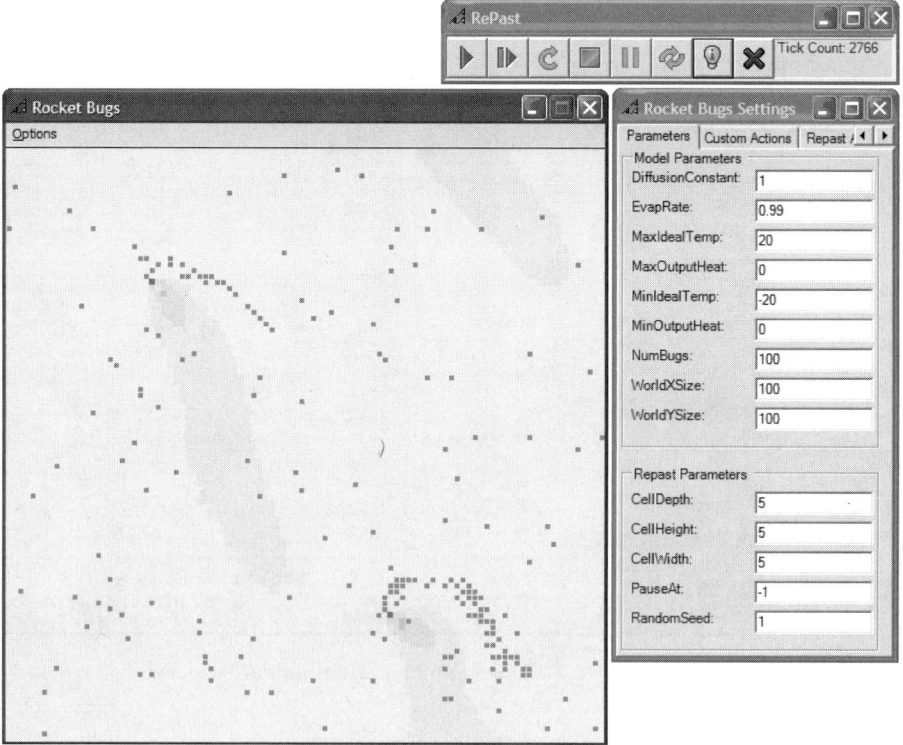

Fig. 6.5. Repast.Net Rocket Bugs model.

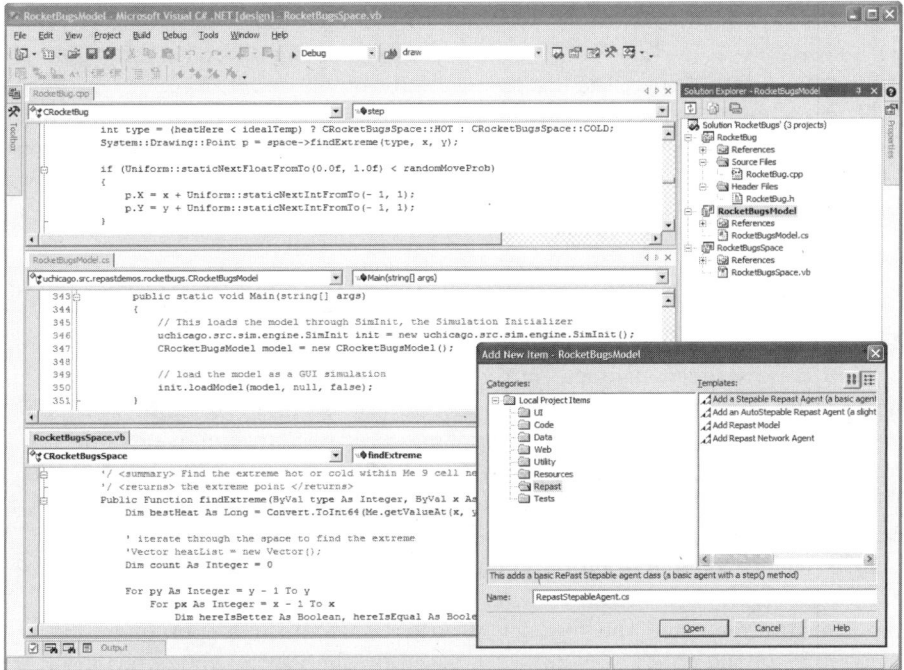

Fig. 6.6. Repast.Net in Microsoft Visual Studio.Net.

Some of the code for this model is displayed in the Visual Studio Environment in Fig. 6.6. It can be seen in the three windows on the left in the figure that the Rocket Bugs simulation uses a combination of Managed C++, C#, and Visual Basic.Net, all in a single seamless model. Additionally, note in the lower right that Repast.Net comes with a full set of specialized Visual Studio templates. These templates automate the initial creation of both Repast.Net models and model components such as agents.

All three versions of Repast are designed to work well with other software development tools. For example, all three versions are integrated with geographical information systems such as the RepastPy Agent Analyst example shown in Fig. 6.1. However, since RepastJ is the most widely used version of Repast, the integration examples will focus on Java. See ROAD for many other examples [41].

RepastJ easily permits aspect-oriented software development. Aspects implement cross-cutting concerns that allow software idioms repeated throughout a model to be factored to reduce redundancy [14]. See Walker, Baniassad, and Murphy for a discussion of the use of Aspects for software development [48].

RepastJ includes its own built-in logging facilities but also works with the high-performance Log4j system and also with the National Center for

Supercomputing Applications' (NCSA) Hierarchical Data Format 5 (HDF5) data storage system [21, 34]. The use of Log4j, among other logging tools, in conjunction with AspectJ is discussed briefly by Cloyer et al. [9].

RepastJ unit testing is performed with JUnit as outlined in Beck and Gamma [3]. Unit testing allows software to be tested on an incremental modular level. The combination of these and other tools with RepastJ allows sophisticated models to be constructed reliably and efficiently.

6.3.1 Repast Concepts

The Repast system has two layers. The core layer runs general-purpose simulation code written in Java or C#. This component handles most of the behind the scenes details. Repast users do not normally need to work with this layer directly. The external layer runs user-specific simulation code written in Java, C#, Python, Managed C++, Managed Lisp, Managed Prolog, Visual Basic.Net, or other languages. This component handles most of the center stage work. Repast users regularly work with this layer.

The Repast system has four fundamental components, as shown in Fig. 6.7. The components are the simulation engine, the input/output (I/O) system, the user interface, and the support libraries. Each of these components is implemented in the core layer and is accessed by the user in the external layer. A Unified Modeling Language (UML) diagram showing the relationships between these components is presented in Fig. 6.8. Information on UML notation can be found in Booch [6].

The Repast simulation engine is responsible for executing simulations. The Repast engine has four main parts, namely the scheduler, the model, the controller, and the agents. The relationship between these components is indicated in Figs. 6.7 and 6.8 and is discussed later in this section.

The Repast scheduler is a full-featured discrete event scheduler. Simulations proceed by popping events or "actions" as they are called in Repast, off an event queue and executing them. These actions are such things as "move all agents one cell to the left," "form a link with your neighbor's neighbor," or "update the display window." The model developer determines the order in which these actions execute relative to each other using ticks. As such, each tick acts as a temporal index for the execution of actions. For example, if event X is scheduled for tick 3, event Y for tick 4, and event Z for tick 5, then event Y will execute after event X and before event Z. Actions scheduled for execution at the same tick will be executed with a simulated concurrency. In this way, the progression of time in a simulation can be seen as an increase in the tick count.

The Repast scheduler includes full support for concurrent task execution. Tasks become concurrent when actions are given both a starting time and duration. When durations are specified, actions that can be started in the background are run concurrently. Actions with nonzero durations will run concurrently with other actions with compatible tick counts as well as block

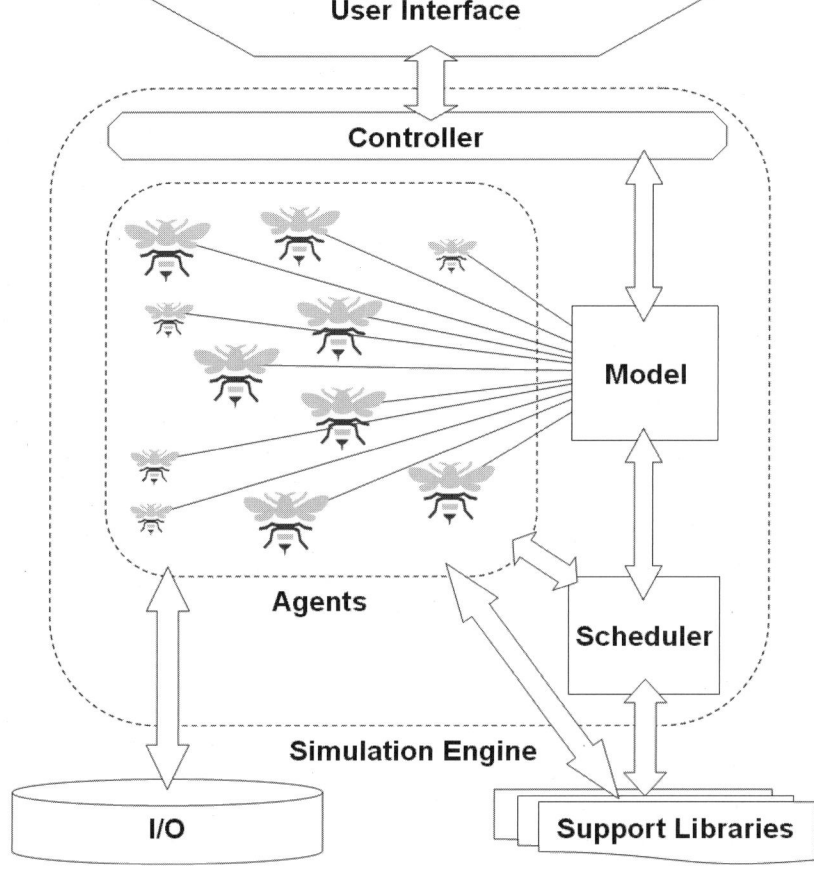

Fig. 6.7. Repast overview diagram.

the execution of other actions with higher tick counts until the current action is completed. For example, consider a process that contains some long-running and complicated behavior that can be started at time (t) with results needed at (t + 5). Imagine that there are actions that can be run concurrently over time (t) to (t + 5). This behavior can modeled as an action with a five-tick duration. In terms of implementation, this action will run in its own thread that is amenable to being run on a separate processor or even on another computer. This allows the natural introduction of complex concurrent and parallel task execution into Repast simulations. Since durations are optional, modelers can begin by creating sequential simulations and then introduce concurrency as needed.

Repast schedulers are themselves actions that can be recursively nested following the composite design pattern [19]. This allows a Repast action to be

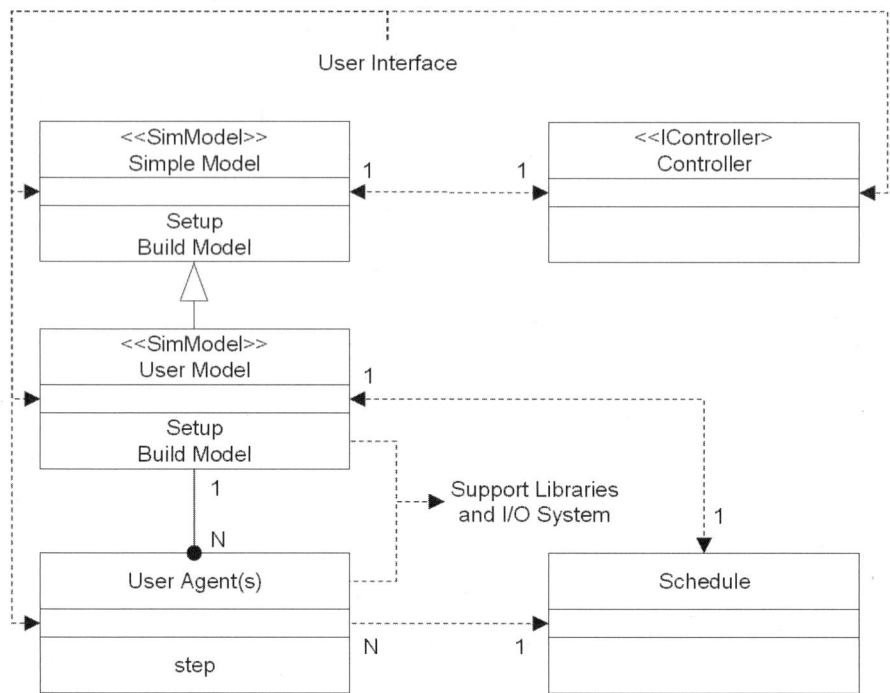

Fig. 6.8. Core Repast UML diagram.

as complex as needed for a given application. It even allows advanced multiscale simulations to be constructed by combining existing models such that the full schedules of lower-level models run as simple actions in higher-level models.

Repast models contain the definition of the simulation to be run by the scheduler. Repast models include the list of agents to be executed, the simulation initialization instructions, and the user interface specification.

Repast controllers connect models and schedulers. They activate the selected model and then manage the interactions between the user or batch execution system and the model.

Repast agents are created by users from components within Repast. A variety of options are available including geographically situated agents and network-aware agents. Agents receive data from and provide results to the Repast I/O system.

The Repast I/O system allows agents to be created based on input properties. It also can store data from both agents and overall models. Repast includes a set of results loggers that support a range of storage formats.

The Repast user interface supports the display of model results and allows user to interact with running models. Repast user interface examples are shown in Figs. 6.1, 6.3, 6.5, 6.9, 6.10, and 6.11. Model user interfaces can

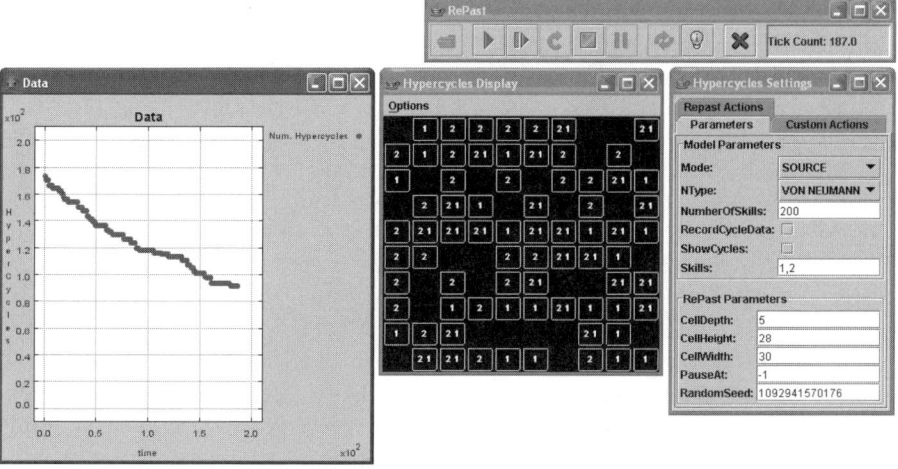

Fig. 6.9. Padgett, Lee, and Collier's RepastJ Hypercycle model.

include graphical outputs or maps of the agent states as well as interactive probes that allow users to view and modify agent states. An agent map is shown in the lower left of Fig. 6.3, and an agent probe is shown in the upper left. Users have full control over what is available through both maps and probes.

The Repast support libraries include a variety of tools for both mathematics and modeling. The mathematics support includes a range of random distribution generators and statistical aggregation tools [30]. The modeling support includes genetic algorithm and neural network tools among other features [24, 49].

6.3.2 Using Repast

As previously mentioned, Repast is distributed under a variation of the BSD license [41]. This license states that Repast can be used for virtually any purpose without fees and without a requirement to release propriety model source code. See ROAD for details [41]. This license allows Repast to be freely used in education, research, and entertainment by nonprofit, government, and commercial organizations.

Many educational institutions are now using or have used Repast for either education or research. These institutions include the University of Chicago, the University of Michigan, Iowa State University, the Swiss Federal Institute of Technology Zurich, the Illinois Institute of Technology, and Harvard University. In particular, the University of Chicago is the birthplace of Repast. The educational uses generally focus on providing students with a laboratory environment for experiments with complex systems and for instructing students on agent-based modeling concepts. The research work includes the development of models in a variety of domains and as well as model theoretic studies. Several of the models are discussed in the following sections. The model theoretic work mostly involves additions to and extensions of the Repast framework itself. This list of educational institutions using Repast is rapidly growing.

A significant number of U.S. federal government agencies and other organizations are using or have used Repast. These organizations include the U.S. Department of Energy, the U.S. Joint Chiefs of Staff, the U.S. Navy, and the U.S. Department of Homeland Security. These users have Repast models that focus on a range of mission-critical applications such as infrastructure security and network communications planning.

Several commercial organizations are working with Repast. These organizations include software developers such as ESRI and other private organizations. These corporations are using Repast for several purposes, including planning and commercial software enhancement.

6.4 Repast Artficial Life Models

Repast has been used for a variety of artificial life applications. There are a large number of applications in areas that range from traditional artificial life modeling to social systems simulation. Selected example areas include the use of Repast for modeling artificial ecosystems, for modeling multiscale biological systems, and for modeling artificial societies.

6.4.1 Artificial Evolution and Ecosystems

There are a variety of pressing reasons to model evolution and ecosystems. According to Wilke and Adami [50]:

> Historically, evolutionary biology has generally been an observational and theoretical science. The experimental verification of evolutionary mechanisms is a challenging undertaking for several reasons: most organisms have comparatively long generation times; there are difficulties in determining important parameters, such as mutation rates or fitness values; and the large variances inherent in evolution lead to poor statistical significance in averages.

Padgett, Lee, and Collier's Hypercycle model uses Repast in combination with analytic methods to investigate autocatalytic co-evolution of complex interconnected production and consumption systems [35]. The Hypercycle model has been used to study the emergence of economic production and consumption in adaptive systems [35]. The long-term goal is to model selected critical features found in real production and consumption systems such as Renaissance Florence [36]. The model is shown in Fig. 6.9.

The Hypercycle model has three components [35]:

1. Products are used and exchanged throughout the Hypercycle world.
2. Rules transform products into other products.
3. Agents use rules to convert products into other products.

The Hypercycle world is a two-dimensional torus with a Moore tessellation. A Moore tessellation creates a Cartesian grid such that each vertex has exactly eight neighbors. One agent resides at each vertex. This agent can exchange products with its eight neighbors or release a product to the outside environment.

Rules and products are initially seeded throughout the Hypercycle world on a random basis. At each time step, agents examine their rules to determine if they can transform any of their products to another product with one of their rules. If so, they do this. The new product is then forwarded to a randomly selected agent among the agent's eight neighbors. Any products that cannot be transformed are ejected to the outside world.

In the Hypercycle model, rules reproduce and die under a carrying-capacity constraint. Rules that are used to transform a product that is in turn transformed by a second rule are considered successful rules. These successful rules are allowed to reproduce. The carrying-capacity constraint requires the total number of rules to remain constant. Therefore, rules that reproduce do so at the expense of other randomly selected rules. The randomly selected rules are killed and removed from the world. Eventually, the accumulating deaths cause some agents to run out of rules. Agents that exhaust their rules die and drop out of the Hypercycle world.

Kampis and Gulyas are applying Repast to investigate evolutionary emergence [25–27]. They are using Repast to study "how is it possible to produce sustained evolution in an artificial system" [26]. They state that [27]

> We developed an agent-based simulation model using the Repast package. Organisms are agents that selectively feed, reproduce and die, based on their phenotypic properties described in variable length records. As adaptation progresses, new property sets extend the records, and as a result, selection can spontaneously switch between the defining properties of an interaction. The aim is to develop functionally disjoint subpopulations specialized for the use of different property sets. The first results have recently been reported, showing the possibility of progressive evolution productive of new selection effects, as an illustration for the causal principles of embodiment.

Riolo at the University of Michigan is currently working on replicating Holland's Echo system, along with extensions to it [23, 40]. The goals are to implement "the Holland Echo system in Repast, use it to replicate the experiments of Bedau et al. on whether open-ended evolution is occurring in Echo and explore how changes to the basic system affect its ability to support open-ended evolution (e.g., as defined by Bedau et al.'s measures)" [4, 40].

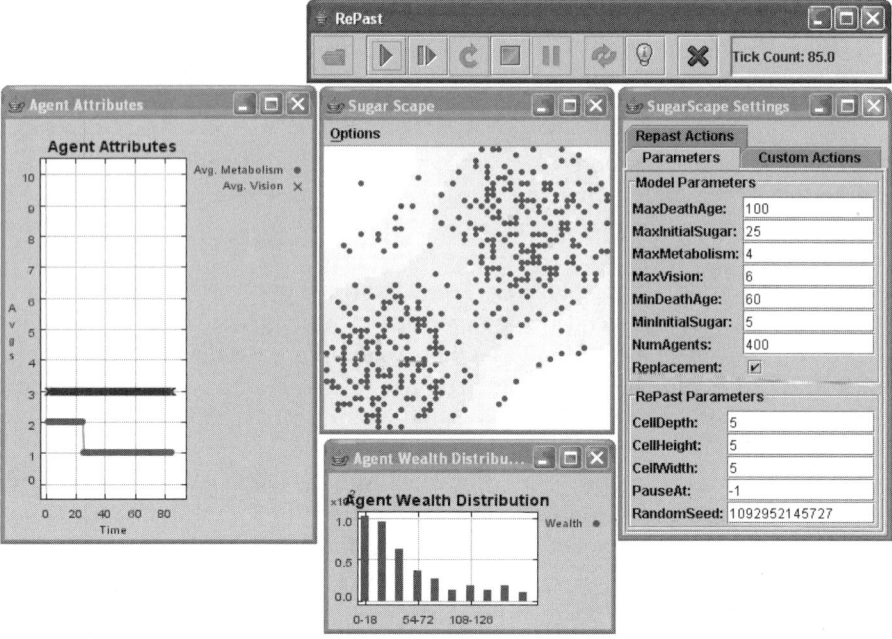

Fig. 6.10. Sugarscape in RepastJ.

6.4.2 Artificial Societies

Repast is used for a range of artificial society simulations. Repast comes with a partial implementation of Epstein and Axtel's Sugarscape model as shown in Fig. 6.10 [16]. Sugarscape was originally implemented using the Ascape ABMS toolkit [38]. In Sugarscape, "fundamental social structures and group behaviors emerge from the interaction of individual agents operating on artificial environments under rules that place only bounded demands on each agent's information and computational capacity" [16].

Sugarscape is a complex model populated by simple agents. The agents live in a simple toroidal world that is covered with varying amounts of sugar cane that grows at varying rates. The agents have several traits including a sugar metabolism, speed, vision, wealth in the form of accumulated sugar, and other factors. The agents live according to simple rules that cause them to collect the sugar at their location, burn some of their accumulated sugar, and then move to the area within their vision that has the highest sugar level. If two agents with enough wealth inhabit the same location, then they can reproduce. The new agent is born with a mixture of its parents' traits and is given some of its parents' wealth. Various versions of the model include externalities such as pollution, simple social identities, social networks, combat, and credit and disease propagation. Sugarscape has been successful in reproducing a variety of social outcomes such as skewed wealth distributions, as can be seen in Fig. 6.10.

Axelrod is using Repast to investigate consumer choice. Some of his other work on adaptive organizational responses is also conceptually related to this research effort [2]. The agents are consumers and the agent environments are markets. The agents seek to maximize their own welfare given the available choices.

Picker of the University of Chicago Law School has used Repast to investigate the endogenous emergence of social norms and the resulting reification of selected norms as law [39]. The agents in his Endogenous Neighborhoods and Norms (ENN) model are individual people. The agent's environment is the forum for interaction. The agents adopt or change norms based on the relative success they experience using those social norms. Success is itself dependent on the level of adoption of the underlying norms.

Cederman is using Repast to study state formation and nationalist movements [8]. In his Repast models, each agent represents a nation. Nations can form alliances with other nations. Nations can also attempt to invade and defeat neighboring states in combat. The agent's environment is a grid covered with variable amounts of resources.

Dibble is using Repast to investigate the spatial effects of technologies and human settlement patterns [11]. Her agents are individual people that can transmit a variety of things around their environment including diseases, resources, and information. The agent environments are generally "small-world" graphs consisting of regular rings modified with small numbers of randomly connected edges [51].

Parker is using Repast to study land use and land-use change [37]. Parker and Najlis' Simulated Land Use Dependent on Edge Effect Externalities (SLUDGE) and related SluGIS models simulate the usage of individual parcels of land in abstract or real geographies. The simulated land uses change over time based on the natural traits of the parcel itself such as size and accessibility; the current usage of the land surrounding each parcel; and either endogenous or exogenous resource demands. The SluGIS model is shown in Fig. 6.1.

Brantingham is applying Repast to investigate stone tool assembly by ancient peoples [7]:

> Stone tool assemblage variability is considered a reliable proxy measure of adaptive variability. Raw material richness, transport distances, and the character of transported technologies are thought to signal (1) variation in raw material selectivity based on material quality and abundance, (2) optimization of time and energy costs associated with procurement of stone from spatially dispersed sources, (3) planning depth that weaves raw material procurement forays into foraging activities, and (4) risk minimization that sees materials transported in quantities and forms that are energetically economical and

least likely to fail. This paper dispenses with assumptions that raw material type and abundance play any role in the organization of mobility and raw material procurement strategies. Rather, a behaviorally neutral agent-based model is developed involving a forager engaged in a random walk within a uniform environment. Raw material procurement in the model is dependent only upon random encounters with stone sources and the amount of available space in the mobile toolkit.

Brantingham reports that the Repast model "richness-sample size relationships, frequencies of raw material transfers as a function of distance from source, and both quantity-distance and reduction intensity-distance relationships are qualitatively similar to commonly observed archaeological patterns" [7]. This success has lead Brantingham to interesting findings including the "possibility that Paleolithic behavioral adaptations were sometimes not responsive to differences between stone raw material types in the ways implied by current archaeological theory" [7].

6.4.3 Artificial Biological Systems

Repast is being applied to study a range of artificial biological systems. The Repast system itself includes the simple Hexabugs model shown in Fig. 6.3 [41]. The Hexabugs model has agents that release individually varying levels of heat into a diffusion space. Each agent has a unique temperature preference. Over time, the agents move toward areas with temperatures closer to their own ideal temperature. Simple adjustments in preferences and heat output can lead to the emergence of either clustering (Fig. 6.11, left) or forward moving fronts of agents (Fig. 6.11, right). In the figure, the agent locations are represented by highlighted points.

The clusters are roughly stable over time, while the running fronts move forward from top to bottom in Fig. 6.11.

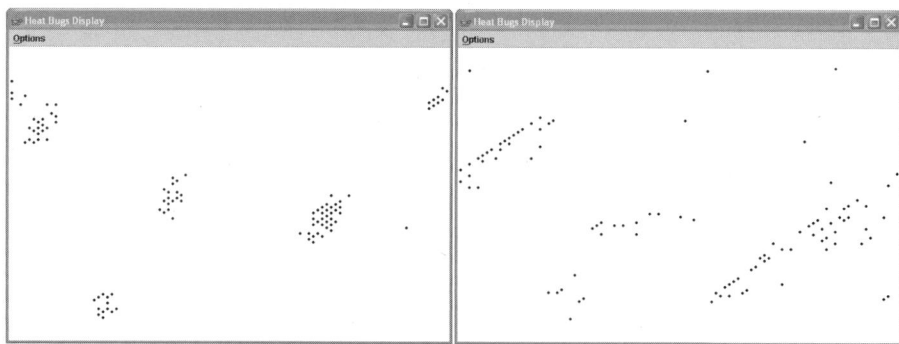

Fig. 6.11. The RepastJ Hexabugs model with clustering (*left*) and fronts (*right*).

Folcik and Orosz of the Department of Surgery at the Ohio State University College of Medicine and Public Health are using Repast to model the antiviral response of human immune systems [17]. They state that

> The immune system is a prime example of a complex adaptive system, with individual cells that follow rules for behavior based upon detection of signals and contacts with other cells in the environment. We have created a simulation of a human anti-viral immune response using the Repast software framework. The agent-based simulation includes three windows that represent a generic tissue site with parenchyma that becomes infected with virus, a lymph node site with cells that can become activated to fight the viral infection, and the peripheral blood that carries the responding immune cells and antibodies back to the site of infection. The simulation uses seven agent types and twenty signals to represent Parenchymal Cells, B-Cells, T-Cells, Macrophages, Dendritic Cells, Natural Killer Cells and the virus, and pro- and anti-inflammatory cytokines, chemokines, and antibodies that such cells use to communicate with each other. The numbers of agents present as well as the quantity and types of signals present depend upon rules for proliferation and the release of cytokines that the agent types follow. Individual agents have various states, migrate from one window to another and live or die as the rules for their behavior dictate.

Folcik and Orosz are using their model to "explore formative patterns of agent behavior that develop within a complex adaptive system, to evaluate how information is used for decision making as responses evolve, and to develop methods of generating and evaluating simulator data that can be used to identify the strengths and weaknesses of clinical and experimental tools that are currently in use" [17].

North and Macal are using RepastJ to model bacteria chemotaxis in *Escherichia coli* (*E. coli*) on multiple simultaneous scales [15]. Chemotaxis is the biological process of moving toward or away from specific chemicals or classes of chemicals [5]. Bacterial chemotaxis in *E. coli* is one of the best-characterized examples of biological information processing [28]. In bacterial chemotaxis, information outside cells is converted into usable information within cells via signal transduction networks. Signal transduction networks allow cells to respond and to adapt to environmental changes. These signal transduction networks are scientifically important since they exhibit the key properties found in most complex biological systems. As part of the multiscale modeling architecture, the AgentCell simulation uses the Stochism model to represent chemical reactions at the molecular level [32].

The AgentCell model simulates the chemistry of bacterial chemical receptors, the effects of receptor signaling on cellular motion and the resulting consequences of cellular motion on population distributions. AgentCell models the relationship between intracellular processes in individual *E. coli* cells and the behavior of a cellular population. Each AgentCell bacterium is an independent agent equipped with its own chemotaxis network, motors, and flagella.

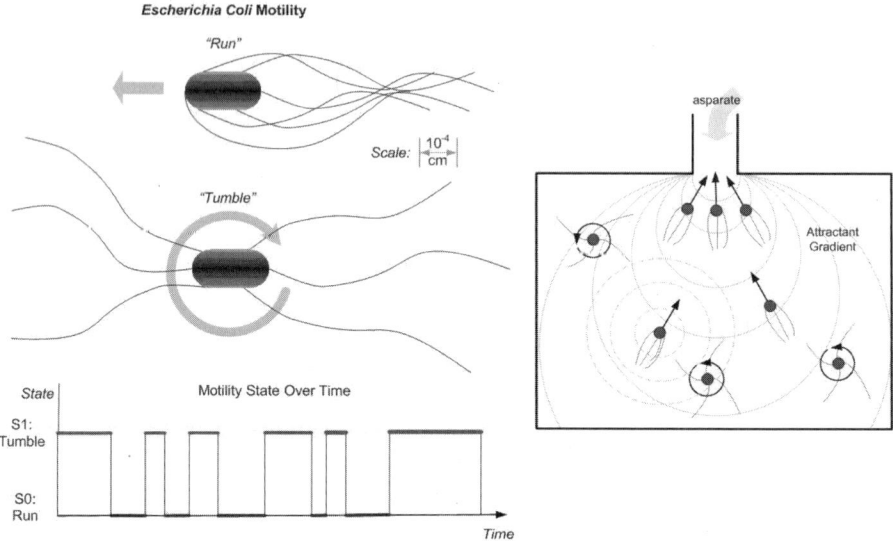

Fig. 6.12. Bacterial structure (*top left*), bacterial motility (*bottom left*), and population response to a stimulus (*right*).

The swimming cells are propelled in three dimensions by their flagella, as shown on the top left of Fig. 6.12. When most of the flagella rotate counterclockwise, the flagella form a bundle and the bacterium runs forward smoothly; when motors rotate clockwise, the bacterium tumbles erratically, as shown on the bottom left of Fig. 6.12. Tumbling randomizes the cell trajectory. Controlling the amount of tumbling allows bacterial populations to perform chemotaxis by individually swimming toward attractants or away from repellents, as shown on the right side of Fig. 6.12.

The AgentCell model was developed on individual personal computers under both Microsoft Windows and Linux. AgentCell was then moved to Argonne's 350 node Argonne "Jazz" Linux computing cluster without substantial modifications. A total of 2,000 cells were simulated for 120,000 time steps each. The simulations took a period of 60 hours on the Jazz cluster. Each time step represented 10 milliseconds. During the time this work was performed, the Argonne Jazz cluster was among the top 250 most powerful computing clusters in the world [46].

The AgentCell model was validated by simulating the collective chemotactic behavior of more than 1000 *E. coli* bacteria as they moved along a linear gradient of attractant and in an environment without attractants. At regular time intervals the position and orientation of all the cells were recorded.

Within each cell, the state of the motors, flagella, receptors and the activity of the proteins involved in the chemotaxis network were also recorded. The simulation was found to reproduce the important statistical features observed in single *E. coli* cells as reported by Korobkova et al. [15, 28].

An example trajectory of an individual cell is shown in Fig. 6.13.

The trajectories of a small population of 25 cells are shown in Fig. 6.14.

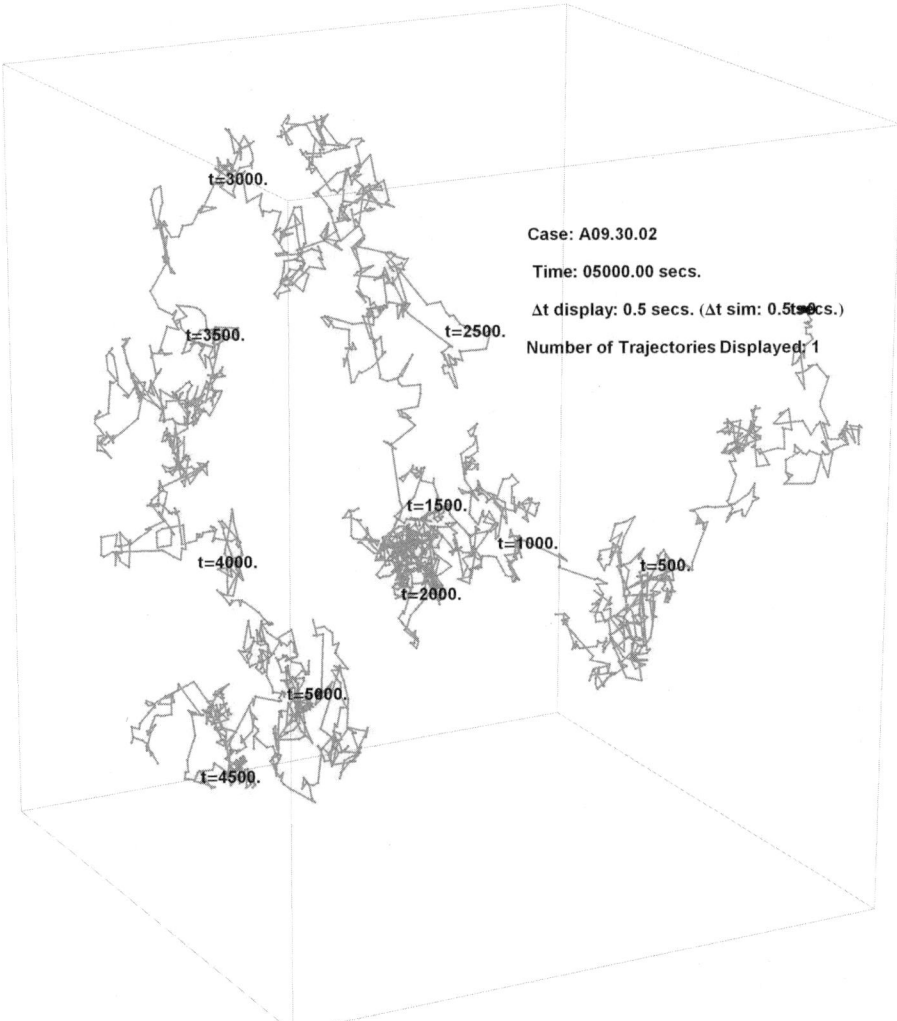

Fig. 6.13. The simulated trajectory of one bacteria.

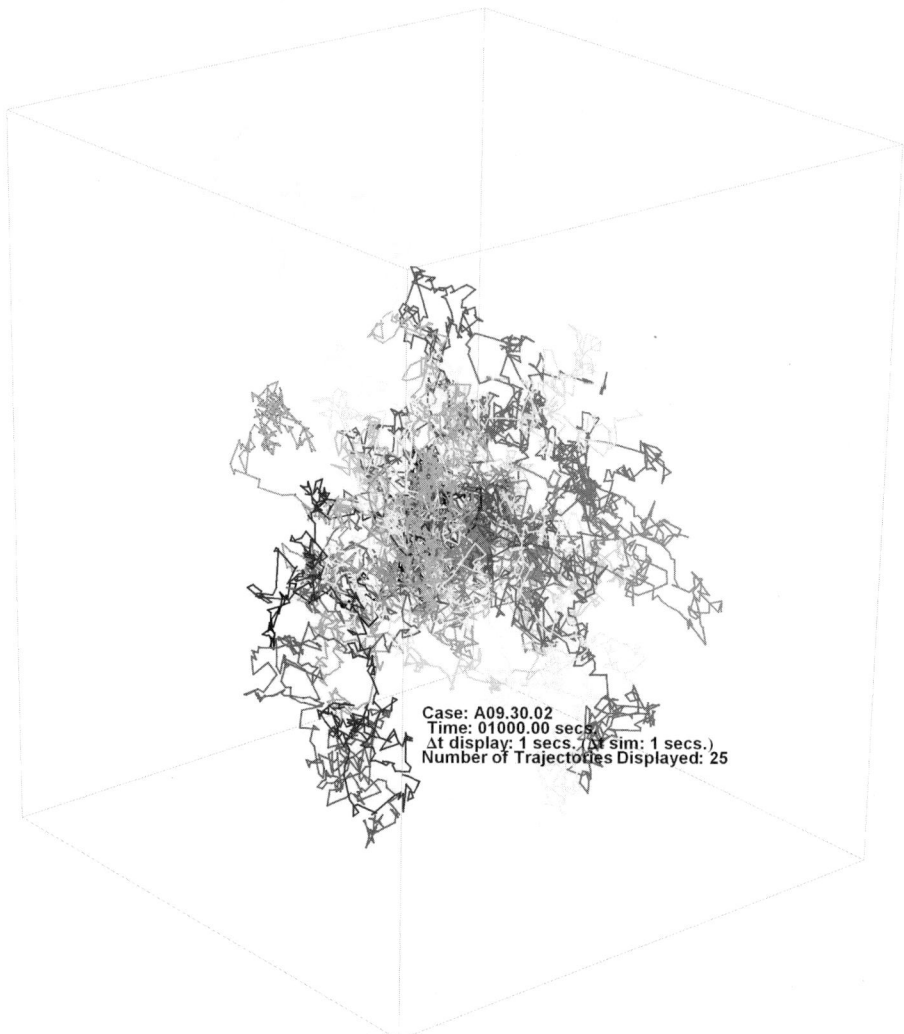

Fig. 6.14. The simulated trajectories of 25 bacteria. See also color plate.

6.5 Conclusions

Artificial life focuses on synthesizing "life-like behaviors from scratch in computers, machines, molecules, and other alternative media" [29]. Artificial life expands the "horizons of empirical research in biology beyond the territory currently circumscribed by life-as-we-know-it" to provide "access to the domain of life-as-it-could-be" [29]. Agent-based modeling and simulation are used to create computational laboratories that replicate selected real or potential behaviors of actual or possible complex adaptive systems. Agent-based models can be used to escape the accident of history in the form of "life-as-we-know-it" by revealing alterative forms of "life-as-it-could-be."

Repast is a free and open source agent modeling toolkit. Repast's features directly support the implementation of models with Holland's three properties and four mechanisms of complex adaptive system [22]. As such, Repast is a natural framework in which to perform artificial life experiments.

Repast toolkit version 3.0 can be thought of as a specification for agent-based modeling services or functions. There are three concrete implementations of this conceptual specification, namely Repast for Java (RepastJ), Repast for the Microsoft.Net framework (Repast.Net), and Repast for Python Scripting (RepastPy). The fourth version of Repast, namely Repast for Oz/Mozart (RepastOz), is an experimental system that partially implements the Repast conceptual specification while adding advanced new features. Repast 3.0 has a variety of features including full object orientation; a concurrent discrete event scheduler; built-in simulation results logging and graphing tools; an automated Monte Carlo framework; two-dimensional agent environments and visualizations; dynamically accessible agent and model properties; libraries for genetic algorithms, neural networks, and specialized mathematics; built-in systems dynamics modeling; social network modeling support; and integrated geographical information systems support.

Repast is fully implemented in a variety of languages including Java and C#. Repast models can be developing in many languages including Java, C#, Managed C++, Visual Baisc.Net, Managed Lisp, Managed Prolog, and Python scripting. Repast is available on virtually all modern computing platforms, including Windows, Mac OS, and Linux. The platform support includes both personal computers and large-scale scientific computing clusters.

Repast has many academic, government, and industry users. These users are involved in a variety of application areas, including educational, research, and commercial uses. In particular, there are many examples in which Repast has been used extensively for artificial life applications in topical areas such as artificial evolution and ecosystems; artificial societies; and artificial biological systems.

References

1. Archer T (2001) Inside C#. Microsoft Press, Redmond, Washington.
2. Axelrod R and Cohen M (2000) Harnessing Complexity: Organizational Implications of a Scientific Frontier. Free Press, New York.
3. Beck K and Gamma E (1998) Test infected: Programmers love writing tests. Java Report 3:37–50.
4. Bedau M, McCaskill J, Packard N, Rasmussen S, Adami C, Green D, Harvey I, Ikegami T, Kaneko K and Ray T (2000) Open Problems in Artificial Life. Artificial Life 6:363–376.
5. Berg HC (1993) Random Walks in Biology. Princeton University Press, Princeton.

6. Booch G (1993) Object-oriented Design with Applications. Addison-Wesley, Reading, MA.
7. Brantingham P (2003) A neutral model of stone raw material procurement. American Antiquity 487–509.
8. Cederman L-E (1991) Modeling the co-evolution of states and nations, Proc. 1999 Workshop on Agent Simulation. University of Chicago, Chicago.
9. Cloyer A, Clement A, Bodkin R, and Hugunin J (2003) Practitioners report: Using aspectJ for component integration in middleware. In: Companion of the 18th Annual ACM SIGPLAN Conf. on Object-Oriented Programming, Systems, Languages, and Applications. ACM, New York.
10. Collier N, Howe T, and North M (2003) Onward and upward: The transition to Repast 2.0. In: Proc. of the 1st Annual North American Association for Computational Social and Organizational Science Conference, Electronic Proceedings. Pittsburgh, PA.
11. Dibble C (1999) Geographic small worlds, agent models on graphs. In: Proc. 1999 Workshop on Agent Simulation. University of Chicago, Chicago.
12. Di Paolo E (2004) Unbinding biological autonomy: Francisco Varela's contributions to artificial Life. J of Artificial Life 231–234.
13. Eclipse Home Page (2004), available at http://www.eclipse.org/.
14. Elrad T, Filman R, and Bader A (2001) Aspect-oriented programming: Introduction. Comm. ACM 44:29–32.
15. Emonet T, Macal C, North M, Wickersham C, and Cluzel P (2004) AgentCell: A Multi-scale agent-based platform for intracellular and extracellular simulations. Joint University of Chicago and Argonne National Laboratory Working Paper, Chicago and Argonne.
16. Epstein J and Axtell R (1996) Growing Artificial Societies Social Science from the Bottom Up. MIT Press, Boston.
17. Folcik V and Orosz C (2004) The immune system as a complex adaptive system: A Repast simulation of the anti-viral immune response. In: Proc. of SwarmFest 2004, University of Michigan, Ann Arbor.
18. Foxwell H (1999) Java 2 Software Development Kit. Linux Journal, Specialized Systems Consultants, Seattle, Washington.
19. Gamma E, Helm R, Johnson R, and Vlissides J (1995) Design Patterns: Elements of Reusable Object-Oriented Software. Addison-Wesley, Reading, MA.
20. Gilbert N and Bankes S (2002) Platforms and methods for agent-based modeling. Proc. National Academy of Sciences of the USA 99:7197–7198.
21. Gülcü C (2003) The Complete Log4j Manual: The Reliable, Fast, and Flexible Logging Framework for Java. QOS Press.
22. Holland J (1996) Hidden Order: How Adaptation Builds Complexity. Addison-Wesley, Reading, MA.
23. Hraber P, Jones T and Forrest S (1997) The ecology of Echo. Artificial Life 3:165–190.
24. Java Object Oriented Neural Engine (Joone) Home Page (2004), available at http://www.jooneworld.com/.
25. Kampis G (2002) A causal model of evolution. In: Proc. 4th Asia-Pacific Conf. on Simulated Evolution and Learning. Singapore, pp. 836–840.
26. Kampis G and Gulyas L (2004) Emergence out of interaction: A Phenotype based model of species evolution. 5th Int. Workshop on Emergent Synthesis.
27. Kampis G and Gulyas L (2003) Causal structures in embodied systems. The European Research Consortium for Informatics and Mathematics News 53.

28. Korobkova E, Emonet T, Vilar J, Shimizu T, and Cluzel P (2004) From molecular noise to behavioral variability in a single bacterium. Nature 428:574–578.
29. Langton C (1994) What is Artificial Life?, The Digital Biology Project, available at http://www.biota.org/papers/cglalife.html.
30. Law AA and Kelton D (1982) Simulation Modeling and Analysis. McGraw-Hill, New York.
31. Lutz M and Ascher D (1999) Learning Python. O'Reilly Press.
32. Morton-Firth C, Shimizu T and Bray D (1999) A free-energy-based stochastic simulation of the tar receptor complex J. Molecular Biology 286: 1059–1074.
33. Mozart Consortium: Mozart Programming System 1.3.1 (2004), available at http://www.mozart-oz.org/.
34. NCSA, HDF 5 Home Page (2004), http://hdf.ncsa.uiuc.edu/HDF5/.
35. Padgett J, Lee D, and Collier N (2003) Economic production as chemistry. Industrial and Corporate Change 12: 843–877.
36. Padgett J (2001) Organizational genesis, identity and control, In: The Transformation of Banking in Renaissance Florence Networks and Markets, Rauch J and Casella A (eds). Russell Sage, New York, pp. 211–257.
37. Parker D, Evans T, and Meretsky V (2001) Measuring emergent properties of agent-based land-cover: land-use models using spatial metrics. In: 7th Ann. Int. Conf. Society for Computational Economics, Yale University, New Haven, CT.
38. Parker M (1999) Ascape: An Agent-based modeling framework in Java. In: Proc. 1999 Workshop on Agents Simulation, University of Chicago, Chicago, IL, USA.
39. Picker R, Baird D and Gertner R (1994) Game Theory and the Law. Harvard University Press, Boston, MA.
40. Riolo R (2004) Repast Mailing List Posting, available at http://repast.sourceforge.net/.
41. ROAD: Repast 3.0 (2004), available at http://repast.sourceforge.net/.
42. Sandler T (2001) Economic Concepts for the Social Sciences. Cambridge University Press.
43. Serenko A and Detlor B (2002) Agent toolkits: A General overview of the market and an assessment of instructor satisfaction with utilizing toolkits in the classroom. Working Paper 455. McMaster University, Hamilton, Ontario.
44. Swarm Development Group: Swarm 2.2 (2004), http://wiki.swarm.org/.
45. Tobias R and Hofmann C (2003) Evaluation of free Java-libraries for social-scientific agent based simulation. J. of Artificial Societies and Social Simulation 7:1.
46. Top 500 Supercomputers for June 2004 (2004), available at http://www.top500.org/lists/2004/06/.
47. Van Roy P and Haridi S (2004) Concepts, Techniques, and Models of Computer Programming. MIT Press, Boston, MA.
48. Walker R, Baniassad E and Murphy G (1999) An initial assessment of aspect-oriented programming. Proc. 1999 Int. Conf. Software Engineering. IEEE, Piscataway, NJ, pp. 120–135.
49. Whitley D (1994) A genetic algorithm tutorial. Statistics and Computing 4:65–85.
50. Wilke C and Adami C (2002) The biology of digital organisms. Trends in Ecology and Evolution 17:528–532.
51. Watts D (2003) Small Worlds: The Dynamics of Networks between Order and Randomness. Princeton University Press, Princeton, NJ.

7

EINSTein: A Multiagent-based Model of Combat

Andrew Ilachinski

Artificial life techniques — specifically, *multiagent-based models* and *evolutionary learning algorithms* — provide a powerful new approach to understanding some of the fundamental processes of war. This paper introduces a simple artificial-like "toy model" of combat called EINSTein. EINSTein is designed to illustrate how certain aspects of land combat can be viewed as self-organized, emergent phenomena resulting from the dynamical web of interactions among notional combatants. EINSTein's *bottom-up, synthesist* approach to the modeling of combat stands in stark contrast to the more traditional top-down, or reductionist, approach taken by conventional military models, and represents a step toward developing a complex systems theoretic toolbox for identifying, exploring, and possibly exploiting self-organized, emergent collective patterns of behavior on the real battlefield. A description of the model is provided, along with examples of emergent spatial patterns and behaviors.

7.1 Background

"War is...not the action of a living force upon lifeless mass...but always the collision of two living forces." — Carl von Clausewitz, *Prussian Military Strategist* (1780–1831)

In 1914, F. W. Lanchester introduced a set of coupled ordinary differential equations — now commonly called the Lanchester equations (LEs) — as models of attrition in modern warfare [1]. In the simplest case of directed fire, for example, the LEs embody the intuitive idea that one side's attrition rate is proportional to the opposing side's size:

$$\begin{cases} \frac{dR}{dt} = -\alpha_B B(t), & R(0) = R_0, \\ \frac{dB}{dt} = -\alpha_R R(t), & B(0) = B_0, \end{cases} \quad (7.1)$$

where R_0 and B_0 are the initial red and blue force levels, respectively, and α_R and α_B represent the effective firing rates at which one unit of strength on one side causes attrition on the other side's forces. The closed-form solution of these equations is given in terms of hyperbolic functions as

$$\begin{cases} R(t) = R_0 \cosh\left(t\sqrt{\alpha_B \alpha_R}\right) - B_0 \sqrt{\alpha_B/\alpha_R} \sinh\left(t\sqrt{\alpha_B \alpha_R}\right), \\ B(t) = B_0 \cosh\left(t\sqrt{\alpha_B \alpha_R}\right) - R_0 \sqrt{\alpha_R/\alpha_B} \sinh\left(t\sqrt{\alpha_B \alpha_R}\right), \end{cases} \quad (7.2)$$

and satisfies the simple "square-law" state equation:

$$\alpha_R \left[R_0^2 - R(t)^2\right] = \alpha_B \left[B_0^2 - B(t)^2\right]. \quad (7.3)$$

Similar ideas were proposed around that time by Chase [2] and Osipov [3]. These equations are formally equivalent to the Lotka–Volterra equations used for modeling the dynamics of interacting predator–prey populations [4]. Despite their relative simplicity, the LEs have since served as the fundamental mathematical models upon which most modern theories of combat attrition are based and are to this day embedded in many "state-of-the art" military models of combat. Taylor [5] provides a thorough mathematical discussion.

On the one hand, there is much to like about the LEs, since they are very intuitive and therefore easy to apply, and provide relatively simple closed-form solutions. On the other hand, as is typically the case in the more general setting of nonlinear dynamical system theory, knowing the "exact" solution to a simplified problem does not necessarily imply that one has gained a deep insight into the problem. Moreover, almost all attempts to correlate LE-based models with historical combat data have proven inconclusive, a result that is in no small part due to the paucity of data. Most data consist only of initial force levels and casualties, and typically for one side only. Moreover, the actual number of casualties is usually uncertain because the definition of "casualty" varies (killed, killed + wounded, killed + missing, etc.).

Two noteworthy battles for which detailed daily attrition data and daily force levels do exist are the battle of Iwo Jima in World War II and Inchon-Seoul campaign in the Korean War. While the battle of Iwo Jima is frequently cited as evidence for the efficacy of the classic LEs, the conditions under which it was fought were very close to the ideal list of assumptions under which the LEs themselves are derived. A detailed analysis of the Inchon-Seoul campaign has also proved inconclusive [6]. Weiss [7], Fain [8], Richardson [9], and others analyze attrition in battles fought from 200 B.C. to World War II.

While the LEs may be relevant for the kind of static trench warfare and artillery duels that characterized most of World War I, they lack the spatial degrees of freedom to realistically model modern combat. They are certainly too simple to adequately represent the more modern vision of combat, which depends on small, highly trained, well-armed autonomous teams working in concert, continually adapting to changing conditions and environments. The fundamental problem is that the LEs idealize combat much in the same way as Newton's laws idealize physics.

The two most significant drawbacks to using LEs to model land combat are that (1) they are unable to account for any spatial variation of forces (no link is established, for example, between movement and attrition), and (2) they do not incorporate the human factor in combat (i.e., the uniquely individual, often imperfect, psychology and decision-making capability of the human soldier.) While there have been many extensions to and generalizations of the LEs over the years, all designed to minimize the deficiencies inherent in their original formulation (including reformulations as stochastic differential equations and partial differential equations), most existing models remain essentially Lanchesterian in nature, the driving factor being force-on-force attrition.

7.2 Land Combat as a Complex Adaptive System

To address all of these shortcomings, the Center for Naval Analyses and the Office of Naval Research are exploring developments in coplex adaptive systems theory — particularly the set of agent-based models and simulation tools developed in the artificial life community — as a means of understanding land warfare in a fundamentally different way.

Military conflicts, particularly land combat, possess the key characteristics of complex adaptive systems (CASs) [10–13]: Combat forces are composed of a large number of nonlinearly interacting parts and are organized in a command and control hierarchy; local action, which often appears disordered, induces long-range order (i.e., combat is self-organized); military conflicts, by their nature, proceed far from equilibrium; military forces, in order to survive, must continually adapt to a changing combat environment; and there is no master "voice" that dictates the actions of each and every combatant (i.e., battlefield action effectively proceeds according to a decentralized control).

A number of recent papers discuss the fundamental role that nonlinearity plays in combat. See, for example, Beckerman [14], Beyerchen [15], Hedgepeth [16], Ilachinski [17, 18], Miller and Sulcoski [19], Saperstein [20], and Tagarev and Nicholls [21]. The general approach of the EINSTein project is to extend these largely conceptual and general links that have been drawn between properties of land warfare and properties of complex systems into a set of practical connections and analytical research tools.

7.3 Agent-based Modeling and Simulation

Models based on differential equations homogenize the properties of entire populations and ignore the spatial component altogether. Partial differential equations — by introducing a physical space to account for movement — fare somewhat better, but still treat the agent population as a continuum. In contrast, agent-based models (ABMs) consist of a discrete heterogeneous set of spatially distributed individual agents, each of which has its own characteristic properties and rules of behavior. These properties can also change as agents evolve in time.

ABMs of CASs are becoming an increasingly popular exploratory tool in the artificial life community and are predicated on the basic idea that the (often complicated) global behavior of a real system derives, collectively, from simpler, low-level interactions among its constituent agents [22]. Insights about the real-world system that an ABM is designed to model can then be gained by looking at the emergent structures induced by the interactions taking place within the simulation, as well as the feedback that these patterns might have on the rules governing the individual agents' behavior.* Agent-based simulations engender a significant shift in the kinds of questions that are asked of the real system being simulated. For example, where traditional models ask, effectively, "How can I characterize the system's top-level behavior with a few (equally top-level) variables?" ABMs instead ask, *"What low-level rules and what kinds of heterogeneous, autonomous agents do I need to have in order to synthesize the system's observed high-level behavior?"*

Perhaps the most important benefit of using an agent-based simulation to gain insight into why a system behaves the way it does — whether that system is a collection of traders on the stock market floor, neurons in a brain, or soldiers on the battlefield — is that once the simulation is used to generate the desired behavior, the researcher has immediate and simultaneous access to both the top-level (i.e., generated) behavior of the system and a low-level description of the system's underlying dynamics. Because they take an actively generative, or synthesist, approach to understanding a system, from the bottom up, ABMs are thus a powerful methodological tool for not just describing behaviors but also explaining why specific behaviors occur. While an analytical solution may provide an accurate description of a phenomenon, it is only with an agent-based simulation that one can fine-tune one's understanding of the precise set of conditions under which certain behaviors emerge.

In the context of modeling combat, agent-based simulations represent a fundamental shift from focusing on simple force-on-force attrition calculations to considering how complex, high-level properties and behaviors of combat emerge out of (sometimes coevolving) low-level rules of behaviors and interactions. The final outcome of a battle — as defined, say, by measuring the surviving force strengths — takes second stage to exploring how two forces might coevolve as a series of firefights and skirmishes unfold. ABMs are designed to allow the user to explore the evolving patterns of macroscopic behavior that result from the collective interactions of individual agents, as

---

* Two excellent recent texts on agent-based modeling, as applied to a variety of disciplines, are by Ferber [23] and Weiss [24]. Collections of papers focusing on systems that involve aspects of "human reasoning" are by Gilbert and Troitzsch [25], Gilbert and Conte [26], and Conte, et al. [27]. More recently, ABMs have been applied successfully to traffic pattern analysis [28] and social evolution [29,30].

well as the feedback that these patterns might have on the rules governing the individual agents' behavior.

7.4 EINSTein

EINSTein (*Enhanced ISAAC Neural Simulation Tool*) is an adaptive ABM of combat, and is an outgrowth of a more far-reaching project to develop a complexity-based fundamental theory of warfare [31]. EINSTein builds upon and extends an earlier proof-of-concept, DOS-based combat simulator called ISAAC (*Irreducible Semi-Autonomous Adaptive Combat*), which was developed for the US Marines Corps [33]. All approved-for-public-release documents, project reports and summaries, tutorials, sample runs, and an auto-install program for Windows-based PCs may be downloaded from http://www.cna.org/isaac/. Details of the EINSTein toolkit are provided in [34].

EINSTein represents one of the first systematic attempts, within the military operations research community, to simulate combat — on a small to medium scale — by using autonomous agents to model individual behaviors and personalities rather than specific weapons. Because agents are all endowed with a rudimentary form of "intelligence," they can respond to a very large class of changing conditions as they evolve during battle. Because of the relative simplicity of the underlying dynamical rules, EINSTein can rapidly provide outcomes for a wide spectrum of tunable parameter values defining specific scenarios, and can thus be used to effectively map out the space of possible behaviors.

Fundamentally, EINSTein addresses the basic question: *"To what extent is land combat a self-organized emergent phenomenon?"* Or, more precisely, "What are the conditions under which high-level patterns (such as penetration, flanking maneuvers, attack, etc.) emerge from a given set of low-lying dynamical primitive actions (move forward, move backward, approach/retreat-from enemy, etc.)." As such, EINSTein's intended use is not as a full system-level model of combat but as an interactive toolbox — or "conceptual playground" — in which to explore high-level emergent behaviors arising from various low-level (i.e., individual combatant and squad-level) interaction rules. The idea behind developing this toolbox is emphatically not to model in detail a specific piece of hardware (an M16 rifle or M101 105mm howitzer, for example). Instead, the idea is to explore the middle ground between — at one extreme — highly realistic models that provide little insight into basic processes and — at the other extreme — ultra minimalist models that strip away all but the simplest dynamical variables and leave out the most interesting real behavior, that is, to explore the fundamental dynamical tradeoffs among a large number of notional variables.

The underlying dynamics is patterned after mobile cellular automata rules [35] and are somewhat reminiscent of Braitenberg's vehicles [36]. Mobile cellular automata have been used before to model predator–prey interactions in natural ecologies [37]. They have also been applied to combat modeling [38], but in a much more limited fashion than the one used by EINSTein.

7.4.1 Features

EINSTein's major features include

- *Dialog-driven I/O, using a Windows GUI front-end*
- *Object-oriented C++ source code base*
- *Integrated natural terrain maps and terrain-based adaptive decision dynamics*
- *Context-dependent and user-defined agent behaviors*
- *Multiple squads, with intersquad communication links*
- *Local and global command-agent dynamics*
- *Genetic algorithm toolkit to tailor agent rules to desired force-level behaviors*
- *Data collection and multidimensional visualization tools*
- *Mission fitness-landscape profilers*
- *Over 250 user-programmable functions on the source code level*

Figure 7.1 provides a screenshot of a typical run-session in EINSTein. The screenshot contains three active windows: main battlefield view (which includes passable and impassable terrain elements); trace view (which shows color coded territorial occupancy), and combat view (which provides a grayscaled filter of combat intensity). All views are simultaneously updated during a run. Toward the right-hand side of the screenshot appear two data dialogs that summarize red and blue agent parameter values. Appearing on the lower left side and along the bottom of the figure are time-series graphs of red and blue center-of-mass coordinates (as measured from the red flag) and the average number of agents within red and blue agent's sensor ranges, and a dialog that allows the user to define communication relays among individual squads.

7.4.2 Source Code

EINSTein is written and compiled using Microsoft's Visual C++** and makes use of Pinnacle Publishing Inc.'s Graphics Server*** for displaying time-series plots and 3D fitness-landscapes. EINSTein consists of roughly 100K lines of object-oriented source code.

The source code is divided into three basic parts: (1) the *combat engine* (parts of which are summarized below); (2) the *graphical user interface* (GUI);

** Microsoft Visual C++, Version 6.0: http://msdn.microsoft.com/developer/
*** Graphics Server is a commercial plug-in, licensed from Pinnacle Publishing, Inc.: http://www.graphicsserver.com

7 EINSTein   149

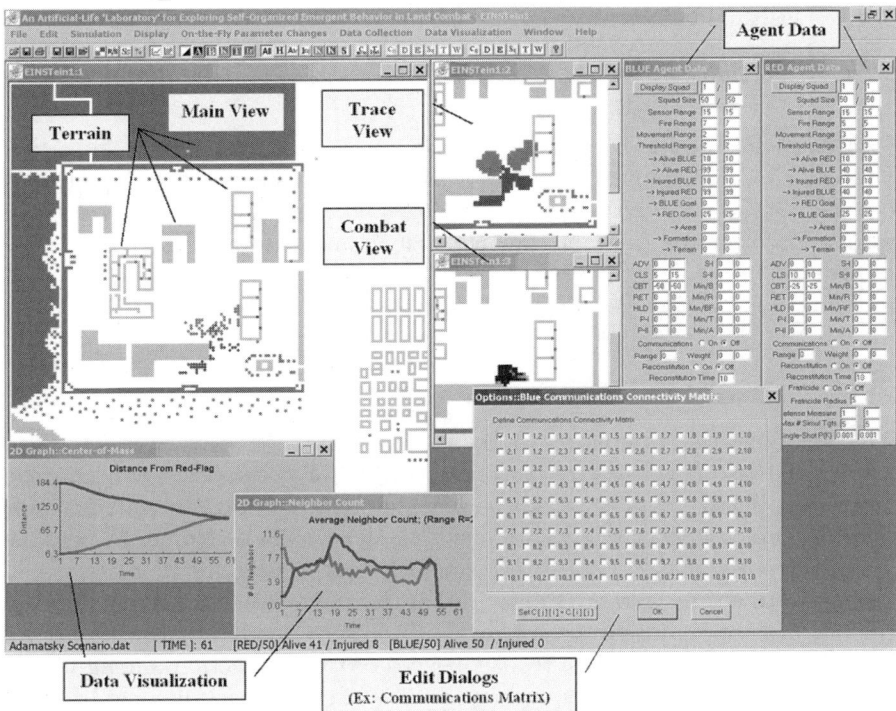

Fig. 7.1. Screenshot of EINSTein's graphical user interface (GUI) front-end.

and (3) the *data-collection/data-visualization functions*. These parts are essentially machine (i.e., CPU and/or operating system) independent and may be compiled separately. EINSTein's source code base is thus highly portable and is relatively easy to modify to suit particular problems and interests. For example, an EINSTein-based combat environment may be developed as a stand-alone program on a CPU platform other than the original MS Windows target machine used for EINSTein's original development. Any developer/analyst interested in porting EINSTein over to some other machine and/or operating system is tasked only with providing his own machine-specific GUI as a "wrap-around" to the stand-alone combat and data-visualization engines (that may be provided as DLLs). Moreover, it is very easy to add, delete, and/or change the existing source code, including making complicated changes that significantly alter how agents decide their moves.

At the heart of EINSTein lies the combat engine (discussed ahead). The combat engine processes all run-time, combat-related logical decisions and is the core script upon which multiple time-series data collection, fitness landscape sweeps over the agents' parameter space, and genetic algorithm searches all depend.

7.4.3 Design Philosophy

"Things should be as simple as possible, but not simpler." — Albert Einstein

EINSTein's design is predicated upon two guiding principles: (1) to keep all dynamical components and rules as simple as possible (with a view toward optimizing the trade-off between run time and realism), and (2) to treat all forms of information (and the way in which all information is processed locally by agents) in a contextually consistent manner. The meaning of this second principle will become clear in the exposition below.

Simplicity

The first guiding principle is to keep things *simple*. Specifically, EINSTein is designed to make it as intuitive as possible for the user to program specific agent behaviors. This is done by deliberately keeping the set of combat and movement rules small and by defining those rules as simply as possible. Thus, the power projection rule is essentially "target and fire upon any enemy agent within a threshold fire range" rather than some other, more complicated (albeit, possibly more physically realistic) prescription. The idea is to qualitatively probe the behavioral consequences of the interaction among a large number of notional variables, not to provide an explicit detailed model of the minutiae of real-world combat.

Consistency

The second guiding principle is keep things *consistent*. All dynamical decisions — whether they are made by individual agents, by local or global commanders, or by the user (when scripting a scenario's objectives) — consist of boundedly rational (i.e., locally optimal) penalty assessments. Actions are based on an agent's *personality* (see ahead), which consists of numerical weights that attach greater or lesser degrees of relative importance to each factor relevant to selecting a particular move in a given local context (from the point of view of a given agent). It is in this sense that all forms of information, on various levels, are treated on a consistent basis.

The decisions taking place on different levels of the simulation all follow the same general template of probing and responding to the environment. Each decision consists of a personality-mediated "answer" to the following three basic questions:

- What are my immediate and long-term goals?
- What do I currently know about my local environment?
- What must I do to attain my goals?

As we shall see in detail ahead, at the most primitive level, each agent cares only about "moving toward" or "moving away from" all other agents and/or his own and the enemy's flag. An agent's personality prescribes the relative weight assigned to each of these immediate "goals." On the other hand, a global commander must weigh such features as overall force strength, casualty rate, rate of advance, and so on in order to attain certain long-term goals. Local and supreme commanders have their own unique concerns. While the actual decisions are different in each case and on each information level — for example, an individual agent's decision to "stay put" in order to survive is quite different and uses a different form of information, from a global commander's drive to "get to the enemy flag as quickly as possible" — the general manner in which these decisions are made is the same.

7.4.4 Program Flow

A typical sequence of programming steps during an interactive run consists of multiple loops through the following basic steps:

1. *Initialize battlefield and agent distribution parameters.*
2. *Initialize time-step counter.*
3. *Adjudicate combat.*
4. *Refresh battlefield graphics display.*
5. *Find context-dependent personality weight vector for each red and blue agent.*
6. *Compute local penalty function to determine best move.*
7. *Move agents to their newly selected position (or leave them where they are).*
8. *Refresh graphics display and loop through steps 3 – 7.*

The most important parts of this skeletal structure are the adjudication of combat, the adaptation of personality weights, and the decision-making process that each agent goes through in choosing its next move. Before describing the details of what each of these steps involves, we must first discuss how each agent partitions its local information. During interactive runs (i.e., whenever the fitness-landscape profiler and genetic algorithm breeder batch modes are both inactive), the user can pause the simulation at any time to make on-the-fly changes to any, or all, agent parameters (including adding or subtracting "playing" agents) and then resume the run with the changed values.

7.5 Combat Engine

7.5.1 Agents

The basic element of EINSTein is an agent, which loosely represents a primitive combat unit (infantryman, tank, transport vehicle, etc.) that is equipped with the following characteristics:

- *Doctrine:* a default local-rule set specifying how to act in a generic environment
- *Mission:* goals directing behavior
- *Situational awareness:* sensors generating an internal map of environment
- *Adaptability:* an internal mechanism to alter behavior and/or rules

Each agent exists in one of three states: alive, injured, or killed. Injured agents can (but are not required to) have different personalities and offensive/defensive characteristics from when they were alive. For example, the user can specify that injured agents are able to move half as far, and shoot half as accurately, as their "alive" counterparts. Up to 10 distinct groups (or "squads") of personalities, of varying sizes, can be defined. The user can also specify how agents from one squad react to agents from other squads.

Each agent has associated with it a set of ranges (sensor range, fire range, communications range, etc.), within which it senses and assimilates various forms of local information, and a personality, which determines the general manner in which it responds to its environment. A global rule set determines combat attrition, reconstitution, and (in future versions) reinforcement. EINSTein also contains both local and global commanders, each with their own command radii, and obeying an evolving command and control (C2) hierarchy of rules.

7.5.2 Battlefield

The putative combat battlefield is represented by a two-dimensional lattice of discrete sites. Each site of the lattice may be occupied by one of two kinds of agents: red or blue. The initial state consists of user-specified formations of red and blue agents positioned anywhere within the battlefield. Formations may include squad-specific bounding rectangles or may be completely random. Red and blue flags are also typically (but not always) positioned in diagonally opposite corners. A typical goal, for both red and blue agents, is to reach the enemy's flag.

EINSTein includes an option to add terrain elements. Terrain can be either impassable or passable. If passable, the user can also tune an agent's behavior to a particular terrain type. For example, if an agent is positioned within "heavy brush," its movement range and visibility (from other nearby agents) may be curtailed.

7.5.3 Agent Personalities

Each agent is equipped with a user-specified personality — or internal value system — nominally defined by a six-component personality weight vector, $\mathbf{w} = (w_1, w_2, \ldots w_6)$, where $-1 \leq w_i \leq 1$ and $\Sigma_i |w_i| = 1$. The components of $\mathbf{w}$ specify how an individual agent responds to specific kinds of local information within its sensor range.

The personality weight vector may be health-dependent. That is, w_{alive} need not, in general, be equal to w_{injured}. The components of **w** can also be negative, in which case they signify a propensity for moving away from, rather than toward, a given entity.

7.5.4 Penalty Function

An agent's personality weight vector is used to rank each possible move according to a penalty function. The simplest penalty function effectively measures the total distance that the agent will be from other agents (including both friendly and enemy agents) and from its own and enemy flags, weighing each component distance by the appropriate component of the personality weight vector, **w**. An agent moves to the position that incurs the least penalty. That is, an agent's move is the one that best satisfies its personality-driven desire to "move closer to" or "farther away from" other agents in given states and either of the two flags. The general form of the penalty function is given by

$$Z(B_{x,y}) = \frac{1}{\sqrt{2}r_S} \left[\begin{array}{c} \frac{\omega_{AF}}{N_{AF}} \sum_{i \in AF}^{N_{AF}} D_{i,B_{x,y}} + \frac{\omega_{AE}}{N_{AE}} \sum_{j \in AE}^{N_{AE}} D_{j,B_{x,y}} \\ + \frac{\omega_{IF}}{N_{IF}} \sum_{i \in IF}^{N_{IF}} D_{i,B_{x,y}} + \frac{\omega_{IE}}{N_{IE}} \sum_{j \in IE}^{N_{IE}} D_{j,B_{xy}} \end{array} \right]$$

$$+ \omega_{FF} \frac{D^{new}_{FF,B_{xy}}}{D^{old}_{FF,B_{x,y}}} + \omega_{EF} \frac{D^{new}_{EF,B_{x,y}}}{D^{old}_{EF,B_{x,y}}}, \qquad (7.4)$$

where B_{xy} is the (x, y) coordinate of battlefield B; AF, IF, AE, and IE represent, respectively, the sets of alive friends, injured friends, alive enemies, and injured enemies within the given agent's sensor range, r_S; w_i are the components of the personality weight vector; $\sqrt{2}r_S$ is a scale factor; N_X is the total number of elements of type X within the given agent's sensor range (for example, N_F is the number of alive friends within range r_S); $D_{A,B}$ is the distance between elements A and B; FF and EF denote the friendly and enemy flags, respectively; and represent distances computed using the given agent's new (candidate move) position and old (current) position, respectively.

A penalty is computed for each possible move. That is, for each of the $N = (2r_m + 1)^2$ possible sites to which an agent can "step" in one time step: $Z_1(B_{x,y})$, $Z_2(B_{x+1,y})$, $Z_3(B_{x-1,y})$..., $Z_N(B_{x+n,y+n})$. The actual move is the one that incurs the least penalty. If there is a set of moves (consisting of more than one possible move) all of whose penalties are within $\epsilon_{\text{Penalty}} \geq 0$ of the minimal penalty, an agent randomly selects the actual move among the candidate moves making up that set. Users can also define paths near which agents must try to stay while maneuvering toward their ultimate goal.

The penalty function shown above includes only a few relative-proximity-based weights. In practice, the penalty function is more complicated, and incorporates more terms, though its basic form is the same. Additional terms can include the propensity for maintaining the minimum distance from friendly or enemy agents, staying near a designated patrol area, the cost of traversing terrain, desire for finding local cover (from fire) and/or concealment (from enemy sensors), and combat intensity (see Table 7.1).

Table 7.1. A Partial List of EINSTein's *Primitive Weight Set*.

Weight	Meaning = Relative Weight for...
$w_{\rm AF}$	...moving toward/away-from alive friendly agents
$w_{\rm IF}$	...moving toward/away-from injured friendly agents
$w_{\rm AE}$	...moving toward/away-from alive enemy agents
$w_{\rm IE}$	...moving toward/away-from injured enemy agents
$w_{\rm FF}$	...moving toward/away-from friendly flag
$w_{\rm EF}$	...moving toward/away-from enemy flag
$w_{\rm BB}$	...moving toward/away-from the boundary of battlefield
$w_{\rm area}$	...staying near some (squad-specific) area
$w_{\rm squad}$	...maintaining formation with own squad-mates
$w_{\rm fire-team}$	...maintaining formation with own fireteam-mates
S_{ij}	... how agents from squad S_i react to agents from squad S_j
SS'_{ij}	... how agents from squad S_i react to agents from enemy squad S_j
$w_{\rm LC}$	...moving toward/away-from local commander
$w_{\rm obeyLC}$	...obeying orders issued by local commander
$w_{\rm terrain}$	...moving toward/away-from terrain elements
$w_{\rm enemy-fire}$	...moving toward/away-from enemy agents that have fired on agent

7.5.5 Meta-Rules

An agent's personality may be augmented by a set of meta-rules that tell it how to alter its default personality according to dynamic environmental contexts. A typical meta-rule consists of altering a few of the components of an agent's personality vector according to a set of associated local threshold constraints. The three simplest meta-rule classes effectively define the local conditions under which an agent is allowed to *advance toward enemy flag* (class 1), *cluster with friendly forces* (class 2), and *engage the enemy in combat* (class 3).

For example, a class-1 meta-rule prevents an agent from advancing toward the enemy flag unless it is locally surrounded by a threshold number of friendly agents; i.e., it is a notional indicator of local combat support. A class-2 meta-rule can be used to prevent an agent from moving toward friendly agents once it is surrounded by a threshold number. Finally, a class-3 meta-rule can be used to fix the local conditions under which an agent is allowed to move toward or away from possibly engaging an enemy agent in combat. Specifically, an agent is allowed to engage an enemy if and only if the difference between friendly and enemy force strengths locally exceeds a given threshold.

Other meta-rule classes include *retreat, pursuit, support,* and *hold position.* A global rule set determines combat attrition (see ahead), communication, reconstitution, and (in future versions) reinforcement. EINSTein also contains both local and global commanders, each of which is equipped with its own unique command-personality and area of responsibility, and obeys an evolving command and control hierarchy of rules. Table 7.2 summarizes some of EINSTein's meta-rules.[†]

Table 7.2. A Partial List of EINSTein's *Meta-Rule* Set.

Meta-rule	Description
w_{AF}	...moving toward/away-from alive friendly agents
Advance	Advance to enemy flag if the number of friends $\geq \tau_{Advance}$
Cluster	Stop seeking friends if number of friends $\geq \tau_{Cluster}$
Combat	Engage enemy if the $N_{friends} - N_{enemies} \geq \Delta_{Combat}$
Hold	Hold current position
Pursuit-I	Temporarily turn off pursuit of enemy agents
Pursuit-II	Temporarily turn exclusive pursuit on
Retreat	Retreat toward own flag
Run Away	Run away, fast, from enemy agents
Support-I	Provide support for nearby injured
Support-II	Seek support from nearby friends
Min-D Friend	Maintain minimum distance from all friendly agents
Min-D Enemy	Maintain minimum distance from all enemy agents
Min-D Flag	Maintain minimum distance from all friendly agents
Min-D Terrain	Maintain minimum distance from terrain
Min-D Area	Maintain minimum distance from a fixed area on battlefield

7.5.6 Combat

During the combat phase of an iteration step for the whole system, each agent X (on either side) is given an opportunity to fire at all enemy agents Y_i that are within a fire range r_F of X's position. If an agent is shot by an enemy agent, its current state is degraded either from alive to injured or from injured to dead. Once killed, an agent is permanently removed from the battlefield. The probability that a given Y_i is shot is fixed by user-specified, single-shot probabilities. Weapons are assigned to individual agents and are either point-to-point (i.e., rifles) or area destruction (i.e., grenades).

[†] Note that threshold constraints ($\tau_{Advance}, \tau_{Cluster}$, and Δ_{Combat}) are explicitly defined only for the first three meta-rules. These meta-rules are used in the sample runs discussed ahead. In fact, each of the meta-rules appearing in Table 7.2 has one or more threshold constraints associated with it, and the set also requires additional logic to dynamically resolve ambiguities as they arise during the course of a run. Details are in [31].

By default, all enemy agents within a given agent's fire range are targeted for a possible hit. However, the user has the option of limiting the number of enemy targets that can be engaged simultaneously. If this option is selected, and the number of enemy agents within an agent's fire-range exceeds a user-defined threshold number (say N), then N agents are randomly chosen among the agents in this set. Grenades include additional targeting logic (to maximize expected inflicted damage on the enemy).

This basic combat logic may be enhanced by three additional functions: (1) *defense*, which adds a notional ability to agents to be able to withstand a greater number of "hits" before having their state degraded; (2) *reconstitution*, which adds a provision for previously injured agents to be reconstituted to their alive state; and (3) *fratricide* ("friendly fire"), which adds an element of realism by making it possible to inadvertently hit friendly forces.

7.5.7 Run Modes

EINSTein can be run in three basic modes (see EINSTein's *User's Guide* [31]):

- *Interactive mode*, in which the combat engine is run interactively using a fixed set of rules. This mode, which allows the user to make on-the-fly changes to the values of any (or all) parameters defining a given run, is particularly well suited for playing simple *"What if?"* scenarios. The interactive mode also makes it easy to search for interesting emergent behavior.
- *Data-collection mode*, in which the user can (1) generate time series of various changing quantities describing the step-by-step evolution of a battle and (2) keep track of certain measures of how well mission objectives are met at a battle's conclusion. Additionally, the user can generate behavioral profiles on two-dimensional slices of EINSTein's N-dimensional parameter space.
- *Genetic algorithm "breeder" mode*, in which a genetic algorithm is used to breed an agent force that is optimally suited for performing a specific mission against a fixed enemy force. This mode is designed to suggest ways in which ABMs may eventually be used to evolve real-world tactics and strategies.

7.6 Sample Patterns and Behavior

EINSTein possesses a large repertoire of emergent behaviors: *forward advance, frontal attack, local clustering, penetration, retreat, attack posturing, containment, flanking maneuvers, "Guerrilla-like" assaults*, among many others. Moreover, behaviors frequently arise that appear to involve some form of intelligent division of red and blue forces to deal with local firestorms and skirmishes, particularly those forces whose personalities have been bred (via a genetic algorithm) to perform a specific mission. It is important to point out

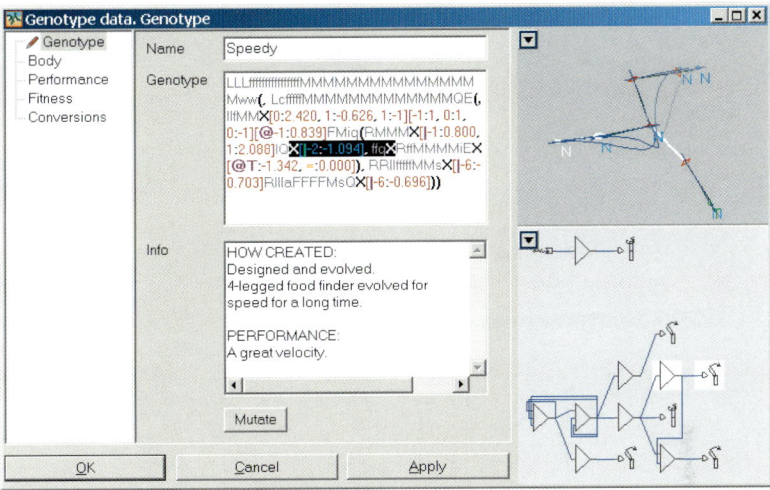

Fig. 2.8. A sample genotype and the corresponding creature (body and brain). Some genes are selected by a user, and the corresponding parts of body and brain are highlighted.

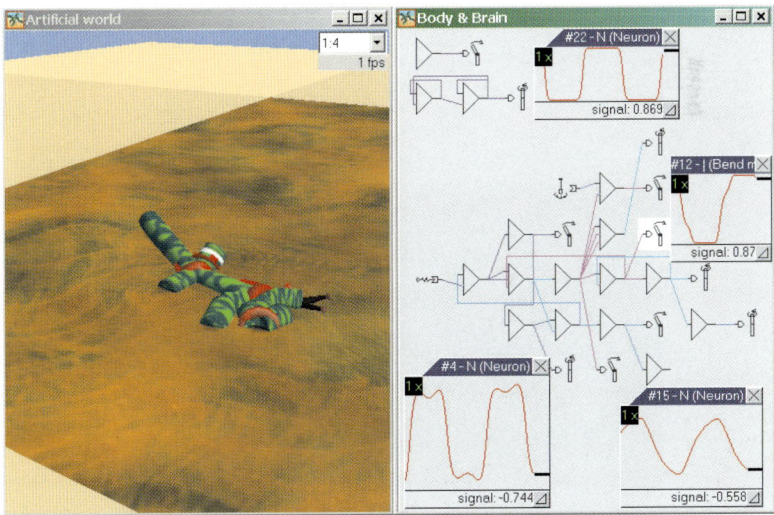

Fig. 2.10. A simulated creature with the control system under investigation. Four neural probes can be seen, showing signals in different locations of the neural network.

Fig. 2.17. Four Framsticks Theater shows: introduction, dance, biomorph, and reproduction.

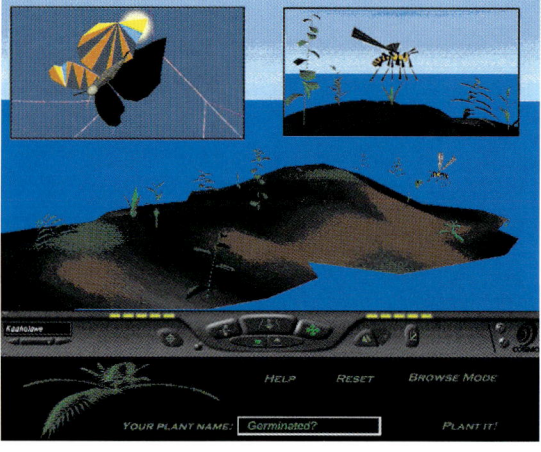

Fig. 3.2. Nerve Garden interface in web browser.

Fig. 3.6. Bee flight through a Nerve Garden island populated by user-generated L-System plants.

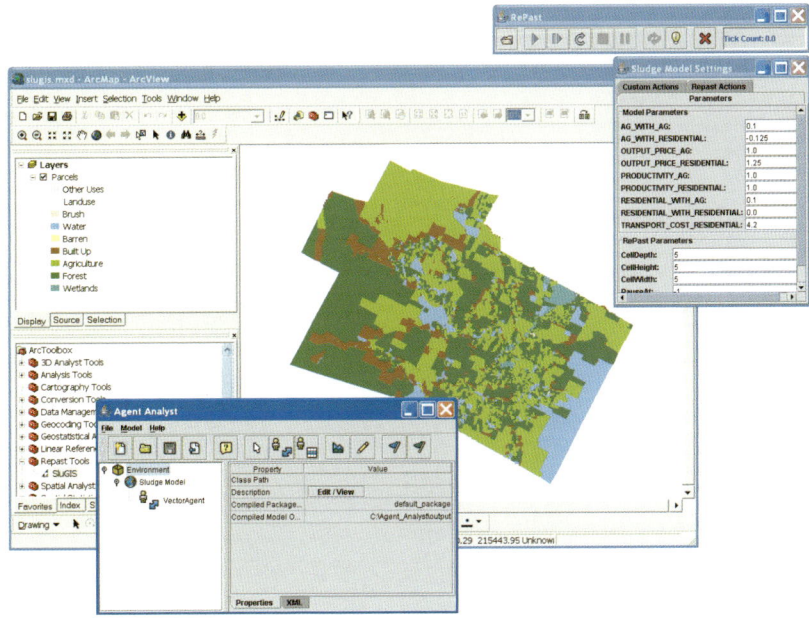

Fig. 6.1. A Repast model user interface.

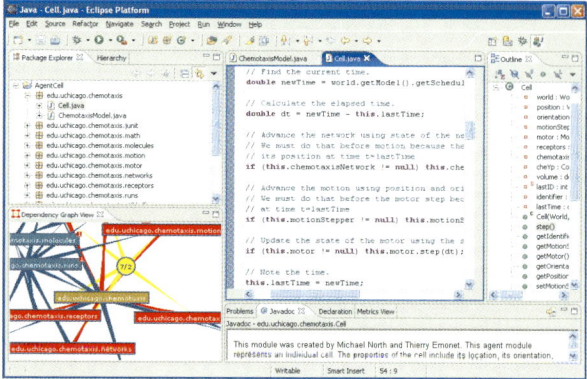

Fig. 6.4. RepastJ in the Eclipse Development Environment.

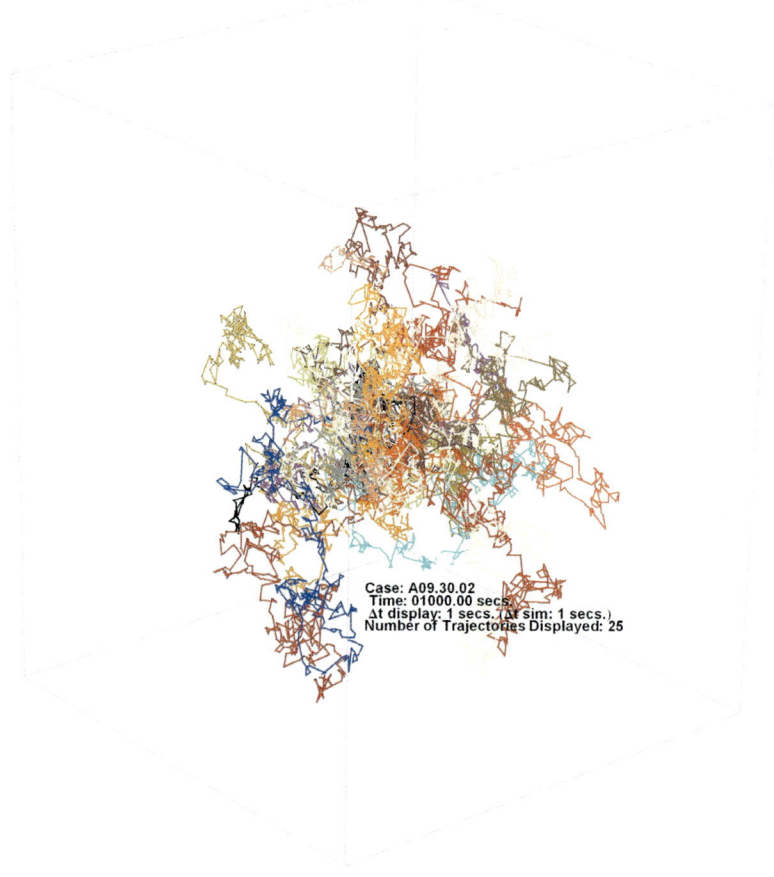

Fig. 6.14. The simulated trajectories of 25 bacteria.

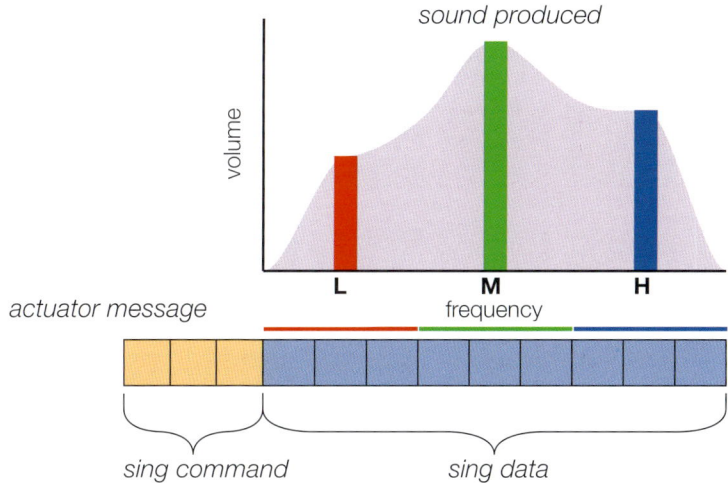

Fig. 9.6. The "sing" actuator message contains two parts. The first is the command requesting the agent to perform a sing operation; the remainder contains the sing data: volume levels for three distinct frequency bands. Using three bits per frequency band results in 2^9, or 512 distinct sounds.

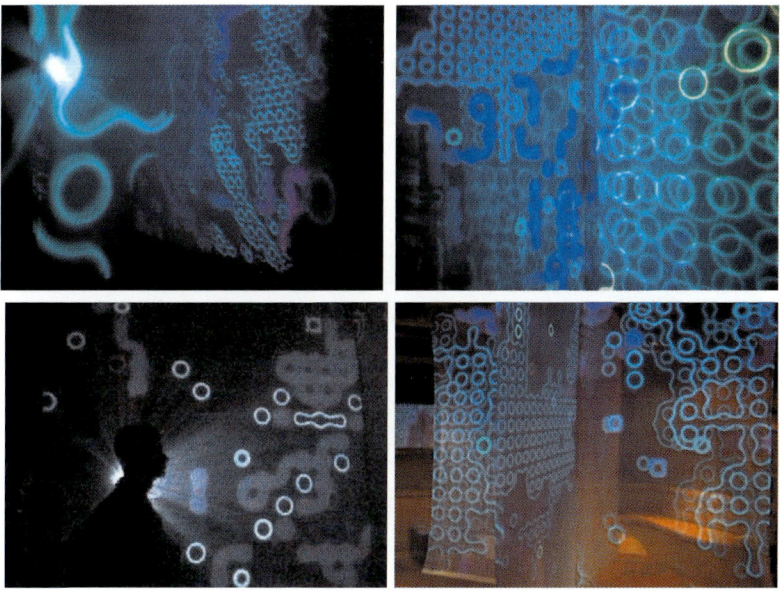

Fig. 9.8. Images of Eden in operation.

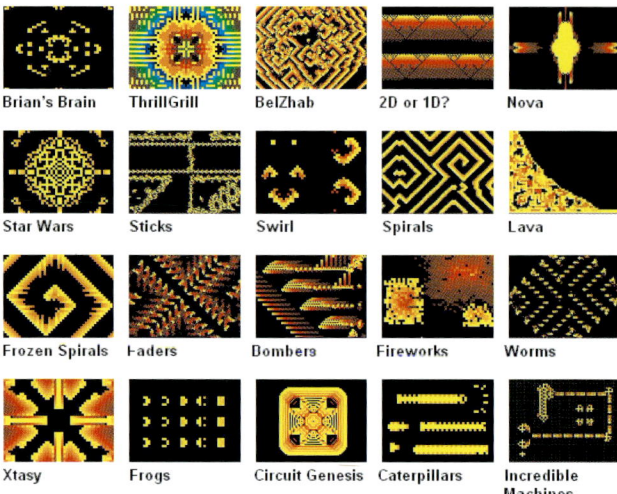

Fig. 10.6. Sample rules from the Generations family.

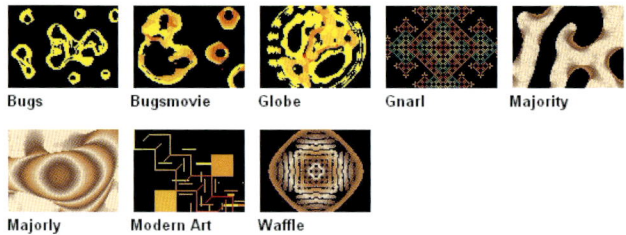

Fig. 10.7. Sample rules from the Larger than Life family.

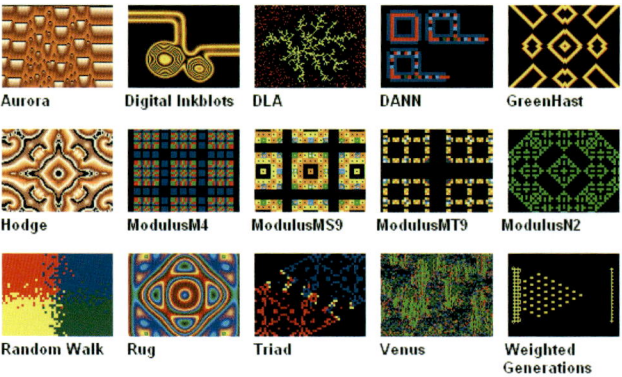

Fig. 10.13. Sample rules from the User DLLs family.

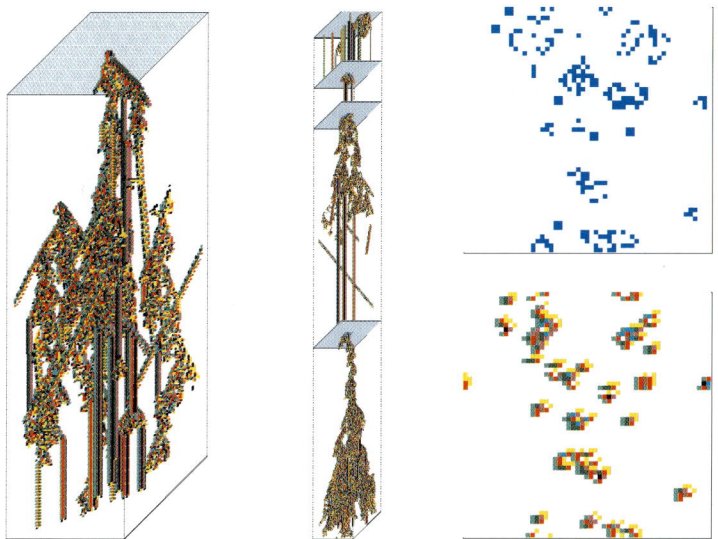

Fig. 11.7. Space-time pattern of the 2D game of Life, (v=2, k=9, $n = 55 \times 55$) in a 3D isometric projection. 2D time steps stack below each other and are shown as if looking up at a transparent shaft. *Left*: Starting from the "r-pentomino" seed. *Center*: Rescaled to the smallest scale, new seeds set at intervals. *Upper right*: A 2D state (time step) colored according to value. *Lower right*: The same state colored according to the neighborhood look-up.

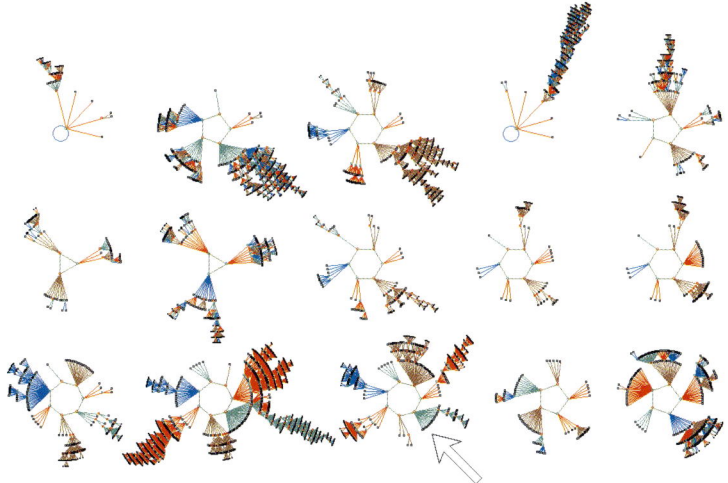

Fig. 11.9. The basin of attraction field of a small random Boolean network, n=13. The $2^{13} = 8192$ states in state space are organized into 15 basins, with attractor periods ranging between 1 and 7, and basin volume between 68 and 2724. The arrow points to the basin shown in more detail.

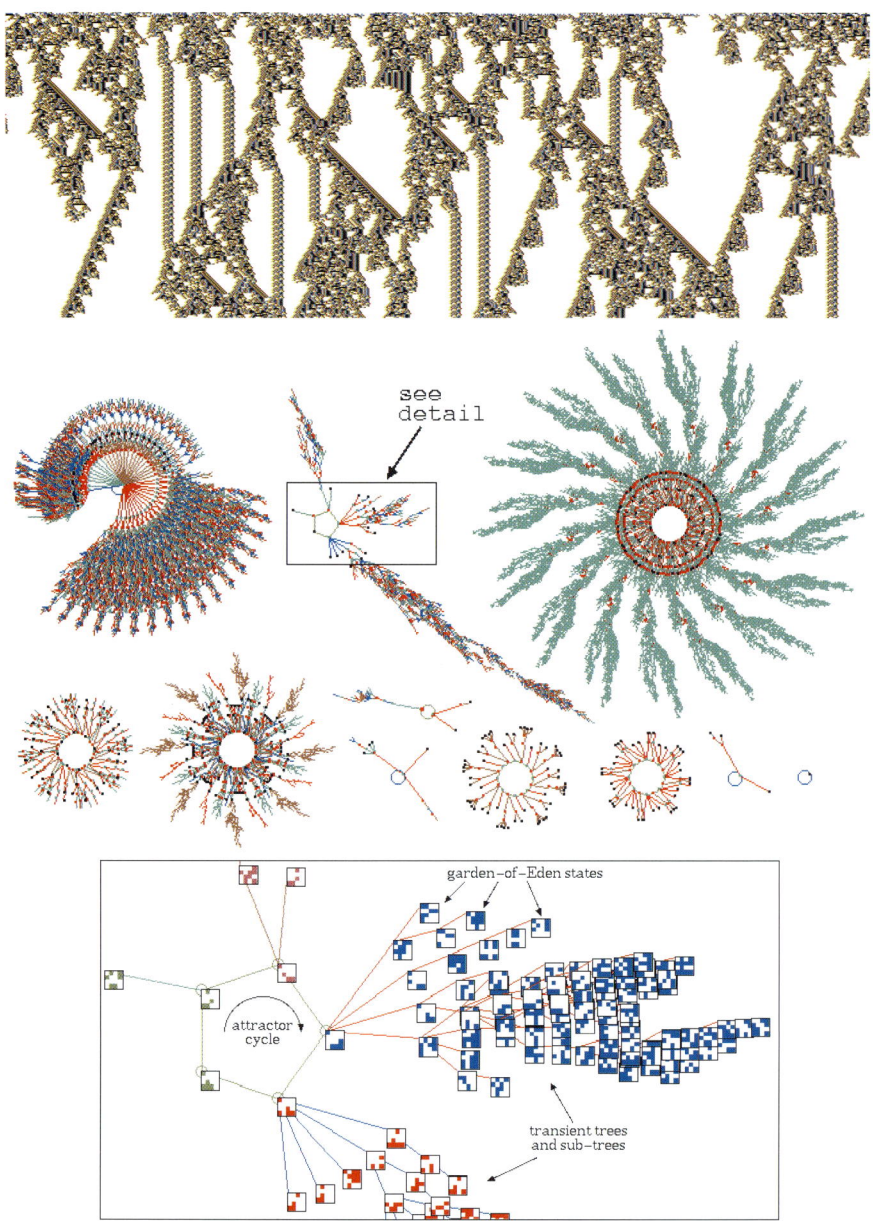

Fig. 11.11. *Top*: The space-time pattern of a 1D complex binary CA where interacting gliders emerge, $n=700$, $k=7$, 308 time steps are shown from a random initial state. *Center*: The basin of attraction field for the same rule, $n=16$. The 2^{16} states in state space are connected into 89 basins of attraction, but only the 11 nonequivalent basins are shown, with symmetries characteristic of CA. *Bottom*: A detail of the second basin in the basin of attraction field, where states are shown as 4×4 bit patterns.

that such behaviors are not hard-wired but are rather an emergent property of a decentralized, but dynamically interdependent, swarm of agents.

Figure 7.2 shows screen captures of spatial patterns resulting from 16 different rules and illustrates the diversity of behaviors that emerges out of a relatively simple set of rules. (Note that the sample patterns shown here are for clashing red and blue forces consisting of a *single* squad. Multisquad scenarios, in which agents belonging to different squads obey different rules, and interact with one another according to an additional layer of micro-rules, often result in considerably more complicated emergent behaviors.) An important long-term goal is for EINSTein to be flexible enough to serve as a general tool (that transcends the specific notional combat environment to which it is obviously tailored) for exploring the still very poorly understood mapping between micro-rules and emergent macro-behaviors in complex adaptive systems.

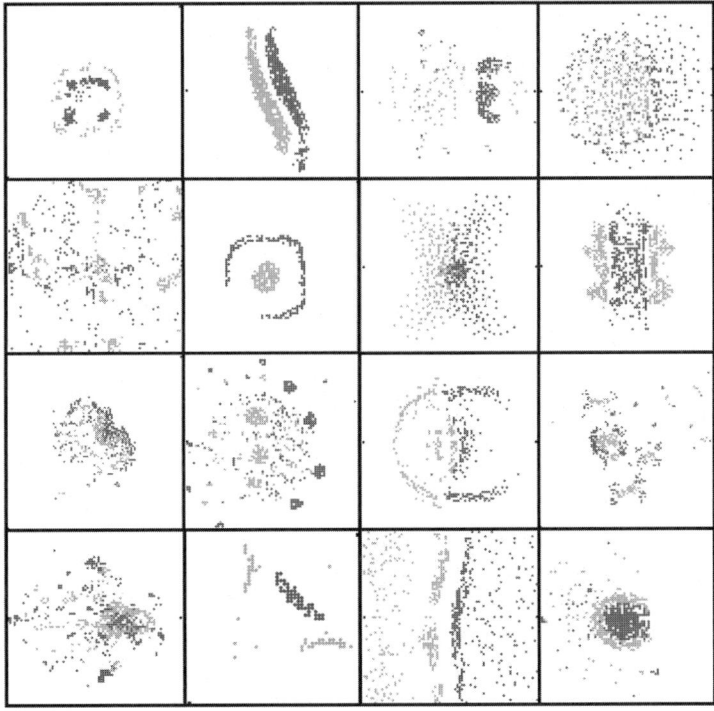

Fig. 7.2. A sampling of emergent spatial patterns of opposing agents obeying EINSTein's micro-rules. Each of the 16 squares represents a different rule and contains a single snapshot of a typical run.

7.6.1 Qualitative Classes of Behavior

Simulations run for many different scenarios and initial conditions suggest that EINSTein's collective behavior generally falls into one of six broad qualitative classes (labeled, suggestively, according to different kinds of fluid flow):

- *Laminar flow*, which typically consists of one (or, at most, a few) well-defined "linear" battlefronts. This class is so named because it is visually suggestive of laminar fluid flow of two fluids, and is reminiscent of static trench warfare in World War I. Laminar rules can actually be divided into two types of behaviors, characterized according to a system's overall stability (i.e., according to whether the system is stable, or not stable, to initial conditions).
- *Viscous flow*, in which the unfolding battle typically consists of a single tight cluster (or, at most, a few clusters) of interpenetrating red and blue agents.
- *Dispersive flow*, in which — as soon as red and blue agents maneuver within view of the opposing side's forces — the battle unfolds as a single, explosive, dispersion of forces. Dispersive systems exhibit little, if any, of the "front-like" linear structures that form for laminar-flow rules.
- *Turbulent flow*, in which combat consists of either spatially distributed, but otherwise confined and/or clustered individual combat zones, or a series of close-to space-filling local firestorms. In either case, there is almost always a significant degree of local maneuvering.
- *Autopoeitic Flow* in which agents self-organize into persistent dissipative structures. These formations typically maintain their integrity for long times (on the scale of individual agents entering and leaving the structure) and undergo "higher level" maneuvering, including longitudinal motion and rotation.‡
- *Swarming*, in which agents self-organize into nested swarms of attacking and/or defending forces.

We should be quick to point out that this taxonomy is neither complete nor well defined, in a mathematical sense. Because of the qualitative distinctions among classes, there is considerable overlap among them. Moreover, a given scenario, as it unfolds in time, usually consists of several phases of behavior during which one class predominates at one time and other classes at other times. Indeed, for such cases, which occur frequently, it is of considerable interest to understand the nature of the transition between distinct behavioral phases. For example, the initial stages of a scenario may unfold in typically laminar fashion and suddenly transition over into a turbulent phase.

A finer distinction among these six classes can be made on the basis of a more refined statistical analysis of emergent behavior. There is strong ev-

---

‡ *Autopoiesis* refers to dynamical systems that are simultaneously self-creating and self-maintaining. It was introduced as an explanatory mechanism within biology by Maturana and Varela [39].

idence to suggest, for example, that while attrition rates for certain classes of rules display smooth Gaussian statistics, other classes (overlapping with viscous flow and turbulent flow rules) display interesting fractal power-law scaling behaviors [40]. Insofar as the "box-counting" fractal dimension [41] is useful for describing the degree of agent clustering on the battlefield, it can also be used as a simple discriminant between laminar and turbulent classes of behavior. Measuring temporal correlations in the time series of various statistical quantities describing combat is also useful in this regard. The case studies presented here are selected mainly to highlight the qualitative behavioral classes described previously.

7.6.2 Lanchesterian Combat

On the simplest level, EINSTein is an interactive, exploratory tool that allows users to take conceptual excursions away from Lanchesterian oversimplifications of real combat. It is therefore of interest to first define a Lanchesterian scenario within EINSTein that can subsequently be used as a test bed to which the outcomes of other, non-Lanchesterian, scenarios can be compared. The set of simulation parameters that are appropriate for simulating a maneuverless, Lanchester-like combat scenario in EINSTein includes a red/blue movement range of $r_m = 0$ (so that the position of all agents is fixed) and a red/ blue sensor range that is large enough so that all agents have all enemy agents within their view (for the example below, $r_S = 40$).

Figure 7.3 shows several snapshots of a typical run. Initial conditions consist of 100 red and 100 blue agents (in a tightly packed block formation, with block-centers 15 units distant on a 60-by-60 battlefield) and a red/blue single-shot probability of hit $P_{\text{hit}} = 0.005$. Note that the outcome of the battle is a function of the initial sizes of red and blue forces and P_{hit} alone, and does not depend on maneuver or any other agent, squad, or force characteristics.

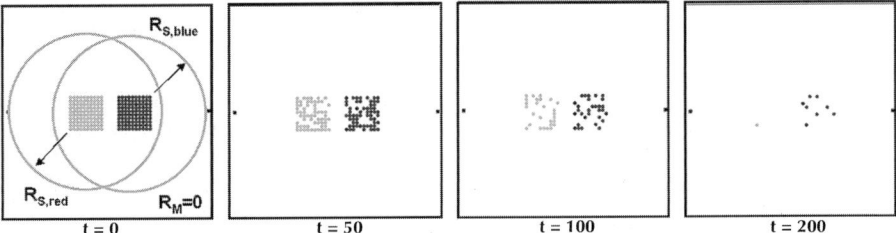

Fig. 7.3. Screenshots of a typical run using an EINSTein rule-set that approximates LE-like combat.

While the Lanchester scenario shown here is highly unrealistic, of course, it is important to remember that most conventional military models (even those that include some form of maneuvering) adjudicate combat by effectively sweeping over a series of similarly idealized maneuver-less skirmishes until one side, or both sides, of the conflict decide to withdraw after sustaining a threshold number of casualties. Most models are still almost entirely attrition-driven. The only substantive role that play maneuver and adaptability is in getting the individual combatants into position to fight.

A typical signature of such Lanchesterian-like combat scenarios is a linear dependence of the *mean attrition rate* — defined as the average number of combatants lost, $\langle \alpha \rangle$, during some specified time interval, $\Delta \tau = t - t_0$ — on the *single-shot kill* (or, in our case here, *single-shot hit*) probability, P_{ss}:

$$\langle \alpha \rangle = \left\langle \frac{\Delta n}{\Delta \tau} \right\rangle = \left\langle \frac{n(t_0 + t) - n(t_0)}{\Delta \tau} \right\rangle = \sum_{i=1}^{N} P_{ss}(i) = N P_{ss}, \quad (7.5)$$

where N is the total number of agents, $n(t)$ is the number of agents at time t, $P_{ss}(i)$ is the single-shot hit probability of the ith agent, and we have assumed, for the final expression on the right, that $P_{ss}(i) = P_{ss}$ for all i.

What happens if agents are allowed to maneuver? If the maneuver is in any sense "intelligent" — i.e., if agents react reasonably intelligently to changing levels of combat intensity as a battle unfolds — intuitively we should not expect the same linear dependence between $\langle \alpha \rangle$ and P_{ss} to hold. In the extreme case of infinitely timid combatants that run away at the slightest provocation, no fighting at all will occur. In the case where one side applies sophisticated targeting algorithms to maximize enemy casualties but minimize friendly casualties, we might expect a marked increase in that force's relative fighting ability.

Lauren [40] has used EINSTein (and other ABMs of combat; see [42]) to identify some significant differences between agent-based attrition statistics and results derived from stochastic LE-based models. For example, he has found evidence to suggest that the intensity of battles obeys a fractal power-law dependence on frequency, and displays other traits characteristic of high-dimensional chaotic systems, such as fat-tailed probability distributions and intermittency. Specifically, the attrition rate appears to depend on the cube root of the kill probability, which stands in marked contrast to results obtained for stochastic variants of LE-based models, in which, typically, the attrition rate scales linearly with an increase in kill probability.[§] If the ABM more accurately represents real combat processes, a 1/3 power-law scaling

---

[§] The key observation is that the attrition rate generally depends not just on P_{ss} (as in eq. 7.5), but on both P_{ss} and the *fractal dimension*, D_F, representing the spatial distribution of agents. To derive eq. 7.5, for Lanchesterian combat, one assumes that one side's attrition rate is proportional to the opposing side's size (and *nothing else*); in the general case, one must assume that the attrition rate also depends on the probability that an agent actually "sees" an enemy (or cluster of enemy agents) in a given period of time. The likelihood of this happening, in turn, may be expressed in terms of D_F. See [34, 42] for details.

implies that a relatively "weak" force, with a small kill probability, may actually constitute a much more potent force than a simple LE-based approach suggests. The potency of the force comes from its ability to maneuver (which is never explicitly modeled by LE-based approaches) and to selectively concentrate firepower on the enemy while maneuvering. This deceptively simple result has an important consequence for peacekeeping activities in the Third World, where a strong, modern force may (and often, does) significantly underestimate the ability of ostensibly poorly trained and/or poorly armed militia to inflict damage.

The appearance of fractal power-law scaling in EINSTein (and other agent-based combat models) is particularly interesting in light of the fact that it has been observed before in real combat [43]. While it has been previously argued, on intuitive grounds, that this must be due to the dynamical coupling between local information processing and maneuver — features that are completely ignored by Lanchesterian models — no generative "explanation" for why fractal power-law scaling appears in combat has heretofore existed. It is therefore tempting to speculate that there are phases of real combat that are poised at *self-organized critical states* (see, for example, [44, 45]).

7.6.3 A Step Away from Lanchester

With an eye toward exploring non-Lanchesterian scenarios, consider an example that includes both simple maneuver and terrain. Figure 7.4 shows the initial state, consisting of 12 red and 12 blue agents positioned near their respective "flags" (in the lower left and upper right corners, respectively). The red agents are arrayed along a berm (i.e., a permeable terrain element, which appears green in the figure), whose dynamical effect is to reduce their visibility to the approaching blue enemy agents to 15% of the nominal value. As blue agents approach the red flag, red agents remain fixed at their positions (simulating a notional "hunkered-down" condition). The red and blue weapon characteristics (probability of hit and range) are equal.

Runs typically proceed as follows. Because of the stealth afforded the dug-in red agents by the berm, red agents are targeted and engaged with a much lower probability than the approaching blue force. The attrition of the attacking force (blue) is significantly higher than the attrition of the defending force (red). When the attackers are able to survive (with some of their force intact) — on some particular run of the scenario — it is because they are able to maneuver out of range (which occurs when the force strength drops below the combat effective threshold of 50% and attempts to withdraw) and red is unable to pursue. (As an aside, EINSTein's ability to prescribe retreat conditions adds a certain realism to the model. Faced with mounting attrition, real squads fall back and regroup.)

The red force usually remains at full strength after the engagement (the probability of zero red casualties is about 80%). This result is intuitively satisfying, since, historically (all other factors being equal), defending forces have

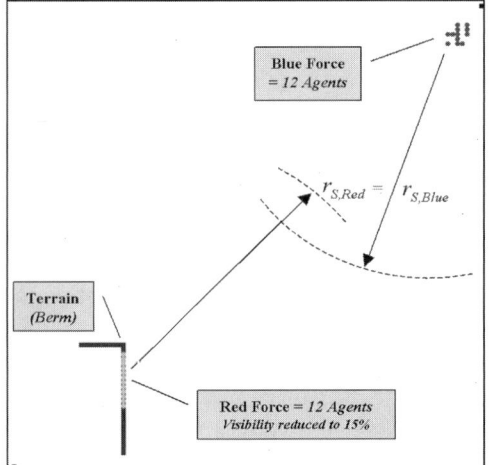

Fig. 7.4. Initial state for simple non-Lanchesterian scenario; see text for details.

the advantage over an attacking force traversing open ground. An obvious question to ask is, *"How large must the blue force be in order to overcome the advantage of the red's terrain?"* Figure 7.5 plots the fraction of the initial forces that remain at the end of the engagement (150 steps) versus the attacker-to-defender force-size ratio (the lines are simple fits to the data to guide the eye). In the runs used to generate this graph, the size of the blue force ranges from 12 to 40 agents, while the red force remains at 12. Note that the red and blue survival curves merge at roughly a 2.8 : 1 ratio; which is interesting in light of the well-known "rule of thumb" that attackers require a 3:1 force ratio against a defended position [46].

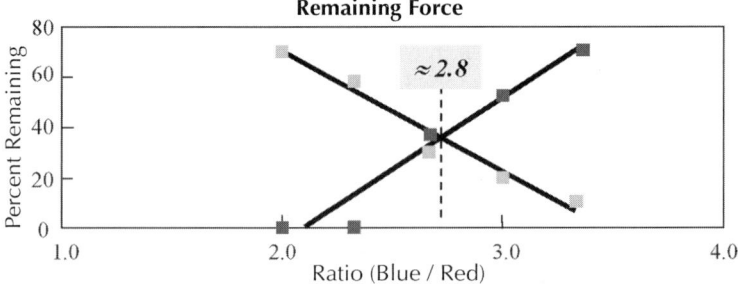

Fig. 7.5. Impact of attacker-to-defender force ratio on survival for the simple non-Lanchesterian scenario shown in the previous figure. The red and blue survival curves merge at about a 2.8 : 1 ratio, which compares favorably to the well-known "rule of thumb" that attackers require a 3:1 force ratio against a defended position [46].

7.6.4 Swarming Forces

One of the first detailed studies of swarming, as a major theme in military history, was recently conducted by Sean Edwards, as part of the *Swarming and the Future of Conflict* project at RAND [47]. Edwards' report focuses on 10 carefully selected historical examples of swarming, includes a series of important lessons-learned distilled from these examples about the advantages and disadvantages of swarming, and provides some examples of successful countermeasures that have been used against swarming in the past.

Edwards notes that swarming consists of four overlapping stages: (1) *location*, (2) *convergence*, (3) *attack*, and (4) *dispersion*. Moreover, swarming forces must be capable of a sustainable pulsing; i.e., networks of swarming agents must be able to come together rapidly and stealthily on a target, then redisperse and finally recombine for a new pulse:

> *The swarm concept is built on the principles of complexity theory, and it assumes that blue units have to operate autonomously and adaptively according to the overall mission statement....It is important that swarm units converge and attack simultaneously. Each individual swarm unit is vulnerable on its own, but if it is united in a concerted effort with other friendly units, overall lethality can be multiplied, because the phenomenon of the swarm effect is greater than the sum of its parts. Individual units or incompletely assembled groups are vulnerable to defeat in detail against the larger enemy force with its superior fire-power and mass.*

The report notes that swarming scenarios have already played a role in certain high-level war-gaming exercises, such as at the *Dominating Maneuver Game*, held at the U.S. Army War College in 1997. Edwards concludes his survey by speculating about the feasibility of a future "swarming doctrine," that would consist of small, distributed, highly maneuverable units converging rapidly on specific targets.

Because of its decentralized rule-base and rich space of behavioral primitives, EINSTein is an ideal test bed with which to explore the nature of battlefield swarming and the efficacy of swarm-like tactics. Typically, but not always, one side appears to swarm the other when there is a significant mismatch in firepower, total force strength, and/or maneuvering ability. (Swarming also occasionally emerges as a useful "tactic" to use against certain opponents when EINSTein's built-in genetic algorithm is tasked with finding optimal attack strategies.) While it is common to find swarm-like behavior for personalities that include large cluster meta-rule thresholds, $\tau_{Cluster}$ (which increases the likelihood that agents will remain in close proximity to friendly agents), the most interesting "self-organized" examples of swarming are those for which $\tau_{Cluster}$ is, at most, a few agents.

Table 7.3 lists some of the parameter values defining four representative swarm scenarios (I–IV). In scenario I, blue attacks red; in scenario II, blue defends. Blue agents are more aggressive than red in all four scenarios (as defined by the values of their respective combat meta-rule thresholds, Δ_{Combat}).

Note that, in scenarios II and III, defending blue agents are able to communicate with other blue agents that are within a range $r_C = 25$ of their position. Figure 7.6 show snapshots of typical runs using parameters for scenarios I–IV, respectively.

Table 7.3. Agent Parameter Values for Scenarios I–IV Shown in Fig. 7.6.

	I	I	II	II	III	III	IV	IV
Force	Red	Blue	Red	Blue	Red	Blue	Red	Blue
Size	150	225	90	125	25	100	200	200
r_S	5	5	5	10	3	7	3	7
r_F	3	3	3	7	2	5	2	5
r_M	1	1	1	2	1	1	1	1
w_{AF}	25	10	10	0	5	0	5	0
w_{AE}	25	50	40	99	40	5	40	5
w_{IF}	75	0	10	0	5	0	5	0
w_{IE}	25	99	40	99	90	50	90	50
w_{FF}	0	0	0	0	0	0	0	0
w_{EF}	75	25	50	0	0	0	0	0
τ_{Advance}	5	1	3	N/A	N/A	N/A	N/A	N/A
τ_{Cluster}	15	3	3	12	5	5	5	5
Δ_{Combat}	5	-7	0	-15	-5	-10	-5	-10
Comms	no	no	no	yes, $r_C = 25$	no	yes, $r_C = 25$	no	no

7.6.5 Non-Monotonicity

For a fixed set of force characteristics, number, type, and lethality of weapon systems, and tactics, one might intuitively expect that as one side's capability is unilaterally enhanced — say, by increasing sensor range or its ability to maneuver — the other side's ability to perform its mission ought to be commensurately diminished. In other words, our expectations are that mission success scales monotonically with force capability.

In fact, non-monotonicities abound in both real-world behavior and simulations. With respect to models and simulations, of course, one must always be on guard against the possibility that non-monotonic scaling is an artifact of the code and therefore does not represent real processes. As pointed out by a RAND study that addressed this issue [48], "a combat model with a single decision based on the state of the battle...can produce non-monotonic behavior in the outcomes of the model and chaotic behavior in its underlying dynamics."

Figure 7.7 shows an instructive example of genuinely non-monotonic behavior; genuine in the sense that the non-monotonicity emerges directly out of the primitive rule set. The three rows in Fig. 7.7 contain snapshots of three separate runs in which red's sensor range is systematically increased in increments of two: $r_{S,\text{red}} = 5$ for the top sequence; $r_{S,\text{red}} = 7$ for the middle

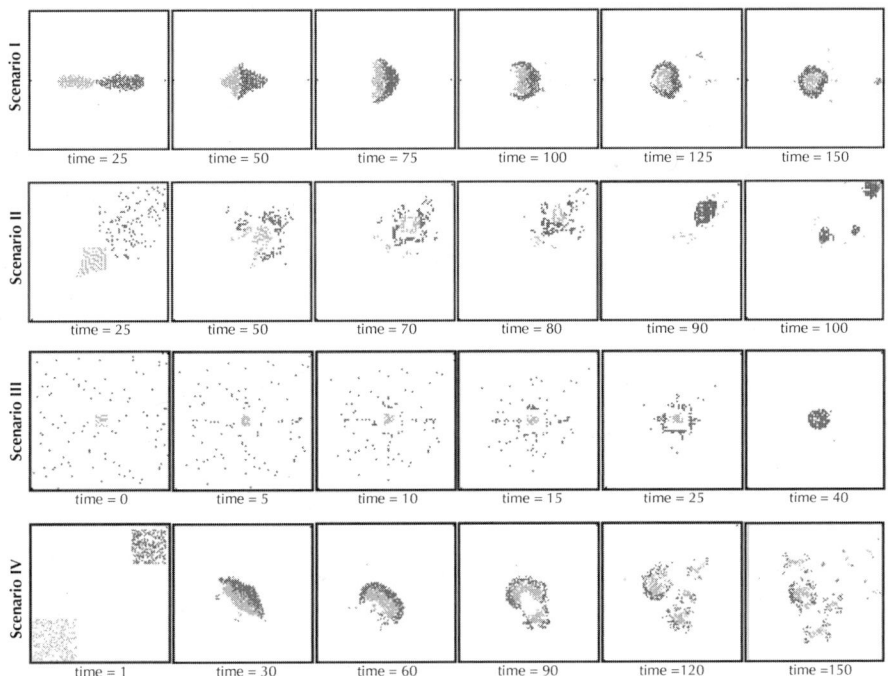

Fig. 7.6. Sample runs of swarm scenarios I–IV. See Table 7.3 for parameter values.

sequence; $r_{S,\text{red}} = 9$ for the bottom sequence. Blue's sensor range, $r_{S,\text{blue}}$, remains fixed at $r_{S,\text{blue}} = 5$ throughout all three runs. The values of other pertinent red and blue agent parameters are given in Table 7.4.

Table 7.4. Agent Parameter Values for *Non-monotonic* Run Appearing in Fig. 7.7.

	N	r_S	r_F	r_M	$\mathbf{w} = (w_{\text{AF}}, w_{\text{AE}}, w_{\text{IF}}, w_{\text{IE}}, w_{\text{FF}}, w_{\text{EF}})$	τ_{Adv}	τ_{Clus}	Δ_{Combat}
Red	100	5,7,9	4	1	$\mathbf{w}_{\text{Red}} = (10, 90, 10, 50, 0, 99)$	2	4	-4
Blue	50	5	4	1	$\mathbf{w}_{\text{Blue}} = (10, 90, 10, 50, 0, 99)$	2	4	0

In each of the runs, there are 100 red and 50 blue agents. Red is also the more the aggressive force. Blue engage red in combat if the number of friendly and enemy agents is locally about even, while red will fight blue even if outnumbered by four enemy combatants. Both sides have the same fire range ($r_F = 4$), and the same single-shot probability ($P_{\text{hit}} = 0.005$) and can simultaneously engage the same maximum of three enemy targets. (Note that the flags for this run are near the middle of the left and right edges of the notional battlefield rather than at the corners.)

The top row of Fig. 7.7 shows screenshots of a run in which red's sensor range is equal to blue's. Here the red force easily penetrates the blue defense

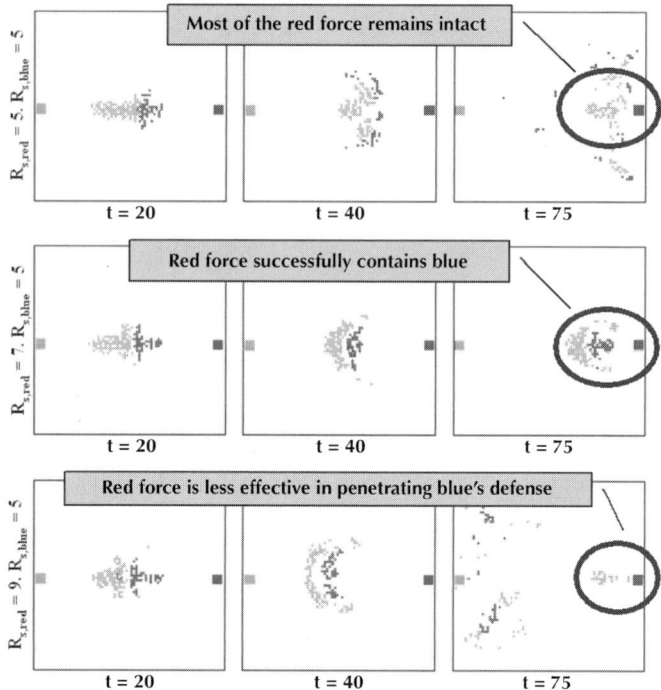

Fig. 7.7. An example of non-monotonic behavior. The three rows contain snapshots of three separate runs in which red's sensor range is increased in increments of two (from $r_{S,\text{red}} = 5$ on the top row, to $r_{S,\text{red}} = 9$ on the bottom). Blue's sensor range is fixed at $r_{S,\text{blue}} = 5$ throughout. Comparing the bottom row to the top two rows, we see that increasing red's sensor appears to have a detrimental effect on red's overall ability to penetrate blue's defense.

as it moves toward the blue flag. During red's advance, a number of agents are "stripped" away from the main red-blue cluster in the center as they respond to the presence of nearby blue agents. The snapshots in the middle row of Fig. 7.7 show that when red's sensor range is two units greater than blue's, red is not only able to mass almost its entire force on the blue flag (by $t = 90$ — not shown — blue's flag is completely enveloped by red forces), but also to defend its own flag from all blue forces as well. In this instance, the red force knows enough about, and can respond quickly enough to, enemy action such that it is able to march into enemy territory effectively unhindered by enemy forces and "scoop up" blue agents as they are encountered.

What happens as red's sensor range is increased still further? One might intuitively guess that red can only do at least as well, certainly no worse — i.e., that red's mission performance scales monotonically with the amount of information that each red agent is allowed to have about the engagement. However, as the snapshots for bottom row of Fig. 7.7 reveal, when red's sensor range is increased to $r_{S,\text{red}} = 9$ — *so that all red agents are locally aware of more information* — red, as a force, turns in an objectively weaker mission performance than on the preceding runs. "Weaker" here meaning that red is less effective in (1) establishing a presence near the blue flag, and (2) defending blue's advance toward the red flag.

The nonmonotonic behavior is immediately obvious from Fig. 7.8, which shows a 3D fitness landscape for mission objective = *maximize number of red agents near blue flag* (where "near" is defined as anywhere within 10 battlefield-units). The landscape sweeps over $r_{S,\text{red}}$ ($= 1, 2, \ldots, 16$) and red combat meta-rule threshold Δ_{Combat} ($= -15, -14, \ldots, +15$). Higher-valued fitness values translate to mean better performance.

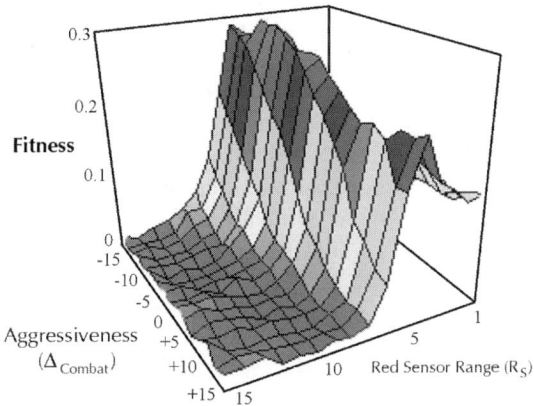

Fig. 7.8. Fitness landscape for mission = *maximize number of red agents near blue flag*, as a function of combat aggressiveness (Δ_{Combat}) and red sensor range ($r_{S,\text{red}}$). Higher-valued fitness values translate to mean better performance. Note that (this particular fitness measure) does not scale monotonically with sensor range.

This example illustrates that when the resources and personalities of both sides remain fixed in a conflict, how well side X does over side Y does not necessarily scale monotonically with X's sensor capability. As one side is forced to assimilate more and more information (with increasing sensor range), there will inevitably come a point where the available resources will be spread too thin and the overall fighting ability will therefore be curtailed. Agent-based models such as EINSTein are well suited for providing insights into more operationally significant questions such as, *"How must X's resources and/or tactics (i.e., personality) be altered in order to ensure at least the same level of mission performance?"*

7.7 Genetic Algorithm Breeding

One of EINSTein's most powerful built-in features is a genetic algorithm "breeder" run-mode. Genetic algorithms (GAs) are a class of heuristic search methods and computational models of adaptation and evolution based on natural selection. In nature, the search for beneficial adaptations to a continually changing environment (i.e., evolution) is fostered by the cumulative evolutionary knowledge that each species possesses of its forebears. This knowledge, which is encoded in the chromosomes of each member of a species, is passed on from one generation to the next by a mating process in which the chromosomes of "parents" produce "offspring" chromosomes. GAs mimic and exploit the genetic dynamics underlying natural evolution to search for optimal solutions of general combinatorial optimization problems. They have been applied to the traveling salesman problem, VLSI circuit layout, gas pipeline control, the parametric design of aircraft, neural net architecture, models of international security, and strategy formulation [49].

Figure 7.9 illustrates how GAs are used in EINSTein. Chromosomes define individual agents. Genes encode the components of the personality weight vector, sensor range, fire range, meta-rule thresholds, etc. The initial GA population consists of a set of randomly generated chromosomes. The fitness function represents a user-specified mission "fitness" (see ahead). The target of the GA search is, by default, the red force. The parameter values defining the blue force — once they are defined at the start of a search — are held fixed.

7.7.1 Search Space

EINSTein uses up to 80 genes to conduct a GA search; the actual number depends on the particular region of the parameter space the user wishes to explore. Some genes are integer-valued (such as the agent-to-agent communication links), while others are real-valued. All appropriate translations to integer values and/or binary toggles (*on/off*) are performed automatically by the program. Typically, each gene encodes the value of a basic parameter defining the red force. For example, g_1 encodes red's sensor range when an agent is in the alive state, g_3 encodes red's alive-state fire range, and so on. Some special genes encode the sign (+ or −) of an associated parametric gene. Thus, the actual value of each of the components of red's personality weight vector, for example, is actually encoded by *two genes*; one gene specifying the component's absolute value, and the other gene its sign.

EINSTein's GA can conduct its search over five spaces:

- *Single-squad personality:* GA searches over the personality-space defining a single squad.
- *Multiple-squad personality:* GA searches over the personality-space defining multiple squads. The number of squads and the size of each squad remain fixed throughout this GA run mode.

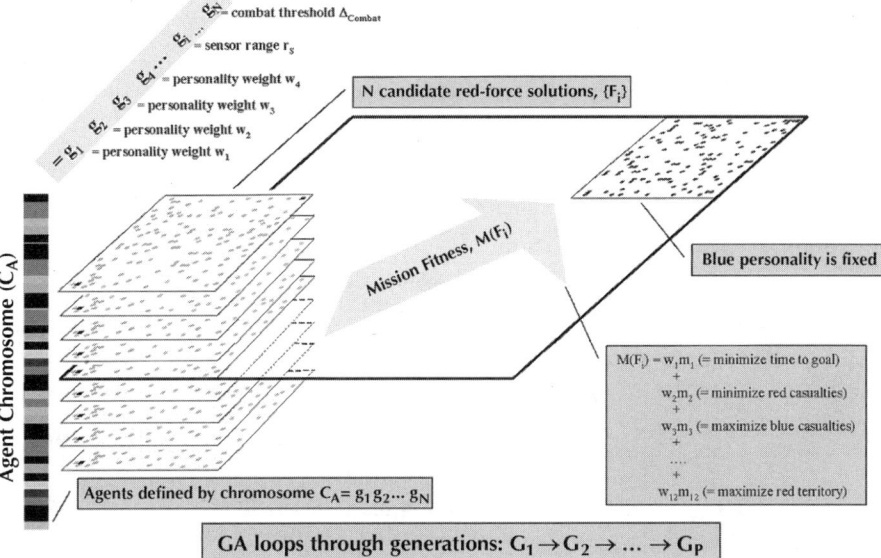

Fig. 7.9. Schematic of EINSTein's GA. The blue force and mission fitness are both fixed by the user. The GA encodes components of the agents' personality weight vector, sensor range, fire range, meta-rule thresholds, etc. and breeds the "best" red force using populations of N red force "candidate" solutions; see text for details.

- *Squad composition:* GA searches over squad composition space. The personality parameters defining squads 1 through 10 are fixed according to the values defined in the default input data file used to start the interactive run. The GA searches over the space defined by the number of squads (1–10) and size of each squad (constrained by the total number of agents as defined by the data file).
- *Inter-squad communications connectivity:* GA searches over the zero-one entries defining the communications matrix. The number of squads and the number of agents per squad are kept fixed at the values defined in the default input data file used to start the interactive run.
- *Inter-squad weight connectivity:* GA searches over (real-valued) entries defining the squad interconnectivity matrix. The number of squads and the number of agents per squad are kept fixed at the values defined in the default input data file.

7.7.2 Mission Fitness

The mission fitness (MF) is a measure of how well agents perform a user-defined mission. Typical missions are *"Get to blue flag as quickly as possible," "Minimize red casualties,"* and *"Maximize the ratio of blue to red casualties,"* or some combination of these. MFs are always defined from red's perspective. The user assigns weights ($0 \leq w_i \leq 1$)¶ to represent the relative degree of importance of each mission fitness primitive, m_i (see Table 7.5). While the mission primitives are relatively few in number and simple, they can be combined to define more complicated multi-objective functions.

Table 7.5. EINSTein's GA Mission Fitness Primitives.

Weight	Primitive	Description
w_1	m_1	Minimize time to goal
w_2	m_2	Minimize friendly casualties
w_3	m_3	Maximize enemy casualties
w_4	m_4	Maximize friendly-to-enemy survival ratio
w_5	m_5	Minimize friendly center-of-mass distance to enemy flag
w_6	m_6	Maximize enemy center-of-mass distance to friendly flag
w_7	m_7	Maximize N_{friends} within distance D of enemy flag
w_8	m_8	Minimize N_{enemy} within distance D of friendly flag
w_9	m_9	Minimize number of friendly fratricide hits
w_{10}	m_{10}	Maximize number of enemy fratricide hits
w_{11}	m_{11}	Maximize friendly territorial possession
w_{12}	m_{12}	Minimize enemy territorial possession

The mission fitness function, M, used by the GA, is a weighted sum of mission primitives: $M = \sum_i m_i$. (It is left up to the user to ensure that mission objectives are both logically consistent and amenable to a "solution.") Future versions of EINSTein will include a richer set of mission fitness primitives, including: locate and kill enemy squad leaders, stay close to friends, stay away from enemies, have combat efficiency (as measured by cumulative number of hits on enemy), clear specified area of enemy agents, occupy area for specified period of time, take the enemy flag under specific conditions (for example, the user is asked to specify the number of agents that must occupy a given area around the enemy flag for a given length of time), among others.

7.7.3 EINSTein's GA Recipe

The GA uses EINSTein's agent-movement/combat engine to conduct its searches. In pseudocode, the main components of EINSTein GA recipe are as follows:

> for generation=1,$G_{\max}$
> > for personality=1,$P_{\max}$
> > > decode chromosome
> > > for initial_condition IC=1 to$IC_{\max}$

¶ *Mission fitness* weights must not be confused with the *personality* weights; **Agent Personalities** discussed earlier.

>   *run combat engine*
>   *calculate fitness (for given IC)*
>   *next initial_condition*
>   *calculate mission fitness*
>   *next personality*
>   *find the best personality*
>   *select survivors from population*
>   *perform (single-point) crossover operation*
>   *perform mutation operation*
>   *update progress/status*
>   *next generation*
>   *write best personality to file*

In words, the GA uses a randomized pool of chromosomes to define an initial generation of red personalities. For each red personality, and for each of the $IC_{\max}$ initial spatial configurations of red and blue forces, the program then runs EINSTein's combat engine to determine the mission fitness. After looping through all personalities and initial conditions, the GA first sorts and ranks the personalities according to their mission fitness values, then selects some to be eliminated from the pool and others to breed. The GA then performs the basic operations of crossover and mutation. Finally, after a new generation of red personalities has been defined, the entire process is repeated until either the user interrupts the evolution or the maximum generation number has been reached (see Fig. 7.9).

7.7.4 Sample GA Breeding Experiment #1

Consider the following mission (as stated from the *red* force's point-of-view): *"Keep blue agents as far away from the red flag as possible, for as long as possible (up to a maximum 100 iteration steps)."* That is, set all GA mission weights to zero, except for $w_6 = w_8 = 1/2$; see Table 7.5). This means that the mission fitness M will be close to its maximal value *one* only if red is able to keep all blue agents pinned near their own flag (at a point farthest from the red flag) for the entire duration of the run, and M will be near its minimal value *zero* if red allows blue agents to advance completely unhindered toward the red flag. Combat unfolds on a 40-by-40 battlefield, with 35 agents per side. The GA is run using a pool of 50 red personalities for 50 generations, and each personality is averaged over 25 initial spatial configurations. Blue agents are each assigned (a fixed) personality weight vector $w_{\text{Blue}} = (w_{\text{AF}}, w_{\text{IF}}, w_{\text{AE}}, w_{\text{IE}}, w_{\text{FF}}, w_{\text{EF}}) = (0, 10, 0, 10, 0, 90)$.

Figure 7.10 shows a typical *learning curve*, where "Best" refers to the fitness of the highest-ranking candidate solution and "Average" refers to the average fitness among all candidate solutions per generation. The GA run described here (using a 1 GHz Pentium IV PC) each requires roughly an hour to complete.

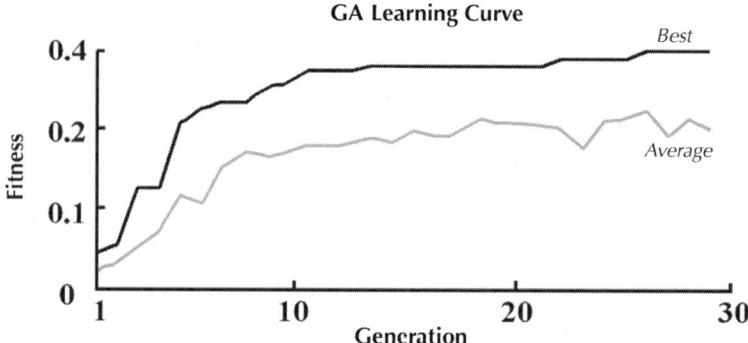

Fig. 7.10. Typical GA learning curve for GA breeding experiment discussed in text.

Screenshots from a typical run using the highest-ranked red personality (as sampled from "solution" pool representing generation 30) that the GA is able to find for this mission are shown along the top row of Fig. 7.11. They show that red is very successful at keeping blue forces away from its own flag; the closest that red permits blue agents from approaching the red flag — during the entire allotted run time of 100 iteration steps — is some point roughly near midfield. In words, the "tactic" here seems to be — from red's perspective — *"fight all enemy agents within sensor range, and move toward the enemy flag slowly enough to drive the enemy along."* Note that this emergent tactic is also fairly robust, in the sense that if the battle is initialized with a different spatial disposition of red and blue forces (while keeping all personality parameters fixed), red performs this particular mission about as well, on average, as evidenced by these screenshots.

Screenshots from a typical run using the second-highest ranking red personality are shown along the second row of Fig. 7.11. These show a slightly less successful, but nonetheless innovative, alternative tactic. Initially, red agents move away from their own goal to meet the advancing blue forces, just as in the first case (at $t = 25$). Once combat ensues, however, any red agents that find themselves locally isolated now "double back" toward their own flag (positioned in the lower left corner of the battlefield) to regroup with other remaining friendly agents. The red force thus, effectively, forms an impromptu secondary defense against possible blue leakers. Because a few blue agents do manage to fight their way near the red flag at later times (at least in the particular run these screenshots have been taken from; see snapshot for $t = 90$), the red agent parameter values underlying this emergent tactic are not as highly ranked as the parameter values underlying the run shown in the top row.

The series of screenshots appearing in the third row of Fig. 7.11 show the emergent tactic used by the highest-ranked red personality found by the GA

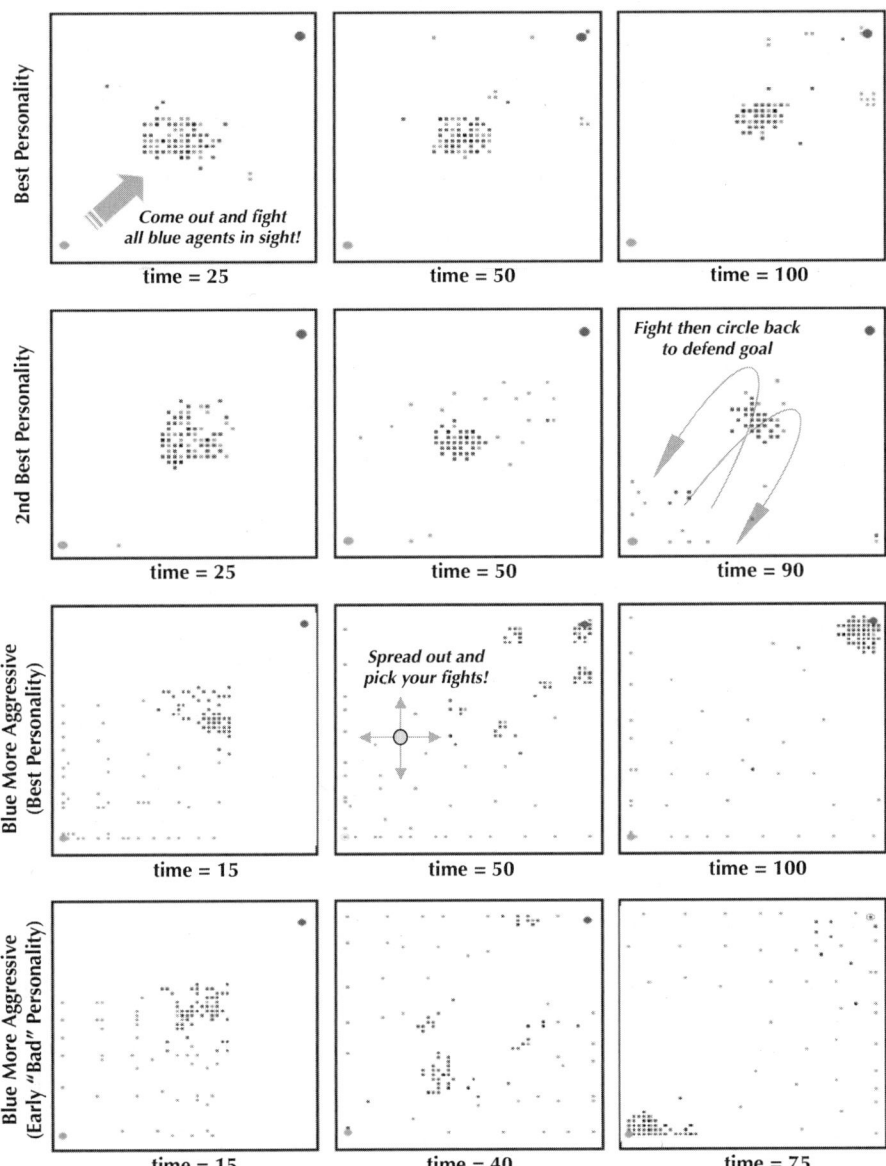

Fig. 7.11. Screenshots from several sample runs of GA breeding experiment #1. The top row shows a run using the highest-ranked red agents after 50 generations. The second row shows the second-highest ranked red force. The third row shows how the red force adapts to a more aggressive blue force. Finally, the fourth row shows an example of how a suboptimal red force performs. It represents a pool of agents occupying an early portion (generation 10) of the GA's learning curve.

after the blue force is made more *aggressive*. For this case, prior to initializing the GA search, blue's personality weight-vector components for moving toward red (i.e., $w_{AE} = w_3$, and $w_{IE} = w_4$) are first increased by 50%. We see that EINSTein's GA discovers an entirely different (and more effective) tactic to use. Here, the red force quickly spreads out to cover as much territory as possible and individual agents attack the enemy as soon as they come within view. As red agents' local territorial coverage is thinned — either through attrition or gradual advance toward the blue flag — other red agents (namely, agents that had previously been positioned near the periphery of the battlefield) move closer to the center of the battlefield, thus filling emerging voids. This tactic succeeds in preventing any blue agents from reaching the red flag and also manages to push most of the surviving blue force back toward its own flag (near the top right corner of the battlefield)! As is true of the other cases in this experiment, this tactic is also fairly robust and is not a strong function of the initial spatial disposition of red and blue forces.

The last row of plots in Fig. 7.11 contains snapshots from a run using interim red agent parameter values, *before* the GA has had a chance to evaluate a large number of candidate solutions. This example illustrates how an obviously suboptimal pool of agents behaves differently from their optimized counterparts. The mission parameters and blue-force agent personalities are the same as in the case represented by the screenshots in the third row. We see that, initially at least, there does not seem to be much difference in the optimal and suboptimal behaviors; red agents quickly disperse outward to cover a large area. However, because the GA has not yet had the time to fine-tune all of red's genes, the red force is in this instance unable to prevent blue agents from penetrating deeply into its territory. The defensive tactic, however it may be characterized, is obviously ineffective.

7.7.5 Sample GA Breeding Experiment #2

Consider a scenario in which the blue force is tasked with defending its flag against a smaller attacking red force. We use the GA to find a red force that is able to penetrate the blue defense. Table 7.6 lists some pertinent parameter values defining the two forces. The middle row of the table (i.e., red trial values) lists baseline red force parameter values (as defined by us, not the GA) used to test the scenario. The bottom row (i.e., GA-bred values) lists the GA bred red force "solution." Notice that, in both cases, the number of agents is the same and is fixed (with blue outnumbering red, 100 to 50 in all runs). (All baseline red-*trial* alive and injured parameter values are equal.)

Figure 7.12 shows screenshots from a typical run using the red-trial values. Red agents attack, unsuccessfully, in a tight cluster. The larger blue force (whose agents initially move about randomly around their starting position until a red agent comes within their sensor range) dispels the red force rather easily (within the 30 time steps shown here).

Table 7.6. Agent Parameter Values for GA Sample Run Appearing in Fig. 7.12 and 7.13.

	Blue Agents	Red *Trial* Agents	Red *GA bred*	
			Alive Agents	*Injured* Agents
N_{Agents}	100	50	50	50
r_S	5	5	8	5
r_F	3	3	8	5
r_M	2	2	2	2
w_{AF}	0	10	3	-22
w_{AE}	100	40	40	95
w_{IF}	0	10	46	-86
w_{IE}	100	40	38	-14
w_{FF}	0	0	-70	14
w_{EF}	0	25	65	31
τ_{Advance}	N/A	3	3	1
τ_{Cluster}	5	10	13	17
Δ_{Combat}	-20	0	-19	+20

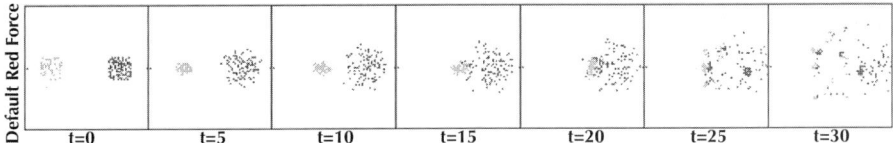

Fig. 7.12. Trial red attacking force (consisting of typical parameter values that are not explicitly tuned for performing any specific mission). Red performance is used simply as a reference for interpreting the output of the sample GA breeding experiment discussed in the text.

The GA-bred parameters listed along the bottom row in Table 7.6 define the highest-ranked red force that EINSTein's GA is able to find (after 30 generations) with respect to performing the mission = *"maximize the number of red agents able to penetrate within a distance $d = 7$ units of the blue flag within 40 time steps."* A population size of 75 was used (i.e., each generation of the GA search consists of 75 red force candidate "solutions") and mission fitness, for a given candidate solution, is averaged over 10 initial configurations of red and blue forces. The fitness equals *one* if a candidate solution performs the specified mission in the best possible manner (i.e., if the red force sustains zero casualties and all agents remain within $d = 7$ of the blue flag starting from the minimal possible time at which they move to within that distance of the flag, for all 10 initial states) and equals *zero* if a candidate solution fails to place a single red agent within $d = 7$ of the blue flag for all 10 initial states (within the mission time limit). Figure 7.13 shows screenshots from a typical run using the GA-bred red force values. (The arrows are included as visual aids and simply trace the motion of the red agent clusters.) Comparing this sequence of steps to those in the trial run shown in Fig. 7.12, it is obvious that the respective "attack strategies" in the two cases are very different. Indeed, the GA has found just the right mix of agent-agent proximity weights and meta-rules to define a red force that effectively exploits a relative weakness in the randomly maneuvering blue defenders. The emergent "tactic" is to *separate into two roughly equal-sized units, regroup beyond enemy sensor range, and then simultaneously strike, as a pincer, into the heart of the defending enemy cluster.*

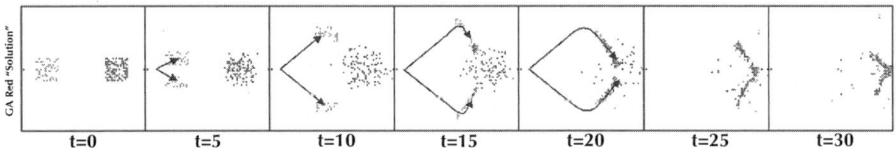

Fig. 7.13. Screenshots from a typical run using the GA-bred red force for the sample GA breeding experiment discussed in the text. Red agents are defined by GA-bred parameter values that are the highest ranked (after 30 generations) with respect to performing the mission = *"maximize the number of red agents able to penetrate within a distance d=7 units of the blue flag within 40 time steps."*

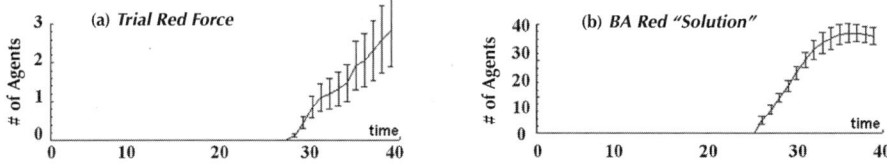

Fig. 7.14. A comparison between the average number of red agents that approach within a distance $d = 7$ of the blue flag for (a) *trial* and (b) *GA-bred* red forces. We see that the GA-bred red force typically performs this mission an order of magnitude more successfully than the trial force.

Apart from the anecdotal evidence supplied by screenshots of this particular run, the efficacy of this simple GA-bred tactic is illustrated by comparing graphs of the number of agents near the blue flag (averaged over 50 runs) as a function of time for the red-*trial* and *GA-bred* cases. Figure 7.14 shows that whereas fewer than three red-trial agents, on average, penetrate close to the blue flag (Fig. 7.14a), almost 80% of the entire GA-bred red force is able to do so (Fig. 7.14b); and begins penetrating at an earlier time. Other (well-performing) tactics are possible, of course. A representative sampling is generally provided by looking at the behaviors of some of the higher-ranking red forces remaining at the end of a GA search. It is interesting to run a series of GA runs to systematically probe how red forces "adapt" to different blue personalities. What one observes, typically, is that as the behavior of the blue agents changes, various — often dramatically different — GA-bred red personalities emerge to exploit any new weaknesses in the blue's defensive posture.

7.8 Discussion

> *The musical notes are only five in number,*
> *but their melodies are so numerous that one cannot hear them all.*
> *The primary colors are only five in number,*
> *but their combinations are so infinite that one cannot visualize them all.*
> *In battle there are only the normal and extraordinary forces,*
> *but their combinations are limitless; none can comprehend them all.*
> — Sun Tzu, *The Art of War*

The high-level, or poetic, description of EINSTein owes much to the suggestive metaphors appearing in the quote from *The Art of War*. In the same way as, for Sun Tzu, rainbows and melodies are all natural outcomes of combining primary colors and musical notes, EINSTein may be viewed as an "engine" that converts a primitive grammar — i.e., a grammar composed of the basic notes and colors of combat — into the limitless patterns and possibilities of war. The researcher chooses and/or tunes primitive, low-level agents and rules; and EINSTein provides the dynamic arena within which these rules interact and spawn high-level patterns and behaviors. On a more practical level, EINSTein was developed with these three important goals in mind:

1. To demonstrate the efficacy of agent-based simulation alternatives to more traditional Lanchester-equation-based models of combat [5].
2. To be used as a general prototype artificial life model/toolkit that can be used as a testbed for exploring self-organized emergent behavior in complex adaptive systems.
3. To provide the military operations research community with an easy-to-use, intuitive agent-based combat-simulation laboratory that — by respecting both the principles of real-world combat and the dynamics of complex adaptive systems — may lead researchers one step closer to a fundamental theory of combat.

To better appreciate how each of these motivations has contributed to EINSTein's (still evolving) architecture, consider the conceptual map of its design, as illustrated schematically in Fig. 7.15. Self-organized patterns emerge out of a set of primitive local rules of combat, both on the individual agent level — via interactions among internal motivations (on the *Phenotype-I* level, which appears as the middle level in Fig. 7.15) — and squad and force levels (labeled *Phenotype-II* in Fig. 7.15, and which appears as the top-most level in the figure) — via mutual interactions among many agents in a changing environment.

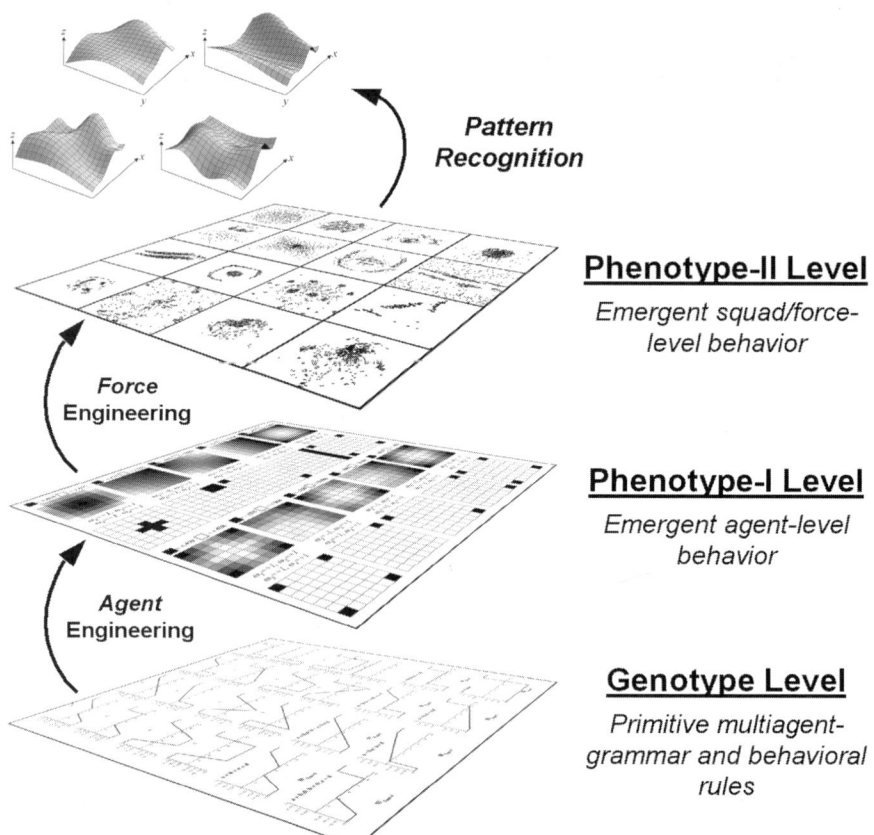

Fig. 7.15. A hierarchy of conceptual levels that illustrate EINSTein's core design.

Of course, a deeper understanding of phenomena governing behaviors on the top-most level can only be achieved by developing a suite of appropriate pattern recognition tools (the need for which is indicated symbolically at the top of Fig. 7.15). Although a number of interesting, and highly suggestive, high-level patterns have already been discovered, much still remains to be done. Consider, for example, the frequent appearance of various power-law scalings and fractal dimensions describing space-time patterns and attrition rates ([34, 40]). The existence of power-law scalings, in particular, strongly suggests that a self-organized, critical-like dynamical mechanism might govern turbulent-like phases of combat. But the data collection and analysis necessary to rigorously establish the nature of these findings (as well as to establish a mathematically precise set of conditions under which power-law scalings either *do* or *do not* occur) has only just started.

One of the directions in which EINSTein's design is moving (some details of which are described in the next section) is toward a fully developed ontological architecture that assigns specific meaning to the symbolic relationship between *environment* and *action*. The hope is to be able to explore the complementary problem of *reverse behavior engineering*; i.e., the problem of finding an appropriate set of primitives (properties and rules) that lead either to empirically observed, or desired, macroscopic patterns of combat (or, in Fig. 7.15, of finding ways of going from either phenotype level I or II to the genotype level).

7.8.1 Other Features and Future Enhancements

Since (as of this writing) EINSTein is still being actively developed, the version of the program described in this paper necessarily represents an incomplete snapshot of an evolving toolkit. Many capabilities — both existing (such as agent↔agent communications and terrain-modeling features) and/or in the design stage (such as endowing agents with both a memory of, and a facility to learn from, their past actions) — have not been discussed. Most of the planned enhancements are natural extensions of EINSTein's current capabilities; future versions are generally shifting toward a more robust, multilayered agent-logic architecture that can more gracefully scale the full spectrum of behaviors from large agent-swarms to intelligent behaviors on the *squad* and *single-agent* levels. Loosely speaking, this shift of emphasis represents a shift away from describing the mutual interactions among many *simple* agents to describing interactions among a relatively few, but *complex* agents (which are also endowed with a richer internal structure and dynamics). Where early versions have focused on the complexity of emergent behaviors on the system level, more recent work adds the ability to explore emergent behaviors on the individual agent level as well. Details are discussed in [34].

Almost all of the features described in this paper were well in place before EINSTein's first version release (v1.0); many additional features and capabilities have been added since then. For example, among the major additions to version 1.1 of the program were (1) an *enhanced weapons class* (that allows users to essentially design their own weapons, with arbitrary properties and lethality characteristics), (2) *intelligent pathfinding* (that uses a priority-queue variant of Dijkstra's optimal path algorithm [50]), and (3) *waypoint scripting* (that can be used to "guide" agents along desired paths). Collectively, these three enhancements make it possible to design scenarios that are considerably more realistic than the pedagogical examples cited in this paper.

Version 1.3 of EINSTein introduced two other important enhancements: (1) *trigger-state-based* action-selection logic, and (2) an adaptive *weapon-targeting logic*. Trigger states generalize EINSTein's meta-rules by allowing users to associate arbitrary conditions (that can be defined by using one or a combination of two or three environmental features) with agent behaviors; i.e., specific behaviors may be "triggered" by specific conditions. Meta-rules have always allowed agents to tailor their behavior to simple contexts — the Δ_{Combat} meta-rule, for example, defines the conditions under which agents either engage (or do not engage) the enemy — but also constrain the user to making basic *either/or* decisions (and limit an agent's context-specific behavior modification to changing a single component of its default personality weight vector). EINSTein's newer trigger-state logic is vastly more flexible and allows essentially arbitrary modifications of an agent's behavior to be made contingent upon arbitrary environmental conditions. Aside from obviously adding a great deal of realism to scenarios, the new logic also allows analysts to more deeply explore interactions between agent personalities and their dynamic environment. For example, one can easily design (using only EINSTein's GUI) a robust *fire suppressed* state in which agents react intelligently to strong local enemy fire by, say, ceasing their own fire on the enemy and advance toward the enemy flag, dropping "to the ground," becoming temporarily immobile, in order to reduce visibility, and disabling communications with squad mates. It is impossible to construct such "mutated" behaviors by using EINSTein's meta-rules alone.

EINSTein's most recently added weapon-targeting logic effectively provides an entirely new dimension to an agent's default "personality" (that adjudicates only movement) by endowing agents with an intelligent targeting capability. With it, agents can discriminate among possible targets by weighing the relative potential benefit of firing at the given coordinate on the battlefield. Agents may consider factors such as the damage likely to be inflicted on friends and enemies near the target coordinate, and the value or threat that specific enemy agents represent. Agents use a "targeting" penalty function (evaluated for each of the possible targeting strategies they may use in a given context) that is an analog of the movement penalty function defined in Eq. (7.4).

7.8.2 Why Are Agent-based Models of Combat Useful?

The most important immediate payoff to using EINSTein is the radically new way at looking at fundamental issues. However, agent-based models are best used to enhance understanding, not as prediction engines. Specifically, EINSTein is being designed to help researchers...

- Understand how all of the different elements of combat fit together in an overall combat phase space: *"Are there regions that are 'sensitive' to small perturbations, and, if so, might there be a way to exploit this in combat (as in selectively driving an opponent into more sensitive regions of phase space)?"*
- Assess the value of information: *"How can I exploit what I know the enemy does not know about me?"*
- Explore trade-offs between centralized and decentralized command-and-control (C2) structures: *"Are some C2 topologies more conducive to information flow and attainment of mission objectives than others?" "What do emergent forms of a self-organized C2 topology look like?"*

- Provide a natural arena in which to explore consequences of various qualitative characteristics of combat (unit cohesion, morale, leadership, etc.).
- Explore emergent properties and/or other "novel" behaviors arising from low-level rules (even combat doctrine if it is well encoded): *"Are there universal patterns of combat behavior?"*
- Provide clues about how near-real-time tactical decision aids may eventually be developed using evolutionary programming techniques.
- Address questions such as *"How do two sides of a conflict coevolve with one another?"* and *"Can one side exploit what it knows of this coevolutionary process to compel the other side to remain out of equilibrium?"*

Command and Control

EINSTein contains embedded code that hard-wires in a specific set of command and control (C2) functions (i.e., both contain a hierarchy of local and global commanders), so that it can be used to explore the dynamics of a given C2 structure. However, a more compelling question is, *"What is the best C2 topology for dealing with a specific threat, or set of threats?"* One can imagine using a genetic algorithm, or some other heuristic tool to aid in exploring potentially very large fitness landscapes, to search for alternative C2 structures. What forms should local and global command take, and what is the optimal communications matrix among individual combatants, squads, and their local and global commanders?

Pattern Recognition

An even deeper issue has to do with identifying the primitive forms of information relevant on the battlefield. Traditionally, the role of the combat operations research analyst has been to assimilate, and provide useful insights from, certain conventional streams of battlefield data: attrition rate, posture profiles, available and depleted resources, logistics, rate of reinforcement, FEBA location, morale, etc. While all of these measures are obviously important, and will remain so, having an ABM of combat permits one to ask the following deeper question: *"Are there any other forms of primitive information — perhaps derived from measures commonly used to describe the behavior of nonlinear and complex dynamical systems — that might provide a more thorough understanding of the fundamental dynamical processes of combat?"* We have already mentioned, for example, that evidence suggests that the intensity of battles — both in the real world and in agent-based models of combat — obeys a fractal power-law dependence on frequency. and displays other traits characteristic of high-dimensional chaotic systems. Are there other, similar but heretofore unexamined, measures that may provide insight into the dynamics of real world combat?

"What If?" Experimentation

The strength of agent-based models lies not just in their providing a potentially powerful new general approach to computer simulation, but also in their infallible ability to prod researchers into asking a host of interesting new questions. This is particularly apparent when EINSTein is run interactively, with its provision for making quick "on-the-fly" changes to various dynamical parameters. Observations immediately lead to a series of *"What if?"* speculations, which in turn lead to further explorations and further questions. Rather than focusing on a single scenario, and estimating the values of simple attrition-based measures of single outcomes ("Who won?"), users of agent-based simulations of combat typically walk away from an interactive session with an enhanced intuition of what the overall combat fitness landscape looks like. Users are also given an opportunity to construct a context for understanding their own conjectures about dynamical combat behavior. The agent-based simulation is therefore a medium in which questions and insights continually feed off one another.

Universal Grammar of Combat?

The last decade has witnessed the development of an entirely new and powerful modeling and simulation paradigm based on the distributed intelligence of swarms of autonomous, but mutually interacting, agents. First applied to natural systems such as ecologies and insect colonies, later to population dynamics and artificial intelligence, and then to social, economic, and cultural evolution, this paradigm has recently finally entered the mainstream consciousness of military operations research.

What lies at the heart of an artificial life approach to simulating combat, is the hope of discovering a fundamental relationship between the set of higher-level emergent processes (penetration, flanking maneuvers, containment, etc.) and the set of low-level primitive actions (movement, communication, firing at an enemy, etc.). Wolfram [51] has conjectured that the macro-level emergent behavior of all cellular automata rules falls into one of only four universality classes, despite the huge number of possible local rules. While EINSTein's rules are obviously more complicated than those of their elementary cellular automata brethren, it is nonetheless tempting to speculate about whether there exists — and, if so, what the properties are, of — a *universal grammar of combat*.

Final Comment

Despite the fact that many of the ideas and tools for studying artificial life systems, not to mention military engagements, are still in their infancy, and the success of multiagent-based modeling depends strongly on developing and nurturing a closeknit but interdisciplinary research community, I am convinced that the role they will play in helping us understand the fundamental processes of warfare will eventually far exceed that of any other mathematical tools heretofore brought to bear on this problem.

As for the present time — following the tragic events of September 11, 2001 — it is hard to overemphasize the critical need for developing new complex systems theory inspired analytical tools and models for understanding the dynamics of the powerful new adversary that has entered our daily consciousness: the *terrorist network*. If ever there was a time for complexity theory to come into its own within the military operations research community — much in the same way as mathematical search theory did in World War II when the need arose for finding and employing novel strategies to search for German U-boats [52] — that time is *now*.

Acknowledgments

I'd like to thank U.S. Marine Corps LtGen (Ret) Paul van Riper, whose vision of applying the lessons of complexity theory to warfare directly inspired the ISAAC and EINSTein projects. I'd also like to thank Lyntis Beard (who coined both of the names ISAAC and EINSTein), Rich Bronowitz, Dave Kelsey, Mike Shlesinger, and David Mazel for encouraging words and many useful discussions. Programming support for EINSTein is very skillfully provided by Fred Richards. Funding was provided, in part, by the Office of Naval Research (contract #N00014-96-D-0001).

References

1. Lanchester FW (1995) Aircraft in Warfare. Lanchester Press.
2. Chase JV (1902) A Mathematical Investigation of the Effect of Superiority in Combats Upon the Sea. In: Fiske BA (1994) The Navy as a Fighting Machine. U.S. Naval Institute Press, Annapolis, MD, Software Pioneers. Springer, Berlin, Heidelberg, New York.
3. Osipov M (1995) The Influence of the Numerical Strength of Engaged Forces in Their Casualties. Naval Research Logistics 42:435–490.
4. Hofbauer J, Sigmund K (1988) Evolutionary Games and Population Dynamics. Cambridge University Press.
5. Taylor JG (1983) Lanchester Models of Warfare. Operations Research Society of America.
6. Hartley DS, Helmbold RL (1995) Validating Lanchester's square law and other attrition models. Naval Research Logistics 42: 609–633.
7. Weiss HK (1957) Lanchester-type models of warfare. Proceedings of 1st Conference on Operations Research, Operations Research Society of America.
8. Fain J (1975) The Lanchester Equations and Historical Warfare. In: Proceedings of the 34th Military Operations Research Symposium. Military Operations Research Society, Alexandria, VA.

9. Richardson LF (1960) Statistics of Deadly Quarrels. Boxwood Press, Pittsburgh.
10. Cowan GA, Pines D, Meltzer D (1994) Complexity: Metaphors, Models and Reality. Addison-Wesley.
11. Kauffman S (1993) Origins of Order. Oxford University Press.
12. Langton CG (1995) Artificial Life: An Overview. MIT Press.
13. Mainzer K (1994) Thinking in Complexity. Springer-Verlag.
14. Beckerman Linda P (1999) The Non-Linear Dynamics of War. Science Applications International Corporation.
15. Beyerchen A (1992) Clausewitz, Nonlinearity, and the Unpredictability of War. International Security 17.
16. Hedgepeth WO (1993) The Science of Complexity for Military Operations Research. Phalanx 26:25–26.
17. Ilachinski A (1996) Land Warfare and Complexity, Part I. CNA Corporation.
18. Ilachinski A (1996) Land Warfare and Complexity, Part II. CNA Corporation.
19. Miller LD, Sulcoski MF (1995) Foreign Physics Research with Military Significance. Defense Intelligence Reference Document.
20. Saperstein A (1995) War and chaos. American Scientist 83:548–557.
21. Tagarev T, Nicholls D (1996) Identification of Chaotic Behavior in Warfare. In: Sulis W, Combs A (eds.) Nonlinear Dynamics in Human Behavior. World Scientific.
22. Maes P (1990) Designing Autonomous Agents. MIT Press.
23. Ferber J (1999) Multi-Agent Systems. Addison-Wesley.
24. Weiss G (1999) Multiagent Systems. MIT Press.
25. Gilbert N, Troitzsch KG (1999) Simulation for the Social Scientist. Open University Press.
26. Gilbert N, Conte R (1995) Artificial Societies. UCL Press.
27. Conte R, Hegselmann R, Terna P (1997) Simulating Social Phenomena. Springer-Verlag.
28. Barrett C (1997) Simulation Science as it Relates to Data/Information Fusion and C2 Systems. Los Alamos.
29. Epstein JM, Axtell R (1996) Growing Artificial Societies. MIT Press.
30. Prietula MJ, Carley KM, Gasser L (1988) Simulating Organizations. MIT Press.
31. Ilachinski A (2000) EINSTein. CNA Corporation.
32. Ilachinski A (1999) EINSTein User's Guide. CNA Corporation.
33. Ilachinski A (1997) Irreducible Semi-Autonomous Adaptive Combat (ISAAC). CNA Corporation.
34. Ilachinski A (2004) Artificial War. World Scientific.
35. Ilachinski A (2001) Cellular Automata. World Scientific.
36. Braitenberg V (1984) Vehicles. MIT Press.
37. Boccara N, Roblin O, Roger M (1994) Automata network predator–prey model with pursuit and evasion. Physical Review E 50:4531–4541.
38. Woodcock AER, Cobb L, Dockery JT (1988) Cellular Automata: A New Method for Battlefield Simulation. Signal 1: 41-50.
39. Varela FJ, Maturana H, Uribe R (1974) Autopoiesis. Biosystems 5:187–196.
40. Lauren MK (2000) Firepower Concentration in Cellular Automata Models. Defense Operational Technology Support Establishment.
41. Krantz H, Schreiber T (1997) Nonlinear Time Analysis. Cambridge University Press.

42. Lauren MK (1999) Characterizing the Difference Between Complex Adaptive and Conventional Combat Models. Defense Operational Technology Support Establishment.
43. Dockery JT, Woodcock AER (1993) The Military Landscape. Woodhead Publishing Limited, Cambridge, England.
44. Bak P (1996) How Nature Works. Springer-Verlag.
45. Roberts DC, Turcotte DL (1988) Fracticality and Self-Organized Criticality of Wars. Fractals 6.
46. Taylor D, Schmal C, Hashim A (2000) Ground Combat Study: Summary of Analysis. CNA Corporation.
47. Edwards SJA (2000) Swarming on the Battlefield. RAND Corporation.
48. Dewar JA, Gillogly J, and Juncosa M (1991) Non-Monotonicty, Chaos, and Combat Models. RAND Corporation.
49. Mitchell M (1996) An Introduction to Genetic Algorithms. MIT Press.
50. Thulasiraman K, Swami M (1992) Graphs: Theory and Algorithms. John Wiley and Sons.
51. Wolfram S (1994) Cellular Automata and Complexity: Collected Papers. Addison-Wesley.
52. Morse PM, Kimball GE (1951) Methods of Operations Research. MIT Press.

8

StarLogo: A Programmable Complex Systems Modeling Environment for Students and Teachers

Andrew Begel and Eric Klopfer

StarLogo is a computer modeling tool that empowers students to understand the world through the design and creation of complex systems models. StarLogo enables students to program software creatures to interact with one another and their environment, and study the emergent patterns from these interactions. Building an easy-to-understand, yet powerful tool for students required a great deal of thought about the design of the programming language, environment, and its implementation. The salient features are StarLogo's great degree of transparency (the capability to see how a simulation is built), its support to let students create their own models (not just use models built by others), its efficient implementation (supporting simulations with thousands of independently executing creatures on desktop computers), and its flexible and simple user interface (which enables students to interact dynamically with their simulation during model testing and validation). The resulting platform provides a uniquely accessible tool that enables students to become full-fledged practitioners of modeling. In addition, we describe the powerful insights and deep scientific understanding that students have developed through the use of StarLogo.

8.1 Background

In the past 20 years a paradigm shift has been taking place in scientific research. A new approach to scientific inquiry has emerged that seeks to understand the intricacies of complex adaptive systems (CAS) by transcending separate disciplines and augmenting traditional experimental methods with the use of sophisticated tools for computer modeling. A growing group of scientists is adopting this approach to understand a range of such systems as varied as the human immune system and the global economy.

Scientists now have more powerful theories and tools for explaining and predicting the behavior of self-organizing, emergent systems, ranging from natural selection and adaptation in local ecologies [15] to economic supply chains [14]. These and many other subjects studied by complexity scientists are introduced to students in middle and high schools. Teachers do not typically teach these subjects as complex systems, but rather as systems that behave more mechanistically. Consequently, students frequently have difficulty understanding the complex dynamics of such systems. For example, most teachers present the topic of ideal gases in physics class as a set of equations to be memorized. Instead, a teacher could present ideal gases as a particular example of a complex system and study it from the point of view of the interactions between gas molecules. Additionally, students tend to hold persistent misconceptions of how complex, adaptive systems work and develop incomplete models of these systems [18]. Moreover, students rarely have the opportunity to understand how to link multiple models together to construct and test alternative representations of situations, something scientists typically do when using models [3].

Using simulations in the classroom can have many advantages. Not only do they allow students to explore systems as coherent bodies of knowledge instead of a disjoint collection of facts, but simulations allow them to explore systems at temporal and spatial scales that are not normally accessible to them in the classroom. Students can examine topics from molecular interactions to the evolution of new species which are difficult or impossible to explore experimentally without the aid of computers. Computer simulations in the classroom can be a pervasive glue that brings together experimental experiences to allow students to construct their own understandings of systems.

In this paper, we describe an approach to modeling, implemented using the StarLogo development environment, that makes it possible for students to study, hypothesize, construct, test, and evaluate their own models of complex systems. First, we show how StarLogo's approach to modeling is different than more traditional modeling environments. Then, we propose criteria that we believe to be important in designing such a modeling environment for students. Next, we introduce the StarLogo platform by way of an example model and describe StarLogo's major actors: the turtles, the patches, and the observer. Viewed from a purely technological perspective, StarLogo has evolved over the past 10 years from its origins running on a massively parallel supercomputer to one that runs on desktop computers of the kind found commonly in schools today. We describe, in a slightly more technical fashion, how StarLogo is structured internally as well as discuss key design decisions that distinguish StarLogo from a professional modeling environment to one that is especially suited for students learning to model. We then talk about our approach to bring StarLogo to schools through workshops utilizing our new book, *Adventures in Modeling*. Finally, we tell some anecdotal stories about our students and their models from past workshops we have given, and then conclude.

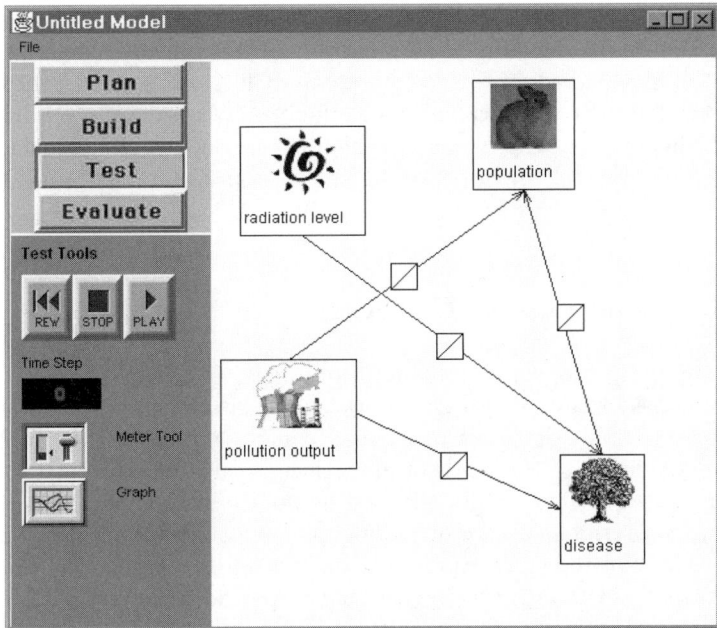

Fig. 8.1. A model built in Model-It that shows the impact of disease, pollution, and radiation on a the numbers of rabbits in a population (courtesy of Model-It).

8.2 Approaches to Modeling

Science has long relied on the use of scientific models based on ordinary differential equations (ODE) that can be solved (in simple cases) without computers. These models describe how aggregate quantities change in a system, where a variable in the model might be the size of a population or the proportion of individuals infected by a disease. The mathematics required for these models is advanced, but several commonly used modeling programs like Model-It 8.1 [16], Stella [10], and MatLab [6] have graphical interfaces that make them easy to construct. These programs have become very popular in the classroom as well as the laboratory. The user places a block on the screen for each quantity and draws arrows between the blocks to represent changes in those quantities. While this interface does not remove the need for the user to learn math, it lowers the barrier for entry. However, the abstraction required to model these systems at an aggregate level is a difficult process for many people, which often limits the utility of this modeling approach.

Additionally, many of the systems studied in the classroom are more amenable to simulation using agent-based modeling. Rather than tracking aggregate properties like population size, agent-based models track individual organisms, each of which can have its own traits. For instance, to simulate how birds flock, one might make a number of birds and have each bird modify its flight behavior based on its position relative to the other birds. A simple rule for the individual's behavior (stay a certain distance away from the nearest neighbor) might lead to a complex aggregate behavior (flocking) without the aggregate behavior being explicitly specified anywhere in the model. These emergent phenomena, where complex macro-behaviors arise from the interactions of simple micro-behaviors, are prevalent in many systems and are often difficult to understand without special tools.

8.3 Additional Design Criteria

In designing an appropriate modeling tool for use in the K–12 classroom, we needed to consider several design criteria. One criterion is the foundation on agent-based as opposed to aggregate-based modeling. This approach is not only more amenable to the kinds of models that we would like to study in the classroom, but it is also readily adopted by novice modelers.

The next criterion is to create a modeling environment that is a "transparent box." Many of the simulations that have been used in classrooms to date are purchased for the purpose of exploring a specific topic such as Mendelian genetics or ideal gases. Modeling software has been shown to be particularly successful in supporting learning around sophisticated concepts often thought to be too difficult for students to grasp [12, 17]. This software allows students to explore systems, but they are "black box" models that do not allow the students to see the underlying models. The process of *creating* models — as opposed to simply using models built by someone else — not only fosters model-building skills but also helps to develop a greater understanding of the concepts embedded in the model [9, 11, 17]. When learners build their own models, they can decide what topic they want to study and how they want to study it. As learners' investigations proceed, they can determine the aspects of the system on which they want to focus, and refine their models as their understanding of the system grows. Perhaps most importantly, building models helps learners develop a sound understanding of both how a system works and why it works that way. For example, to build a model of a cart rolling down an inclined plane in the population Interactive Physics program, a student could drag a cart and a board onto the screen and indicate the forces that act about each object. In doing so, the student assumes the existence of an unseen model that incorporates mass, friction, gravity, etc. that calculates acceleration of the cart. It would be a much different experience to allow the student to construct the underlying model herself and have that act on the objects that she created.

We also considered the level of detail that we felt would be appropriate in student-built models. All too often, students want to create extremely intricate models that exhaustively describe systems. But it is difficult to learn from these "systems models" [13]. It is more valuable for students to design and create more generalized "idea models" that abstract away as much about a

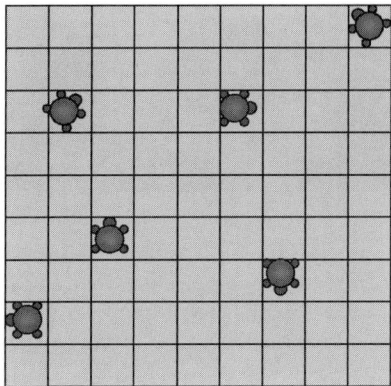

Fig. 8.2. Turtles move around on a grid of patches.

system as possible and boil it down to the most salient element. The ability to make these abstractions and generalize scientific principles is central to the idea of modeling. For example, a group of students might want to create a model of a stream behind their school, showing each species of insect, fish, and plant in the stream. Building such a model is not only an extremely large and intricate task, but the resulting model would be extremely sensitive to the vast number of parameters. Instead, the students should be encouraged to build a model of a more generalized system that includes perhaps one animal and one plant species. The right software should support the building of such "idea models."

Based on these criteria and our approach to modeling, we created a computer modeling environment, named StarLogo, that we describe in the next section.

8.4 The StarLogo Platform

To enable students to build their own CAS models, we developed StarLogo, a programming language and environment specifically designed to support simulation design, construction, and testing [8]. While there have been several versions of StarLogo on different platforms through the years (detailed ahead), they have each striven to meet the design goals described above and provide a program language and development platform that is accessible to students of a broad age range. Each version of StarLogo has shared many common language features and an underlying metaphor that describes the StarLogo world in terms of three entities — turtles, patches, and an observer. "Turtles" is our term for all entities that move. On other platforms these might be called "agents." But StarLogo's lineage brings with it the turtles that defined Logo, along with much of that language as well. While we call them "turtles" generically, they might be rabbits, atoms, or cars in any particular model.

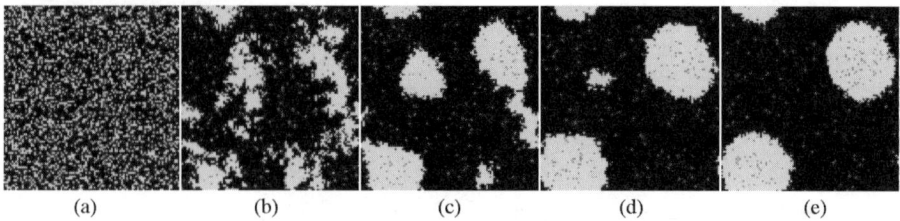

(a)   (b)   (c)   (d)   (e)

Fig. 8.3. This figure shows the time evolution of the termites project. At the beginning (a), all termites and wood chips are randomly scattered over the patches. As the termites pick up and drop the wood chips (b), the number of piles begins to decrease (c). Small piles shrink (d) and eventually disappear (e). If we run this further, all of the wood chips will end up in one pile.

The turtles walk around on top of a grid composed of patches. If you think of the grid as a large checkerboard, each square on the checkerboard is a patch (and the turtles would be the checkers moving over the board: see Fig. 8.2). The turtles can interact with the patches by responding to their features, or even modifying their features. One way for turtles to modify the patches is by using the pen that each turtle carries to draw on the patches. The patches are also able to run their own instructions, through which they can modify themselves or the turtles that are standing on them.

Finally, there is a single observer that watches over the entire grid. Continuing with the checkers metaphor, the observer might be thought of as a person playing (solitaire) checkers on this checkerboard filled with the turtles and patches. The observer takes care of certain operations like clearing the whole board, creating new turtles, and keeping track of time that either cannot be done by individual turtles, or are easier to conduct through the observer.

8.4.1 Termites Example

To familiarize readers with StarLogo, we present a small StarLogo project about termites. This project is inspired by the behavior of termites gathering wood chips into piles. The termites follow a set of simple rules. Each termite wanders randomly. If it bumps into a wood chip, it picks the chip up and continues to wander around. When it bumps into another wood chip, it finds a nearby empty space and puts its wood chip down. We show a run of this simulation in Fig. 8.3.

We look at the StarLogo source code to get a feel for what the language feels like. The following is the setup procedure for termites.

```
to setup
    clearall
    if (random 100) > 80 [setpatchcolor yellow]
    create-turtles 200
```

```
ask-turtles
   [ setcolor red
      setxy random (screen-edge * 2)
            random (screen-edge * 2) ]
end
```

To begin, we kill all of the turtles and set the patch colors to black. Then, on each patch, we throw a random 100-sided die. If it exceeds a threshold, we set the patch's color to yellow (i.e., we give it a wood chip). We then create 200 turtles (termites), ask them to color themselves red, and scatter them around the screen.

```
to go
   search-for-chip
   find-new-pile
   find-empty-spot
end
```

The go procedure is the main loop. First, a termite looks for a wood chip and picks it up. Then it wanders until it finds another wood chip in a pile and finds a place to put it down.

```
to search-for-chip
   if patchcolor = yellow
      [ stamp black jump 20 stop ]
   wiggle
   search-for-chip
end
```

In search-for-chip, a termite wanders around, wiggling, until it is standing on a yellow patch. That means there is a wood chip there. It picks up the wood chip and jumps 20 turtle steps away.

```
to wiggle
   forward 1
   right random 50
   left random 50
end
```

A termite wiggles by moving forward one turtle step, then turning right and left a random number of degrees.

```
to find-new-pile
   if patchcolor = yellow [ stop ]
   wiggle
   find-new-pile
end
```

The termite then wiggles around until it finds a pile to put down the wood chip.

```
to find-empty-spot
   if patchcolor = black
      [ stamp yellow get-away stop ]
   setheading random 360
   forward 1
   find-empty-spot
end
```

A termite does not want to put a wood chip down on top of another one, so it moves forward in a random direction until it finds an empty patch. Once it finds that spot, it stamps the patch to make it yellow (giving it the wood chip), and then jumps away to look for new wood chips.

```
to get-away
   setheading random 360
   jump 20
   if patchcolor = black [ stop ]
   get-away
end
```

To get away, a termite keeps jumping 20 steps in random directions until it lands on a spot without any wood chips. Then it starts the cycle over again, looking for another wood chip to pick up.

One interesting thing to notice about this model — over time, the number of piles of wood chips decreases. Why? There's certainly nothing obviously programmed into the model to make this happen. But, inevitably, when the simulation is finished, the termites will be left with one pile. How does this happen? First, ask yourself how a pile can disappear. A pile disappears when termites carry away all of the chips. Can a new pile be formed? No, there is no way to start a new pile by a deliberate termite action, since termites only put their wood chips next to other wood chips. This behavior will only increase an existing pile's size; it will not create a new separate pile. In fact, the only way to create a "new" pile is to take away enough wood chips to split an existing pile into two. However, this is quite rare except when a pile gets very small. So, overall, the number of piles must decrease until there is only one left. This is known as an emergent property of the model — an aggregate behavior that is unexpected given the simple rules programmed into the model.

Next, we will begin the discussion of how StarLogo works internally. This discussion will be more technical than the rest of this article, but will reveal some interesting design tradeoffs that are visible directly to the user and affect the fidelity of the models that can be built.

8.5 StarLogo Design Through the Ages

Building an agent-based modeling environment like StarLogo is not a trivial task. It involves balancing the pedagogical needs of students with the efficiency requirements of running *thousands* of agents at the same time. In this section, we will give a little flavor of what actually runs under the hood to make StarLogo go.

There are three main pieces of work: the design of the StarLogo virtual machine (which has changed over time as the technology has improved); the process scheduler, which determines the order in which turtle, patch, and observer operations run; and the turtle, patch and observer data structures (which form the core data of the StarLogo runtime system).

8.5.1 The StarLogo Virtual Machine

StarLogo has more going on in parallel than most other computer environments. Several thousand turtles move about on a grid of over 10,000 patches, each one independently executing code. Our first implementation of this system was on an actual parallel computer called the Connection Machine. With 16,384 physical processors, each running at 8 MHz, we could devote one processor to each turtle and have plenty to spare. This gave us plenty of parallelism, but the machine's bulk and extreme cost made it all but inaccessible to schoolchildren.

To solve this problem, we brought StarLogo to the Apple Macintosh in 1994. Our challenge was to bring our parallel environment to the moderately underpowered, single-processor, desktop computers that were common in schools at the time (our target platform at the time was a Mac IIfx, with only a single 25 MHz processor and 16 MB of RAM). A single processor would have to be made to emulate thousands of "virtual processors."

How does a computer run more than one thing at a time? Instead of trying to run all programs at the same time (which is impossible on a computer with only one processor), we run a single program by itself for a short amount of time and then switch to the next one. Each program is deceived into thinking it is the only program running on the processor. Most operating systems such as Windows, UNIX, or MacOS are designed to run tens or hundreds of these programs (called processes) at a time, each one getting one little slice of the processor's time (usually around 16 milliseconds per slice). Since they are switching so fast, the user perceives everything on the computer as running in parallel. StarLogo's needs require that a processor be able to switch between tens of thousands of processes at a time, which is beyond the capabilities supported by any operating system.

To achieve the desired performance, we created a *virtual machine* — a simulation of one computer within another — to run the StarLogo programming language. Within this machine (written in extremely low-level machine language for performance), we implemented a large number of turtle, patch, and observer commands and created an extremely lightweight multiprocessing system to run all its processes.

The StarLogo virtual machine is very similar to the one developed for the Cricket [7], a project run by the Lifelong Kindergarten Group at the MIT Media Laboratory. A Cricket is a tiny computer powered by a 9-volt battery that can control two motors and receive information from two sensors. Crickets are equipped with an infrared communication system that allows them to communicate with each other. Powered by a Microchip PIC processor, the virtual machine in Cricket Logo holds about 1000 words of instruction memory and only a few dozen words of RAM. Even though a modern desktop computer is much more powerful than a PIC microcontroller, we can justify using a similar virtual machine for both the Cricket and StarLogo. Even though the desktop computer is much faster than the PIC, the PIC only has to run one process, while the desktop computer has to run thousands. Similar memory constraints hold as well.

For several years after the initial Macintosh version of StarLogo, we received requests by an increasing number of users who wished to see StarLogo on a Windows PC. Around this time (1995), the Java programming language was introduced by Sun Microsystems, Inc., so we decided to take the opportunity and rewrite StarLogo in this new cross-platform language. Designing it in the same way as our Macintosh version, we were able to directly port over all of the code for StarLogo's virtual machine into Java fairly quickly, and within three days of programming, we had a first implementation of a turtle world running. Gradually, over a period of a few years, we recreated the rest of the StarLogo experience in the Java realm. This is the version now available at our web site: http://education.mit.edu/starlogo.

8.5.2 The Anatomy of a Virtual Machine

What exactly is a virtual machine? A virtual machine is a computer program that simulates the behavior of a physical processor. An example of a commercial virtual machine is Virtual PC for MacOS, which simulates an Intel Pentium processor on a Macintosh computer. Simulations of commercial processors make up a small number of the kinds of virtual machines available, however. Designers take advantage of the inherent flexibility of software to create virtual machines that simulate processors never before found in the market. The StarLogo virtual machine is this kind of virtual machine; it simulates a Logo processor.

Logo is a programming language invented in the 1960s by Wallace Feurzig and Seymour Papert. A variant of the Lisp programming language, Logo was designed to be easy to learn and use by children. It also tends to be easy to implement using a virtual Logo processor (a piece of software that our group at MIT has created numerous times for almost every project we undertake). StarLogo's Logo processor contains two types of commands: Logo language operations, and StarLogo primitive commands. Ten commands are used for implementing Logo; these handle procedure invocation and returns and manage data and instruction lists. The other 300 primitives provide support for moving the turtle around on the screen, communicating among the turtles, patches, and observer, observing and modifying the turtle's environment, reading and writing turtle, patch, and observer state, and user variables, and executing mathematics and control functions.

All modern machines (including simulated processors such as the one we built) execute in similar fashion. A user begins by starting a program (often by double-clicking on an icon). The operating system loads the program's code into memory, creates a new process to store the program's execution state, and jumps to the program's starting point. The processor loads the program's instructions, one by one, into its execution unit. After each instruction runs, the processor increments its instruction pointer (which points to the next instruction to be executed) and continues. After some amount of time, a timer goes off and signals to the processor that the current process has been running for too long. The *process scheduler* captures the run-time state of the current process, stores it, finds another process that is ready to execute, and swaps it in. This swap is known as a *context switch*. The process scheduler is responsible for performing context switches, as well as for determining the order of the processes that get to execute.

The StarLogo virtual machine adds three more pieces to this generic processor: the turtles, the patches, and the observer. Each of these entities is an object in memory. Turtles are made up of turtle state (the coordinates of the turtle on the screen, its id number, its color, heading, breed, shape, pen state (up or down), visibility (shown or hidden), and a timer), bookkeeping data (a pointer to the patch the turtle is currently standing on, a set of "underme" and "overme" pointers to keep track of turtles stack on top of one another, a pointer to the partner turtle used when this turtle is communicating with another one, and a true-false variable that indicates when this turtle is alive (useful for generating proper error conditions)), and a collection of user-defined variables (in StarLogo terminology, *turtles-own* variables).

A patch is like a turtle in structure, but contains less information. Patch state consists of the patch's coordinates on the screen, a patch color, and a pointer to the first turtle standing on the patch. Patches contain less bookkeeping data as well, only requiring a pointer to a partner turtle used when the patch is communicating with a turtle. Finally, patches also contain a collection of user-defined variables called *patches-own* variables.

The observer contains only a collection of user-defined variables called *globals*.

8.5.3 The Process Scheduler and Its Processes

An important part of the design of StarLogo is the process scheduler. As we discussed above, the scheduler controls the order of execution of the processes that are running. It also controls how long a process gets to run before being swapped out for another. Both of these tasks are controlled by a carefully chosen policy. We will discuss the rationale for our particular choices ahead.

Recall that StarLogo is intended to run the turtle and patch processes fast enough to appear to be running in parallel. In order to maintain the fiction of parallelism with a single physical processor, we must context-switch rapidly among all the processes that all turtles, patches, and the observer are executing. There are two forms of context-switching that we could choose from. We could support *preemptive* multiprocessing, in which a timer goes off every few milliseconds and causes the virtual machine to context-switch, or we could choose *cooperative* multiprocessing, and only context-switch at carefully chosen points in the program.

We chose the latter for several reasons, but the most important is that under the former (preemptive multiprocessing), synchronization issues would become unnecessarily exposed to the user. For instance, the following common StarLogo idiom would not work as expected:

```
if count-turtles-here > 1
    [mate-with one-of-turtles-here]
```

A turtle is looking for another with whom to mate. It looks on the current patch to see if there is any other turtle there. If there is, it mates with it by asking for its turtle id and calling a user-defined procedure mate-with. Under preemptive multiprocessing, it is possible for the virtual machine to context-switch between the condition `count-turtles-here > 1` and the consequent of the if statement, *mate-with one-of-turtles-here*; if this happens, in one glance the first turtle might see the other one on its patch, but in the next, the other turtle may have moved before the first turtle has had to a chance to mate with it!

To avoid this kind of problem, we only allow context switches at "safe" times such as the end of each command. A *command*, in Logo, is what we call a primitive operation or user function that does not return a value (e.g., `setcolor blue`, `forward 10`). In contrast, a *reporter* is a primitive or user function that does return a value (e.g., 3, 5 + 7, `color-of 5`). In our cooperatively multiprocessing virtual machine, we elect to context-switch between commands, but not after reporters. This gives the if statement above a guarantee of *atomicity* (meaning that the two statements must execute together without any context switching in between). The reporter in the predicate is guaranteed still to be true when the first command in the consequent executes. This policy also enables the fairly common idiom of fetch and update (e.g., `setfoo foo + 1`) to work without user-supplied synchronization, as well.

Several primitives interact with context switches. One in particular is the forward command. When a turtle wants to move in the direction of its current heading, it calls forward with a number of turtle steps. If we implemented this by context switching after each turtle went forward the full number of turtle steps, we would see (if we slowed the computer down) individual turtles scooting, one by one, to their final locations. We wish to maintain an illusion of realistic-looking parallelism, so we want to see all of the turtles move forward one step at a time. To do this, we context-switch in the middle of the forward primitive after the turtle has taken one step. We jump back to the middle of the forward primitive when the turtle is rescheduled. Context switching on this granularity gives us the nice-looking parallel behavior we want.

StarLogo has two scheduling policies that can be selected by the user. The scheduling policies influence the order of process execution during each *once-through*. A once-through is one complete iteration of all of the processes — a unit of execution in our scheduler, where we are sure that we have given each process one unit of time to execute. Between consecutive once-throughs, the particular scheduling policy chosen may affect the order of process execution without accidentally starving any particular processes of a chance to run. The first scheduling policy executes each process *in-order* as it appears in the scheduler. This policy gives reasonable user-visible behavior in many cases; however, it sometimes introduces artifacts into a user's program.

For example, consider a rope made up of individual turtles spread across the screen. If we jiggle one of the turtles, it should exert a spring force on its two neighbors. If we force the leftmost turtle to move up and down in a sine wave, it will send a sine wave down the right side of the rope. To make this happen, each turtle computes its change in velocity as a function of its distance from its two neighbors, and then moves. If we run this spring force process for each turtle, and the turtles execute it from left to right across the screen, the first turtle to move is the one directly to the right of the sine wave turtle. This turtle's motion propagates to the right and the sine wave appears to travel to the right across the turtles. Consider what would happen if the spring force process instead executed from right to left. The rightmost turtle will not move, because its left neighbor has not moved. Its left neighbor will not move either. In fact, no turtle will move until we execute the spring force function for the turtle directly to the right of the sine wave turtle. The next iteration repeats this nonmotion except where the wave has propagated to the right by one turtle. This kind of artifact can be completely unexpected but occurs because the turtle processes are executing in series, rather than in parallel.

To eliminate this artifact, we support a *randomized* scheduling policy. Before each once-through, we randomize the order of all processes in the scheduler. This produces somewhat more disconcerting appearing behavior (a more jagged motion when you see a line of turtles do something), but it removes order-dependent artifacts and more accurately simulates parallelism in most models.

8.5.4 The StarLogo Interface

The implementation of the StarLogo virtual machine is critical to its operation. But to most users, these details are transparent, allowing them to take on the modeling challenge at hand. Instead, what most users experience is

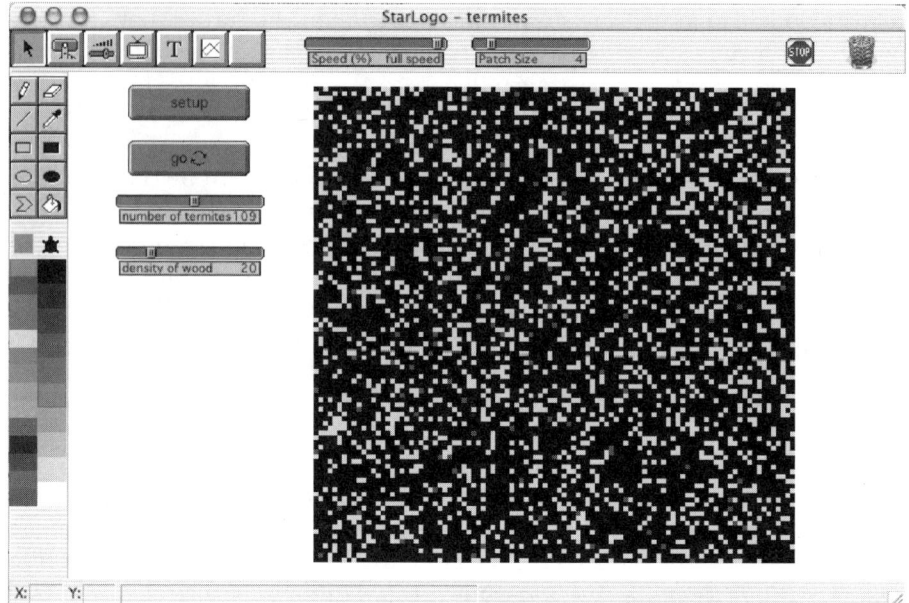

Fig. 8.4. The StarLogo 2.0 user interface for the Termites project. There are two user-created buttons: setup runs the user's setup procedure, and go is a forever button that execute the main loop of the model. There are two sliders that enable a user of the model to control the initial number of termites created as well as the density of the wood chips in the environment.

a user-friendly graphical environment that simultaneously facilitates the creation of models and an accompanying user interface. A user of a model is presented with a screen that displays the running model along with the interface elements that control it (Fig. 8.4).

All user interface elements are placed on the screen by merely clicking on the appropriate tool and then on a blank space in the StarLogo window. The creator of the model can then specify the instructions or values associated with that user interface element. There are several types of user interface elements in StarLogo, including tools for input, output, and help. The primary user interface elements in StarLogo are buttons and sliders.

Buttons control the execution of procedures. For example, in the termites model there is a button that controls the setup procedures, which creates the initial distribution of termites and wood. (A button behaves similarly to an icon in Windows or MacOS. When it is pushed, StarLogo creates one process for every turtle that exists and starts to execute the instructions in the virtual machine.) The termites model also contains a go button that executes the instructions for the termites to move around and pick up wood. This button is different than the setup button in that once it is pressed down it stays down until it is pressed again. This kind of button, known as a forever button and represented by the two looping arrows, causes the turtles to continuously follow the prescribed instructions, until the user pops the button using the mouse. (When the user pops a button, it causes the StarLogo process scheduler to find the processes associated with the button, and remove them from the running process list.)

Sliders allow the user to control global variables in the model. The sliders might affect the model at setup time (e.g., by controlling the initial distribution of termites and wood) or dynamically at run time (e.g., by changing the probability that a termite picks up wood when it sees it). The slider values are changed by clicking and dragging on the slider to manipulate the designated variable. For example, in the termites model the user can specify the number of initial termites or the density of wood.

The ability to design and implement a simple user interface makes the StarLogo modeling experience highly interactive. In addition to buttons and sliders, modelers can place monitors that provide continuously updated numeric output, labels and legends that assist in the operation and interpretation of the model, and graphs that give visual feedback from the models. Together these tools allow developers to rapidly create useful models.

8.6 Learning to Model Through *Adventures in Modeling*

Using computer simulations of complex adaptive systems as a platform, we have crafted an introduction to scientific modeling [4, 5]. We have found that these tools can enable students to become full-fledged practitioners of modeling [1]. Students design scientific models and then go on to investigate and explore those same models. The use of these tools allows nonexperts to act as scientists, creating and exploring models of phenomena in the world around them, evaluating and critiquing those models, refining and validating their own mental models, and improving their understandings [1].

The StarLogo Workshops are designed to introduce participants to the computational and cognitive aspects of modeling complex, dynamic systems. During these workshops, participants work together to design, build, and analyze agent-based computer models. Participants engage in an iterative process of model creation and scientific investigation as they explore important scientific principles and processes. We design the workshops to foster a playful, cooperative, creative spirit, while at the same time providing adequate structure for learning how to build models. To accomplish this balance between structure and exploration, we organize the workshops around a set of open-ended StarLogo design challenges on the computer and a series of off-computer activities in which participants enact and analyze a simulation.

Each challenge is a problem statement that is meant to guide participants' explorations and get their creative juices flowing. For example, one challenge asks participants to build a model in which creatures change their environment and subsequently react to those changes. In response to this challenge, one might create a model of a beaver, altering its environment by cutting down trees to build a dam, or termites chewing on a log to create passageways. Every challenge includes sample projects, which teachers are encouraged to explore. The challenges and accompanying sample projects facilitate model design and construction, build familiarity with the StarLogo environment, and introduce the principles of complex systems.

Though "on-screen" computer modeling is one focus of our workshops, "off-screen" activities provide another way to connect abstract notions of scientific systems to personal experience [1]. These activities allow participants to think about concepts like exponential growth, local versus global information, and group decision-making from a personal perspective. For instance, in one activity, participants "fly" around a parking lot trying to form cohesive "bird flocks" without the assistance of a leader.

Recently, we have captured the essentials of our workshops in the book *Adventures in Modeling: Exploring Complex, Dynamic Systems with StarLogo* [2] published by Teachers College Press. This book brings the design challenges and supporting activities to students and educators everywhere. *Adventures in Modeling* includes a series of 10 StarLogo design challenges, and a complementary set of ten participatory activities. Additionally, we provide guidelines for educators in facilitating the challenges and activities, for integrating them into a variety of classes, and for mapping them to state curriculum standards. As a package, it provides a flexible but well-defined pathway for teachers to follow.

8.7 Lessons Learned

It is difficult to appreciate the many ways that people use and learn from StarLogo without seeing it in action. In the following section we relate several stories of how we have observed people use and learn from StarLogo. Each of the stories highlights aspects of our software and our approach to modeling that we have found to be unique and enlightening.

8.7.1 Fire

Often science classes dictate the explorations that students undertake during their laboratories. Typically these "experiments" follow a prescribed set of instructions outlined in a cookbook fashion. These experiences leave little room for the students to inject any of their own personal interests or fascinations into the experiments. Not surprisingly, students often lose interest in these experiments and lose sight of the real scientific method as they search for the "right" answer to the experiment.

One of the powers of StarLogo is that it allows students to conduct explorations of systems that are interesting to them. Students can explore systems that are personally interesting. This brings the flexibility of a science fair to

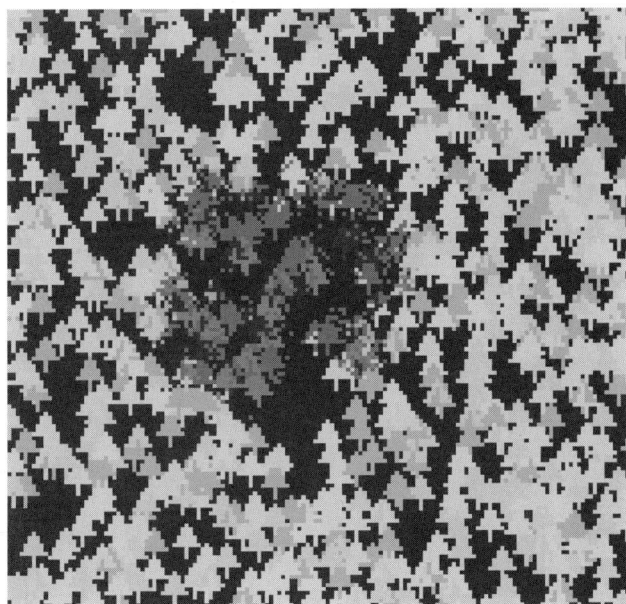

Fig. 8.5. A student-generated model of a forest fire. The different color trees have variable flammability. The dark gray trees in the middle are burning, and the lighter gray trees are already burned.

the classroom, but removes the constraints of the size, location, time scale, or cost of the system that the student wants to explore. A student could easily explore the interactions of protons and electrons in an atom, or the evolution of a trait over hundreds of generations — systems that normally could not be explored in a classroom.

During the summer of 2000 forest fires raged across New Mexico, causing extensive damage across thousands of acres and making national news headlines. At that time a student summer school was taking place in Santa Fe, New Mexico. One group of three ninth-grade girls was intrigued by the forest fires that summer. There were often small forest fires in that area at that time of year, but what made them so bad this time? They decided to create a model of forest fires to explore this phenomenon.

The model that they created initially included many factors. After some exploration they narrowed down the factors of interest to wind, rain, and density of trees. They made sliders that controlled each of these factors and recorded the number of trees burned, number of trees alive, and time to extinguishing of fire for several combinations of these parameters. In the end they were able to develop an understanding of each of the factors in isolation, as well as in combination such as high density of trees, low rain, and high winds.

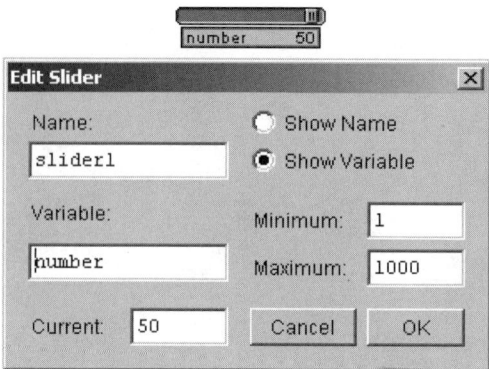

Fig. 8.6. A StarLogo slider (top) is clicked on to change the maximum value from 50 to 1000.

8.7.2 But This One Goes to 1000

One of the most important design features of StarLogo is that all aspects of the models and modeling environment are open to user inspection and manipulation. While the designer of a model might set parameters or specify particular behaviors, this information is always accessible to the user and can be changed.

Recently, a fifth-grade class that was beginning to learn StarLogo by playing with a sample project from the *Adventures in Modeling* book. The model included many buttons and sliders that controlled the movement and creation of turtles. One boy was fiddling with the slider that controlled the numbers of turtles that were on the screen, which, by default, ranged from 1 to 50. At some point, he double-clicked on the slider to see what it would do. He was then presented with a dialog box that controlled the minimum and maximum values for that slider. Being a fifth-grade boy, he immediately replaced the seemingly small value of 50 turtles with a new maximum of 1000 turtles. He tried out the new value and quickly proclaimed his finding as "cool" since the new patterns were much different than the old ones with 50 turtles.

While this innovation was interesting, it might have taken quite some time for others in the room to make similar changes if each one of them had to independently discover this same mechanism. But the accessibility of StarLogo, and the social atmosphere that it facilitates in the classroom, permits and encourages the sharing of information. Within minutes of the boy's discovery of the way to change the slider, nearly half the class had changed their sliders in a similar way. Of course, this being a fifth-grade class the idea never jumped the boy–girl divide, and until they were forced to share, the girls were left out of the loop.

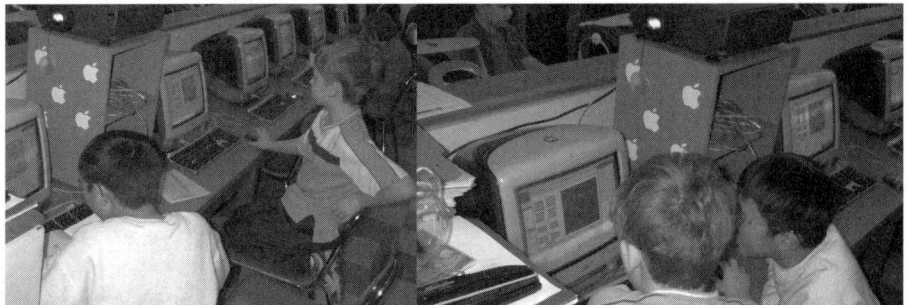

Fig. 8.7. Two students working exploring a StarLogo model. A student makes a discovery (left) and shares it with his neighbor (right).

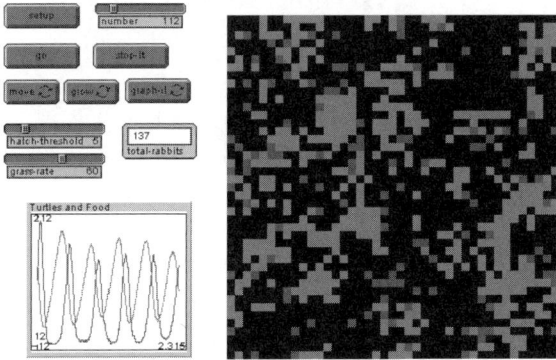

Fig. 8.8. The *Rabbits and Grass* model showing the oscillations in predator–prey populations over time. The rabbits (red) increase as grass disappears (green is plentiful). The rabbits soon deplete their resources, and die off, allowing the grass to return. The return in food is followed closely by a return of rabbits.

8.7.3 The Evolution of Rabbits and Grass

StarLogo models have an advantage over off-the-shelf simulations when it comes to integrating them into the curriculum. Unlike typical purchased simulations that are closed off from being changed by the user, StarLogo models can be customized to fit the unique needs of each classroom. One good example of this customization started with our *Rabbits and Grass* project that has long been a part of StarLogo. In *Rabbits and Grass* the rabbits (represented by red turtles) move around randomly on the screen, using up small amounts of energy as they move, but gaining energy as they eat grass (green patches) when they encounter it. If the rabbits gain enough energy, they can reproduce (by binary fission), but if they lose all of their energy, they will die. These rules lead to the classic predator–prey oscillations that are characteristic of the Lotka–Volterra equations often studied in beginning calculus.

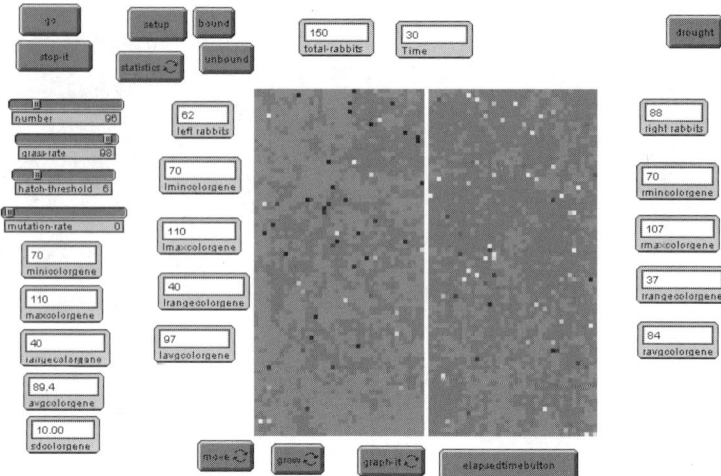

Fig. 8.9. The speciation model, showing the two populations of rabbits and grass divided by an impassable white barrier. The two populations can be given the same, or different selection pressures, and students can observe how long it takes to create a new "species."

Some time ago, Noah, a biology teacher who was in one of the *Adventures in Modeling* workshops, was tinkering around with the *Rabbits and Grass* model and decided to make a small change. Instead of the rabbits, all being red when they were created, they were randomly assigned a color. When the modified model ran for a couple of oscillations, quickly there were only one or two colors of rabbits left. After searching through the code for a possible bug that would lead to this behavior, Noah realized that this was indeed not a bug, but a feature of his new model. The predator–prey model was now a model of genetic drift. As the rabbit population got very small on the downside of the population oscillations, there would only be a few rabbits left. Those remaining rabbits would found the next generation of rabbits that would reproduce rapidly when the food became more plentiful. The offspring of these rabbits would be the same colors as they were, leading to a population in the next generation with limited colors.

Noah said that the students in his class rarely understand this bottleneck effect after reading it in their texts. But there are no traditional laboratories that can help the students explore this and related phenomena first-hand. So Noah set out to build an entire suite of *Rabbits and Grass* models for teaching ecology and evolution to his students. He built models with sexual and asexual reproduction, selection, mutation and genetic drift; and his model that put it all together was a model of speciation. In the speciation model, students can apply different selection pressures to a population of rabbits that is split due to an earthquake that isolates the two populations. These principles are difficult to teach to high school students, perhaps because the time scales are so long. As students experience evolutionary phenomena in real time through these models, Noah says that his students are developing a much deeper understanding of the concepts, and enjoying themselves in the process. In fact, a neighboring biology class complained that Noah's class was having too much fun.

8.7.4 The Tides Are Turning

In another of our recent *Adventures in Modeling* workshops, two of the participants were interested in exploring the patterns in formation of tidal sandbars. This phenomenon is difficult to study in nature because of the large temporal and spatial scales required. Most modeling tools are not applicable to this purpose either, because this process is intensely visual. So these participants were excited to be able to have an opportunity to explore this phenomenon.

The modelers started their project by borrowing a landscape generation procedure from another project. This gave them the capability to create underwater terrains with some existing variation in sand height. From there they set out to implement wave action. They represented waves by a line that swept from left to right on the screen, moving some of the underlying sand to adjacent patches. After exploring this version for some time, they weren't satisfied with the scale at which they saw the sandbars changing. So they decided to add another feature that they thought might be important — tides. Tides were implemented by rising and falling water tables that caused underlying larger-scale changes in the sand and also interacted with the waves as they moved across the water. The resulting model produced some striking visualizations of tidal and wave movement of sandbars.

8.8 Conclusion

StarLogo provides many unique benefits to students when used in the classroom. It can change the way that kids view both science and technology as well as the relationship between the two. By empowering kids to "take over the technology," StarLogo allows students to become creators, not just consumers of technology. It also helps students develop a deep understanding of scientific concepts as they design, build, and explore models of systems in which they are personally invested. Further, StarLogo provides an opportunity to engage students in what we deem "the real scientific method," the messy process of iteratively designing experiments, learning about systems, and subsequently modifying experiments.

While StarLogo has met with much success in many classrooms, there are still a lot of students left to reach. But we, too, are engaged in an iterative process of model building, where the StarLogo world is our model. As we learn from our own experiments in the classroom use of StarLogo, we modify the tool to better meet the needs of our audience. This means providing greater accessibility and applicability through the development of new tools and techniques. This spring, we once again enter the design phase for "StarLogo: The Next Generation" and will begin constructing the software and developing new workshops later on this year.

Acknowledgments

Mitchel Resnick, Vanessa Colella, Brian Silverman, and countless MIT undergraduate student researchers have provided inspiration and ideas for the StarLogo project. We are grateful to C. Andrew Frank for helpful comments on an earlier draft of this paper. The LEGO Company and the National Science Foundation provided financial support.

References

1. Colella V (2000) Participatory simulations: Building collaborative understanding through immersive dynamic modeling. Journal of the Learning Sciences 9:471–500.
2. Colella V, Klopfer E and Resnick M (2001) Adventures in modeling: Exploring complex, dynamic systems with StarLogo. Teachers College Press, New York.
3. Frederiksen JR and White BY (2000) Sources of difficulty in students' understanding causal models for physical systems. In: Proceedings of the Annual Meeting of the American Educational Research Association. New Orleans, LA.
4. Klopfer E and Colella V (1999) Structuring collaboration in workshops and classrooms: The starlogo community of learners. In: Proceedings of Computer Supported Collaborative Learning Conference. Palo Alto, CA.
5. Klopfer E and Colella V (2000) Modeling for understanding. In: Proceedings of the Society for Information Technology and Teacher Education (SITE) Conference. San Diego, CA.
6. Mathworks, http://www.mathworks.com/.
7. Mikhak B, Berg R, Martin F, Resnick M and Silverman B (2000) Robots for Kids: Exploring New Technologies for Learning Experiences. In: Mindstorms and Beyond: Evolution of a Construction Kit for Magical Machines. Morgan Kaufman, Academic Press, San Francisco.
8. Resnick M (1994) Turtles, Termites, and Traffic Jams: Explorations in Massively Parallel Microworlds (Complex Adaptive Systems). MIT Press, Cambridge, MA.
9. Resnick M, Bruckman A, and Martin F (1996) Pianos not stereos: Creating computational construction kits. Interactions 3:40–50.
10. Roberts M, Anderson D, Deal R, Garet M, and Shaffer W (1983) Introduction to computer simulation: A system dynamics modeling approach. Addison-Wesley, Reading, MA.
11. Roschelle J (1996) CSCL: Theory and practice of an emerging paradigm. In: Learning by collaborating: Convergent Conceptual Change. Lawrence Erlbaum, Mahwah, NJ, pp 209–248.

12. Roschelle J and Kaput J (1996) Educational software architecture and systemic impact: The promise of component software. J. of Education Computing Research 14:217–228.
13. Roughgarden J, Bergman A, Shafir S and Taylor C (1996) Adaptive computation in ecology and evolution: A guide for future research. In: Belew RK and Mitchell M (eds) Adaptive Individuals in Evolving Populations: Models and Algorithms. Addison-Wesley, Reading, MA, pp 25–30.
14. Roy B (1998) Using agents to make and manage markets across a supply web. Complexity 3:31–35.
15. Salthe SN (1993) Development and evolution: Complexity and change in biology. MIT Press, Boston, MA.
16. Soloway E, Pryor A, Krajik J, Jackson S, Stratford SJ, Wisnudel M and Klein JT (1997) Scienceware model-it: Technology to support authentic science inquiry. T.H.E. Journal 25:54–56.
17. White B (1993) Thinkertools: Causal models, conceptual change, and science education. Cognition and Instruction 10:1–100.
18. Wilensky U and Resnick M (1999) Thinking in levels: A dynamic systems approach to making sense of the world. Journal of Science Education and Technology 8:3–19.

9

On the Evolution of Sonic Ecosystems

Jon McCormack

This chapter describes a novel type of artistic artificial life software environment. Agents that have the ability to make and listen to sound populate a synthetic world. An evolvable, rule-based classifier system drives agent behavior. Agents compete for limited resources in a virtual environment that is influenced by the presence and movement of people observing the system. Electronic sensors create a link between the real and virtual spaces, virtual agents evolve implicitly to try to maintain the interest of the human audience, whose presence provides them with life-sustaining food.

9.1 Introduction

> *One thing that foreigners, computers and poets have in common is that they make unexpected linguistic associations.*
> Jasia Reichardt [25]

Music and art are undoubtedly fundamental qualities that help define the human condition. While many different discourses contribute to our understanding of art making and art interpretation, two implicit themes connect all artworks. The first is the act of creation. Even the most abstract or conceptual artworks cannot escape the fact that, as ideas, objects, or configurations, they must be made. Secondly, the importance of novelty, either perceived or real, is a fundamental driving force behind any creative impetus or gesture. Artists do not seek to create works that are identical to their previous creations or the previous work of others.

Artificial life (AL) methodologies can play an important role in developing new modes of artistic enquiry and musical composition. For artists, AL can offer new methodologies for the creative arts. For the first time in the history of art, AL suggests that, in theory at least, it may be possible to create artificial organisms that develop their own autonomous creative practices —

to paraphrase the terminology of Langton [16], *life-as-it-could-be* creating *art-as-it-could-be*.

In addition, AL has important contributions to make in our understanding of genuine novelty,* often referred to under the generalized term *emergence* [6, 11, 20].

9.1.1 Artificial Life Art

Techniques from cybernetics and artificial life have found numerous applications in the creative arts. General contemporary overviews can be found in [2, 3, 31, 38], for example.

Cybernetics has a rich and often overlooked history in terms of computing and the arts. The seminal ICA exhibition *Cybernetic Serendipity*, held in London in the summer of 1968, was one of the first major exhibitions to look at connections between creativity and technology [24]. Even the title suggests notions of novelty and discovery, a key theme for many works and critics in the decades that have followed the exhibition. Interestingly, the curators shunned distinctions between art and science and instead focused on ideas and methodologies that connected the two.

One particularly relevant concept from cybernetics is that of *open-ended behavior*, what Ashby referred to as *Descartes dictum:* how can a designer build a device that outperforms the designer's specifications [1]. Cyberneticist Gordon Pask built an "ear" that developed, not through direct design, but by establishing certain electrochemical processes whereby the ear formed and developed in response to external stimuli [7].

The goal of the work described here is to create an open-ended artistic system that is *reactive* to its environment. In order to address this goal, two important problems were explored during the design and development of the work. First, how we can create a virtual AL world that evolves toward some subjective criteria of the audience experiencing it, without the audience needing to explicitly perform fitness selection. Second, how the relationship between real and virtual spaces can be realised in a way that integrates those spaces phenomenologically. The resultant artwork developed by the author is known as *Eden*.

---

* The concept of novelty is a vexed one with many different interpretations in the literature and could easily occupy an entire chapter in itself. Some authors argue that novelty and emergence have no relation [22] whereas others see them as fundamentally the same [6]. In the sense the term is used in this chapter, novelty suggests that which has never existed before, hence the issues surrounding novelty are connected with determinism [11]. For art, almost every new artwork is in some sense novel, however, we may at least be able to apply criteria that suggest a degree of novelty, such as descriptive causality and explainable causality. Moreover, in an AL sense, we require not only the artwork to be novel, but the behavior of the virtual agents to be novel as well.

In terms of software, *Eden* is an AL environment that operates over a cellular lattice, inhabited by agents who have, among other capabilities, the ability to make and "listen" to sound. Agents use an internal, evolvable, rule-based system to control their behavior in the world. The virtual environment that the agents inhabit develops in response to the presence and movement of people experiencing the system as an artwork.

This software system will be described more fully in Sections 9.2 and 9.3 of the chapter. Interaction with the work is detailed in Section 9.4, with a summary of results and brief conclusion in Sections 9.5 and 9.6.

9.1.2 Related Work

The software system described in this chapter, draws its technical inspiration from John Holland's *Echo* [15], particularly in the use of classifier systems for the internal decision-making system of agents. Many others have used evolutionary systems as a basis for musical composition, but in the main for compositional *simulation* [32, 37], rather than as a new form of creative tool for the artist and audience.

The *Living Melodies* system [9] uses a genetic programming framework to evolve an ecosystem of musical creatures that communicate using sound. *Living Melodies* assumes that all agents have an innate "listening pleasure" that encourages them to make noise to increase their survival chances. The system described in this paper, *Eden,* contains no such inducement, beyond the fact that some sonic communication strategies that creatures discover should offer a survival or mating advantage. This results in the observation that only some instances of evolution in *Eden* result in the use of sonic communication, whereas in *Living Melodies, every* instance evolves sonic communication. *Living Melodies* restricts its focus to music composition, whereas *Eden* is both a sonic and visual experience.

9.2 *Eden*: An Artificial Life Artwork

Eden is a "reactive" artificial life artwork developed by the author. The artwork is typically experienced in an art gallery setting, but in contrast to more traditional artworks is designed as an *experiential* environment, whereby viewers participation and activity within the physical space have important consequences over the development of the virtual environment.

The artwork is exhibited as an installation and experienced by any number of users simultaneously. It consists of multiple screens, video projectors, audio speakers, infrared distance sensors, computers, and custom electronic systems. Figure 9.1 shows a floor plan and simulated visualization of the work. As shown in this figure, physically the work consists of two semitransparent screens suspended from the ceiling of the exhibition space. The screens are positioned at 90° to each other, forming an X shape when viewed in plan. The

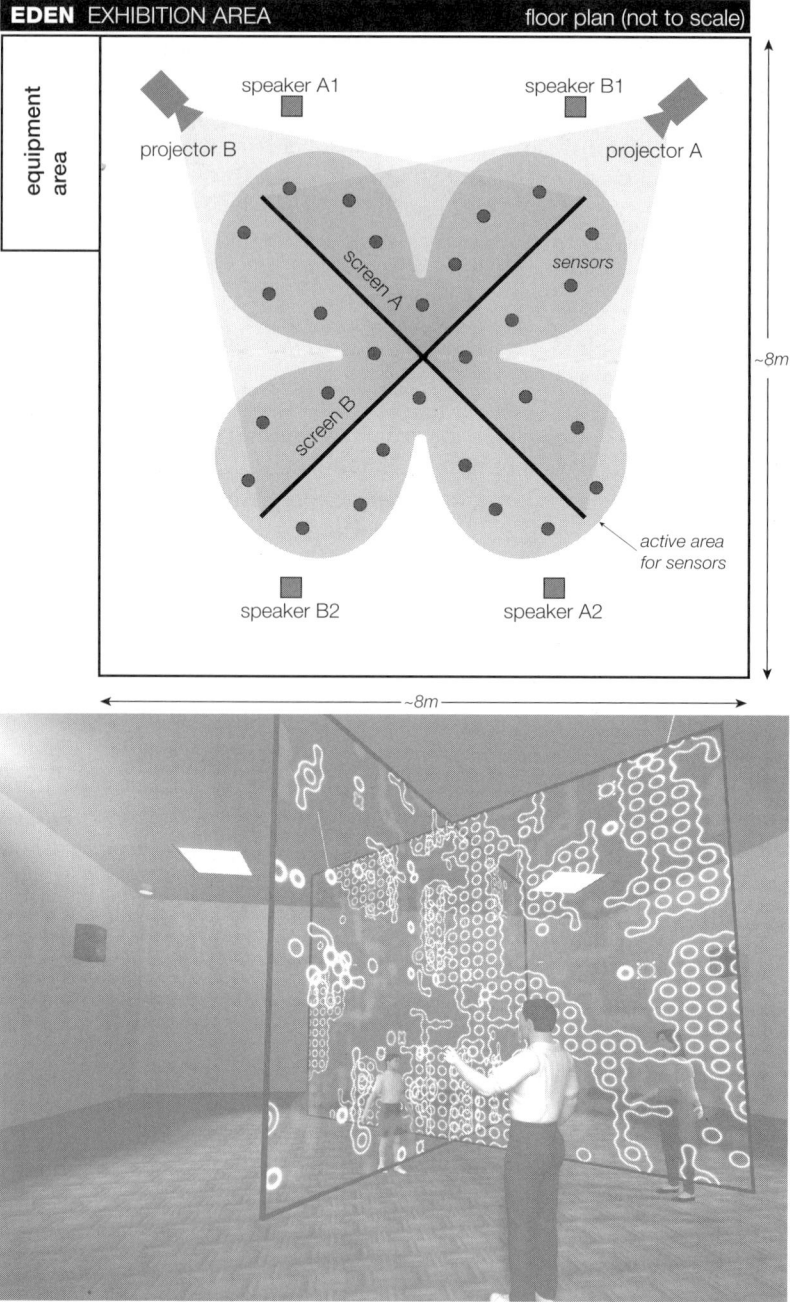

Fig. 9.1. Floor plan of Eden (top) showing the layout screens, speakers, projectors, and sensors. The active sensor area is shown in red. The image (bottom) is a simulation of the work running in a typical gallery environment, illustrating the effect of using transparent screens to visualize the work.

ambient lighting is minimal; making the screens and the light they reflect and transmit the predominant source of visual interest in the space. The screens' transparency enables them to be viewed from either side and creates a layered visual effect that merges the real and virtual boundaries. Multichannel audio is provided by a number of speakers placed on the periphery of the main screen area.

In addition to this audio-visual infrastructure, a series of infrared range sensors are placed around the screen area. The purpose of these sensors is to measure the position and movement of people experiencing the work. The sensors themselves are not visible to the audience. They function as an environmental stimulus for the virtual agents' world and ultimately contribute to selective pressures that aim to encourage a symbiotic relationship between people experiencing the work and the agents populating the virtual world. The role of the sensors and their effect on the development of the virtual environment portrayed in the work are detailed in Section 9.4.

9.3 Agents and Environments

This section gives technical details on the major software components of the system, with particular emphasis on the mechanisms that facilitate development of sonic agents within the system. Further details, particularly the *payoff* and *bidding* processes for rule selection, may be found in [18].

9.3.1 The Eden World

The environment projected onto the screens is known as the Eden *world*. In implementation terms, the world consists of a two-dimensional cellular lattice that develops using a global, discrete, time-step model — a popular AL model based on the theory of cellular automata [8, 34]. Each cell in the lattice may be populated by one of the following entities:

- *Rock:* inert matter that is impervious to other entities and opaque to sound and light. Rock is placed in cells at initialization time using a variation of the *diffusion limited aggregation* (DLA) model [39]. Rocks provide refuge and contribute to more interesting spatial environmental behavior of the agents.
- *Biomass:* a food source for evolving entities in the world. Biomass grows in yearly** cycles based on a simple feedback model, similar to that of *Daisyworld* [35]. Radiant energy (in "infinite" supply) drives the growth of biomass. The amount of radiant energy falling on a particular cell is dependent on a number of factors, including the local absorption rate of

---

** An *Eden* year lasts 600 *Eden* days, but passes by in about 10 minutes of real time.

the biomass and global seasonal variation. Probabilistic parameters can be specified at initialization time to control these rates and variations. The efficiency at which the biomass converts radiant energy into more biomass is also dependent on the presence of people in the real space of the artwork. This dependency is detailed in Section 9.4.

- *Sonic agents:* mobile agents with an internal, evolvable *performance system*. Agents get energy by eating biomass or by killing and eating other agents. More than one agent may occupy a single cell. Since these agents are the most complex and interesting entity in the world, they are described in detail in Section 9.3.2.

A real-time visualization of the world produces images that are projected onto the screens, as illustrated in Fig. 9.1 (in this case there are two worlds, each running on a separate computer, but connected as a single logical world running over two computers). The visualization process is described more fully in Section 9.3.3. The sound the agents make as they move about the world is played with approximate spatial correspondence by a series of loudspeakers.

9.3.2 Agent Implementation

Sonic agents are the principal evolving entity in the world. Essentially, the agent system uses classifiers similar to that of Holland's *Echo* system [15]. An agent consists of a set of *sensors*, a rule-based *performance system*, and a set of *actuators*. This configuration is illustrated in Fig. 9.2. Sensors provide measurement of the environment and internal introspection of an individual agent's status. The performance system relates input messages from the sensors to desired actions. The actuators are used to show intent to carry out actions in the world. The success or failure of an intended action will be dependent on the physical constraints in operation at the time and place the intent is instigated. Actuators and actions are detailed later in this section.

At initialization of the world, a number of agents are seeded into the population. Each agent maintains a collection of internal data. These data includes:

- *Current age*, an integer measured in time steps since birth. Agents live up to 100 years and cannot mate in their first year of life.
- *Health index:* an integer value indicating the overall health of the agent. A value of 100 indicates perfect health; if the health index falls to 0, the agent dies. An agent can lose health via a sustained negative *energy level* differential (explained ahead); by bumping into solid objects, such as rocks; or by being hit by other agents. In addition, the loss in health from being hit by another agent depends on both its mass and health index.
- *Energy level:* a measure of the amount of energy the agent currently has. Agents gain energy by eating biomass or other agents. Energy is expended attempting to perform actions (regardless of their success); a small quantity of energy is expended even if no action is performed at a given time

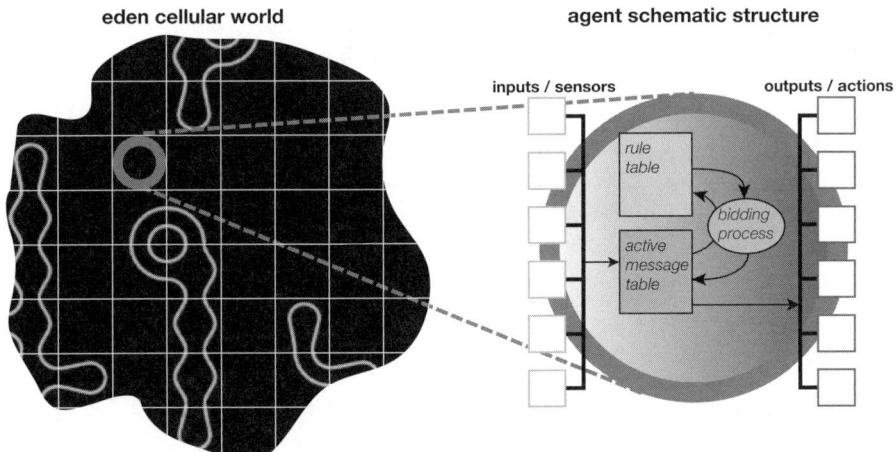

Fig. 9.2. Shows a section of the Eden cellular lattice in visual form (left). To emphasize the lattice structure, grid lines have been layered over the image. The image shows rocks (solid), biomass (outline), and an agent (circle). The diagram (right) shows the agent's internal schematic structure, consisting of a number of sensors, a performance system that evolves, and a set of actuators.

step. If an agent's energy level falls to zero, the agent dies and its body is converted to new biomass in the cell in which it died.
- *Mass*: an agent's mass is linearly proportional to its energy level, plus an initial "birth mass" that is normally distributed over the population.

Sensors

Sensors provide a way for an agent to measure itself and its environment [23]. Sensor data are presented as bit strings constructed from local environmental conditions and from the internal data structures held by the agent. Sensor data are updated once every time step. An agent can use a range of sensor types, but the sensors themselves do not undergo any evolution and are fixed in function, sensitivity, and morphology. It is up to an individual agent's performance system to make use of a particular sensor, so sensor data will only be used in the long term if they provide useful information that assists the agent's survival or mating prospects. Sensor use does not incur any cost to the agent.

Sensor information available to an agent consists of

- A simple local vision system that detects the "color" of objects on facing and neighboring cells (the range is limited to a single cell). Rocks, biomass, and agents all have different "colors", which enables an agent to distinguish between them.

- A sensor to detect the local cell nutritional value. Cells that contain biomass or dead agents have a high nutritional value, rocks do not.
- A sound sensor that detects sound pressure levels over a range of frequency bands. Sound can be detected over a much larger spatial range than vision and also with greater fidelity.
- An introspection of *pain*. Pain corresponds to a negative health index differential and would usually indicate attack by another agent or that the agent is bumping into rocks.
- An introspection of the current energy level.

Actuators

Actuators are used to signal an agent's intent to carry out an action in the world. The physical laws of the world will determine whether the intended action can be carried out or not. For example the agent may intend to "walk forward one cell", but if that cell contains a rock, the action will not be possible. Furthermore, all actions cost energy, the amount dependent on the type of action and its context (e.g., attempting to walk into a rock will cost more energy than walking into an empty cell).

As with the sensors, the number and function of actuators are fixed and do not change as the performance system evolves. Actions will only be used in the long term if they benefit the agent. Analysis of actions used by agents who are successful in surviving shows that not all agents make use of the full set of actuators.

Actions an agent may perform consist of

- *Move* forward in the current direction.
- *Turn* left or right.
- *Hit* whatever else is in the cell occupied by the agent. Hitting another agent reduces that agent's health level using a nonlinear combination of the mass, health, and energy level of the agent performing the hit. Hitting other objects or being hit will cause pain and a loss of health.
- *Mate* with whatever is currently occupying the current cell. Obviously, this is only useful if another agent is in the same cell. In addition, mating is only possible if the age of both agents is greater than one year.
- *Eat* whatever is currently occupying the current cell. Agent's can only eat biomass, or dead agents (which turn into biomass shortly after death).
- *Sing*: make a sound that can be heard by other agents. Sound is detailed more fully in Section 9.3.4.

Performing an action costs energy, so agents quickly learn not to perform certain actions without benefit. For example, attempting to eat when your nutritional sensor is not activated has a cost but no benefit. Attempting to move into a rock has a cost greater than moving into an empty cell.

Agents may also choose not to perform any action at a given time step (a "do nothing" action), but even this costs energy (although less than any other action).

Performance System

The performance system connects an agent's sensors to its actuators (Fig. 9.2). It is based on the classification system of [15]. Sensory data arrive from the sensors in the form of a *message*, a binary string of fixed length.*** Messages are placed in an *active message table*, a first-in, first-out (FIFO) list of messages currently undergoing processing. Each agent maintains a collection of *rules*, stored in a database or *rule table*. Rules consist of three components: a *condition string*, an *output message*, and a *credit*. Condition strings are composed from an alphabet of three possible symbols: $\{1,0,\#\}$. At each time step, the message at the head of the active message table is processed by checking for a match with the condition string of each rule in the rule table. A 1 or 0 in the condition string matches the corresponding value in the message at the same index. A # matches either symbol (0 or 1). So for example, the message 10010111 is matched by any of the condition strings 10010111, 10010##1, ########. The condition string #######0, however, would not match.

Rules whose condition strings match the current message bid for their output message (also a bit string of the same length as sensor messages) to be placed in the active message table. This bid is achieved by calculating the rule's *strength*. Strength is the product of the rule's credit (detailed shortly) and its *specificity*. Specificity is a unit normalized value, inversely proportional to the total number of # symbols in the condition string. So for example, a condition string consisting entirely of # symbols has a specificity of 0; a string with 75% # symbols has a specificity of 0.25; and so on.

For each rule that matches the current message under consideration, its strength is calculated. The rule with the highest strength is selected and then places its output message into the active message table. If more than one rule has the highest strength, then a uniform random selection is made from the winning rules. The selected rule places its output message into the active message table. Most output messages are *action messages*,[†] i.e., they trigger an actuator. Action messages are removed from the table once they have been translated into actuator instructions.

The process outlined in this section is illustrated in Fig. 9.3.

[***] Currently a message length of 32 bits is used, but the actual length does not concern the processes described. Larger message lengths allow more bandwidth in sensor messages, but require more storage.

[†] Action messages are distinguished from other messages by a marker bit in the string being set — all other message types are guaranteed not to set this bit.

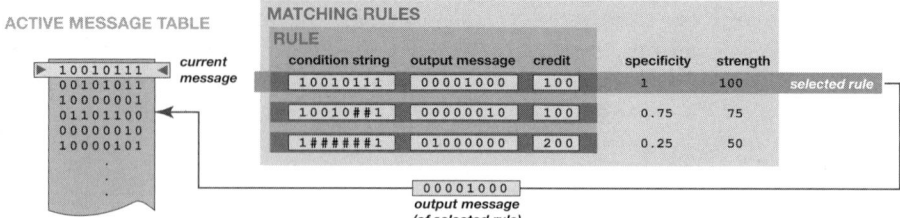

Fig. 9.3. The rule matching and bidding process. The top message from the active message table is selected and becomes the current message. Rules whose condition string matches the current message have a strength calculated as the product of their credit and specificity. The rule with the highest strength then becomes the selected rule and its output message is added to the active message table. The current message is then discarded and the process repeats. Some messages are action messages and trigger actions.

Credits and Payoffs

Each rule maintains a credit, essentially a measure of how useful this particular rule has been in the past. Rules begin with a default credit value and earn or lose credit based on how useful the rule is in assisting the agent to live and mate in the world. As described earlier in this section, agents maintain an energy level and health index. The differentials of these quantities are monitored, and when they reach a certain threshold, a *credit payoff* is performed. The credit payoff rewards or punishes rules that have been used since the last payoff (held in a separate list), by altering their credit according to frequency of use and the magnitude of the change in energy since the last payoff. Further details regarding this process may be found in [18].

The credit payoff system enables rules that, over time, assist in increasing health and energy to be rewarded; those that decrease health and energy will decrease in credit. The rationale being, that the next time rules have a chance to bid, if they have been useful in the past, they'll probably be useful in the current situation.

The number of time steps between successive payoffs will be dependent on how quickly or slowly the agent's health is changing. For example, if a creature is being attacked and losing health quickly, payoffs will be more frequent. The rules involved in letting the agent get hit will also decrease in credit quickly (hopefully soon being outbid by other rules that may prove more successful if the agent is to survive).

Maintaining a list of rules that have been used since the previous payoff allows rules that indirectly increase health to receive appropriate credit. For example, while the rule to "eat when you find food" is a good one, you may need to walk around and look for food first to find it. The rules for walking and turning, although they decrease health in the short term, may result in finding food. This increases health in the longer term. Overall, if such rules are helpful in increasing health, their credit will increase. A rule whose strength falls to zero will be automatically removed from the agent's rule table, since it is on longer able to bid to be used.

As specified in Section 9.3.2, a rule's strength is the product of its credit and specificity. This is necessary, since rules that are more specific will be used less often as they match fewer messages. Rules that are more specific will have less chance to receive credit payoffs but still may be useful. When two or more rules with the same credit match a message, the more specific rule will have greater strength and thus will be selected over the more general one.

Agent Evolution

The credit payoff system allows rules that have contributed to the agent's survival to be used more often. However, this will only select the best rules from the currently available set. The problem remains as to how the agent can discover better rules than those it currently uses.

Genetic algorithms follow a Darwinian metaphor in that they operate as a search method over the phase space of possible phenotypes in a given system — searching over the *fitness landscape* for individuals of higher *fitness* [12,21]. In the *Eden* system, a rule functions as the genetic unit of selection and new rules are brought into an agent's genome via the standard operations of *crossover* and *mutation* (see the references for explanations of these terms).

Recall from Section 9.3.2 that mating is a possible action an agent can perform. If two agents successfully mate, they produce a new agent whose rule table is a combination of the parents' tables. A proportion of rules from each parent is selected, based on the strength of the rules — the rules of highest strength from each parent being selected. These selected rules undergo crossover and mutation operations, as per the schema system of Holland [14] resulting in the creation of new rules. Mutation rates vary according to the behavior of people experiencing the artwork in the exhibition space.

Since rules of highest strength are selected from each parent, and those rules may have been discovered during the parents' lifetime, the evolutionary process is Lamarckian [4]. This design decision was used to allow more rapid adaptation to changing environmental conditions — a necessary feature if the agents' in the artificial ecosystem are to adapt to the behavior of people experiencing the work in real time.

9.3.3 Image

Representation of the entities of *Eden* is achieved using tiling patterns, loosely based on Islamic ornamental patterns [13]. Only the representation of biomass will be considered here. The visual representation of the biomass is based on a 16-tile set. A tile is chosen for a particular cell based on the neighbor relationships of adjacent cells. For the purposes of tile selection, tiles are selected based on the binary occupancy condition of the cell's neighbors, considering only cells of the same type. For the 16-tile set, only immediate orthogonal cells are considered — thus there are 16 possible configurations of neighboring cells. Fig. 9.4 shows the individual tiles and the neighbor relation necessary for the tile to be used. The resultant images formed by a grid of cells (illustrated in Fig. 9.5) form a continuous mass of substance, as opposed to squares containing individual entities. These minimalist geometric textures suggest abstract landscapes rather than the iconic or literal individual representations that are common in many artificial life simulations. This design decision forms an integral aesthetic component of the work.

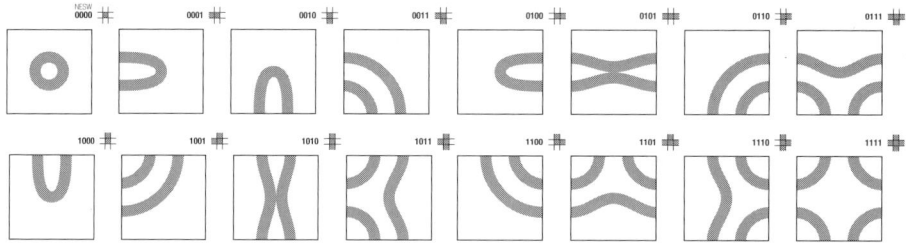

Fig. 9.4. Cellular tiling set for Eden's biomass. Each cell considers the four immediate neighboring cells (north, south, east, and west). The neighboring relations determine the image used for each cell. A function returns the bit pattern representing the neighborhood state for the cell and the tile is selected based on the supplied index. Four bits are required, each representing the four directions. The bits are encoded NESW (from MSB to LSB). The symbols above each cell pattern shown here illustrate the bit pattern and corresponding neighborhood relationships.

9.3.4 Sound

One of the key elements of *Eden* is the ability of agents to create and listen to sound. A large proportion of sensor bandwidth is devoted to sound, allowing orthogonal sensing of both frequency and sound pressure (volume). Some basic physical modeling is performed on sound pressure levels. However, many physical sound propagation aspects are simplified in the interests of efficiency.

Sound Generation

Actuator messages requesting sound generation need to be converted into a generated sound. As described in Section 9.3.2, actuator messages are bit strings. A portion of the string encodes the sound generation command ("sing"), the remainder the sound generation data (energy levels over a range of frequency bands). The current implementation has three distinct frequency

Fig. 9.5. This figure illustrates the visualization of the Eden world, showing rocks (solid shapes), biomass (outline shapes), and agents (circular elements).

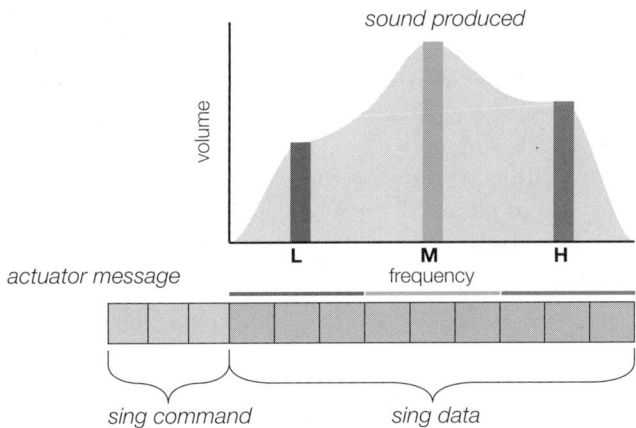

Fig. 9.6. The "sing" actuator message contains two parts. The first is the command requesting the agent to perform a sing operation; the remainder contains the sing data: volume levels for three distinct frequency bands. Using three bits per frequency band results in 2^9, or 512 distinct sounds. See also color plate.

bands, each occupying one third of the total of the sound generation data for the "sing" actuator message (see Fig. 9.6).

When an agent "sings" the spectral signature determined by the sing data in the actuator message is registered for the current time step. In addition, the same signature is used to drive a sonification process, so that people in the exhibition space can hear sounds that correspond to the "singing" activities of the agents. To drive this sonification process, the three frequency bands are assigned labels L, M and H corresponding to low, medium, and high pitched sounds (for example, the majority of spectral energy in the 100, 1000 and 10,000 Hz regions, respectively). When an agent makes a sound, the corresponding selection from a precomputed library of sounds is triggered and sent to the audio subsystem. The audio subsystem does basic sound spatialization using the four-channel audio system that is part of the artwork. Sounds are spatialized according to the position of the agent making the sound on the screen. Thus, as an agent making sound moves across the screen, that sound will appear to move with the agent to human observers. The audio subsystem allows many agents to be making sound simultaneously.

Sound Reception

Agents have a significant amount of sensor bandwidth devoted to sound reception. An agent's sound reception area is a forward-facing conical pattern that, like the sound generation, is sensitive across three separate frequency bands (see Fig. 9.7). Each band has the same propagation and reception pattern, i.e., there are no frequency-dependent differences in the modeling.

At each time step, the conical reception area for each agent is checked for any other agent that is singing within that area. A simple physical model [27] controls the propagation of sound through the environment.[‡] Sounds arriving at the agent's cell are summed on a per-frequency basis and the resultant sensor message instantiated.

9.4 Interaction

The *Eden* system has a unique relationship between the physical and virtual components of the system. As shown in Fig. 9.1, a series of infrared sensors[§] are placed around the screens in the exhibition space. These sensors measure

---

[‡] When sound propagates in a medium such as air at standard temperature and pressure, the perceptual mechanism for loudness behaves in an exponential way, as it does for humans. The relationship between distance and perceived levels is $L = 20 \log_{10}(P/P_o)$, where L is the sound pressure level in decibels (dB), P_o a reference pressure corresponding roughly to the threshold of hearing in humans [26].

[§] The use of the term "sensors" here referrers to physical devices and should not be confused with the sensors described in Section 9.3.2, which are virtual (i.e., simulated).

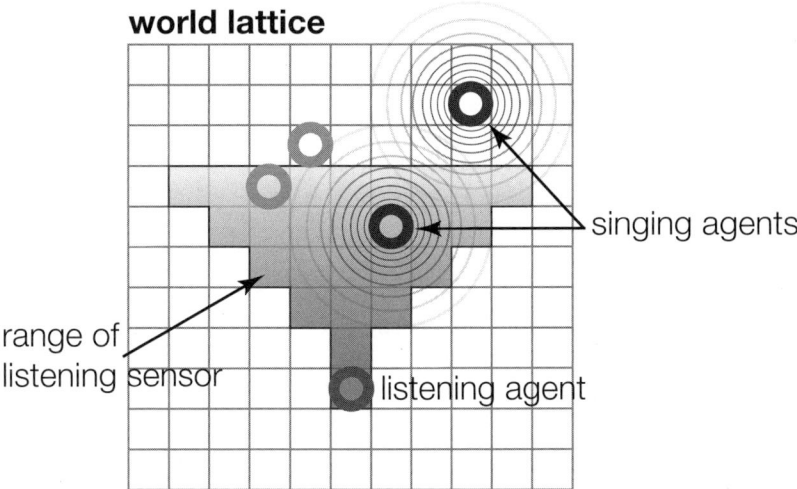

Fig. 9.7. The reception area of an agent. The listening agent will hear agents who are making sound within the blue area only. A simple physical model controls the perceptual volume levels for the agent.

distance. Each sensor has a range of approximately 150 cm. Data collected from individual sensors are digitized in a data collection subsystem that is then used to infer the presence and movement of people in the space. These data are used to drive environmental parameters in the virtual simulation. Before discussing the details of the mappings between sensor data and the simulated environment, we will present a background discussion on the rationale for such mappings.

9.4.1 The Problem of Aesthetic Evolution

Typically, genetic algorithms evolve toward finding maxima in *fitness*, where fitness is some criterion that can be evaluated for each phenotype of the population. Many systems define an explicit *fitness function* that can be machine evaluated for every phenotype at each generation [21].

Aesthetic evolution or *aesthetic selection* is a popular technique that replaces the machine-evaluated fitness function with the subjective criteria of the human operator. Aesthetic evolution was first used by Dawkins [10] in his "Blind Watchmaker" software to evolve two-dimensional, insect-like shapes. Aesthetic selection has been used to successfully evolve images [28, 29], dynamic systems [30], morphogenic forms [17, 33], even musical patterns and structures [5]. Regardless of the system or form being evolved, aesthetic selection relies on the user to explicitly select the highest fitness phenotypes at each generation. Users typically evolve to some subjective criteria — often described as "beautiful", "strange" or "interesting" — criteria that prove difficult to quantify or express in a machine representable form (hence the use of the technique in the first place).

However, aesthetic evolution has two significant problems:

- The number of phenotypes that can be evaluated at each generation is limited by both screen area (in the case of visual representation) and the ability of people to perform subjective comparisons on large numbers of objects (simultaneously comparing 16 different phenotypes is relatively easy; comparing 10,000 would be significantly more difficult).
- The subjective comparison process, even for a small number of phenotypes, is slow and forms a bottleneck in the evolutionary process. Human users may take hours to evaluate many successive generations that in an automated system could be performed in a matter of seconds.

What we would like is a system that combines the ability to subjectively evolve toward phenotypes that people find "interesting" without the bottleneck and selection problems inherent in traditional aesthetic evolution.

9.4.2 *Eden* as a Reactive System

The solution to the problem described in the previous section is to map the presence and motion data of people experiencing the artwork to the environmental parameters of the virtual environment. Thus, the virtual world in which sonic agents live and evolve is dependent not only on the simulated qualities discussed so far, but also on the presence (or absence) of people experiencing the work and their behavior within the exhibition space.

Eden has no explicit fitness function. Agents continue to be part of the system based on how well they can survive and mate in the current environment. If certain selection pressures are applied, such as food becoming scarce, only those agents who can adapt and find food will prosper. By driving environmental conditions from the presence and movement of people in the exhibition space, agents must implicitly adapt to an environment that includes aspects of the world outside the simulation.

In the current system, the following mappings are used:

- *Presence in the real environment maps to biomass growth rates.* The presence of people around the screen area affects the rate of biomass growth in that local area of the *Eden* world. Areas with no people correspond to a barren environment — little biomass will grow without the presence of people in the real environment.
- *Movement in the real environment maps to genotype mutation rates.* The greater the movement of people in the space, the higher the mutation rate for rule evolution (see Section 9.3.2).

These mappings are based on certain assumptions. First, people will generally spend time experiencing something only if it interests them. In the context of experiencing an artwork, people generally may spend a short time evaluating their interest in an artwork, but after a short time, if it no longer interests them, they will leave. There may be other reasons for leaving, but in general the duration of stay will have some relation to how "interesting" the experience is.

Agents require food to survive. If people are in the real environment, then food will grow at a more rapid rate. An agent who is making "interesting" noises, for instance, would have a better chance of keeping a person's attention than one who is not. Moreover, an agent making a progression of sounds, rather than a just a single, repeating sound, is likely to hold a person's attention even longer. Agents who encourage and hold a person's attention in the space implicitly give the environment a more plentiful food supply.

The movement of people in the space mapping to mutation rates is based on the assumption that people will move over an area looking for something that interests them and, when they find it, will stay relatively still and observe it. Hence, the movement of people within the real space serves to inject "noise" into the genome of agents who are close to the source of movement. Higher mutation rates result in more variation of rules.¶ If an agent or group of agents are holding the viewer's attention, then less rule discovery is needed in the current environment, whereas if people are continually moving, looking for something "interesting", this will aid in the generation of new rules.

Further details on the dynamics of this component of the system can be found in [19].

9.5 Results

At the time of this writing, a number of exhibitions of the work have been completed. Images from an exhibition of the work are shown in Fig. 9.8. A typical exhibition may last several weeks, giving plenty of opportunity for the agent evolutionary system to take into account the behavior of people experiencing the work. Certain factors have a marked effect on this behavior and need to be compensated for. For example, when the gallery is closed, there will be no people in the space anyway.‖

Analysis of the rules agents use show that sound is used to assist in mating as would be expected [36] and with the influence of people, sound is used in other ways as well. Once the environmental pressures from audience behavior are incorporated into the system, the generation of sound shows a marked increase and analysis of the rules discovered shows that making sound is not only used for mating purposes.

¶ Most child rules that mutate will not be "better" than the parent rule, but in general, the use of mutation does provide the possibility for the system to discover rules that would not be possible by crossover alone.

‖ Without compensation for gallery opening hours, the entire population dies out each night!

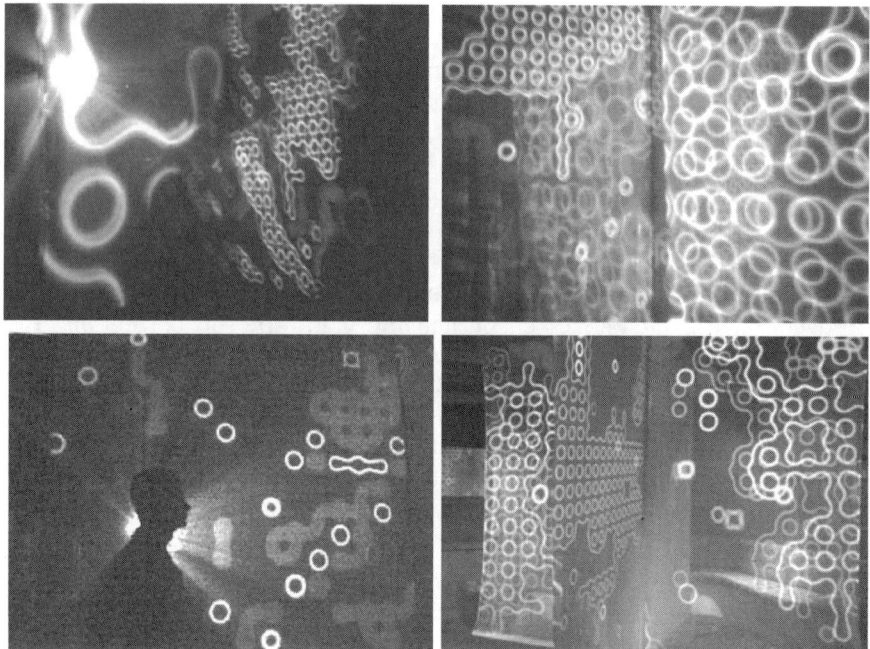

Fig. 9.8. Images of Eden in operation. See also color plate.

9.6 Conclusion

This chapter has described a novel evolutionary system, where agents make use of sound to assist in survival. While the main impetus and methodologies are based around the development of an artistic system, it is hoped that some of the ideas presented here may be of interest to those interested in artificial life from other perspectives or with different agendas and applications.

In summary, a system has been produced that attempts to integrate the open-ended nature of synthetic evolutionary systems into a reactive virtual space. The approach used here has been to measure components of the real environment, incorporating them into that of the virtual one, thus enabling a symbiotic relationship between virtual agents and the artwork's audience, without need for explicit selection of phenotypes that engage in "interesting" behavior.

Further information, including sample sound recordings and video documentation of the work, is available online at http://www.csse.monash.edu.au/~jonmc/projects/eden.html.

References

1. Ashby WR (1956) An Introduction to Cybernetics. Chapman & Hall, London.
2. Bentley PJ (1999) Evolutionary Design by Computers. Morgan Kaufmann Publishers, San Francisco, CA.
3. Bentley PJ and Corne DW (eds.) (2002) Creative Evolutionary Systems. Academic Press, London.
4. Bowler PJ (1992) Lamarckism, In: Keller EF and Lloyd EA (eds.). Keywords in Evolutionary Biology, Harvard University Press, Cambridge, MA, pp. 188–193.
5. Bulhak A (1999) Evolving Automata for Dynamic Rearrangement of Sampled Rhythm Loops. In: Dorin A and J McCormack (eds.) First Iteration: a conference on generative systems in the electronic arts, CEMA, Melbourne, Australia, pp. 46–54.
6. Cariani P (1991) Emergence and Artificial Life. In: Langton CG et al. (eds.) Artificial Life II, SFI Studies in the Sciences of Complexity, vol 10, Addison-Wesley, pp. 775–797.
7. Cariani P (1993) To Evolve an Ear: Epistemological Implications of Gordon Pask's Electrochemical Devices. Systems Research 10:19–33.
8. Conrad M and Pattee HH (1970) Evolution Experiments with an Artificial Ecosystem. Journal of Theoretical Biology 28:393.
9. Dahlstedt P and Nordahl MG (1999) Living Melodies: Coevolution of Sonic Communication. In: Dorin A and McCormack J. (eds.) First Iteration: A conference on generative systems in the electronic arts, Centre for Electronic Media Art, Melbourne, Australia, pp. 56–66.
10. Dawkins R (1986) The Blind Watchmaker. Longman Scientific & Technicial, Essex, UK.
11. Emmeche C, Køppe S and Stjernfelt F (1997) Explaining Emergence: Towards an Ontology of Levels. Journal for General Philosophy of Science 28:83–119.
12. Goldberg DE (1989) Genetic Algorithms in Search, Optimization, and Machine Learning. Addison-Wesley Pub. Co., Reading, MA.
13. Grünbaum B and Shephard GC (1993) Interlace Patterns in Islamic and Moorish Art. In: Emmer M (ed.) The Visual Mind: Art and Mathematics, MIT Press, Cambridge, MA.
14. Holland, JH (1992) Adaptation in Natural and Artificial Systems: An Introductory Analysis with Applications to Biology, Control, and Artificial Intelligence. MIT Press, Cambridge, MA.
15. Holland JH (1995) Hidden Order: How Adaptation Builds Complexity, Addison-Wesley, Reading, MA.
16. Langton CG (1989) Artificial Life. In: Langton CG (ed.) Artificial Life, SFI Studies in the Sciences of Complexity, vol. 6, Addison-Wesley, pp 1–47.
17. McCormack J (1993) Interactive Evolution of L-System Grammars for Computer Graphics Modelling. In: Green D and Bossomaier T. (eds.) Complex Systems: From Biology to Computation, ISO Press, Amsterdam, pp 118–130.
18. McCormack J (2001) Eden: An Evolutionary Sonic Ecosystem. In: Kelemen J and Sosík P. (eds.) Advances in Artificial Life, 6th European Conference, ECAL 2001, Springer, Prague, Czech Republic, pp 133–142.
19. McCormack J (2002) Evolving for the Audience. International Journal of Design Computing 4 (Special Issue on Designing Virtual Worlds). Available online: http://www.arch.usyd.edu.au/kcdc/journal/vol4/index.html.

20. McCormack J and Dorin A (2001) Art, Emergence and the Computational Sublime. In: Dorin A (ed.) Second Iteration: a conference on generative systems in the electronic arts, CEMA, Melbourne, Australia, pp 67–81.
21. Mitchell M (1996) Introduction to Genetic Algorithms. MIT Press, Cambridge, MA.
22. Nagel E (1961) The Structure of Science: Problems in the Logic of Scientific Explanation. Routledge, London.
23. Pattee HH (1988) Simulations, Realizations, and Theories of Life. In: Langton CG (ed) Artificial Life, vol. VI, Addison-Wesley, pp 63–77.
24. Reichardt J (1971) Cybernetics, Art and Ideas. New York Graphic Society, Greenwich, CT.
25. Reichardt J (1971) Cybernetics, Art and Ideas. In: Reichardt J (ed.) Cybernetics, Art and Ideas, Studio Vista, London, pp 11–17.
26. Roads C (1996) The Computer Music Tutorial. MIT Press, Cambridge, MA.
27. Roederer J (1975) Introduction to the Physics and Psychophysics of Music. Springer-Verlag, New York.
28. Rooke S (2002) Eons of Genetically Evolved Algorithmic Images. In: Bentley PJ and Corne DW (eds.) Creative Evolutionary Systems, Academic Press, London, pp 339–365.
29. Sims K (1991) Artificial Evolution for Computer Graphics. Computer Graphics 25:319–328.
30. Sims K (1991) Interactive Evolution of Dynamical Systems. In: First European Conference on Artificial Life. MIT Press, Paris, pp 171–178.
31. Sommerer C and Mignonneau L (eds.) (1998) Art@Science. Springer-Verlag, Wien, Austria.
32. Todd PM and Werner GM (1998) Frankensteinian Methods for Evolutionary Music Composition. In: Griffith N and Todd PM (eds.) Musical Networks: Parallel Distributed Perception and Performance. MIT Press/Bradford Books, Cambridge, MA.
33. Todd S and Latham W (1992) Evolutionary Art and Computers. Academic Press, London.
34. Ulam S (1952) Random Processes and Transformations. Proceedings of the International Congress on Mathematics, vol 2, pp. 264–275.
35. Watson AJ and JE Lovelock (1983) Biological Homeostasis of the Global Environment: The Parable of Daisyworld. Tellus 35B:284–289.
36. Werner GM and Dyer MG (1991) Evolution of Communication in Artificial Systems. In: Langton CG (ed.) Artificial Life II, Addison-Wesley, Redwood City, CA, pp. 659–682.
37. Wiggins G et al (1999) Evolutionary Methods for Musical Composition. Proceedings of the CASYS98 Workshop on Anticipation, Music & Cognition.
38. Wilson S (2002) Information Arts: A Survey of Art and Research at the Intersection of Art, Science, and Technology. MIT Press, Cambridge, MA.
39. Witten TA and Sander LM (1981) Diffusion-Limited Aggregation, a Kinetic Critical Phenomenon. Phys Rev Letters 47:1400–1403.

Part III

Magic of Discrete Worlds

10
Exploring Cellular Automata with MCell

Mirek Wojtowicz

Cellular automata (CA) are dynamical systems that are discrete in space and time, operate on a uniform, regular grid, and are characterized by local interactions. Each point in a regular spatial grid, called a cell, can have any one of a finite number of states. The states of the cells in the grid are updated according to a local rule — the state of a cell at a given time depends only on its own state and the states of its nearby neighbors at the previous time step. All cells on the grid are updated synchronously [3].

Cellular automata were conceptualized by John von Neumann [1] and Stanislaw Marcin Ulam [2] in the 1940s. von Neumann was mainly interested in self-reproducing automata, while Ulam liked to invent pattern games using a computer at Los Alamos. CA were next studied by several other scientists, but they got very popular thanks to John Horton Conway, who in 1970 defined and with his students explored the famous Conway's Game of Life, and Martin Gardner, who published the game in Mathematical Games column in *Scientific American* the same year.

The articles in the Mathematical Games column were a direct inspiration for programming MCell.

10.1 What Is MCell?

MCell (Mirek's Cellebration) [4] is a free, 32-bit Windows application allowing active exploration of a wide range of one-dimensional (1D) and two-dimensional (2D) cellular automata. Starting with version 4.20, MCell became open source and is distributed under the GNU General Public License (GPL).

MCell has not been programmed by a scientist, but rather by a programmer, amazed by the beauty and richness of CA, unpredictable evolution of chaotic states, and precision of designed patters. Because of this, MCell differs from programs like DDLab where the stress has been put on analyses of the dynamics. MCell focuses on visual exploration. It offers a number of easy-to-use tools for browsing patterns, changing neighborhoods' parameters and rules, zooming and panning the animation, or designing new patterns. Furthermore, an open interface made it possible to add research instruments with successful application of the program in scientific experiments with CA.

10.1.1 Program Interface

MCell is a native Windows application and as such can be comfortably handled using the mouse. Experienced users will also find keyboard shortcuts to virtually all functions, including the board panning and zooming. Figure 10.1 presents the main window of the program, with an experiment running within.

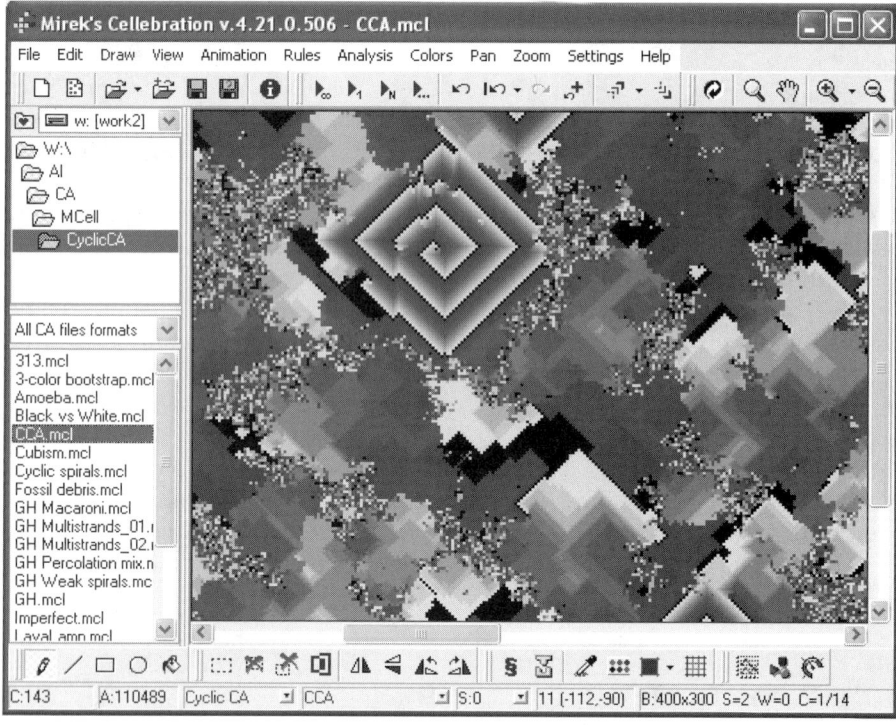

Fig. 10.1. MCell's user interface.

The most often accessed functions are available from a set of toolbars that can be freely placed, can be docked to any program window edge, or can remain floating. All program functions are available from the main menu. Nearly each menu option has a corresponding keyboard shortcut assigned. The program package contains a large number of sample patterns for all rules, so high priority has been set for comfortable browsing and loading the patterns. Most of the operations on files can be accomplished using the File Manager

— a vertical panel placed to the left of the main area. The status bar shows the most important information about the program and experiment state, like the cycle number, count of alive cells, active rules family and the rule name, focused cell coordinates and state, and the universe details.

10.1.2 Some History

The first version of MCell was designed in 1999 as a very simple program allowing users to play with Conway's Game of Life on a 100×100-cell board, but it quickly started to evolve. The author spent much time exploring available Internet resources and expanding the program to cover more general CA. The program soon became known, and the CA community started to contribute to the resources collected in the package. A milestone in MCell's development was meeting with David Griffeath [5], who selected the program as a tool for his studies on new 1D CA — Traffic and Aggregation-Fragmentation. This motivated further development of MCell and resulted in a number of new generalisations, features, and scientific tools. Soon Rudy Rucker [6] found MCell to be a good candidate for carrying over his older experiments implemented in CelLab, thus initiating the development of external DLLs in MCell. External DLLs were the feature that allowed users to run even a wider range of CA in MCell, including nondeterministic experiments. There were many more people who had significant influence on today's shape of the program. Among them were John Elliott, Tim Tyler, George Maydwell, Johan Bontes, and others, too many to list all of them here. But one more fact needs mentioning: In 2002 MCell was used by Stephen Wolfram's team when working on "A New Kind of Science" [7].

10.1.3 Other Popular CA Simulators

There exist many other CA simulators, available for various platforms. Some of them are listed below.

- "CelLab" by Rudy Rucker and John Walker [13] (DOS, Windows)
- "Cellsprings" by John Elliott [14] (Java)
- "Cellular" by J. Dana Eckart [15] (Unix, Windows)
- "Collidoscope" and "SARCASim" by George Maydwell [16] (Windows)
- "Discrete Dynamics Lab" by Andy Wuensche [17] (DOS, Unix, Linux, Solaris)
- "Life32" by Johan Bontes [18] (Windows)
- "StarLogo" [19] (Java)
- "Tim Tyler's CA simulators" collection [20] (Java)

10.2 Description of the Software

MCell is capable of running CA on a board up to 50,000×5,000-cell large. Cells can take up to 256 distinct states. Experiments can be run in Moore, von Neumann, hexagonal, extended Moore or von Neumann (with range up to 10) and Margolus cell neighborhoods. The universe can be optionally toroidal (wrapped at edges). MCell supports both deterministic and nondeterministic rules.

The current version of MCell (4.31) contains 340 built-in cellular automata rules, organized in 15 families [8]. Families do not organize rules by their behavior, but rather by the way the rules are being defined using the program's user interface. Families also reflect important fundamental types of cellular automata, like 1D binary, cyclic, or Larger than Life. Nearly every family can define CA rules falling into all four general Wolframs classes. MCell allows defining new rules either by parameterizing existing families, or by writing custom evaluators using high-level languages like C or Pascal.

10.2.1 Areas of Application

MCell has several areas of application. Based on user feedback, the program is most often used in education, research, art, patterns design, rules exploring, and entertainment.

MCell contains a huge built-in library of classic CA rules and patterns, useful in *education*. Some user-interface and output features (like dynamic zoom, adjustable cells shape, customizable grid, single-step and slow motion) were especially designed to make the program comfortable for being used during presentations. Open OLE automation interface made it possible to prepare fully automatic presentations using any tool offering scripting, like MS Word. Self-contained and documented experiment files can be easily collected from students or exchanged.

Researchers use the built-in analyzing tools, like density statistics, population log, transitions, correlations, or joint correlations. Open OLE automation interface and external DLLs make it possible to construct new measurement tools. Comfortable input/output functions allow users to quickly rerun experiments with changed conditions.

Artists capture beautiful images of running experiments and enrich them by applying custom color palettes.

Pattern designers use many graphics editor-like tools, allowing for the designing and manipulating of patterns: free-hand drawing, lines, rectangles, ovals, filling, block copy and move, copy & paste, or unlimited undo and redo. Period checker and ships detector tools make it easier to find objects with long periods. Thanks to the text format used for storage, designed patterns can be published on Usenet or exchanged in e-mails.

Rules explorers experiment with existing families of CA and/or develop custom DLLs to implement new rules. The Rules setup dialog window allows to fine-tune parameters of all built-in CA rules and apply them to running experiments to see the results. The "Random parameters" function allows users to find new, interesting rules using the coin-tossing method. Although not many explorers admit it, the function has proved to be useful.

MCell also serves well the *entertainment* purpose. Watching the evolution of patterns of many rules is delightful (and addictive; the author still remembers long hours spent just watching the StarWars rule evolution) and doesn't need any CA background. Thanks to complying to Windows software interface standards, even nonexperienced users can easily browse the provided ready-to-run experiments.

10.2.2 Supported Cellular Automata Rules

The currently supported families of CA rules are 1D binary CA, 1D totalistic CA, cyclic CA, general binary, generations, larger than life, life, Margolus, von Neumann binary, rules tables, special rules, user DLLs (with weighted generations subfamily), vote for life, and weighted life. MCell defines a compact textual notation of rules for each family in order to be able to save self-contained pattern files. Such pattern files define the layout and state of living cells, the rule, universe size, and optional experiment parameters. Full details of the families' notation can be found in the corresponding sections of [8].

A brief discussion on all families of rules follows.

1D Totalistic CA

Type: 1D, totalistic, or outer totalistic with optional decay.

This family allows exploring a wide range of 1D totalistic CA. The neighborhoods can be specified in a range of 1–10, allowing up to 21 cells to be considered. One can specify independently the necessary totals of alive neighbors for cells to survive and to be born, in a similar to "Life" S,B manner. It is also possible to specify if the center cell should be taken into account or ignored. No references to 1D totalistic CA have been found on the Internet. The family design and nearly all included rules come from the author. Rules supported by the 1D totalistic CA family fall into all four Wolframs classes and are of exceptional beauty.

Notation: [R]ange, [C]ount of states, [M]idle cell activity, [S]urvival, [B]irth
Example: R3,C0,M1,S3,S6,S7,B0,B1 (Champagne)

1D Binary CA

Type: 1D, binary, with optional decay.

1D binary CA are probably one of the most explored cellular automata. Some rules of this family, like the famous chaotic rule 110, appeared in many

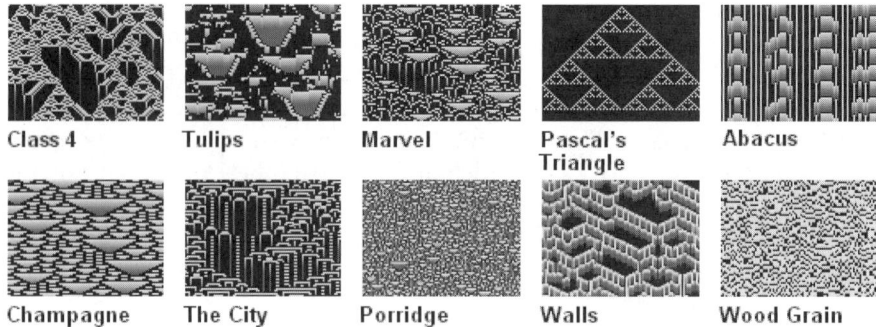

Fig. 10.2. Sample rules from the 1D totalistic CA family.

publications. The neighborhood in 1D binary CA family can be defined in a range of 1 to 4, allowing up to nine cells to be considered. Rules specify the state of new cells for each possible configuration of existing cells found in the defined neighborhood. MCell's extension of this classical family is the possibility to define optional decay states.

Notation: [R]ange, [W]olfram's hexadecimal code, [H] optional count of states

Example: R2,W9D041AC8 (Solitons F)

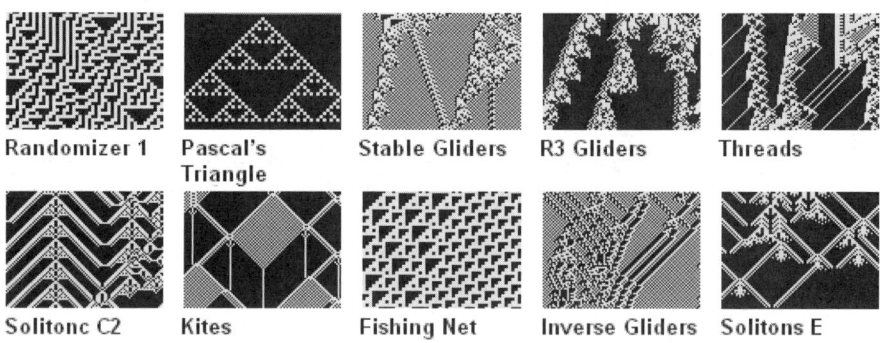

Fig. 10.3. Sample rules from the 1D binary CA family.

Cyclic CA

Type: 2D, cyclic totalistic, in extended Moore and von Neumann neighborhood.

Cyclic cellular automata (CCA) exhibit complex self-organization by iteration of an extremely simple update rule. A specified number of colors are arranged cyclically in a "color wheel." Each color can only advance to the next, the last cycling to 0. At each update a cell's color advances by 1 if there are at least *threshold* cells of the next color within its neighbor set of size Range in extended Moore or von Neumann neighborhood. These simple dynamics exhibit complex self-organization starting from randomness. This class of CA was discovered and explored by David Griffeath [5]. The family also supports the simpler Greenberg-Hastings model, where only cells in state 0 must have the "threshold" count of neighboring 1's to advance to the next state, all other cells advance automatically.

Notation: [R]ange / [T]reshold / [C]ount of states / [N]eighborhood type / [GH]optional Greenberg–Hastings model

Example: R2/T4/C5/NM/GH (GH Macaroni)

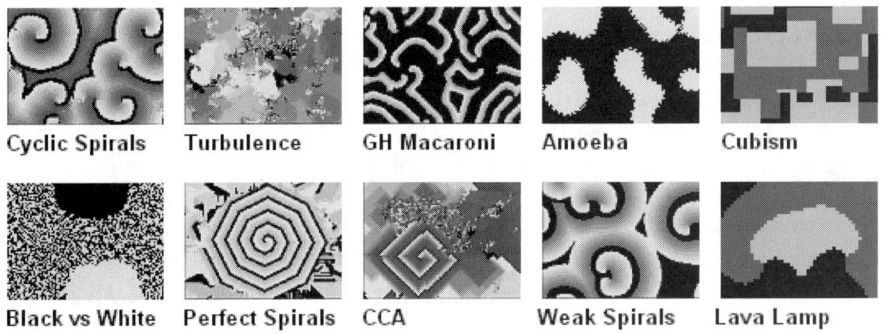

Fig. 10.4. Sample rules from the cyclic CA family.

General Binary

Type: 2D, binary, in Moore and von Neumann neighborhood, with optional decay.

General binary family allows defining a wide range of rules in both Moore and von Neumann neighborhood. In contrast to totalistic CA, general binary rules distinguish not only the count of neighboring cells, but also their location, thus allowing for defining anisotropic (configuration-specific) rules.

Notation: [C]ount of states / [N]eighborhood type / [S]urvival (compressed) / [B]irth (compressed)

Example: C0, NN, S3babbabbabba3b, B7ab3aba3b (Banks)

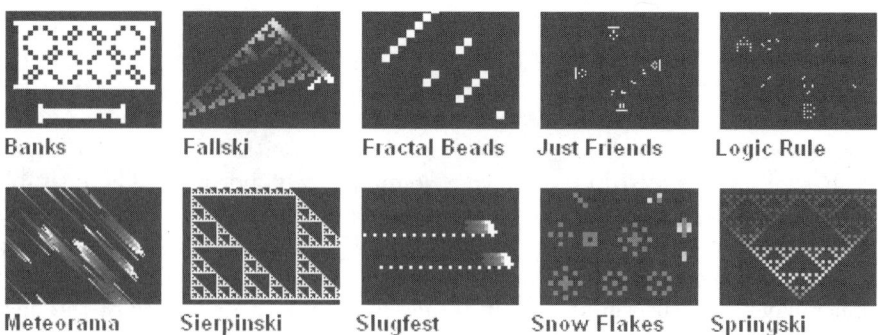

Fig. 10.5. Sample rules from the general binary family.

Generations

Type: 2D, outer totalistic with decay, in Moore and von Neumann neighborhood.

Generations is perhaps the most beautiful family of rules in MCell. The family rules are very close to those from Life, with one addition: the cells' history. Cells that would simply die in "Life" are only getting older in Generations. They cannot give birth to new cells, but they occupy the space of the lattice, thus changing the rules radically. The author defined the family as a generalization of several existing rules extending the Game of Life — BelZhab, Brian's Brain, Frogs, RainZha, Sticks, and Swirl. Today the family contains over 40 interesting rules. A special option in the Rules setup dialog box (see Fig. 10.22) allows specifying many Generations rules using Rudy Rucker's popular NLUKY format.

Notation: Survival / Birth / Count of states
Example: 345/2/4

Larger than Life

Type: 2D, totalistic or outer totalistic with or without decay, in extended neighborhood.

This family extends Conway's Game of Life to larger neighborhoods given by Range and one of two available neighborhoods. A birth occurs at x if the population within its neighborhood (x included or not) lies in the interval [BMin, BMax]. Site x stays occupied if the count is in [SMin, SMax]. Thus Conway's Game is range 1 Box with values [3,3], [3,4], respectively. Additionally, the history known from the Generations family can be defined.

Notation: [R]ange, [C]ount of states, [M]idle cell, [S]urvival, [B]irth, [N]eighborhood type
Example: R4,C0,M1,S41..81, B41..81,NM (Majority)

10 MCell 241

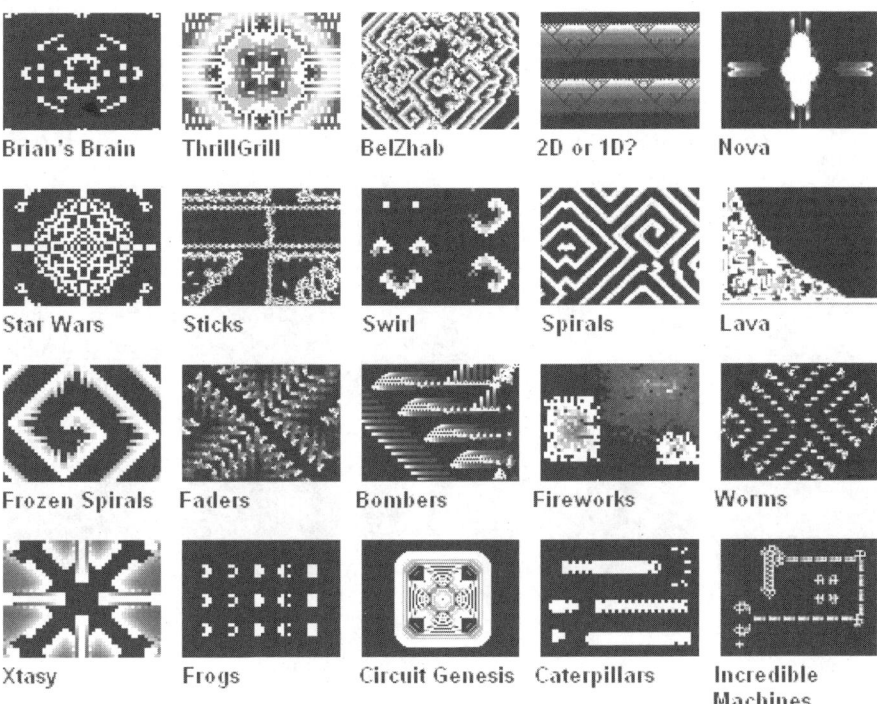

Fig. 10.6. Sample rules from the generations family. See also color plate.

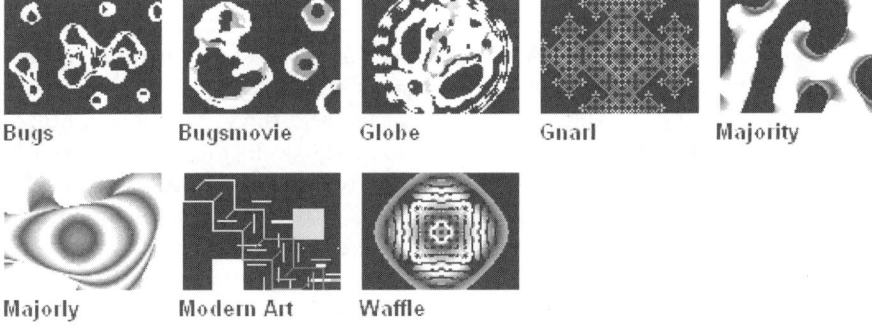

Fig. 10.7. Sample rules from the Larger than Life family. See also color plate.

Life

Type: 2D, outer totalistic, in Moore neighborhood.

Life rules family allows defining the widest-known 2-bit outer totalistic cellular automata, including the mythical Conway's Game of Life.

Notation: Survival / Birth

Example: 23/3 (Conway's Game of Life)

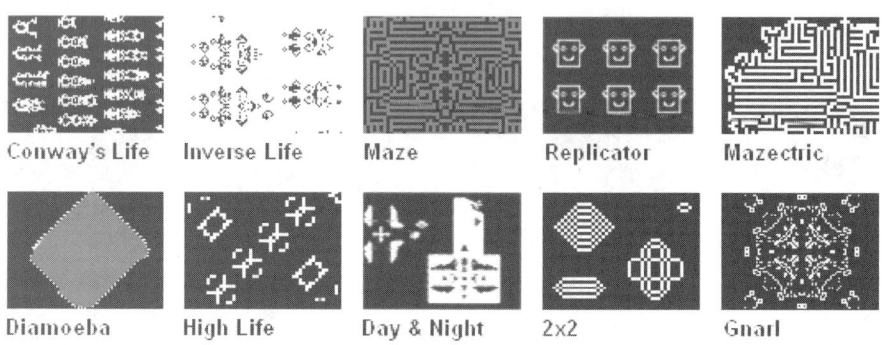

Fig. 10.8. Sample rules from the Life family.

Margolus

Type: 2D, binary, in Margolus neighborhood.

Margolus neighborhood CA family uses the simplest partitioning scheme where the lattice is divided in isolated blocks of size 2×2. Each block moves down and to the right with the next generation, and then moves back. Margolus neighborhood rules define transitions applied to cells found in 2×2 blocks. This simple partitioning scheme turned out to be very useful for modeling physical systems. Another important property of the Margolus neighborhood is that it allows for very easy creation of reversible rules.

Notation: Mx,Dn1;n2;n3;..;n16, where M is family subtype and D is transitions of all 16 possible neighborhood configurations

Example: MS,D0;8;4;3;2;5;9;7;1;6;10;11;12;13;14;15 (BBM, Billiard Ball Machine)

Neumann Binary

Type: 2D, binary, in von Neumann neighborhood.

Neumann binary family of rules allows defining binary (configuration-specific) rules in von Neumann neighborhood. MCell's implementation allows defining rules with up to four states of cells.

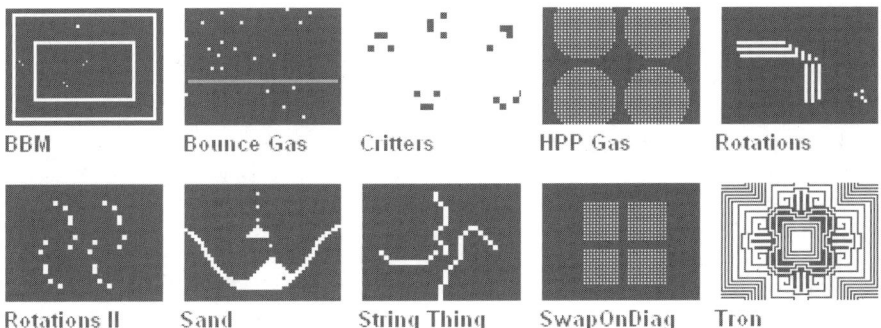

Fig. 10.9. Sample rules from the Margolus family.

Notation: Count of states, transition table
Example: 2011010011001011010010110011010011

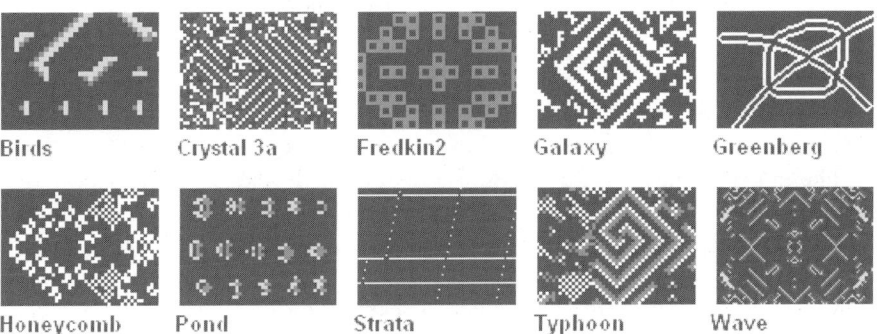

Fig. 10.10. Sample rules from the von Neumann binary family.

Rules Tables

Type: 2D, totalistic or outer totalistic rules table, in Moore neighborhood.

Rules tables family allows users to define totalistic rules by creating special transitions tables. Rules tables remove all limits from totalistic rules, allowing users to define any rules, where states of cells can advance, but can also jump, forward and backward. The idea of the rules table is simple. It describes what new state should get the cell having state S, providing it has N firing neighbors.

Notation: [N]eighborhood type, [M]idle cell activity, [F]irst bitplane firing, [T]able

Example: 1,0,1,0,0,0,1,0,0,0,0,0,0,2,2,1,1,2,2,2,2,2,0,2,2,2,1,2,2,2,2,2 (Historical Life)

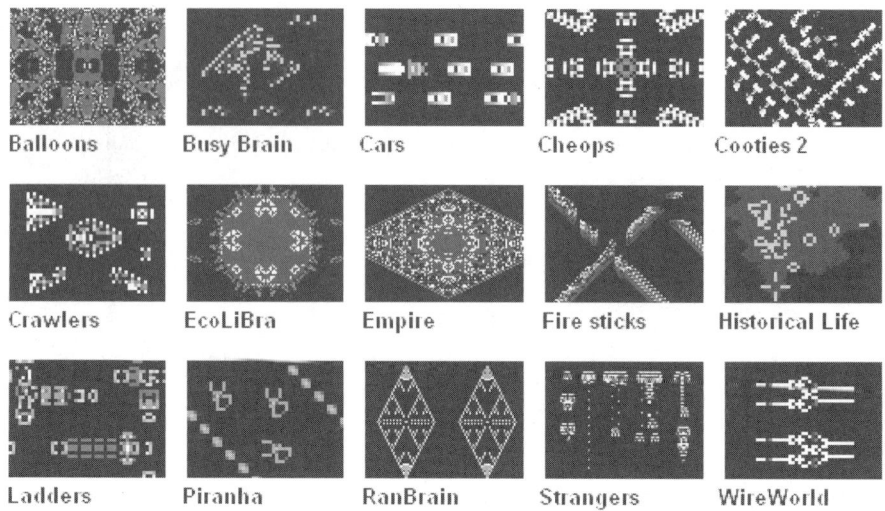

Fig. 10.11. Sample rules from the Rules tables family.

Special Rules

Type: depends on the rule.

The special rules family contains nonstandard rules that cannot fit into any other family and cannot be programmed as external DLLs due to violation of syntax or MCell principles. One of these special rules is "Traffic CA" by David Griffeath and Larry Gray [5]. It's a probabilistic 1D rule that cannot be programmed as an external DLL because it can modify two cells when certain neighborhood conditions are met.

Traffic CA notation: TRCA, acceleration, braking, congested, driving
Example: TRCA,0.11,0.05,0.1,0.1,0.2,0.2 (TRCA)

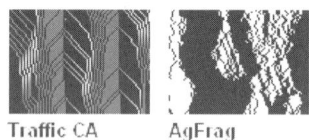

Fig. 10.12. Sample rules from the Special rules family.

User DLLs

Type: 1D and 2D, any neighborhood supported in MCell.

User DLLs family allows MCell users to program rules otherwise impossible to specify in the program. External DLLs can be programmed using any language and compiler producing 32-bit Windows standard DLL files. For detailed instructions of programming user DLLs, refer to [9]. Starting with version 4.20 of MCell, it is also possible to program user DLLs that define new parameterized families of rules. One such family, Weighted Generations, is described in Section 10.2.2.

Notation: DLL name, optional parameters specific to the DLL

Example: WeightedGen,C6,SW0;2;1;1;1,1, PW1;1;1;1;1;1;1, RS4;5, RB5

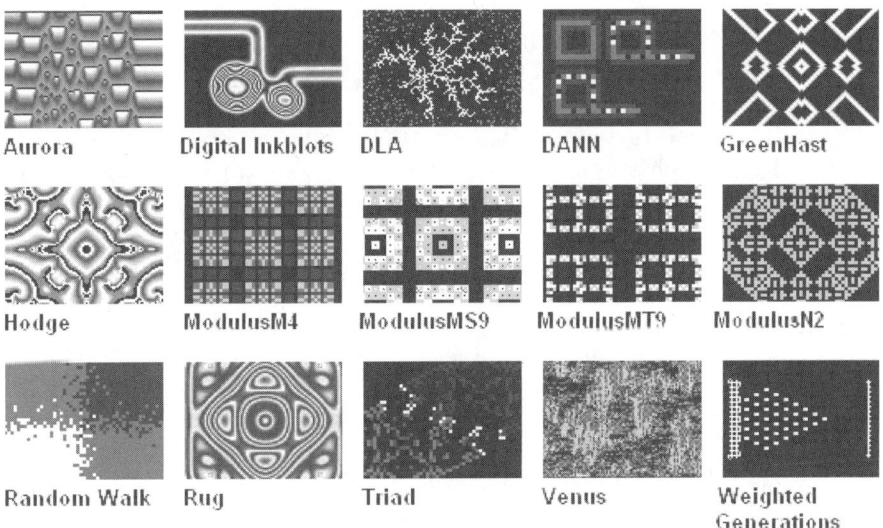

Fig. 10.13. Sample rules from the User DLLs family. See also color plate.

Vote for Life

Type: 2D, totalistic, in Moore neighborhood.

The Vote for Life family is by far the simplest family of rules in MCell. Its rules specify only how many alive neighbors (including the cell itself) must exist for the cell to be "on." Since cells consider their own state, the total number of neighbors can be 9 (not 8 as in "Life" rules). Every rule in this family can be also represented in the "Life" syntax. For example, Vote 46789 is equivalent to Life S35678/B4678.

Notation: states

Example: 46789 (Vote 4/5)

Feux Fredkin Vote Vote 4/5

Fig. 10.14. Sample rules from the Vote for Life family.

Weighted Generations

Type: 2D, totalistic or outer totalistic parameterization with optional decay, in Moore, von Neumann, and hexagonal neighborhood.

The Weighted Generations family, defined and explored in 2001 by Brian Prentice, is a natural extension of the Generations family. The extension simply permits any state to contribute to the neighbor's count using weights associated with each state. If a weight is n, and the corresponding state occurs m times in a cells neighborhood then the neighbor count is incremented by $n \times m$. If a state's weight is 0, then that state does not contribute to the neighbor count. Position weights identical to those used in the Weighted Life family are also supported.

The Weighted Generations family is implemented as a configurable user DLL, supported by MCell starting with version 4.20. The rule setup is controlled by DLL's own custom dialog box.

Notation: [C]ount of states, [SW]weights of states 0..C-1, [PW]position weights, [RS]survivals, [RB]births

Example: WeightedGen,C4,SW0;2;0;1,PW1;1;1;1;1;1;1;1, RS6;7;8;9;10;11, RB4 (WG Rule004)

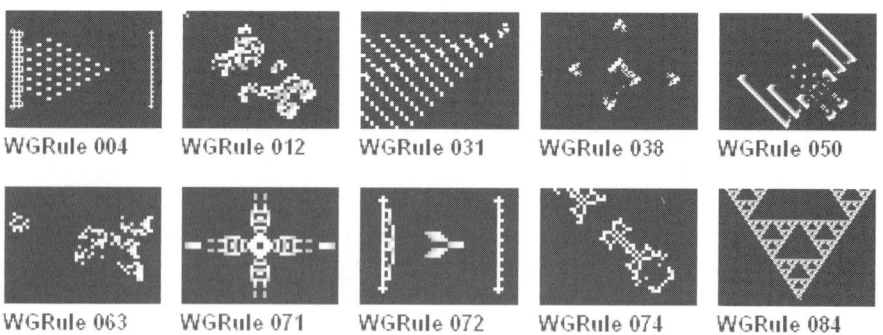

WGRule 004 WGRule 012 WGRule 031 WGRule 038 WGRule 050
WGRule 063 WGRule 071 WGRule 072 WGRule 074 WGRule 084

Fig. 10.15. Sample rules from the Weighted Generations family.

Weighted Life

Type: 2D, totalistic or outer totalistic parameterization with optional decay, in Moore, von Neumann and hexagonal neighborhood.

Weighted Life allows users to apply different weights to particular neighbors, including the cell itself. The weight of neighbors can be set within a range of -256 to 256. When calculating the count of neighbors, the sum of weights of alive neighbors is taken into account. The sum should be within a range of -2048 to 2048. Another extension of Weighted Life is the History, known already from the Generations family.

Weighted Life is one of the more complex families of rules in MCell. The rules of many other families (Life, Generations, Vote for Life, General binary) can be realized in it. For example, in order to realize Life rules, it's enough to assign 1 to all neighbors, 0 to the center cell and to switch off the history. One can also define hexagonal rules by defining NE and SW neighbors as 0.

Notation: NW, NN, NE, WW, EE, SW, SS, SE, ME-weights, HI-states, RS-survival, RB-birth

Example: NW0, NN1, NE0, WW1, ME0, EE1, SW0, SS1, SE0, HI7, RS2, RB1, RB2, RB3 (Cyclish)

10.2.3 Cellular Automata Patterns

One of the goals when programming MCell was to create a standard syntax for exchanging cellular automata patterns between different programs and operating systems. A text format has been selected as it is most portable, and patterns can even be embedded into e-mail and posted on newsgroups and forums. Several popular formats for storing Conway's Life patterns (LIFE1.05, LIFE1.06, RLE, XLife, ProLife, dbLife) already existed; however, none was suitable for storing patterns of general cellular automata. Finally, the RLE format was selected as a base and was next extended into MCL format [10].

The following listing shows the contents of a simple file defining a pattern for the Worms rule:

```
#MCell 4.00
#GAME Generations
#RULE 3467/25/6
#SPEED 20
#BOARD 300x300
#WRAP 1
#D
#D The universe of Worms.
#D
#D Discovered by Mirek Wojtowicz
#D 1999.04.08
```

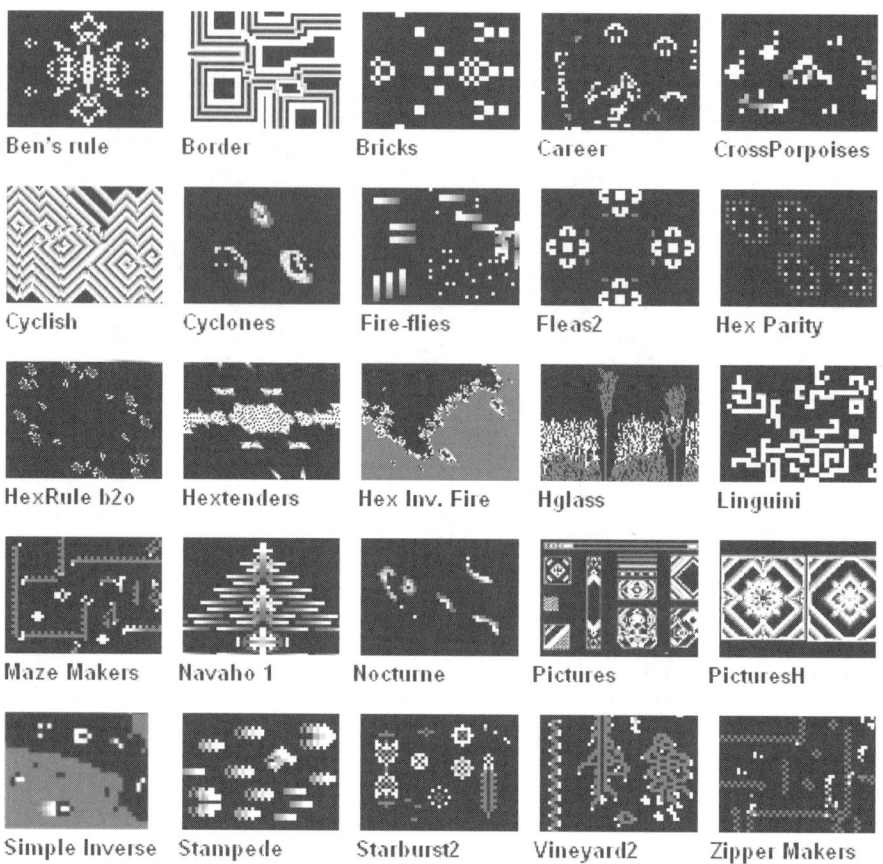

Fig. 10.16. Sample rules from the Weighted Life family.

```
#L  ..DE.DED$.CE.E.DD$BDBABBC$.CACCEC$.A.BD.B$..B3C$3.3A
#L  $..4A$3.AA31$8.AA$7.4A$7.3A$7.3CB$6.B.DB.A$6.CECCAC$
#L  6.CBBABDB$5.DD.E.EC$5.DED.ED
```

The above listing contains only the very basic elements of a pattern file. Full MCL format supports many more keywords and advanced features [10].

A large collection of patterns for supported rules has been collected. Many people have focused on particular rules and created amazing and beautiful patterns. The author has spent a lot of time browsing all available resources and recreating patterns stored on BBS and FTP servers, mentioned on Usenet, or embedded into older DOS-based software packages. The full collection is available in the MCell package. All readers are kindly requested to submit their collections and references to unsupported cellular automata resources.

10.2.4 Interesting Rules and Experiments

The full package of MCell contains a huge collection of more than 1700 CA patterns, illustrating over 30 years of research on CA rules. Many patterns were constructed with great accuracy by their authors to show special features of particular CA rules. To encourage the reader to browse the collection, several experiments are presented here.

Conway's Life

This is the CA rule that has started it all. It was defined in 1970 by the mathematician J. H. Conway, who was searching for a cellular automaton to be on the boundary between unbounded growth and decay into dullness. The rules are really simple:

- If a dead cell has 3 living neighbors, it will become alive in the next generation.
- If an alive cell has 2 or 3 living neighbors, it survives; otherwise, it dies in the next generation.

It was proven that Conway's Life CA chaotic behavior is unpredictable and it could be used to build a universal Turing machine and even a universal constructor. The contrast between the simplicity of this rule and the complexity of the behavior it produces is a constant source of wonder, which is reflected in patterns designed by enthusiasts from all over the world. The patterns contain ships (moving objects), oscillators, guns, reflectors, breeders, and even much more complicated structures, like the binary adder shown in Fig. 10.17.

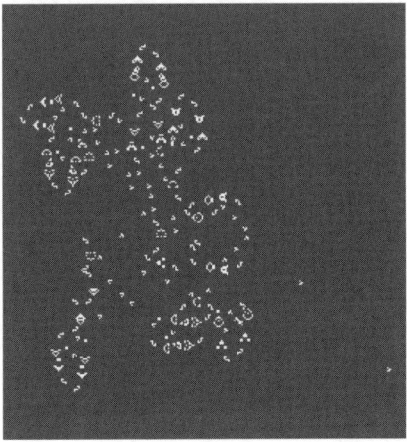

Fig. 10.17. Conway's Life rule — binary adder.

The presented binary adder was designed by David Buckingham in 1975 and next optimized by Mark Niemec. On the pattern two glider streams enter the lower right, representing the binary numbers 1110 and 0011. The sum, 10001, appears from the middle right side after about 1000 generations. The gliders go in and come out backward — that is, 1's place first. That way, the numbers to be added can be arbitrarily large.

WireWorld Rule

WireWorld is one of the oldest and well-explored cellular automata rules. The automaton was designed by Brian Silverman and was included in his program PHANTOM FISH TANK in 1987. A. K. Dewdney publicized WireWorld in his "Computer Recreations" column (*Scientific American*, January 1990). Cells in WireWorld have one of four possible states: background (0), electron head (1), electron tail (2), and wire (3). The rules for updating cells are

- Background (0) always remains background.
- Electron head (1) always changes to electron tail.
- Electron tail (2) always changes to wire.
- Wire (3) changes to electron head if one or two of its neighbors are electron heads.

These simple rules allow fairly complicated logic circuits to be constructed. The fascinating pattern presented in Fig. 10.18 comes from a "Cellular" package by Dr. J. Dana Eckart [15]. MCell is equipped in a large number of WireWorld patterns.

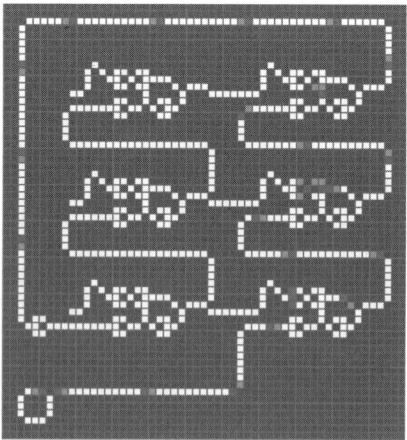

Fig. 10.18. WireWorld rule — sample circuit.

Cyclic Cellular Automata

The next experiment (Fig. 10.19) was created using the cyclic CA rule by David Griffeath [5] and illustrates a complex self-organization. Starting from a uniform random distribution over 14 colors, droplets of color waves nucleate fairly quickly. Soon virtually all of the initial "debris" are overrun by the droplets. As the last vestiges of debris are eliminated, vortices emerge from the disordered wave fronts, creating diamond-shaped spirals. By about time 300 the array is completely covered with periodic spirals, out of phase with one another, and not all of minimal period 14. Typically it takes much longer for the period 14 spiral cores to displace their feebler competitors.

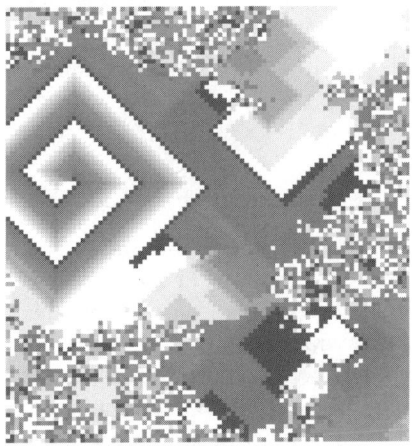

Fig. 10.19. Cyclic cellular automata — complex self-organization.

Rug

The last experiment presented here, Rug (Fig. 10.20), falls into the "beauty" category. It was defined by Rudy Rucker [6]. Rug rules are averaging rules using the full range of 256 possible states. To update itself in a Rug rule, every cell takes four steps:

1. Every cell calculates the sum of its eight nearest neighbors' states.
2. Every cell calculates the average neighbor state by dividing the sum by eight and throwing out any remainder.
3. Every cell computes its new state by adding an *increment* (usually the increment is 1) to the average neighbor state.
4. As a final step, new state is taken modulo 256.

The image presented in Fig. 10.20 was created from a single cell seed.

Fig. 10.20. Rug rule — beautiful kaleidoscopic images.

10.3 Program Usage

The program usage is rather intuitive and shouldn't pose significant difficulties to even nonexperienced users of MS Windows. After automatic installation the program can be conveniently launched from the created desktop icon or from Menu Start. For easy browsing of pattern files the program registers the .MCL extension in the system, thus allowing users to open patterns directly from the Windows Explorer, Web pages, or e-mails.

All program commands are available from the main menu. Most often used options are also available directly from toolbars, keyboard shortcuts, and local menus opened with the right mouse button click.

10.3.1 Browsing Cellular Automata Patterns

Browsing collected cellular automata patterns is probably the most popular and enjoyable application of MCell, so much effort has been put into making it easy and comfortable.

Most input/output operations on pattern files can be realized using the built-in File Manager — the vertical panel to the left of the program window. The main function of the File Manager is opening patterns. Right-clicking on any pattern file in the files panel will reveal additional functions — appending patterns to the active one, viewing pattern descriptions, extracting rule definitions only, getting only the cell's configuration without changing the active rule, and many more. In general, local menus opened with the right-click over the objects offer many object-related functions. Additionally, files can be loaded using the standard Open dialog, can be dropped from the Windows Explorer, can be pasted from the Clipboard or can be even opened from Internet locations.

The program offers many view manipulation functions. In addition to standard zooming and panning, it is also possible to fit the universe to the current window size or activate the auto-fit feature that will fit the world into the screen so that one can see the entire world to the maximum zoom possible during the whole experiment.

10.3.2 Designing Cellular Automata Patterns

MCell is also a comfortable pattern editor that offers drawing tools similar to those known from the graphical programs: a freehand pen, an eraser, tools for drawing line sections, circles, squares and rectangles, or the fill tool. Rectangular portions of patterns can be marked and freely manipulated: moved, replicated, rotated, mirrored, inverted, frozen, or copied to the Clipboard. The color palette allows fast active-state switching.

One very important feature for pattern designers is Undo. Undo can take snapshots of the experiments at specified times (either in terms of seconds, or generations), after specified events took place, or manually. The Undo stack can be viewed and can be undone to a certain point instantly. One can decide what events (from 13 predefined) can cause the Undo stack to auto-expand. Undone snapshots do not disappear — they can be restored with the Redo button or from the snapshots list. A snapshot is always taken of Generation 0, enabling the user to "Replay" the whole pattern repeatedly. The count of stored Undo snapshots is limited by memory.

Before saving, designed patterns can be provided with comprehensive descriptions telling, for example, the purpose of the experiment or how it should be performed. A pattern's descriptions can be viewed using the MCell's File Manager without opening the pattern.

Initial patterns are essential to exploring CA rules. Some rules (for example, Conway's Life) show most interesting results only when applied to carefully designed patterns. Other rules (for example, StarWars) produce fascinating output also when applied to random patterns. The built-in, fully configurable Seeding dialog box offers many ways of initializing the universe or its portions with random or designed patterns. Selected randomizing / seeding parameters can be saved with any name and later restored with one click. The dialog box offers many sophisticated area / coloring / density / mode selections and statistical (Bernoulli) and exact seeding, as shown in Fig. 10.21.

10.3.3 Exploring Cellular Automata Rules

One of the key features of MCell is exploring existing and designing new CA rules. The collected library of rules is briefly described in Section 10.2.2. Existing rules can easily be activated either by selecting them directly from the lists available on the status bar (Fig. 10.1) and in the Rules setup dialog

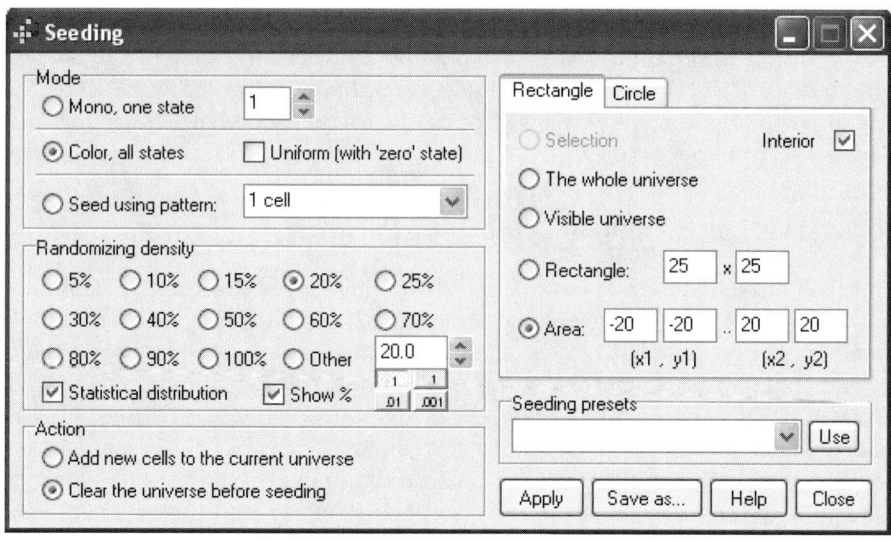

Fig. 10.21. Seeding dialog box.

box (Fig. 10.22), or simply by loading pattern files, which also contain full rules definitions.

The Rules setup dialog box (Fig. 10.22) is a central point for designers of rules. The dialog box is nonmodal and offers access to the main MCell window without closing it, which allows for easy exploring of the existing rules and testing of the new rules.

The exact layout of the Rules setup dialog box depends on the selected family. Figure 10.22 shows the dialog with the "Hexrule b2o" rule of the "Weighted Life" family active. For rules in this family one can define the count of states (also known as cell size), "weights" of all eight neighbors and of the center cell, the survival and births totals. Regardless of the active rules family, a text version of the currently active rule is shown. Rules can be defined either by changing their parameters using available widgets (which update the text version), or by modifying the text version (which updates the widget's state). This way, rules can even be copied and pasted into the text box.

Patterns explorers often use the "Random rule" function. It does not select from available rules, but rather allows creating new rules for the active family using random parameters. A great number of really impressive rules have been discovered this way.

Additional to the rule and universe parameters, the program offers several possibilities for adding subtle disturbances to the running experiments, handled by a Diversities dialog box. The Diversities dialog box allows users to enable/disable any combination of four available disturbances: Noise (adding random alive cells), Black hole (a square area of the lattice with permanent

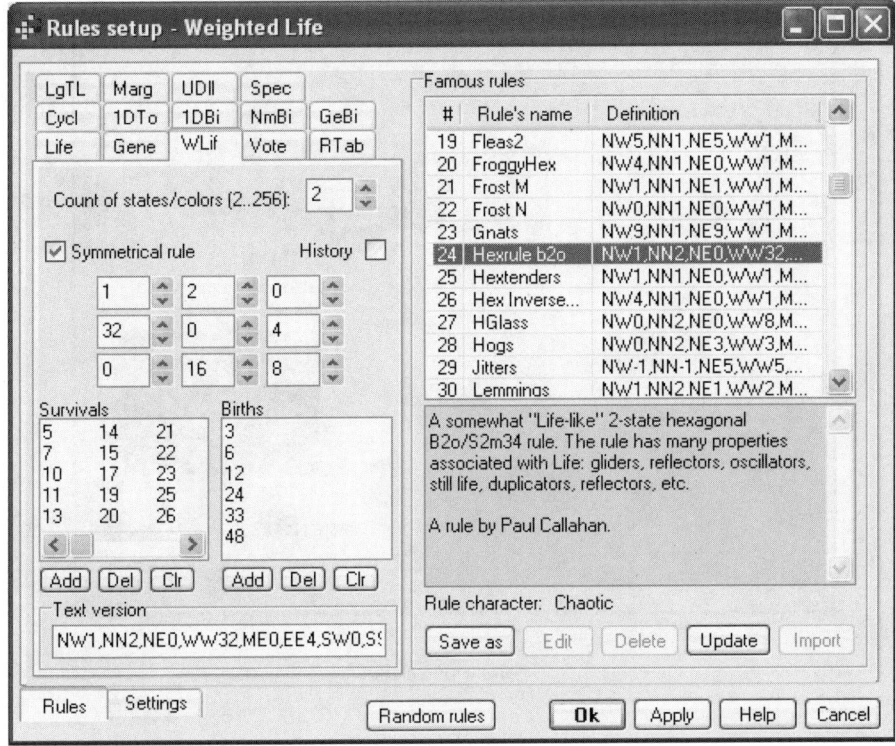

Fig. 10.22. Rules customization dialog box.

state 0), SuperNova (a square area of the lattice with permanent state 1), and an Input stream (a sequence of cells that will be injected at a specified location). It is possible to save the state of diversities with the pattern files.

10.3.4 Program Configuration

The program is highly configurable, from the user interface to cell shapes and colors, board parameters, open/save functionality, or Undo settings. Separate settings dialog tabs allow associating common CA files extensions with the program. One can also decide how and what to save with the pattern. A screenshot of the color customization screen is shown in Fig. 10.23.

10.3.5 Analyses

MCell is equipped with a number of tools performing basic analytical examinations. The simplest tool, Period checker, allows for an easy and fast detection of oscillators and ships and, when found, measures their periods and speeds.

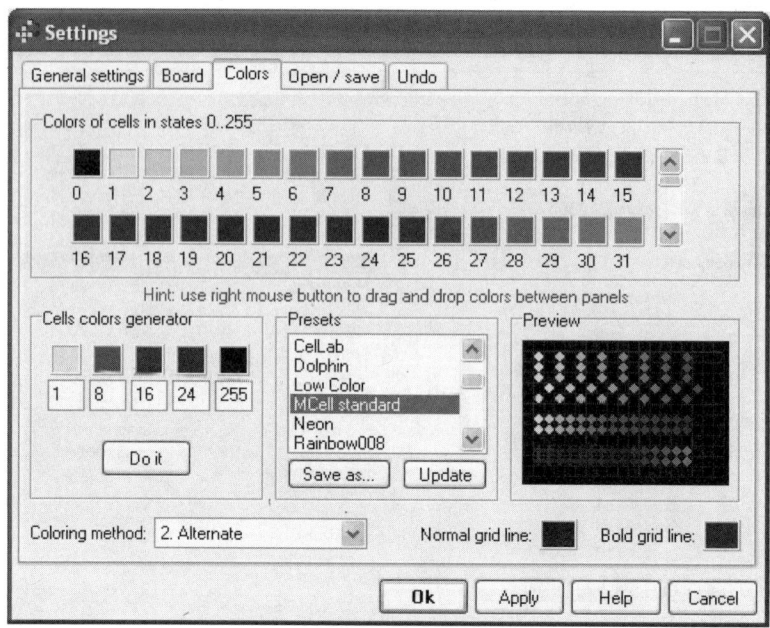

Fig. 10.23. color customization screen.

The Period checker allows users to run experiments with full speed, without updating the view of the pattern.

In some experiments the number of cells in each state is more important than the actual pattern. Figure 10.24 illustrates the basic density statistics window. The dialog box shows the states distribution of the current pattern, and some statistical information, like the board size, current count of cells, and maximum count of cells in the current run of the pattern. The statistics window can stay open and be automatically updated while the pattern is running.

Another option allows users to create a population log that saves statistics on the states as the CA updates. This text file can be easily imported into applications like Microsoft Excel (using semicolons as data delimiter). Figure 10.25 illustrates the dynamics of the 2-cell seeding of the StarWars rule.

More advanced analyses can be performed with two other tools — Transitions and Correlations. The Transitions tool performs a calculation on how often the given site (x, y) changes the state from state c1 to state c2. Up to nine transitions can be tracked simultaneously. The (pair spatial) Joint Correlations tool measures the proportion of times t that cell (x1, y1) takes on the value c1 AND cell (x2, y2) takes on the value c2. The Centered (normalized) Correlations tool performs a slightly more complicated calculation that

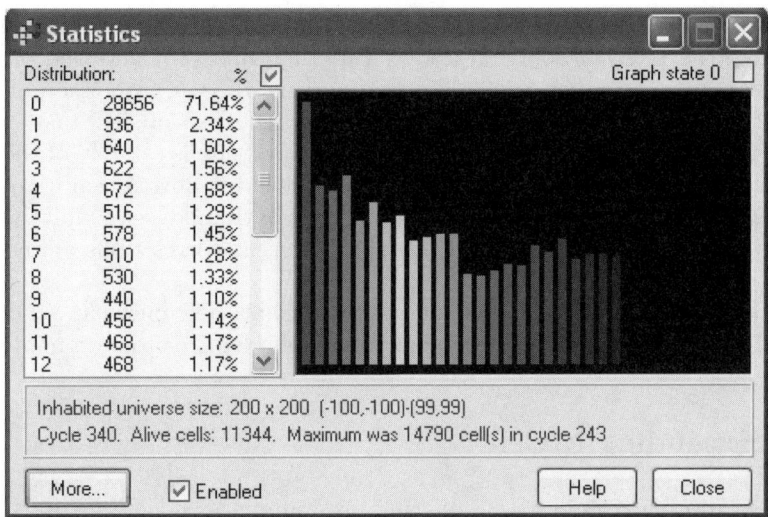

Fig. 10.24. Density statistics.

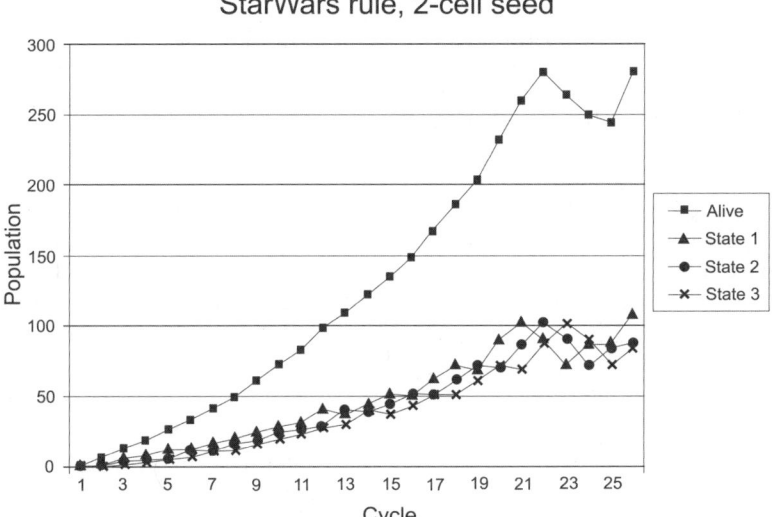

Fig. 10.25. Sample population graph.

indicates positive, negative, or 0 correlations. As in Joint Correlations one computes the AND proportion above. But then one subtracts the product: "proportion of times (x1, y1) takes on the value c1" × "proportion of times (x2, y2) takes on the value c2." For instance, if the pair of sites takes on the ordered pair of values (1, 2) 5% of the time, the first site is a 1 25% of the time, and the second site is a 2 20% of the time, then this normalized correlation is 0. The Correlations dialog allows performing both analyses simultaneously. It also allows users to measure up to nine different correlations at the same time.

If the built-in analytical tools are not sufficient, new ones can be created that will communicate with the program using the OLE Automation interface.

10.4 Extending MCell

MCell is an open CA platform offering programmers and power users many possibilities for extending the program capabilities. It's possible to write your own rules overcoming MCell limitations, create utilities automating often performed tasks, program analyzing plugins, demo shells, and many others. Finally, the source code (Delphi 7) of the program is available, which allows users to extend the program in virtually unlimited directions.

10.4.1 Programming User Rules

User rules are programmed as standalone DLLs that are dynamically loaded by MCell at run time. One can compile them using any Windows 32-bit compiler supporting __stdcall (or _pascal) method of passing parameters. Provided examples show programming user DLLs in Microsoft Visual C 6.0, Borland Delphi 4.0/5.0, and in Borland C++ Builder 3.0/4.0. Despite many efforts, we didn't succeed yet with programming compatible DLLs with Visual Basic. One should, however, have no such problems with other compilers capable of creating DLLs.

The user DLLs mechanism is very powerful. It is even possible to program interactive rules that read parameters from disk files or prompt the user for input. The whole user DLLs specification is available at [9], as well as step-by-step procedures for creating simple DLLs in many programming environments. The MCell package contains full sources of 25 user DLLs.

10.4.2 Extending the MCell Interface

The automation interface implemented in MCell makes it possible for external applications to control MCell through its exposed methods and properties. Almost every 32-bit programming language can be used to write applications controlling MCell. The most popular ones are Visual Basic, Visual C++,

Borland Delphi, Borland C++ Builder, or even Microsoft Word and Excel (through macros).

MCell exposes nine objects (*theApplication, theUniverse, theWindow, thePalette, theSelection, theSeeding, theUndo, theTransitions, theCorrelations*), each with many properties and methods. For a full documentation of MCell's Automation interface and samples, refer to [12].

The following simple example shows an MS Word Basic macro, which starts MCell, creates a new pattern, activates the Game of Life rule, draws 60 cells in a line, and runs the created pattern.

```
Dim objUni As Object
Dim objWin As Object
Public Sub RunLineOfCells()
   'create Automation objects, start MCell
   Set objUni = CreateObject("MCell.theUniverse")
   Set objWin = CreateObject("MCell.theWindow")
   'prepare an empty universe
   objUni.Clear
   'activate the Conway's Game of Life rule
   objUni.Game = "Life"
   objUni.Rule = "23/3"
   'add 60 cells in a line
   Dim i As Integer
   For i = 0 To 59
     Call objUni.SetCell(i, 0, 1)
   Next i
   'redisplay the board
   objWin.Refresh
   'run
   objUni.Run
End Sub
```

10.4.3 Going Java

As a companion to Windows MCell, a Java applet has been developed [11] that allows the running of nearly all rules supported by MCell under the control of other operating systems. The applet is programmed in a very basic version of Java, AWT 1.1, and has been confirmed to run under all versions of Windows, and under Linux and Macintosh using browsers supporting AWT 1.1. The applet handles all rules from 13 CA families and is equipped with over 1500 patterns. Although not as rich in features as MCell, MJCell also allows users to experiment with new patterns and rules.

Figure 10.26 shows the main screen of the MJCell applet.

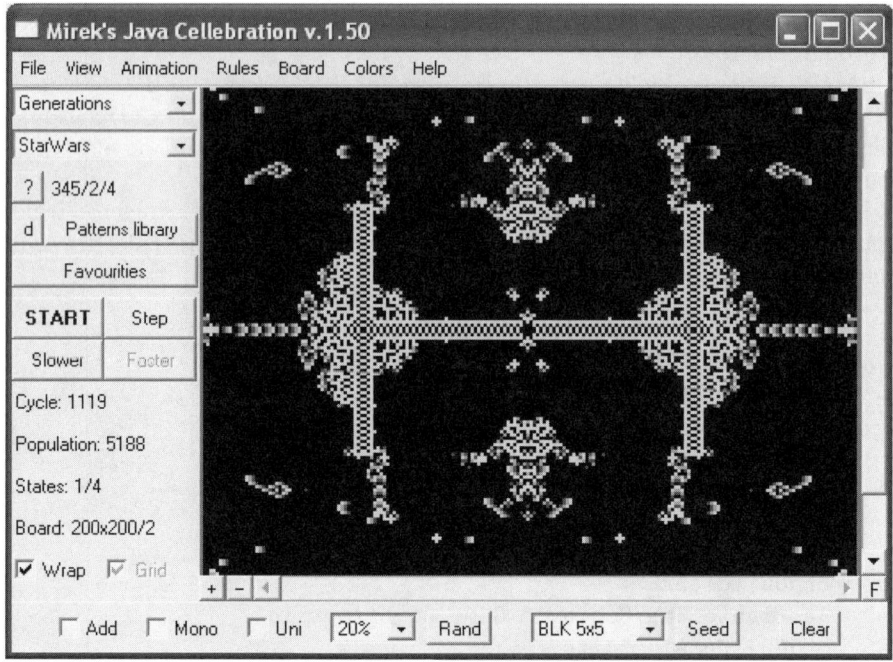

Fig. 10.26. MJCell's main screen.

10.5 Summary

After five years of development MCell has become a mature software allowing active exploration of a wide range of CA. It has not only brought satisfaction to the author, but has also allowed users to perform many scientific experiments, has been a source of enjoyment for many people, and has become popular among students all over the world. The last category of users may not necessarily share my enthusiasm about MCell since I receive lots of desperate e-mails asking me for help with their school assignments.

MCell isn't perfect, however, and will never be finished. Still in 2004 a new version was released that removes some universe restrictions, thus allowing for even more experiments to be run. The program is in use in many countries, often using languages other than English, so full localization of the program is planned. Some volunteers have also started porting the program to Linux.

References

1. John von Neumann
   http://www-groups.dcs.st-and.ac.uk/~history/Mathematicians/Von_Neumann.html

2. Stanislaw Marcin Ulam
   http://www-groups.dcs.st-and.ac.uk/~history/Mathematicians/Ulam.html
3. Cellular Automata by Tim Tyler
   http://cell-auto.com/
4. MCell home page,
   http://www.mirekw.com/ca/
5. David Griffeath, The Primordial Soup Kitchen,
   http://psoup.math.wisc.edu/kitchen.html
6. Rudy Rucker's Home Page,
   http://www.mathcs.sjsu.edu/faculty/rucker/
7. Stephen Wolfram's "A New Kind of Science",
   http://www.wolframscience.com/thebook.html
8. Cellular Automata rules lexicon,
   http://www.mirekw.com/ca/ca_rules.html
9. Programming user DLLs,
   http://www.mirekw.com/ca/user_rules.html
10. Cellular Automata files formats,
    http://www.mirekw.com/ca/ca_files_formats.html
11. MJCell, Java applet,
    http://www.mirekw.com/ca/mjcell/mjcell.html
12. MCell Automation interface,
    http://www.mirekw.com/ca/automation.html
13. CelLab's home page,
    http://www.fourmilab.ch/cellab/
14. Cellsprings' home page,
    http://jmge.net/java/csprings/
15. Cellular's home page,
    http://staff.vbi.vt.edu/dana/ca/cellular.shtml
16. Collidoscope and SARCASim's home page,
    http://www.collidoscope.com/ca/
17. DDLab's home page,
    http://www.ddlab.com/
18. Life32's home page,
    http://psoup.math.wisc.edu/Life32.html
19. StarLogo's home page,
    http://education.mit.edu/starlogo/
20. Tim Tyler's home page,
    http://timtyler.org/

11

Discrete Dynamics Lab: Tools for Investigating Cellular Automata and Discrete Dynamical Networks

Andrew Wuensche

Networks of sparsely interconnected elements with discrete values and updating in parallel are central to a wide range of natural and artificial phenomena drawn from many areas of science; from physics to biology to cognition; to social and economic organization; to parallel computation and artificial life; to complex systems in general.

"Decision-making" networks like this are applied as idealized models in the study of complexity and emergence, and in the behavior of networks in general, including biomolecular networks such as neural and genetic networks [3,4,6,10,12]. The networks themselves have intrinsic interest as mathematical, physical, dynamical, and computational systems with a large body of literature devoted to their study [1,7,8]. Because the dynamics is difficult to describe by classical mathematics, computer simulation is required, and there is a need for simulation software for nonexperts in programming to model networks in their particular fields.

Discrete Dynamics Lab (DDLab) is able to construct these networks (Fig. 11.1) and investigate many aspects of their dynamical behavior. DDLab is interactive graphics software, widely used in research and education, for studying cellular automata (CA), random Boolean networks (RBN) [4], and discrete dynamical networks in general (DDN), where the "Boolean" attribute is extended to multivalue. There are currently versions of DDLab for Mac, Linux, Unix, Irix, and DOS. The source code is written in C. It may be made available on request, subject to various conditions.

As well as generating space-time patterns in one, two, or three dimensions, DDLab is able to construct attractor basins, graphs that link network states according to their transitions (Fig. 11.2), analogous to Poincaré's "phase portrait" that provided powerful insights in continuous dynamics. A key insight is that the dynamics on the networks converges, thus fall into a number of basins of attraction. This is the network's memory, its ability to hierarchically categorize its patterns of activation (state-space), as a function of the precise network architecture [10].

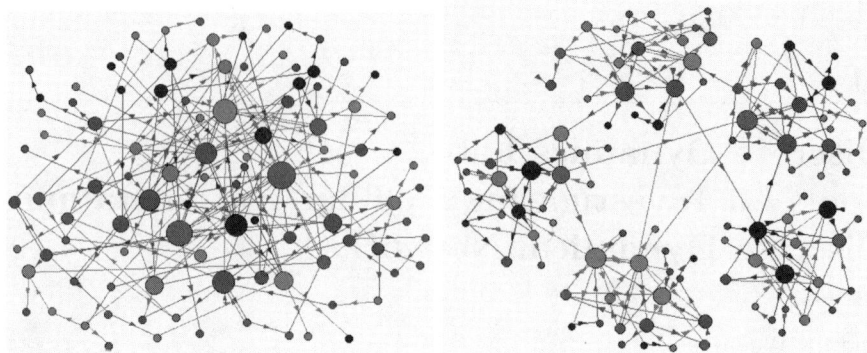

Fig. 11.1. Hypothetical networks of interacting elements (size $n=100$) with an approximate power-law distribution of connections, both inputs (k) and outputs, are represented by directed links (with arrows). Nodes are scaled according to k and average $k \simeq 2.2$. *Left*: A fully connected network. *Right*: A network made up of five weakly interlinked $n=20$ subnetworks or modules.

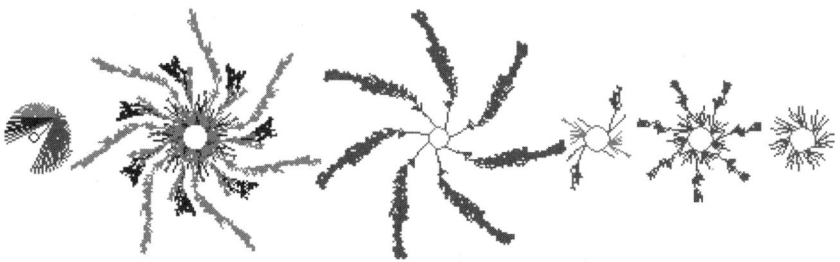

Fig. 11.2. The basin of attraction field of a binary (value range $v=2$) Cellular automaton (CA), $k=3$, $n=14$, rule 193, with equivalent basins suppressed.

Relating this to space-time patterns in CA, high convergence implies order, low convergence implies disorder or chaos [8]. The most interesting emergent structures occur at the transition, sometimes called the "edge of chaos" [5,13].

DDLab has recently been generalized for multivalue logic. Up to eight values (or colors) are now possible, instead of just Boolean logic (two values — 0,1). Of course, with just two values selected, DDLab behaves as before [15]. Multivalues open up new possibilities for dynamical behavior and modeling.

Another major update is an option to constrain DDLab to run forward-only, to generate space-time patterns for various types of totalistic rules, reducing memory load by cutting out all basin of attraction functions. This allows larger neighborhoods (max-k=25, instead of 13). In 2D the neighborhoods are predefined to make hexagonal as well square lattices. Many interesting cellular automaton rules with "life"-like and other complex dynamics can be found in totalistic multivalue rule-space, in 3D as well as 2D [16].

DDLab is an applications program, it does not require writing code. Network parameters and the graphics presentation can be flexibly set, reviewed and altered interactively, including changes on-the-fly. There are built-in tools for constructing and manipulating networks. A wide variety of measures, data, analysis, and statistics are available. For small networks, it is possible to compute and draw basins of attraction, and measure their convergence and stability to perturbation. For larger networks, basins of attraction can be investigated statistically. This chapter provides some general background and gives the flavor of DDLab with a range of examples; the figures shown were all produced within DDLab. The operating manual [14] describes all of DDLab's many functions and includes a "quick start" chapter. DDLab is available at www.ddlab.org and www.cogs.susx.ac.uk/users/andywu/ddlab.html.

DDLab remains free shareware for personal, noncommercial, users. Any other users, including commercial users, companies, government agencies, research or educational institutions, must register and pay a license fee (see www.ddlab.org/ddinc.html).

11.1 Basins of Attraction

Figure 11.4 provides a summary of the idea of state-space and basins of attraction in discrete dynamical networks, sometimes called decision-making networks. The dynamics depends on the connections and update logic of each element, which "decides" its next value based on the values of the few elements that provide its inputs, which might include self-input. The result is a complex web of feedback making the dynamics difficult to treat analytically, despite the simplicity of the underlying network. In fact, although the dynamics is deterministic, the future is in general unpredictable. Understanding these systems relies chiefly on computer simulation.

11.2 Discrete Dynamical Networks

Acronym glossary:

- CA: Cellular automata: nearest-neighbor wiring and a homogeneous rule.
- RBN: random Boolean networks: random wiring and heterogeneous rules, possibly heterogeneous neighborhoods k.
- DDN: discrete dynamical networks: including RBN, but allowing a value range $v \geq 2$. CA and RBN are special cases of DDN.

A discrete dynamical network in DDLab can be imagined as a software simulation of a collection of light bulbs that transmit information to each other about their color state (on/off for binary), and change color according to the arriving signals. More abstractly, the network is made up of elements or "cells," connected to each other by directed links or "wires," where a wire has

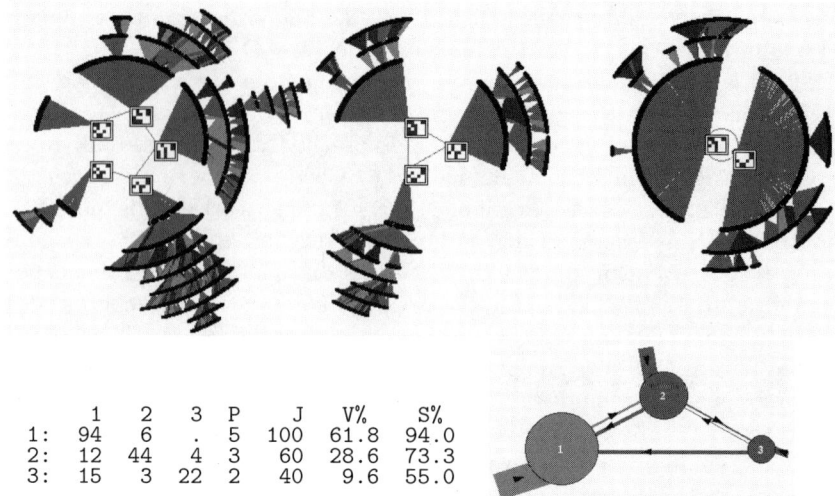

	1	2	3	P	J	V%	S%
1:	94	6	.	5	100	61.8	94.0
2:	12	44	4	3	60	28.6	73.3
3:	15	3	22	2	40	9.6	55.0

Fig. 11.3. The basin of attraction field of one of the $n=20$ subnetworks shown in detail in Fig. 11.1. The binary rules were assigned at random. State-space (size $2^{20} \simeq$ 1.05 million) is partitioned into three basins of attraction. The attractor states are shown as 5×4-bit patterns. The table, and diagram lower right, show the probability of jumping between basins due to one-bit perturbations of their attractor states. P = attractor period, J = possible jumps ($P \times n$), $V\%$ is the basin "volume" as a percentage of state-space, and $S\%$ is the percentage of self-jumps for each basin. All three basins are relatively stable because $S > V$. The lower right diagram, the "attractor jump-graph," shows the same data graphically; node size reflects basin volume, link thickness percentage jumps, arrows the direction, and the short stubs self-jumps.

an input and output terminal. A cell takes on a value (or color) and transmits this value down its output wires. Its value is updated as a function of the values on its input wires. Updating is usually done in parallel, in discrete "timesteps," but may also be sequential in a predetermined order.

This is the system in a nutshell. It remains to set up the network according to its various parameters.

- The value-range, v. The range of values available to a cell. In other words, the number of possible internal states of the cell, or colors, or letters in its "alphabet." In older versions of DDLab this was limited to just 2 values (0,1), but can now be selected from 2 to 8.
- The number of network elements, the system size, n.
- How the elements are arranged in space: in a 1D, 2D, or 3D lattice with axial dimensions i, j, h, or some other arrangement. This network "geometry" may have real meaning (depending on the "wiring scheme" below), or it may simply allow convenient indexing and representation.

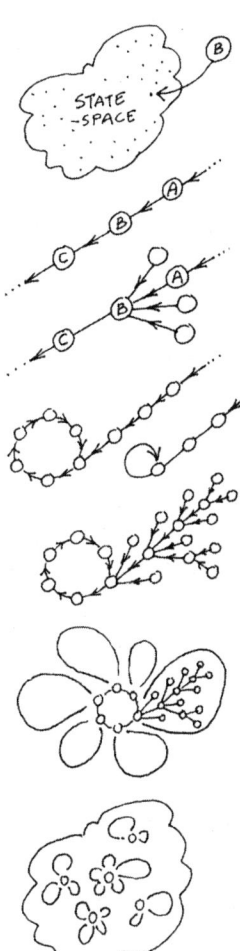

For a binary network size n, an example of one of its states B might be $1010\ldots0110$. *State-space* is made up of all 2^n states, the space of possible bitstrings or patterns.

Part of a *trajectory* in state-space, where C is a successor of B, and A is a predecessor (*pre-image*) of B, according to the dynamics on the network.

The state B may have other pre-images besides A, the total is the *in-degree*. The pre-image states may have their own pre-images or none. States without pre-images are known as *garden-of-Eden* states.

Any trajectory must sooner or later encounter a state that occurred previously — it has entered an attractor cycle. The trajectory leading to the attractor is a *transient*. The period of the attractor is the number of states in its cycle, which may be just one — a point attractor.

Take a state on the attractor, find its pre-images (excluding the pre-image on the attractor). Now find the pre-images of each pre-image, and so on, until all garden-of-Eden states are reached. The graph of linked states is a *transient tree* rooted on the attractor state. Part of the transient tree is a subtree defined by its root.

Construct each transient tree (if any) from each attractor state. The complete graph is the *basin of attraction*. Some basins of attraction have no transient trees, just the bare "attractor."

Now find every attractor cycle in state-space and construct its basin of attraction. This is the *basin of attraction field* containing all 2^n states in state-space, but now linked according to the dynamics on the network. Each discrete dynamical network imposes a particular basin of attraction field on state-space.

Fig. 11.4. State-space and basins of attraction.

- The number of input wires, k, to each cell, or the "k-mix" if k is not homogeneous. k may vary from 0 to 25. Maximum k is reduced for greater value-range v.
- The "wiring scheme": defining the location of the output terminals of each cell's input wires, the element's "neighborhood." CA have a homogeneous "nearest-neighbor" (local) neighborhood throughout the network. RBN and DDN may have a completely arbitrary wiring scheme (a "pseudo-neighborhood"). The wiring scheme can be assigned at random, or may be biased in some way, for example, by confining an element's pseudo-neighborhood close to itself. The wiring scheme also defines boundary con-

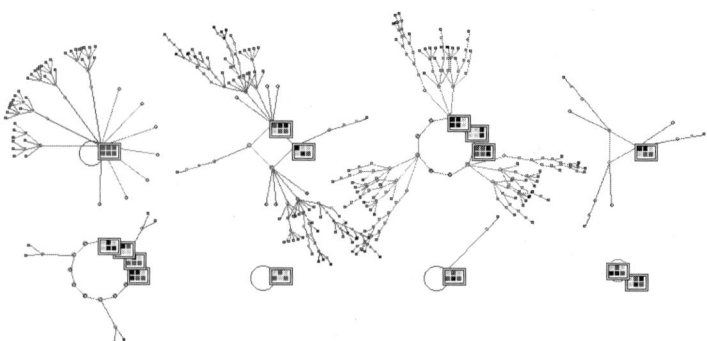

Fig. 11.5. The basin of attraction field of a multivalue $v=3$ $n=6$, $k=3$ CA. The look-up table is 120201201020211201022121111 (1886122584a655 in hex). Just the 8 nonequivalent basins are shown from a total of 23, and attractor nonequivalent states are shown as a 2D pattern. State-space $= v^k = 3^6 = 729$.

ditions. CA wiring usually requires periodic boundary conditions, where an array's edges wrap around to their opposite edges.

- The "rule scheme": the rules or logical functions in the network. Each element applies a rule to its inputs to compute its output. Usually this is made into a look-up table, the "rule table," listing the outputs of all possible input patterns. CA have a homogeneous rule scheme, the same rule throughout the network. RBN and DDN may have a completely arbitrary, heterogeneous, rule scheme, or again, it may be biased in some way.

DDlab is able to create networks with any combination of these parameters, and graphically represent and analyze both the networks themselves and the dynamics resulting from the changing patterns as the complex feedback web unfolds. Network updating may be sequential as well as parallel, noisy as well as deterministic.

11.3 Space-Time Patterns and Basins of Attraction

DDLab has two alternative ways of looking at network dynamics: *local* dynamics, running the network forward, and *global* dynamics, which entails running the network backward.

Running forward generates the network's space-time patterns from a given initial state. Many alternative graphical representations of space-time patterns, and methods for gathering and analyzing data, are available to illustrate different aspects of local network dynamics, including "filtering" to show up emergent structures more clearly as in Fig. 11.8.

Running "backward" generates multiple predecessors rather than a trajectory of unique successors. This procedure reconstructs the branching subtree

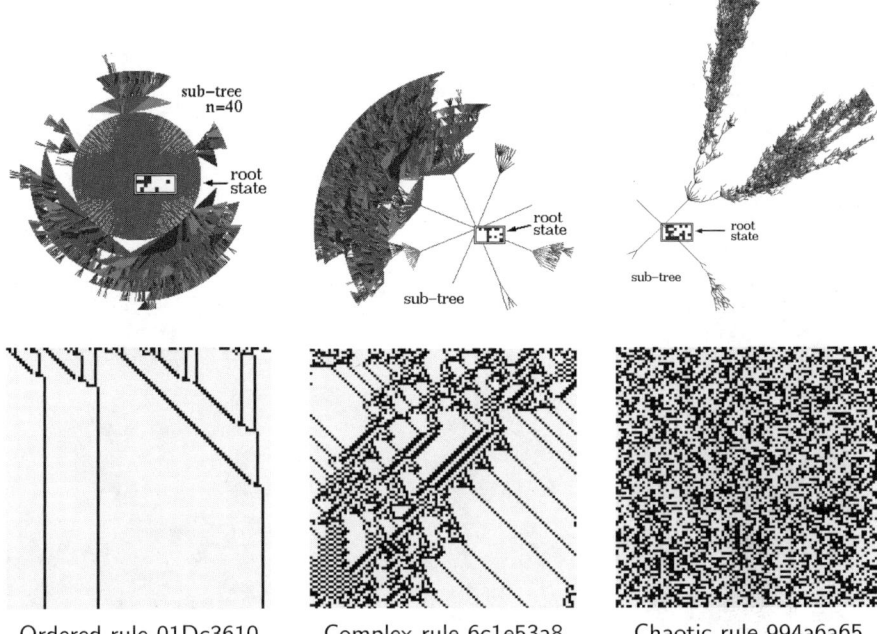

Fig. 11.6. Ordered, complex, and chaotic dynamics of 1D binary CA are illustrated by the space-time patterns and subtrees of three typical $k=5$ rules (shown in hex). The bottom row shows the space-time patterns from the same random initial state. The bit-strings ($n=100$) of successive time steps (represented by white and black dots) are shown horizontally one below the other; time proceeds down. Above each space-time pattern is a typical subtree for the same rule. In this case $n=40$ for the ordered rule, and $n=50$ for the complex and chaotic rules. The root states were reached by first iterating the system forward by a few steps from a random initial state, then tracing the subtree backward. Note that the convergence in the subtrees, their branchiness or typical in-degree, relates to order-chaos in space-time patterns, where order has high, chaos low, convergence.

of ancestor patterns rooted on a particular state. States without predecessors are disclosed, the so-called "garden-of-Eden" states, the leaves of the subtrees. Subtrees, basins of attraction (with a topology of trees rooted on attractor cycles), or the entire basin of attraction field can be displayed as directed graphs in real time, with many presentation options, and methods for gathering/analyzing data. The attractor basins of "random maps" may be generated, with or without some bias in the mapping.

Attractor basins represent the network's "memory" by their hierarchical categorization of state-space; each basin is categorized by its attractor and each subtree by its root. Learning/forgetting algorithms allow attaching/detaching sets of states as predecessors of a given state by automatically mutating rules or changing connections.

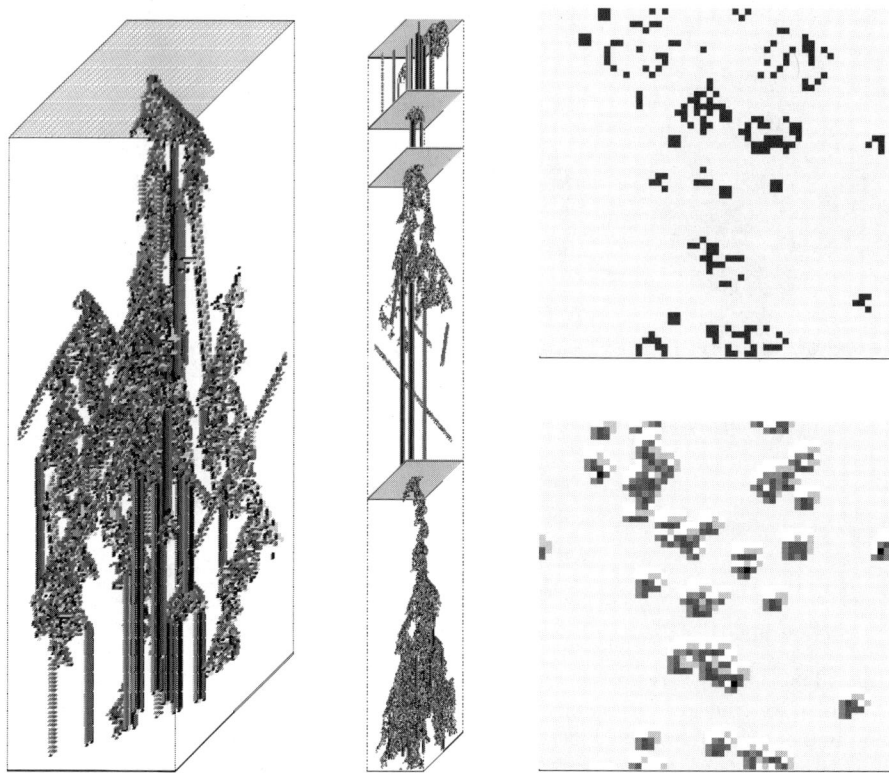

Fig. 11.7. Space-time pattern of the 2D game of Life [2], ($v=2$, $k=9$, $n = 55 \times 55$) in a 3D isometric projection. 2D time steps stack below each other and are shown as if looking up at a transparent shaft. *Left*: Starting from the "r-pentomino" seed. *Center*: Rescaled to the smallest scale, new seeds set at intervals. *Upper right*: A 2D state (time step) colored according to value. *Lower right*: The same state colored according to the neighborhood look-up. See also color plate.

11.4 DDLab User Interface

DDLab is an interactive applications program that does not require writing code. The graphical user interface allows setting, viewing, and amending network parameters, and the various presentation and analysis functions, by responding to prompts or accepting defaults.

The prompts present themselves in a main sequence for the most common 1D CA parameters. and also in a number of context-dependent pop-up windows for DDN, 2D and 3D networks, and various special settings.

A flashing cursor prompts for input. Just enter **return** if in doubt, or the appropriate input from the keyboard. Press **q**, **backspace** (or the right mouse button) to revise. **return** (or the left mouse button) to accept and move on to the next prompt or routine. Just **return** (or left mouse button) automatically

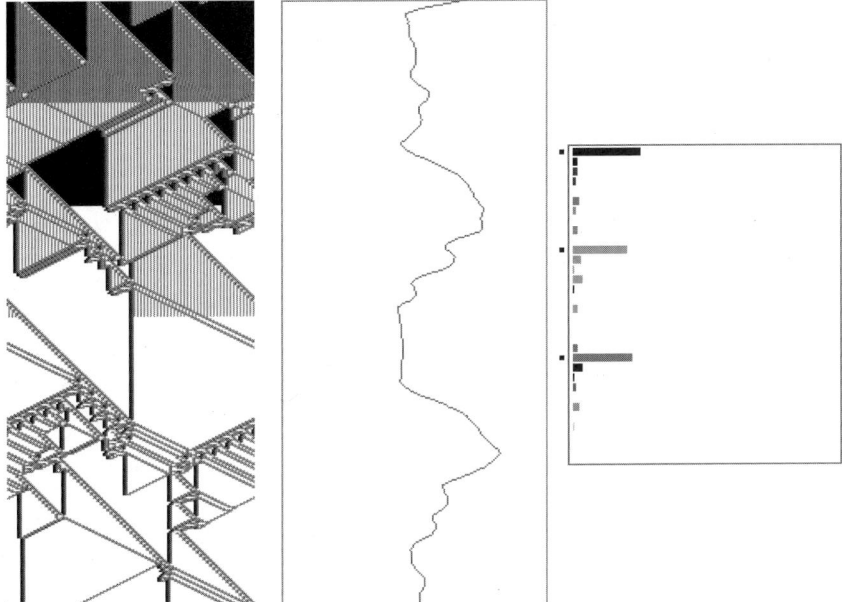

Fig. 11.8. A space-time pattern of a complex 1D CA, $v = 2$, $k = 5$, hex rule e9 f6 a8 15, $n = 150$. About 360 time steps, and some analysis shown by default: *Left*: The space-time pattern colored according to neighborhood look-up, and progressively "filtered" on-the-fly at three times, suppressing the background domain to show up "gliders" more clearly. *Center and right*: The input-entropy plot of the look-up frequency histogram, relative to a moving window of 10 time steps.

selects a default. To backtrack to the preceding prompt, revise, or interrupt a running process such as space-time patterns or attractor basins being generated, press **q** or the right mouse button. To quit DDLab immediately (except for DOS), enter **Ctrl-q** at any prompt, followed by **q**. Otherwise backtrack with **q** to the start of the program.

11.5 Initial Choices

Some initial choices in the prompt sequence set the stage for all subsequent DDLab operations, There is a choice to constrain DDLab to run forward-only for various types of totalistic rules; this reduces memory load by cutting out full look-up tables and all attractor functions; it allows larger neighborhoods, up to max-k=25 instead of max-k=13.

If DDLab is not constrained as above, there is a further choice; either to show the whole basin of attraction field, or alternatively to show something

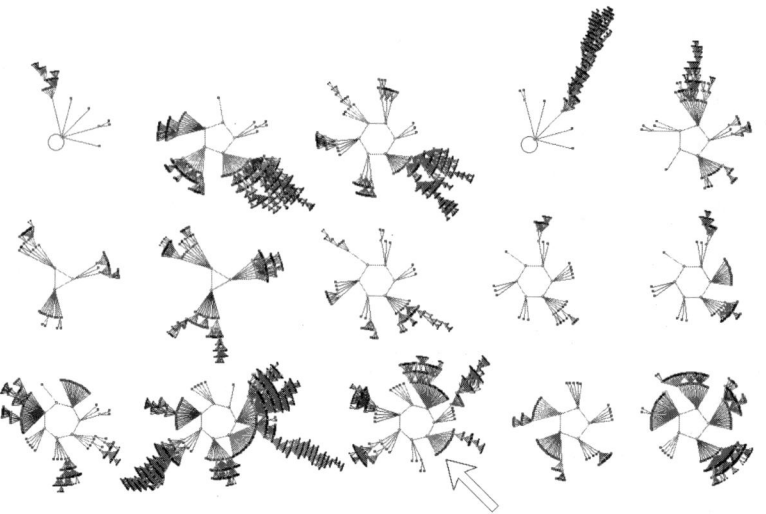

Fig. 11.9. The basin of attraction field of a small random Boolean network, $n=13$. The $2^{13} = 8192$ states in state space are organized into 15 basins, with attractor periods ranging between 1 and 7, and basin volume between 68 and 2724. The arrow points to the basin shown in more detail in Fig. 11.10. See also color plate.

that requires an initial state: a single basin of attraction, a subtree, or just space-time patterns.

The value-range v can be set from 2 to 8. If $v=2$, DDLab behaves as in the old binary version. Note that as v is increased, the size of max-k will diminish, but this also depends on whether DDLab was constrained to run forward-only for totalistic rules. For example, for $v=8$ and unconstrained, max-$k=4$ to handle the large look-up table; if constrained, max $k=11$.

11.6 Setting the Network Size

The network size n for 1D is set early on in the prompt sequence, but this is superseded if a 2D (i,j) or 3D (i,j,h) network is selected in a subsequent prompt window.

For space-time patterns, the network size is limited to $n=65{,}025$, based on the maximum size of a 2D network $(i,j)=255\times 255$. This limit also applies for single basins and subtrees, though in practice much smaller sizes are appropriate, except when generating subtrees for maximally chaotic CA "chain rules".

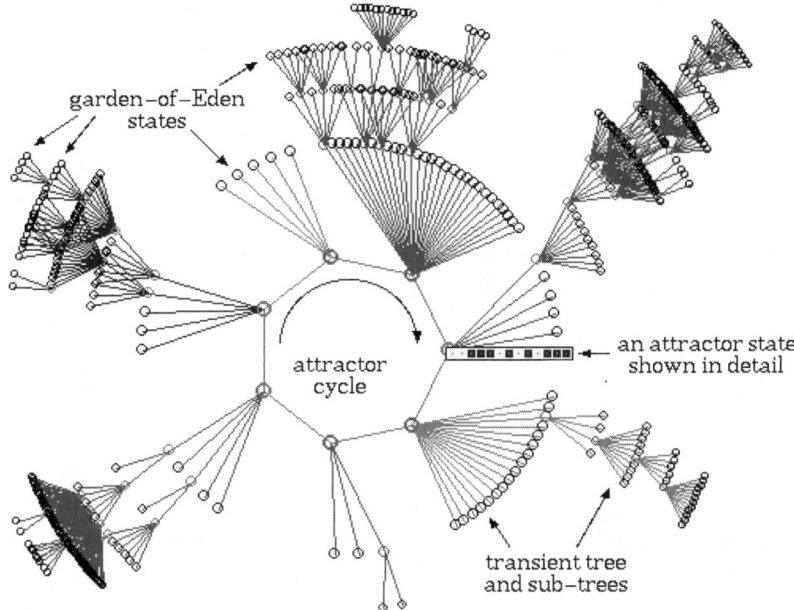

Fig. 11.10. One of the basins of attraction in Fig. 11.9, indicated by an arrow. The basin links 604 states, of which 523 are garden-of-Eden states. The attractor period is 7. One attractor state is shown in detail as a bit pattern. The direction of time is inwards from garden-of-Eden states to the attractor, then clockwise.

For basin of attraction fields, however, the maximum network size, max-n, is much smaller, and depends on the value-range v as set out below:

```
    v:  2   3   4   5   6   7   8
max-n: 31  20  15  13  12  11  10
```

11.7 The Neighborhood k or k-mix

The size of the neighborhood k, the number of inputs each cell receives, can vary from 0 to max-k. Max-k itself depends on the value-range v and also on whether or not DDLab was constrained to run forward-only for totalistic rules. This is set out ahead, showing also the size of the corresponding look-up tables S (Fig. 11.15).

k can be homogeneous, or there can be a mix of k-values in the network. The k-mix may be set and modified in a variety of ways, including defining the proportions of different k's to be allocated at random in the network, or a "scale-free" distribution. A k-mix may be saved/loaded but is also implicit in the wiring scheme. Figure 11.14 shows some predefined neighborhoods, designed to maximize symmetry. In 2D the layout can be either square or hexagonal.

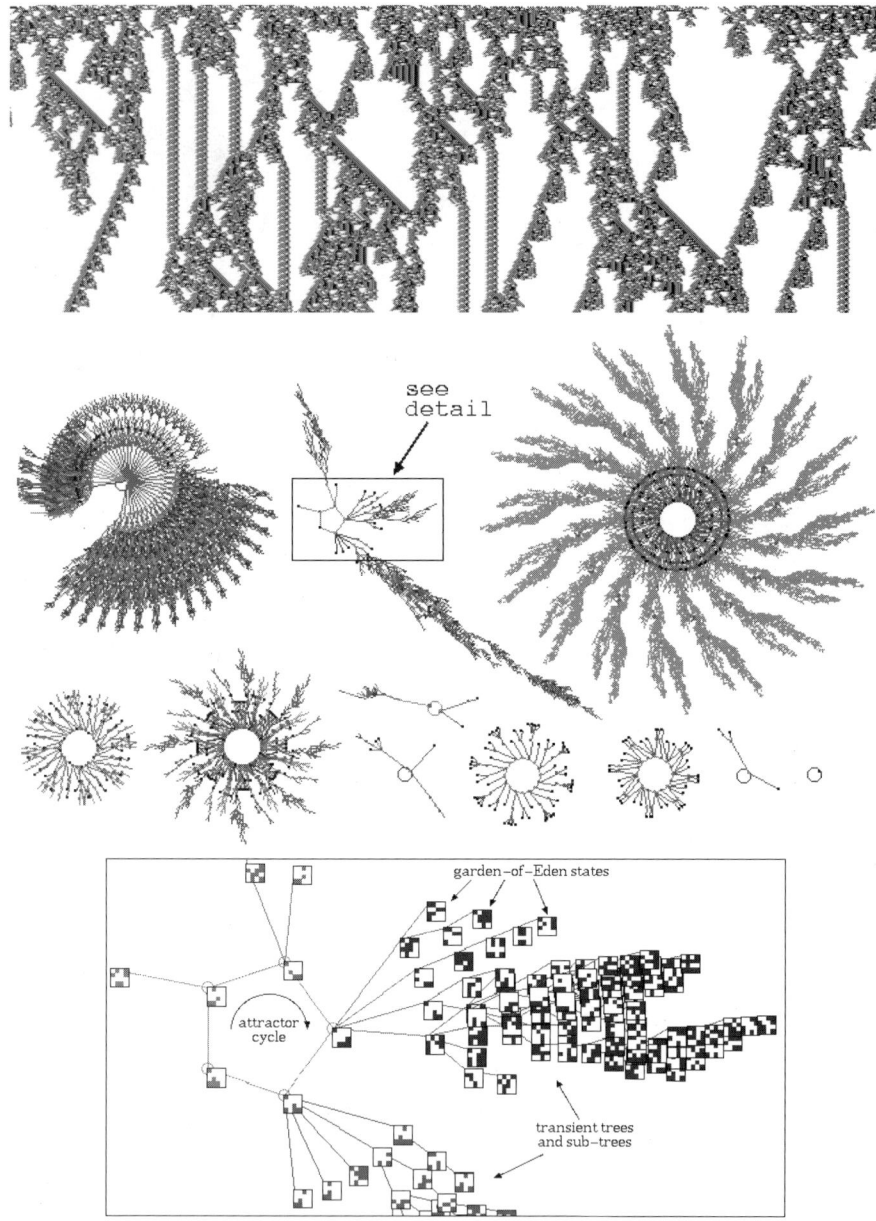

Fig. 11.11. *Top*: The space-time pattern of a 1D complex binary CA where interacting gliders emerge [13], $n=700$, $k=7$, 308 time steps are shown from a random initial state. *Center*: The basin of attraction field for the same rule, $n=16$. The 2^{16} states in state space are connected into 89 basins of attraction, but only the 11 nonequivalent basins are shown, with symmetries characteristic of CA. *Bottom*: A detail of the second basin in the basin of attraction field, where states are shown as 4×4 bit patterns. See also color plate.

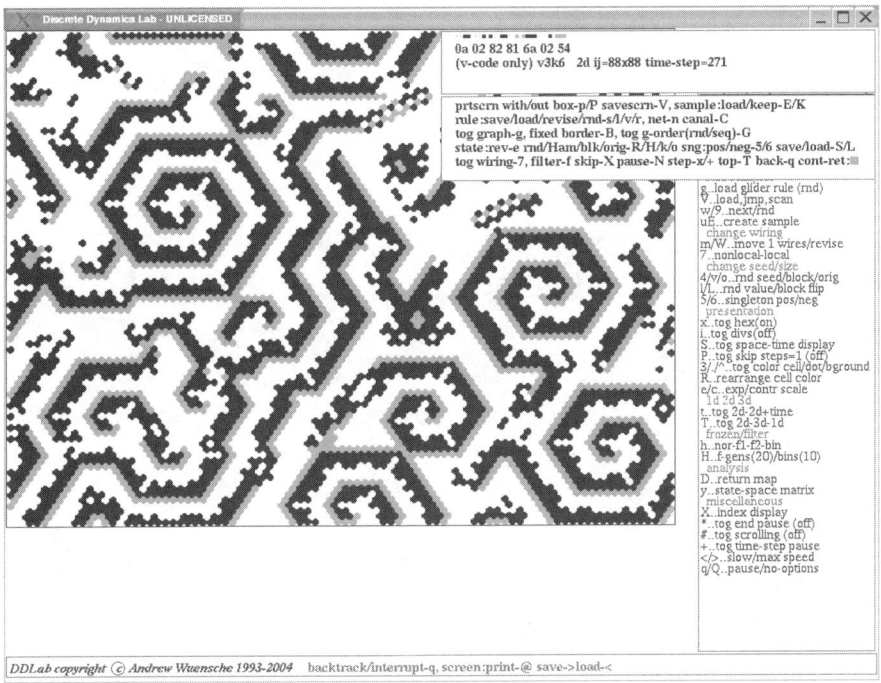

Fig. 11.12. The DDLab window showing an evolving 2D CA space-time pattern, in this case on a hexagonal grid. $n = 88 \times 88$, $v=3$, $k=6$. The k-totalistic rule (00220002200220011222000021110, 0a0282816a0254 in hex) first makes gliders emerge, but spirals eventually take over. When the space-time pattern run is interrupted (with q), top right windows appear, giving the rule details and interrupt options; on-the-fly options are listed on the the right. A k-totalistic look-up table depends on just the frequency of the $v=3$ colors (2,1,0) in the $k=6$ neighborhood, as shown below

```
black: 2: 6 5 5 4 4 4 3 3 3 3 2 2 2 2 2 1 1 1 1 1 1 0 0 0 0 0 0 0 -
  red: 1: 0 1 0 2 1 0 3 2 1 0 4 3 2 1 0 5 4 3 2 1 0 6 5 4 3 2 1 0 - frequencies
white: 0: 0 0 1 0 1 2 0 1 2 3 0 1 2 3 4 0 1 2 3 4 5 0 1 2 3 4 5 6 -
          | | | | | | | | | | | | | | | | | | | | | | | | | | | |
          0 0 2 2 0 0 0 2 2 0 0 2 2 0 0 1 1 2 2 2 0 0 0 2 1 1 1 0 - rule table
```

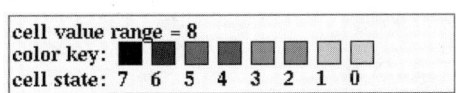

Fig. 11.13. The cell value color key window that appears when the value-range is selected, here for $v=8$. The values themselves are indexed from 7 to 0.

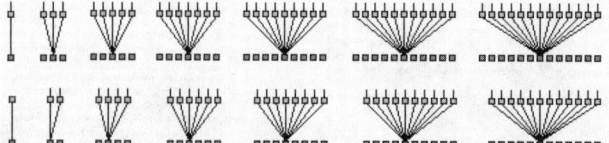

1D neighborhoods: for even k the extra asymmetric cell is on the right.

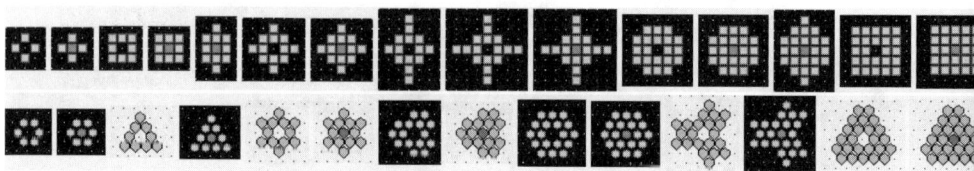

2D neighborhoods k=4-25: top row square; bottom row hex; black indicates the default.

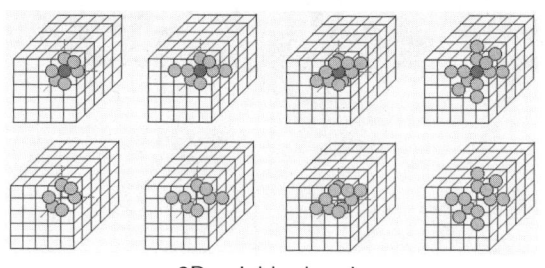

3D neighborhoods

Fig. 11.14. Predefined 1D, 2D, and 3D neighborhoods. For 1D and 2D, $k \leq 25$ if totalistic-rules-only are set, otherwise $k \leq 13$. For 3D $k \leq 13$. For 2D the lattice/neighborhood can be either square or hexagonal.

```
        unconstrained              constrained
        -------------              -----------
             max   look-up              max   look-up
        v    k      S             v     k      S
        -    --    -----          -     --    -----
        2    13    8162           2     25     26
        3     9   19683           3     25    351
        4     7   16484           4     25   3276
        5     6   15629           5     25  23551
        6     5    7776           6     17  26334
        7     5   16807           7     13  27132
        8     4    4096           8     11  31824
```

Fig. 11.15. Look-up tables S.

11.8 Wiring

The network's wiring scheme, its connections, has default settings for regular CA (for 1D, 2D, and 3D), with periodic boundary conditions, for each neighborhood size, as shown in Fig. 11.14. Wiring can also be set at random, with a wide variety of constraints and biases, or by hand. The predefined neighborhoods in this case act as pseudo-neighborhoods to which the rule is applied. A wiring scheme can be set and amended just for a predefined subnetwork within the network, and may be saved/loaded.

Random wiring can be constrained in various ways, including confinement within a local patch of cells with a set diameter in 1D, 2D, and 3D. Part of the network only can be designated to accept a particular type of wiring scheme, for example, rows in 2D and layers in 3D. The wiring can be biased to connect designated rows or layers.

The network parameters can be displayed and amended in a 1D, 2D, or 3D graphic format as in Fig. 11.16, in a "spreadsheet" as in Fig. 11.26, or as a network graph which can be rearranged in various ways, including dragging nodes with the mouse as in Figs. 11.1 and 11.28.

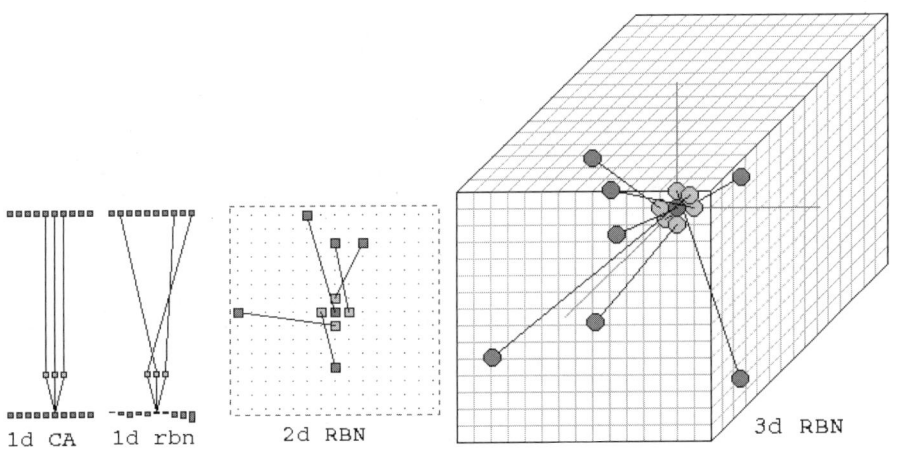

Fig. 11.16. RBN/DDN network wiring: Cells anywhere in the network are wired back to each position in a "pseudo-neighborhood." *Left:* 1D: The wiring is shown between two time steps. *Center:* 2D: $k=5$. *Right:* 3D: $k=7$.

11.9 Rules

The most general update logic or rule is expressed as a full look-up table. However, there are useful subsets of the general case, two types of totalistic

Fig. 11.17. A 2D CA space-time pattern, on a hexagonal grid. $n=88\times88$, $v=3$, $k=6$. The k-totalistic rule 00220002200220011222000021210 (0a0282816a0264 in hex) allows the emergence of gliders, glider-guns, and self-reproduction by glider collisions [16]. This look-up table differs by just one value from the spiral rule in Fig. 11.12.

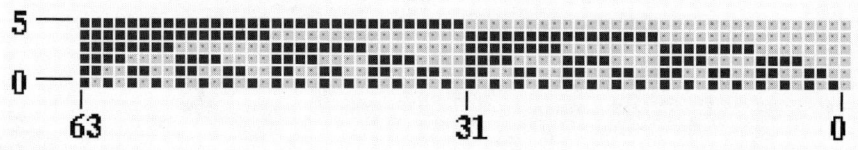

Fig. 11.18. The neighborhood matrix for a full look-up table for $n=2$ $k=6$. All 64 possible neighborhoods from 111111 to 000000 (63 to 0) are shown vertically. The position of each neighbor is indexed 5-0. Assigning an output to each neighborhood makes the look-up table with 64 bits.

rules, and "outer" versions of each type. The simplest, a t-totalistic rule, depends on the sum of values in the neighborhood. k-totalistic rules depend on the frequency of each value (color) in the neighborhood (see Fig. 11.12). If $k=2$, these two types are identical.

In addition, both types of totalistic rules can be made into outer-totalistic rules (also called semitotalistic), where a different rule applies for each value of the central cell; the Game of Life is one such rule.

For these various types of totalistic rules, DDLab can be constrained to run forward-only. This allows greater $[v, k]$ networks than for a full look-up table. Transformations and mutations then apply to just the constrained look-up table.

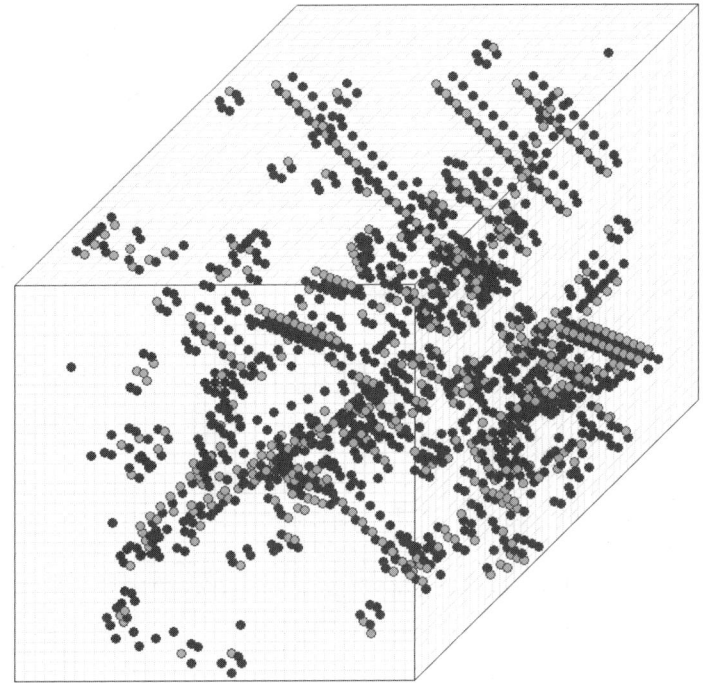

Fig. 11.19. A 3D CA space-time pattern, $n=40\times40\times40$. $v=3$, $k=6$ (nearest neighbors in 3D). The k-totalistic rule 02000010201002000022001201110 (200484200a0614 in hex) allows the emergence of gliders and other complex structures as in the 2D example in Fig. 11.17.

If DDLab remains unconstrained, the totalistic rules can still be selected, but they will be transformed into a full look-up table (which allows attractor basins). Transformations and mutations will then apply to this full look-up table. Within the full look-up table there are also subsets of rules that can be automatically selected at random, including symmetric rules, maximally chaotic "chain rules," Altenberg rules (Fig. 11.29), and others. The rules can be biased by various parameters, *lambda*, Z, and canalizing inputs. The "Game of Life," "majority," and other predefined rules or rule biases can be selected.

A network may have one homogeneous rule, as for CA, or a rule mix as for RBN and DDN. The rule mix can be confined to a subset of preselected rules. Rules may be set and modified in a wide variety of ways, in decimal, hex, as a rule-table bit pattern, at random, or loaded from a file. A rule scheme can be set and amended just for a predefined subnetwork within the network and may be saved/loaded.

Rules may be changed into their equivalents (by reflection and negative transformations) and transformed into equivalent rules with larger or smaller neighborhoods. Rules transformed to larger neighborhoods are useful to achieve finer mutations (see Fig. 11.25). Rule parameters λ and Z, and the frequency of canalizing inputs in a network, can be set to any arbitrary level.

11.10 The Initial Network State, the Seed

An initial network state, the seed, is required to run a network forward and generate space-time patterns. A seed is also required to generate a single basin, by first running forward to find the attractor, then backward from each attractor state.

A seed is, of course, required to generate a subtree, by simply running backward from the seed. However, for most CA rules, most states in state space have no predecessors; they are the leaves of a subtree, "garden-of-Eden" states, so from a random seed its usually necessary to run forward by a few steps to penetrate the subtree before running backward, and an option is provided to do this. This was done to generate the subtrees in Fig. 11.6.

A basin of attraction field does not require setting a seed, because appropriate seeds are automatically provided.

Fig. 11.20. Drawing a 2D initial state (seed) $n=88\times88$, the number of colors $v=8$. Select the color 0 to $(v-1)$; draw with the mouse or keyboard. The image/seed can be moved, rotated, and complemented. Subpatterns saved earlier can be loaded into specified positions within the main pattern. In this example there are 8 colors. Drawing the seed also applies for 1D and 3D.

As in setting a rule, there is a wide variety of methods for defining the seed: in decimal or hex, as a bit pattern in 1D, 2D, or 3D, at random (with various constraints or biases), or loaded from a file. The bit pattern method is a mini-paint program, using the keyboard to set colors (values), and the mouse or keyboard to draw those colors as in Fig. 11.10.

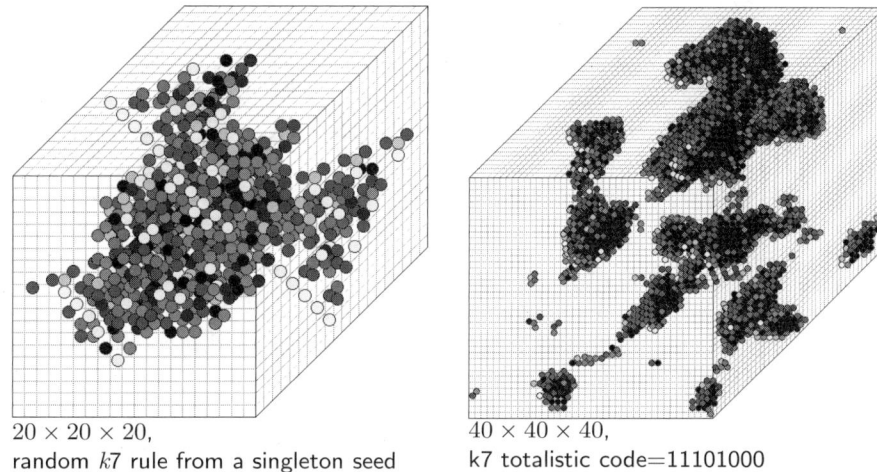

20 × 20 × 20,
random k7 rule from a singleton seed

40 × 40 × 40,
k7 totalistic code=11101000

Fig. 11.21. Examples of 3D CA, $v=2$ $k=7$. The projection is axonometric seen from below, as if looking up at the inside of a cage. Cells are shown colored according to neighborhood look-up for a clearer picture (instead of by value: 0,1). *Left*: $n=20\times20\times20$, with a randomly selected rule. The initial state is a "singleton seed", a single *on* cell in an otherwise empty array. *Right*: $n = 40\times40\times40$ (the maximum size DDLab supports). The initial state was set at random, but with a bias of 45% of *on* cells.

11.11 Networks of Subnetworks

It is possible to create a system of independent or weakly coupled subnetworks (as in Fig. 11.1), either directly, or by saving smaller networks to a file, then loading them at appropriate positions in a base network. Thus a 2D network can be tiled with subnetworks, and 1D, 2D, or 3D subnetworks can be inserted into a 3D base network.

The parameters of the subnetworks can be totally different from the base network, provided the base network is set up appropriately, with the right attributes to accommodate the subnetwork. For example, to load a DDN into a CA, the CA may need be set up as if it were a DDN. To load a mixed-k subnetwork into single-k base network, k in the base network needs to be at least as big as the biggest k in the subnetwork. Options are available to set up networks in this way. Once loaded, the wiring can be fine-tuned to interconnect the subnetworks.

A network can be automatically duplicated to create a total network made up of two identical subnetworks. There is a function to see the difference pattern (or damage spread) between two networks from similar initial states.

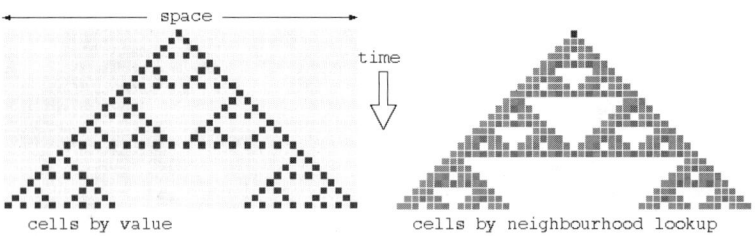

Fig. 11.22. Space-time patterns of a binary 1D CA ($n=24$, $k=3$, rule 90). Twenty four time steps from an initial state with a single central 1. Two alternative presentations are shown. *Left*, cells by value, *Right*, cells colored according to their look-up neighborhood.

11.12 Presentation Options for Space-Time Patterns

Many options are provided for the presentation of space-time patterns. Again, many of these settings can be changed on-the-fly.

Cells in space-time patterns are colored according to their value, or alternatively according to their neighborhood at the previous time step, the entry in the look-up table that determined the cell's value. A key press will toggle between the two. Space-time patterns can be filtered to suppress cells that are updated according to the most frequently occurring neighborhoods, thus exposing "gliders" and other structures, as in Fig. 11.8.

The presentation can be set to highlight cells that have not changed in the previous x generations, where x can be set to any value. The emergence of such frozen elements (order) depends on "canalizing inputs," and is applied in Kauffman's RBN model of gene regulatory networks [3, 4].

A 1D space-time pattern may be presented in successive vertical sweeps, or may be continuously scrolled. 2D networks can be toggled between square and hexagonal layout. 2D networks can also be displayed with a time dimension (2D+time) in a 3D isometric projection, as is Fig. 11.7 for the "Game of Life". 3D networks are presented within a 3D "cage" (Figs. 11.19 and 11.21). The presentation of space-time patterns can be switched on-the-fly between 1D, 2D, 2D+time, and 3D, irrespective of their native dimensions. DDLab automatically unravels or bundles up the dimensions.

There are many other on-the-fly options, including skipping time steps, reversing to previous time steps, changing the scale of space-time patterns, changing the seed, rule/s, wiring, and the size of 1D networks.

Concurrently with these standard presentations, space-time patterns can be displayed in a separate window according to the network graph layout. This can be rearranged in any arbitrary way, including various default layouts. For example, a 1D space-time pattern can be shown in a circular layout.

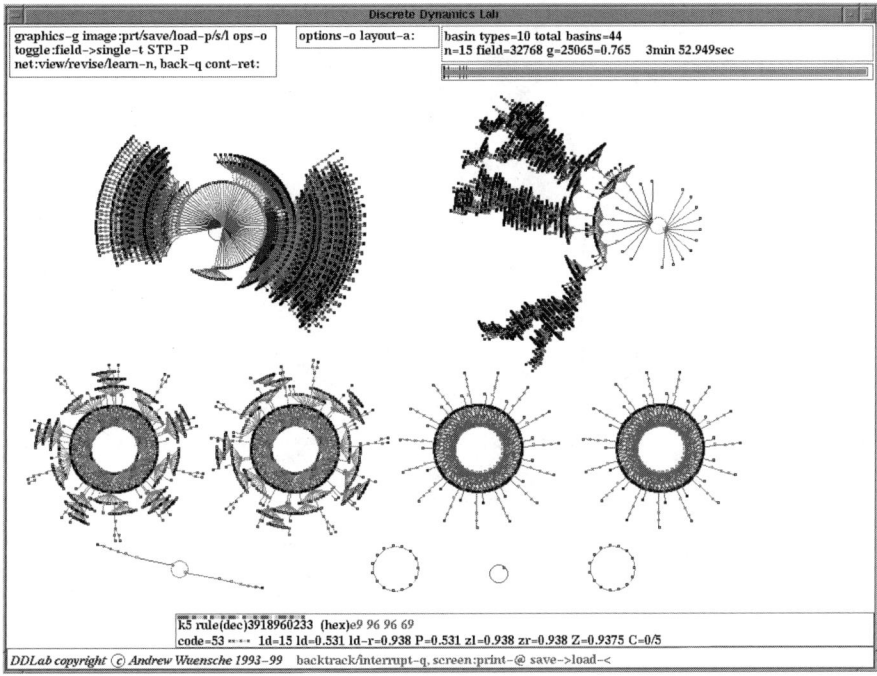

Fig. 11.23. The DDLab screen showing a basin of attraction field. This example is for a binary 1D CA, $n=15$, $k=5$ totalistic code 53. To achieve this layout, a pause was selected after each basin, and the position and spacing of basins were amended on-the-fly.

11.13 Presentation Options for Attractor Basins

Options for attractor basins allow the selection of the basin of attraction field, a single basin (from a selected seed), or a subtree (also from a seed). Because a random seed is likely to be a garden-of-Eden state, to generate subtrees an option is offered to run the network forward a given number of steps to a new seed before running backwards. This guarantees a subtree with at least that number of levels.

Options (and defaults) are provided for the layout of attractor basins, their size, position, spacing, and type of node display (as a spot, in decimal, hex, or a 1D or 2D bit pattern, or none). Regular 1D and 2D CA produce attractor basins where subtrees and basins are equivalent by rotational symmetry. This allows "compression" of basins (by default) into nonequivalent prototypes, though compression can be turned off. Attractor basins are generated for a given system size, or for a range of sizes. As attractor basins are generating, the reverse space-time pattern can be simultaneously displayed.

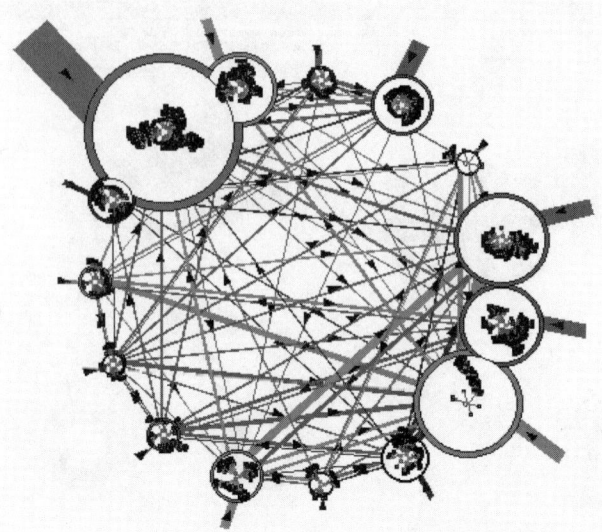

Fig. 11.24. The basin of attraction field (in Fig. 11.9) with each basin redrawn within the nodes of the attractor jump-graph. The jump-graph shows the probability of jumping between basins due to single bit-flips to attractor states. Nodes representing basins (shown inside each node) are scaled according the number of states in the basin (basin volume). Links are scaled according to both basin volume and the jump probability. Arrows indicate the direction of jumps. Short stubs are self-jumps. Note that the jump-graph itself can be suppressed, making this an alternative, flexible method for positioning basins.

An attractor basin run can be set to pause to see data on each transient tree, each basin, or each field. Any combination of these data, including the complete list of states in basins and trees, can be saved to a file.

Normally a run will pause before the next "mutant" attractor basin, but this pause may be turned off to create a continuous demo of new attractor basins. A "screensave" demo option shows new basins continually growing at random positions.

11.14 Filing

DDLab allows filing a wide range of internally defined file types, including network parameters, data, and the screen image. Network parameters and states can be saved and loaded for the following: k-mix, wiring schemes, rules, rule schemes, wiring/rule schemes, and network states. Data on attractor basins, at various levels of detail, can be automatically saved. A file of "exhaustive pairs," made up of each state and its successor, can be created.

Various data including mean entropy and entropy variance of space-time patterns can be automatically generated and saved. This allows a sorted sample of CA rules to be created, discriminating between order, complexity, and chaos [13], as in Fig. 11.31. A large collection of complex rules, those featuring "gliders" or other large-scale emergent structures, can be assembled. Pre-assembled files of CA rules sorted by this method are provided with DDLab.

The screen image is saved and loaded using an efficient homemade compressed format that is only applicable within DDLab. Alternatively, the DDLab window or part of it can be saved and printed using any external screen grabber.

11.15 Mutations

Fig. 11.25. Thirty-two mutant basins of attraction of the $v=2$, $k=3$ rule 195 ($n=8$, seed all 0s). *Top left*: The original rule, where all states fall into just one very regular basin. The rule was first transformed to its equivalent $k=5$ rule (f00ff00f in hex), with 32 bits in its rule table for finer mutations. All 32 one-bit mutant basins are shown. If the rule is the genotype, the basin of attraction can be seen as the phenotype.

As well as on-the-fly changes to presentation, a wide variety of on-the-fly network "mutations" can be made.

When running forward, key-press options allow mutations to wiring, rules, and current state. A number of "complex" CA rules (with glider interactions) are provided as files with DDLab, and these can be activated on-the-fly.

When running backwards and attractor basins are complete, a key press will regenerate the attractor basin of a mutant network. Various mutation options can be preset, including random bit-flips in rules and random rewiring of a given number of wires. Sets of states can be specified and highlighted in the attractor basin to see how mutations affect their distribution. The complete set of one-bit mutants of a rule can be displayed on a single screen as illustrated in Fig. 11.25.

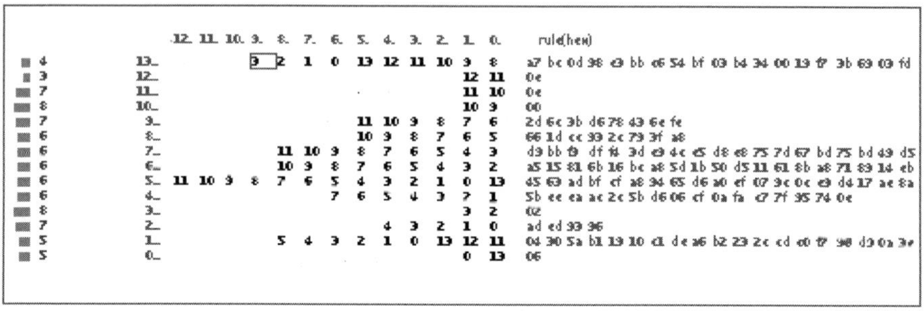

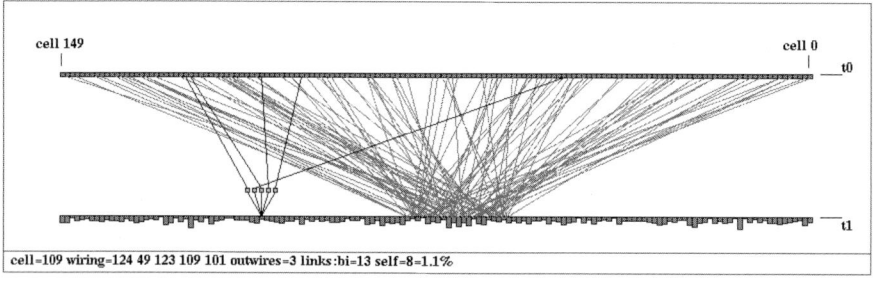

Fig. 11.26. The wiring matrix for a mixed k network with random wiring. $n=14$, $k=2\text{-}13$, with binary rules. $k\text{-}12...0$, indexes columns, $n\text{-}13...0$, indexes rows. The column on the left shows the "out-degree" of each cell, the number of output wires that link to it, also shown as a histogram. If rules have been set, they are shown in hex (as much as will fit) on the right, in the column "rule(hex)." It is possible to move around the wiring matrix as in a spreadsheet to change wiring settings.

Fig. 11.27. The 1D wiring graphic, showing wiring to a block within a 1D network. $k=5$, $n=150$. The block was defined from cells 60–80. Revisions to rules and wiring can then be confined just to the block. The 1D wiring graphic can also be shown as a circle. The "active cell" (109) is still visible and can be moved as usual.

11.16 Network Architecture

DDLab provides methods for reviewing and amending network architecture: both wiring and rules: from the wiring matrix (Fig. 11.26) and from the network architecture graphic (Fig. 11.27), which can be displayed in 1D, 2D, or 3D. The network's connections and rules can be examined, changed, and tailored to requirements, including biased random settings to predefined parts of the network. These are very flexible methods, and for RBN/DDN it is usually easier to set up a suitable dummy network initially, then tailor it here.

Network connectivity measures from the network architecture graphic include the following:

- Average k (inputs), and the number of reciprocal links, and self-links.
- Histograms of the frequency distribution of inputs (i.e., k), outputs, or both (i.e., all connections) in the network.
- The recursive inputs/outputs to/from a network element, whether direct or indirect, showing the "degrees of separation" between elements.

11.17 The Network Graph

Another method of reviewing network architecture is an adjacency matrix and network graph (see Figs. 11.3 and 11.28) that looks just at the network connections, nodes linked by directed edges. It does not allow changes to the underlying network, but includes flexible methods for representing the network, and rearranging and unraveling its graph.

For example, single nodes, connected fragments, or whole components can be dragged with the mouse to new positions with "elastic band" edges. Fragments depend on inputs, outputs, or both, and the distance of fragment links from a node can be defined.

Dragging can include the node + its immediate links (step 1), the node + immediate links + their immediate links (step 2), etc. The average directed shortest path and nondirected small world distance can be calculated. Arbitrary 1D, 2D, and 3D blocks can be dragged. Nodes with the fewest links can be automatically moved to the outer edges. This makes it possible to unravel a graph. The preprogrammed graph layouts available are a circle of nodes, a spiral, or 1D, 2D, or 3D. The graph can be rotated, expanded, contracted, and various other manipulations can be performed. The graph layout can be saved/loaded. An "ant" can be launched into the network that moves according to the link probabilities (as in a Markov chain) keeping a count of node hits.

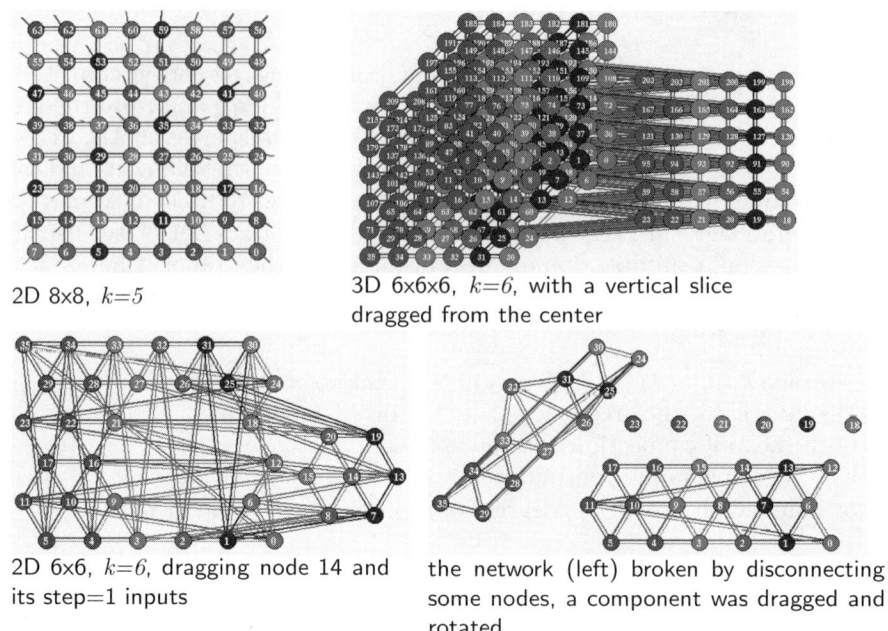

Fig. 11.28. Network graphs of a 2D and 3D CA. *Top left*: a 2D CA. *Top right*: a 3D CA, an axonometric projection seen from below as if looking up into a cage. A vertical slice has been defined and dragged from the graph. *Bottom left*: a 2D CA where the links follow a hexagonal lattice, showing a node and its 1-step inputs dragged out, and *Bottom right*: various manipulations to the graph. Note that breaking and creating new connections affect only the graph, not the underlying network, which can be restored.

11.18 Static Parameters Measures

Various static parameter measures on rule look-up tables include the λ-parameter and equivalent P-parameter, the Z-parameter, which is generalized for multivalue, and the (weighted) average λ and Z for mixed rule networks; the frequency of canalizing "genes" and inputs [3,4], and Post functions.

Single rules or a rule-mix can be tuned to adjust any of these measures to any arbitrary level.

11.19 Measures on Space-Time Patterns

Some measures on space-time patterns are listed here:

- The rule-table look-up frequency histogram in a moving window of time steps, and its entropy plot (Fig. 11.8). This is the basis of the method for automatically filtering space-time patterns [13], as in Fig. 11.32.

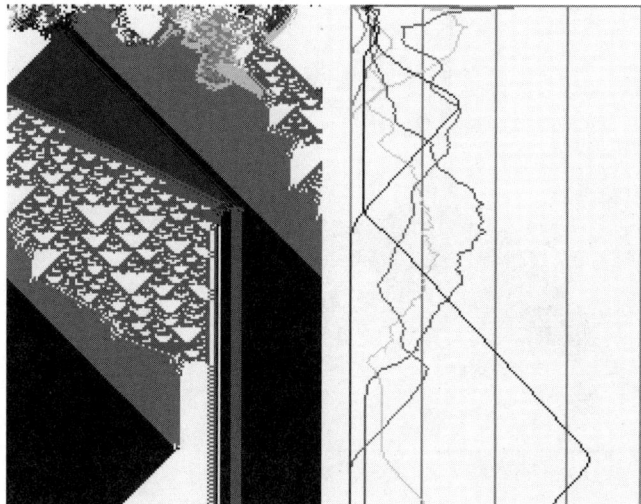

Fig. 11.29. A 1D CA of an Altenberg rule ($v=8$, $k=7$, $n=150$), where the probability of a rule-table output depends on the fraction of colors in its neighborhood. On the right the color density is plotted for each of the 8 colors, relative to a moving window of 10 time steps.

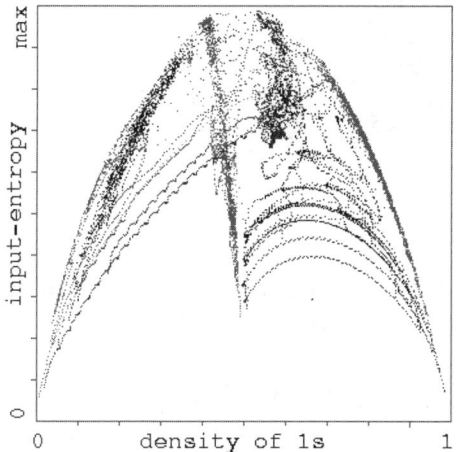

Fig. 11.30. Entropy/density scatterplot [13]. Input-entropy is plotted against the density of 1s relative to a moving window of 10 time steps. Plots for a number of $k=5$ complex rules ($n=150$) are show superimposed, each of which has its own distinctive signature, with a marked vertical extent, i.e., high input-entropy variance. About 1000 time steps are plotted from several random initial states for each rule.

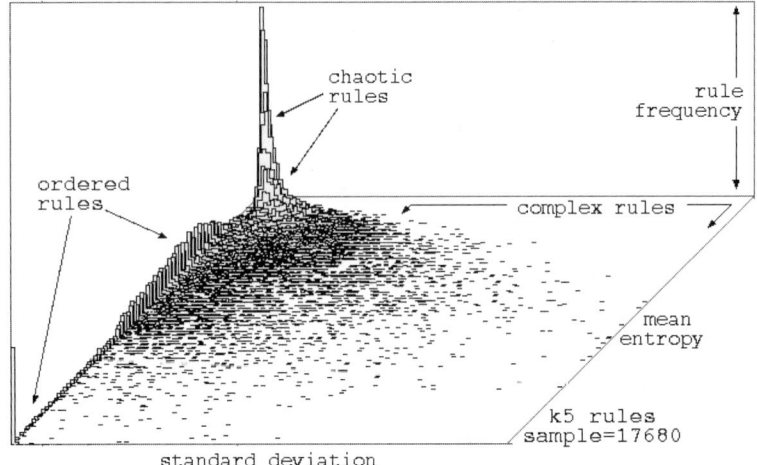

Fig. 11.31. Classifying a random sample $k=5$ rules by plotting mean entropy against the standard deviation of the entropy, with the frequency of rules within a 128 × 128 grid shown vertically.

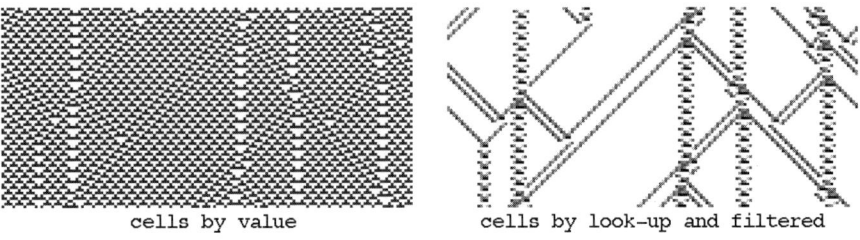

Fig. 11.32. Filtering a binary 1D space-time pattern with interacting gliders embedded in a complicated background *left*, and the same space-time pattern filtered *right*. Filtering is done on-the-fly for any rule. In this example, $k=3$ rule 54 was first transformed to its equivalent $k=5$ rule (hex: 0f3c0f3c). $n=150$.

- The space-time color density in a moving window of time steps(Fig. 11.29).
- The variance of the entropy, and an entropy/density scatterplot, where complex rules have their own distinctive signatures (Fig. 11.30).
- A scatterplot of mean entropy against the standard deviation of the entropy for an arbitrarily large sample of CA rules, which allows ordered, complex, and chaotic rules to be classified automatically, also shown as a 2D frequency histogram (Fig. 11.31). Ordered, complex, and chaotic dynamics are located in different regions, allowing a statistical measure of their frequency. The rules can be sorted by entropy variance, allowing complex rules to be found automatically.
- Various methods for showing the activity/stability of network elements.

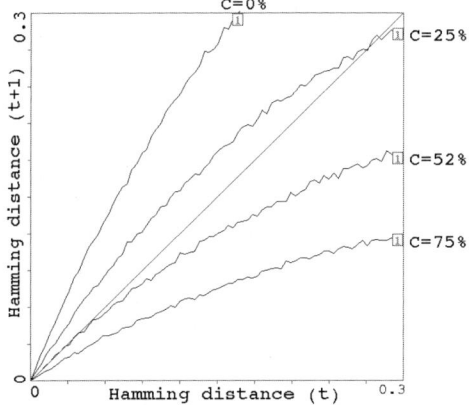

Fig. 11.33. Derrida plots for random Boolean networks (36×36, k=5). This is a statistical measure of how pairs of network trajectories diverge/converge in terms of their Hamming distance. A curve above the main diagonal indicates divergence and chaos, below — convergence and order. A curve tangential to the main diagonal indicates balanced dynamics. This example shows 4 plots where the the percentage of canalizing inputs in the randomly biased network is 0%, 25%, 52%, and 75%, showing progressively greater order.

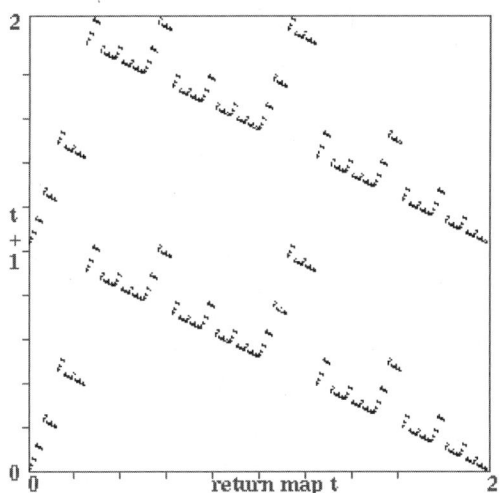

Fig. 11.34. The return map for binary 1D k=3 rule 30, n=150, for about 10,000 time steps. Note the fractal structure. Each state (bit string) $B_0, B_1, B_2, B_3 \ldots B_{n-1}$ is converted into a decimal number 0–2 as follows, $B_0 + B_1/2 + B_2/4 + B_3/8 + \cdots + B_{n-1}/2^{n-1}$. As the network is iterated, this value at time step t (x-axis) is plotted against the value at time step $t+1$ (y-axis).

- The damage spread, or pattern difference, between two networks in 1D or 2D. A histogram of damage spread frequency can be automatically generated for identical networks with initial states differing by 1 bit.
- The Derrida plot [3,4], and Derrida coefficient, analogous to the Liapunov exponent in continuous dynamical systems, which measures how pairs of network trajectories diverge/converge in terms of their Hamming distance. This indicates if a random Boolean network is in the ordered or chaotic regime (see Fig. 11.33), and is also generalized for multivalue.
- A scatterplot of successive iterations in a 2D phase plane, the "return map" (Fig. 11.34), which has a fractal structure, especially for chaotic rules.

11.20 Measures on Attractor Basins

Some measures on attractor basins (i.e., measures on subtrees, basins of attraction, and the basin of attraction field) are listed below:

- Data on attractor basins. The number of basins in the basin of attraction field, their size, attractor period, and branching structure of transient trees. Details of states belonging to different basins, subtrees, their distance from attractors or the subtree root, and their in-degree.
- A histogram showing the frequency of arriving at different attractors from random initial states. This provides statistical data on the basin of attraction field for large networks. The number of basins, their relative size, period, and the average run-in length are measured statistically. The data can be used to automatically generate an attractor jump-graph as in Figs. 11.3 and 11.24. An analogous method shows the frequency of arriving at different "skeletons," partially frozen patterns.
- Garden-of-Eden density plotted against the λ and Z parameters and against network size.
- A histogram of the in-degree frequency in attractor basins or subtrees.
- The state-space matrix, a plot of the left half against the right half of each state bit string, using color to identify different basins, or attractor cycle states.
- The attractor jump-graph (see Figs. 11.3 and 11.24): an analysis of the basin of attraction field, tracking where all possible 1-bit flips (or 1-value flips) to attractor states end up, whether to the same or to which other basin. The information is presented in two ways, as a jump-table: a matrix showing the jump probabilities between basins, and as a jump-graph: a graph with weighed vertices and edges giving a graphic representation of the jump-table. The jump-graph itself can be analyzed and manipulated in various ways, and rearranged and unraveled, including dragging vertices and defined components to new positions with "elastic band" edges; the same methods as for the network graph, Section 11.8.

11.21 Reverse Algorithms

There are three different reverse algorithms for generating the pre-images of a network state. These have all been generalized for multistate networks.

- An algorithm for 1D CA, or networks with 1D CA wiring but heterogeneous rules.
- A general algorithm for RBN/DDN, which also works for the above.
- An exhaustive algorithm that works for any "random mapping" including the two cases above.

The first two reverse algorithms generate the pre-images of a state directly; the speed of computation decreases with both neighborhood size k and network size. The speed of the third, exhaustive, algorithm is largely independent of k, but is especially sensitive to network size.

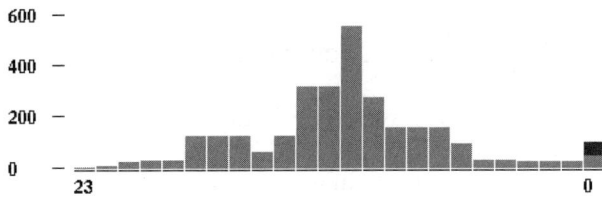

Fig. 11.35. Computing RBN pre-images. The changing size of a typical partial pre-image stack at successive elements. $n=24$, $k=3$. This histogram can be automatically generated for a look at the inner workings of the RBN/DDN reverse algorithm.

The method used to generate pre-images will be chosen automatically, but can be overridden. For example, a regular 1D CA can be made to use either of the two other algorithms for benchmark purposes and for a reality check that all methods agree. The time taken to generate attractor basins is displayed in DDLab. For the basin of attraction field, a progress bar indicates the proportion of states in state space used up so far.

The CA reverse algorithm applies specifically to networks with 1D CA wiring (local wiring) and homogeneous k, though the rules may be heterogeneous. This is the most efficient thus fastest algorithm, described in [8, 13]. Furthermore, compression of 1D CA attractor basins by rotation symmetry speeds up the process [8].

Any other network architecture, RBN or DDN, with nonlocal wiring, will be handled by a slower *general* reverse algorithm described in [9, 13]. A histogram revealing the inner workings of this algorithm can be displayed as in Fig. 11.35. Regular 2D or 3D CA will also use this general reverse algorithm. Compression algorithms come into play in orthogonal 2D CA to take advantage of the various rotation symmetries on the torus.

The third, brute-force, exhaustive, reverse algorithm first sets up a mapping, a list of "exhaustive pairs," each state in state space and its successor (this can be saved). The pre-images of states are generated by reference to this list. The exhaustive method is restricted to small systems because the size of the mapping increases exponentially as v^n, and scanning the list for pre-images is slow compared to the direct reverse algorithms for CA and DDN. However, the method is not sensitive to increasing neighborhood size k and is useful for small but highly connected networks. The exhaustive method is also used for sequential updating.

A random mapping routine can assign a successor to each state in state space, possibly with some bias. Attractor basins can then be reconstructed by reference to this random map with the exhaustive algorithm. The space of random maps for a given system size corresponds to the space of all possible basin of attraction fields and is the superset of all other deterministic discrete dynamical networks.

11.22 Chain Rules and Encryption

The CA reverse algorithm is especially efficient for a subset of maximally chaotic 1D CA rules, the "chain rules," which can be automatically generated in DDLab for any v, k. The approximate number of chain rules is $\sqrt[v]{rulespace}$.

These rules are special because in contrast to the vast majority of rule space, the typical number of predecessors of a state (in-degree) is extremely low, *decreasing* with system size. For larger systems the in-degree is likely to be exactly one. Consequently, the garden-of-Eden density is also very low and *decreasing* with system size; becoming vanishingly small in the limit. This means nearly all states have predecessors, embedded deeply along chain-like transients. Large 1D CA can be run backward very efficiently for these rules, generating a chain of predecessors. As the rules rapidly scramble patterns, they allow a method of encryption which is available in DDLab; run backward to encrypt, forward to decrypt (Figs. 11.36 and 11.37).

11.23 Sequential Updating

By default, network updating is synchronous, in parallel. DDLab also allows sequential updating, both for space-time patterns and attractor basins. Default updating orders are forward, backwards, or a random order, but any specific order can be set from the $n!$ possible orders for a network of size n. The order can be saved/loaded from a file.

An algorithm in DDLab computes the neutral order components (limited to network size $n \leq 12$). These are sets of sequential orders with identical dynamics. DDlab treats these components as subtrees generated from a root

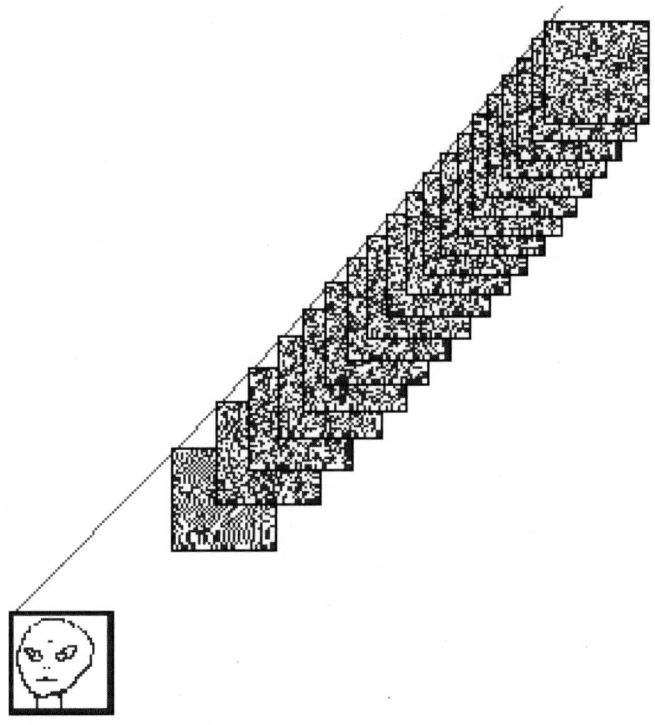

Fig. 11.36. A 1D pattern is displayed in 2D ($n=1600$, 40×40); the "alien" seed was drawn as in Fig. 11.10. The seed could also be an ASCII file, or any other form of information. With a $v=2$, $k=7$ chain rule selected at random, and the alien as the root state, a subtree was generated with the CA reverse algorithm; note that the subtree has no branching, and branching is highly unlikely to occur. The subtree was set to stop after 20 backward steps, which took about 12 seconds. The state reached is the encryption.

order, and can generate a single component subtree, or the entire set of components subtrees making up sequence space (the neutral field) which are drawn in an analogous way to attractor basins.

11.24 Sculpting Attractor Basins

Learning and forgetting algorithms allow attaching and detaching sets of states as predecessors of a given state by automatically mutating rules or wiring couplings. This allows "sculpting" the attractor basin to approach a desired scheme of hierarchical categorization. Because any such change, especially in a small network, usually has significant side effects, the methods are

Fig. 11.37. To decrypt, starting from the encrypted state in Fig. 11.36, the CA with the same rule was run forward by 20 time steps, the same number that was run backwards, to recover the original image or bit-string. This figure shows time steps 17 to 25 to illustrate how the "alien" image was scrambled both before and after time step 20.

not good at designing categories from scratch, but might be useful for fine tuning a network that is already close to where it is supposed to be.

More generally, a very preliminary method for reverse engineering a network, also known as the inverse problem, is included in DDLab, by reducing the connections in a fully connected network to satisfy an exhaustive map (for network sizes $n \leq 13$). The inverse problem is how to find a minimal network that will satisfy a full or partial mapping, fragments of attractor basins such as trajectories.

11.25 Acknowledgments

DDLab has been evolving since the early 1990s, mainly at the Santa Fe Institute following the publication of the "The Global Dynamics of Cellular Automata" [8] and at COGS, University of Sussex.

Many people have influenced DDLab by contributing ideas, suggesting new features, providing encouragement and criticism, and helping with programming. I reserve all the blame for its shortcomings. I would like to thank Mike Lesser, Grant Warrel, Crayton Walker, Chris Langton, Stuart Kauffman, Wentian Li, Pedro de Oliviera, Inman Harvey, Phil Husbands, Guillaume Barreau, Josh Smith, Raja Das, Christian Reidys, Brosl Hasslacher, Steve Harris, Simon Frazer, Burt Voorhees, John Myers, Roland Somogyi, Andy Adamatzky, Mark Tilden, Rodney Douglas, Terry Bossomaier, Ed Coxon, Oskar Itzinger, Pietro diFenizio, Pau Fernandez, Ricard Sole, Antonio Lafusa, Paolo Patelli, Jose Manuel Gomez Soto, and many other friends and colleagues (to whom I apologize for not listing). Thanks also go to DDLab users who have provided feedback.

DDlab continues to be developed; updates and news can be found at www.ddlab.org and www.cogs.susx.ac.uk/users/andywu/ddlab.html.

References

1. Adamatzky A (1994) Identification of Cellular Automata. Taylor and Francis, London.
2. Conway JH (1982) What Is Life? In: Winning ways for your mathematical plays, Berlekamp E, Conway JH and Guy R (eds.). Academic Press, New York.
3. Harris ES, Sawhill BK, Wuensche A, and Kauffman S (1997) Biased eukaryotic gene regulation rules suggest genome behavior is near edge of chaos. Santa Fe Institute Working Paper 97-05-039.
4. Kauffman SA (1993) The Origins of Order. Oxford University Press.
5. Langton CG (1990) Computation at the edge of chaos: phase transitions and emergent computation. Physica D 42:12–37.
6. Somogyi R and Sniegoski C (1996) Modeling the complexity of genetic networks. Complexity 1:45–63.
7. Wolfram S (ed) (1986) Theory and Application of Cellular Automata. World Scientific.
8. Wuensche A and Lesser MJ (1992) The Global Dynamics of Cellular Automata. Addison-Wesley, Reading, MA.
9. Wuensche A (1994) The ghost in the machine: Basin of attraction fields of random Boolean networks. In: Artificial Life III, Langton CG (ed.). Addison-Wesley, Reading, MA.
10. Wuensche A (1994) The emergence of memory. In: Towards a Science of Consciousness. Hameroff SR, Kaszniak AW and Scott AC (eds.). MIT Press.
11. Wuensche A (1997) Attractor basins of discrete networks: Implications on self-organisation and memory. Cognitive Science Research Paper 461., D. Phil Thesis, University of Sussex.
12. Wuensche A (1998) Genomic regulation modeled as a network with basins of attraction. In: Proc. 1998 Pacific Symposium on Biocomputing. World Scientific, Singapore.
13. Wuensche A (1999) Classifying cellular automata automatically: Finding gliders, filtering, and relating space-time patterns, attractor basins, and the Z parameter. Complexity 4:47–66.
14. Wuensche A (2001) The DDLab Manual, PDF available at www.ddlab.org.
15. Wuensche A (2003) Discrete Dynamics Lab: Tools for investigating cellular automata and discrete dynamical networks. Kybernetes 32.
16. Wuensche A (2004) Self-reproduction by glider collisions: The beehive rule. In: Proc. Alife9, J. Pollack et al. (eds.), 286–291. MIT Press.

Part IV

Artificial Life Arts

12

Simulated Breeding — A Framework of Breeding Artifacts on the Computer

Tatsuo Unemi

This chapter describes a basic framework of simulated breeding, a type of interactive evolutionary computing to breed artifacts, whose origin is *Blind Watchmaker* by R. Dawkins. These methods make it easy for humans to design a complex object adapted to his/her subjective criteria, just similarly to agricultural products we have been developing over thousands of years. Starting from randomly initialized genome, the solution candidates are improved through several generations with artificial selection. The graphical user interface helps the process of breeding with techniques of multifield user interface and partial breeding. The former improves the diversity of individuals that prevents being trapped at local optimum. The latter makes it possible for the user to fix features he/she already satisfied. These methods were examined through artistic applications by the author, SBART for graphics art and SBEAT for music. Combining with direct genome editor and exportation to another graphical or musical tool on the computer, they can be powerful tools for artistic creation. These systems may contribute to the creation of a type of new culture.

12.1 Introduction

For over a thousand years, mankind has been utilizing the technique of breeding to obtain useful plants and animals to help human life. Almost all agricultural products and domesticated animals we see now are the results of these processes of many generations. Even in the new century of highly improved genetic engineering, it is still impossible to build such a complex living system by human hands in a similar manner with mechanical and electric machines.

It is also a fact that we already have highly sophisticated technologies in our hands to make complex machines and systems, such as robots, transportation control systems, hi-tech aircrafts, space shuttles, and so on. Many researchers and developers are struggling and competing with each other to design and implement amazing gadgets day by day in laboratories and private companies. Recent improvement of information technologies accelerates this movement. However, it is hard to say that we are receiving enough results on these technologies because of the bottleneck of the developmental cost. The more complex the product gets, the more time we need for design and implementation.

One method to overcome this bottleneck may be to introduce a method of breeding we have been using for living organisms. Some of the currently developed machines are complex enough for objects of breeding. Features that enable us to breed organisms are reproduction with changes, the essential functions for evolvability. All living systems on the Earth intrinsically have this mechanism supported by genetic inheritance and mutation. Artifacts have no ability to reproduce itself in nature, but the computer can help us to realize it. If we build an interactive software to simulate breeding process, it might enable us to obtain our desired design in a reasonable time. In addition, there is the possibility to give us new products that we have unconsciously given up because of the developmental cost.

This chapter presents a framework of *simulated breeding* that realize breeding the artifacts on the computer through an overview of two sorts of applications. One is SBART for drawing abstract computer graphics, and another is SBEAT for composing short musical pieces.

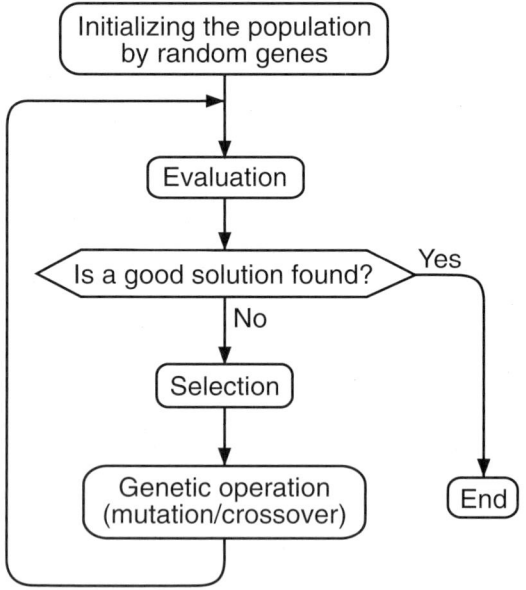

Fig. 12.1. A flowchart of a simple genetic algorithm.

12.2 Basic Framework of IEC

Research on computational intelligence and artificial life has brought some useful algorithms to produce complex systems inspired from biological mechanisms such as morphology, evolution, learning, herding, and so on. One of the most successful technique in terms of engineering applications may be evolutionary computing for optimization in a various types of problems that had been thought difficult to solve. This method was originally developed from a type of optimization of morphological design of living organisms to gain high a rate of reproductive success in the physical and ecological environment. Figure 12.1 shows a flowchart of a simple genetic algorithm, a typical evolutionary computing scheme, consisting of a loop of evaluation, selection, crossover, and mutation.

An ordinary type of evolutionary algorithm uses a predefined fitness function to give a criterion of optimization. It just corresponds to the condition of natural selection. This framework works well if the human designer can draw an appropriate procedure to compute fitness values to evaluate each individual. However, we often go through difficulties in figuring it out explicitly by some reasons, such as multi-objectivity, subjective criteria, dynamic environment, and so on. In a design of room arrangement of a house, for example, each member of the resident family has different preference criteria from others. They are, of course, subjective and often dynamically changing with the natural and social environment.

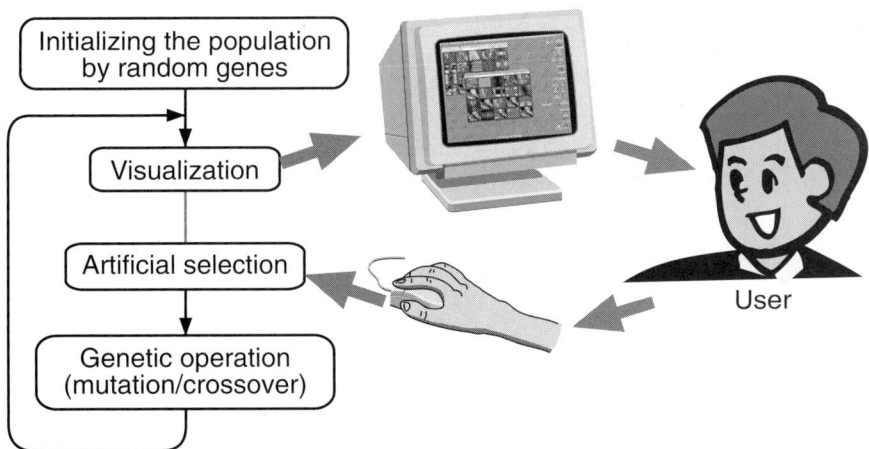

Fig. 12.2. A schematic framework of interactive evolutionary computing (IEC).

Interactive evolutionary computing (IEC) [13] is a promising technique to find better solutions in the domains for optimization by user's subjective criteria, of whose root can be found in *Blind Watchmaker* by R. Dawkins [3].

Differently from ordinary methods of evolutionary computing, fitness values are not calculated automatically by the predefined evaluation function but are given by the user for each individual in some manner. Some researchers are calling this method as the *interactive genetic algorithm* (IGA) [12], because it can be seen as a modified version of the *genetic algorithm* (GA) [4]. Usually, the application systems have a method for the user to rate each individual, typically a graphical user interface using a slider or a set of radio buttons. In the method named *simulated breeding*, the user directly picks up his/her favorite individuals as parents for the next generation. This means the fitness values can take only one (selected) or zero (not selected). It disables stochastic selection, but has an advantage to reduce the number of user's operations to assign the fitness values. Figure 12.2 shows a schematic framework of IEC, where the phases of evaluation and selection in simple GA are replaced with visualization and artificial selection.

Another source of advantage of IEC compared to the other types of design support framework of *generate and test* is explicit separation between genotype and phenotype. Genotype is information on genome that changes through genetic operation. Phenotype is the object of evaluation that performs in the environment. In natural living organisms, genotype is genetic information on DNA, and phenotype is the body and its performance for survival and reproduction. This separation makes it flexible to design the search space for an application domain.

12.3 SBART and SBEAT

The author developed several types of applications of simulated breeding over the years. One is named SBART for computer graphics, and another is named SBEAT for computer music. These artistic domains are mostly suitable for IEC because they are strongly dependent on subject criteria of evaluation.

12.3.1 SBART

SBART [20] is an application of simulated breeding to breed an abstract image of 2D computer graphics. The basic mechanism is based on the idea by K. Sims [11], who implemented his system on a combination of a supercomputer and graphic workstations in 1991. Some researchers who wanted to experience this innovative system developed their small system on personal computers. SBART is one of these systems that was developed in 1993 on a Unix workstation and was exported to MacOS in 1998. The basic idea is the same between Sims's system and SBART, but some features described here were uniquely modified and added in SBART. This software has been widely distributed through the Internet and CD-ROMs attached with some books and journals.

Fig. 12.3. A field window of SBART containing 20 individuals.

Fig. 12.3 shows an example of field window that contains 20 individual drawings, each of which is a candidate of parents for the next generation. The user selects one or more of his/her favorite individuals to reproduce offspring. Through some iterations of generation changes, the user can obtain satisfactory results.

The structure of a genotype is a mathematical expression that calculates color value for each pixel from the two-dimensional coordinates x and y. Each of the intermediate values in the calculation is a three dimensional vector that is interpreted as a color in hue, saturation, and brightness at the result. For example, the genotype of the bottom left individual in Fig. 12.3 is

$$\text{and}(-(1.180), \text{and}(0XY, XY0) + XY0 - \text{hypot}(\text{hypot}(Y0X, 0XY), 1.680))$$

where four types of binary functions $+$, $-$, "and," and "hypot," and one unary function $-$, are used. 0XY, XY0, and Y0X are variable vectors that mean $\langle 0, x, y \rangle$, $\langle x, y, 0 \rangle$, and $\langle y, 0, x \rangle$, respectively. SBART has six types of variables in all permutations of x, y, and 0. Constant scalar values are expanded into a vector containing three same values, that is, 1.180 in the above expression is expanded into $\langle 1.180, 1.180, 1.180 \rangle$. Almost all functions calculate each element values in a vector independently, that is, $\langle x, y, 0 \rangle + \langle 1.180, 1.180, 1.180 \rangle = \langle x + 1.180, y + 1.180, 1.180 \rangle$. Some exceptional functions calculate the result by combination of elements of argument vectors. In the case of the function named "max," for example, the value is defined as

$$\max(\langle x_1, x_2, x_3\rangle, \langle y_1, y_2, y_3\rangle) = \begin{cases} \langle x_1, x_2, x_3\rangle & \text{if } x_1 > y_1 \\ \langle y_1, y_2, y_3\rangle & \text{otherwise.} \end{cases}$$

When more than one individual is selected, crossover operation is applied. When only one individual is selected, the mutants are produced as the population of the next generation. These genetic operations are done in a style of *genetic programming* [5]. Crossover is exchange of subtrees between parents. Mutation is replacement of a node: function, variable or constant with randomly selected one. The target subtree and node are selected randomly.

SBART has not only a breeding mechanism but also some utilities to import some image files and a single movie file to produce a type of collage, to draw arbitrary size of product image to export to another graphics tool, and to create a movie allocating time variable into the 0 element of variable vectors. Some visual jockeys (VJs) are using this system to produce stuff of their own video clips for playing at a dance club.

12.3.2 SBEAT

Sound and music are also attractive targets for the application of IEC techniques because they also strongly depend on subjective criteria for artistic production. One of the key issues for building a successful system in this domain is how the user checks and selects suitable individuals from a population.

J. A. Biles [1] has proposed an alternative method to solve this problem and implemented it in his system, named GenJam. This system helps the user to create improvisational phrases in Jazz music. In GenJam, the user listens to endless phrases generated from individual genotypes in turn. The user pushes the "g" or "b" key according to his/her good or bad feelings about the phrase. It is not necessary for the user to assign fitness values explicitly, or to know the correspondence between the individual and the phrase.

Another type of implementation of musical application of IEC has been developed as the Sonomorph system by G. L. Nelson [6, 7]. It shows nine candidates on the screen by drawing the scores in the form of a collection of horizontal line segments just like piano roll paper. SBEAT [18] was developed by the author in 2000 independently with Sonomorph, which means the author had no knowledge about Sonomorph when considering the basic idea. SBEAT shows nine individuals on a field window shown in Fig. 12.4. A phenotype of each individual is a score of 16 beats and several parts, maximally 23 parts in version 3. Four of the whole parts chosen by the user are shown in the subwindow. The first version of SBEAT treated only three parts, guitar, bass, and drums. It was extended to eight parts, five solos, piano, drums and percussion in the second version SBEAT2 [19]. The next version, SBEAT3 [22], handles 13 solo parts, 2 piano (or chord) parts, and 8 drums and percussion parts.

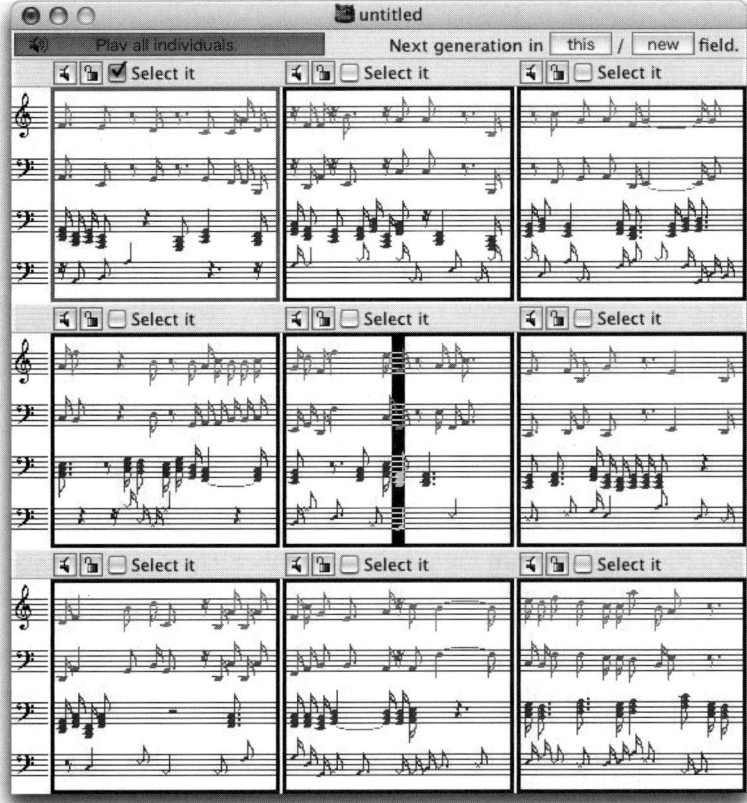

Fig. 12.4. A typical field window of SBEAT containing nine initial individuals.

The genotype of SBEAT3 is a set of three two-dimensional arrays for pitches, rhythm, and velocity. Each array contains 16 by 23 elements for each beat and part. It uses a type of recursive algorithm to produce a basic melody from genotype to guarantee a natural similarity between parents and children. It is also useful to produce individuals in the initial population acceptable for the user.

SBEAT2 and 3 have some utilities to set tempo and scale, to change the instruments set for each part, to integrate the result scores into a longer tune, and to save the score into a file of standard MIDI format (SMF). It is possible to compose a complete tune only by these systems, but the users may export the result in an SMF file to another application, the so-called Desk Top Music, to mix with another kind of composition and to add a various types of effects.

12.4 Breeding in a Field Window

Visualized phenotypes of a population are displayed together in a *field window* as shown in Figs. 12.3 and 12.4. We assume that it is possible to visualize each phenotype with not too high of a computational cost and that the population size is about from 9 to 30. A field window is divided into from 3×3 to 5×6 grids, showing each individual in each rectangle of grid. These 9 to 30 individuals are the members of the current population and there is no other member of the population. The user explicitly selects one or more individuals from the field as parents for the next generation. When only one individual is selected, all individuals except the selected one are replaced by mutants of the selected individual in the next generation. When more than one individual is selected, all individuals are replaced by the children of selected parents produced with crossover operation.

From the results of various settings of experimental implementation of SBART, the appropriate number of individuals simultaneously shown on the screen should be in the range from 16 to 30. The user often had to produce alternative children to obtain improved candidate if the number was less than 16. Some good individuals were ignored if the number was greater than 30.

There is another issue in the domain of sound and music. It is possible to select favorite graphical drawings in seconds, but the user needs a longer time to evaluate sound and music. It is possible to compare candidates simultaneously in graphics domains, but individuals must be examined independently in sound and musical domains. So a system for sound and music has to have two types of selection methods for each individual. One is for selection as a parent, and the other one is for selection for playing. In the case of SBEAT, three types of buttons are attached to each individual subwindow as shown in Fig. 12.4, a play button with speaker icon, a protection button with lock icon, and a selection checkbox. The role of protection is described in the later Sec. 12.5.2.

The collection of genotypes in a field population can be recorded in a disk file similarly to any other document files of a word processor, a drawing tool, and so on. It can be opened again as a field window later if the user saved it. Menu items entitled "New," "Open," "Save," "Save as ...," and "Reset" are available with functions that can be easily guessed from an analogy with other documentation tools. A field is always filled with a fixed number of individuals, so the "New" field is not empty but initialized with individuals of random genes.

12.5 Multifield User Interface

In [17], we propose a design of a graphical user interface using *multifield* for simulated breeding method. The term *field* is used here as a population of visualized individuals that are candidates of selection from an analogy

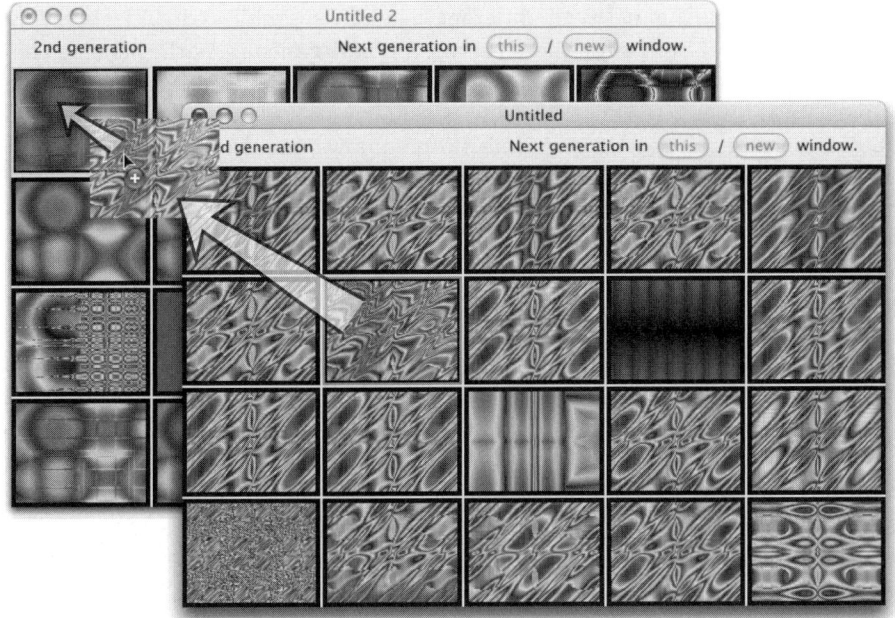

Fig. 12.5. Migration of an individual by *drag & drop*.

with fields in an experimental farm. A multifield interface enables the user to breed his/her favorite phenotypes by selection independently in each field, and he/she can copy arbitrary individuals into another field. As known among the researchers of evolutionary computing, a small population likely leads to premature convergence trapped by a local optimum, and migration among plural populations is useful to escape from this trap. For IEC applications, it is impossible to take a large size of population because the user has to observe all phenotypes in the population as possible to evaluate them instead of predefined fitness function in the ordinary framework of evolutionary computation. The multifield user interface is a suitable method for IEC to provide easy implementation of migration and wider diversity.

We often suffer a complicated multimodal landscape in a structural optimization problem because the search space constructed by solution candidates is usually high-dimensional. It is necessary to examine as many candidates as possible to find the best solution because each candidate has a lot of neighbors in a high-dimensional space. One of the key techniques for successful search is a method to keep diversity of individuals in population. *Island model* [9] is one of the methods to keep diversity.

After geographical separation of a continent into islands, a population of species that lived in a continent is divided into subpopulations in each island, and they usually reach distinct organisms through independent evolutionary process since mating between different islands is prohibited and there are many suboptimal points for the structure of an organism. As the scheme theory [4] in the genetic algorithm indicates, a crossover operation, a combination of parts of different genomes, has the possibility to spawn a better individual by combination of good genes from different individuals. We can expect to get better solutions by migration of individuals among different islands after reaching some convergence in each island. The multifield user interface is a method to bring a similar effect with the island model.

12.5.1 Migration Among Fields

The user can open an arbitrary number of field windows by choosing the "New" and "Open" items from the File menu if the memory capacity is adequate. In addition to these operations, a new field window spawns when the user clicks the "new" button at the top right of each field window instead of "this" to generate a population of the next generation. The new field window is filled with the children of selected parents.

SBART and SBEAT have two types of methods to migrate an individual between fields. The first one is to move it by *copy & paste*. The operation includes four steps:

1. Select the individual that the user wishes to move on the field.
2. Copy it into the copy buffer.
3. Select the individual that should be discarded by overwriting.
4. Paste it.

Selection of an individual on the field is done simply by clicking the subwindow. A red border frame of a rectangle area indicates that the individual is selected. It takes six steps if the user uses the Edit menu to both copy and paste because of invoking the Edit menu from the menu bar. Shortcut keys can reduce it by two steps.

The other way is *drag & drop*. As Fig. 12.5 shows, the user can copy any individual by pointing to it with the mouse cursor, pressing the left button, moving the mouse pointer keeping the mouse button pressed, and releasing the button at the destination rectangle. A small individual image moves following the mouse's move. This method needs a fewer number of operations than the first one. It is easier for the user who well knows another application with similar operation such as a file manager.

12.5.2 Protection of Individual

Not only to save genes in a disk file, the user sometimes wish to keep some interesting individuals without modification temporally. It is realized by *protection* of individual. The user can protect his/her selected individual by pushing "Protect" button in the "Edit menu" and the "Context menu"* in SBART

---

* "Context menu" is a term in MacOS that is called "pop-up menu" in Motif.

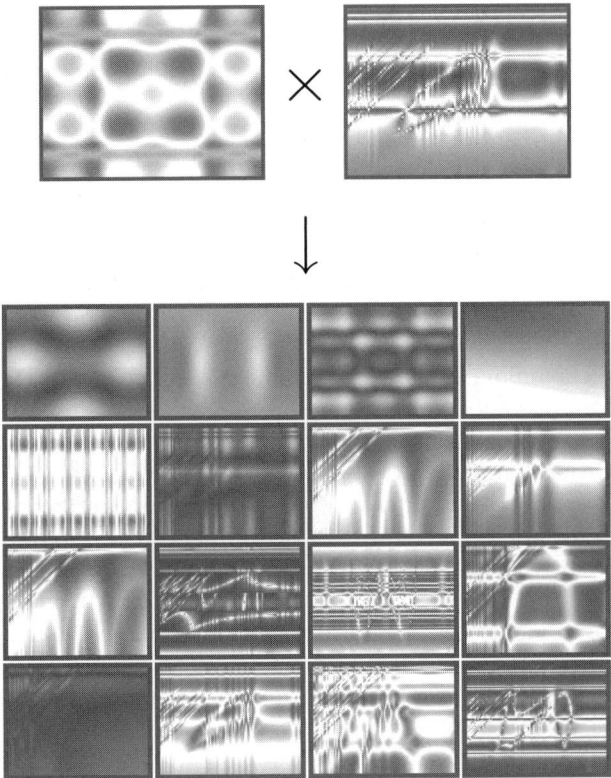

Fig. 12.6. An example of offspring spawned by migration and crossover between two individuals bred independently in the different fields.

and attached each subwindow in SBEAT. Protected individuals can neither be overwritten by migration nor replaced by offspring.

An alternative design of individual protection is to facilitate the other type of window that keeps the arbitrary number of genome as a profile. This method may lead to a filing system including library files; however, we have not tried to implement it yet. Some method for efficient retrieval for the desired genome from a large-scale database will be needed for this type of filing system.

12.5.3 Effects of Multifiled Interface

Populations processed through independent evolution usually reach unique features for each. In these cases, we can expect a new one will be produced by migration among independent fields. Figure 12.6 shows offspring produced by crossover between individuals that came from different fields. Some part of features of both parents pass to the children, but it is unknown which feature remains because the crossover points are determined randomly. If the gene coding allows redundant representation or noneffective part, it may produce children of more unexpected features.

12.6 Partial Breeding

It is a good method to divide a large problem into independent subproblems to solve it efficiently. But it is often difficult because of dependency among parts of the problem features. Musical tune consists also of a complex information including melody, rhythm, tempo, timbre, and so on. We can easily divide information into these functional parts, but evaluation of the tune usually depends on the combination of them. Combination of good melody and good timbre is not always good.

One of the advantages of evolutionary computation comparing with the other optimization technique by search is that we can design different structure of search space than the structure of solution space using mapping between genotype and phenotype. Phenotype corresponds to the solution candidate, and genotype corresponds to the search point. Musical tune can be divided into sections, parts, bars, and so on. It is also helpful to build each of the parts or sections independently and to combine them later. In addition, we can independently breed each of the functional features of music, rhythm, melody, timbre, and so on by encoding them in separate parts of the genotype.

Because of dependency among features in terms of the effect for the quality of the solution, it is difficult to obtain good solution by optimizing each feature step by step independently. We often need to revise a feature previously optimized during optimization of another feature. Even in the ordinary style of evolutionary computation, it is still a research theme how we should apply evolutionary computation to multi-objective optimization problems. Fortunately in IEC, the user can control the evolutionary process by indicating which parts and features should be fixed and which parts should be modified if the system has a user interface of partial protection.

We designed the structure of a genotype for SBEAT as it consists of three types of chromosomes for rhythm, pitches, and velocity, as shown in Fig. 12.7. Velocity, which means loudness of the sound of note as a technical term in music, is an important factor for tune to sound natural for humans' ears. The individual in SBEAT population is a bar of 16 beats and 23 parts. Each of the chromosomes is a two-dimensional array of 16 by 23 to include information for each possible note. Some loci in the pitches and velocity chromosomes are ignored if the corresponding loci of rhythm chromosome indicate rest or continuation.

We designed a graphical user interface to make it possible for the user to indicate which part should be the object of genetic operation. In ordinary cases, all features are the objects of mutation. So we introduced check buttons to indicate protection against mutation. Figure 12.8 shows the dialog window of SBEAT, which includes many buttons, sliders, and menus. The short slider

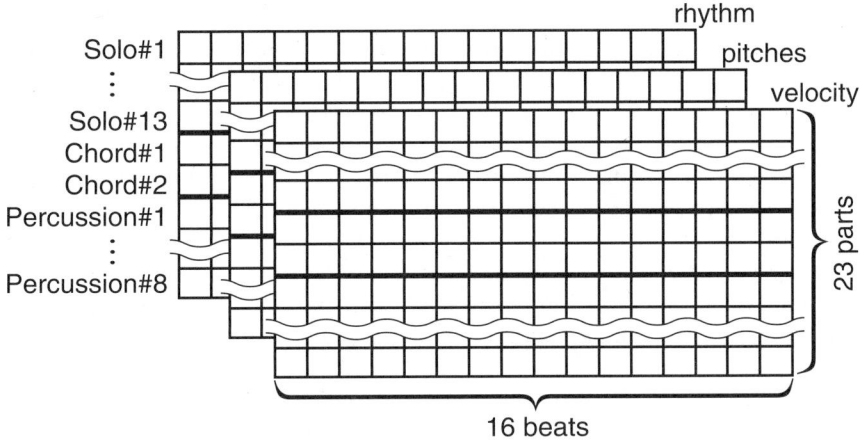

Fig. 12.7. Structure of a genotype in SBEAT3.

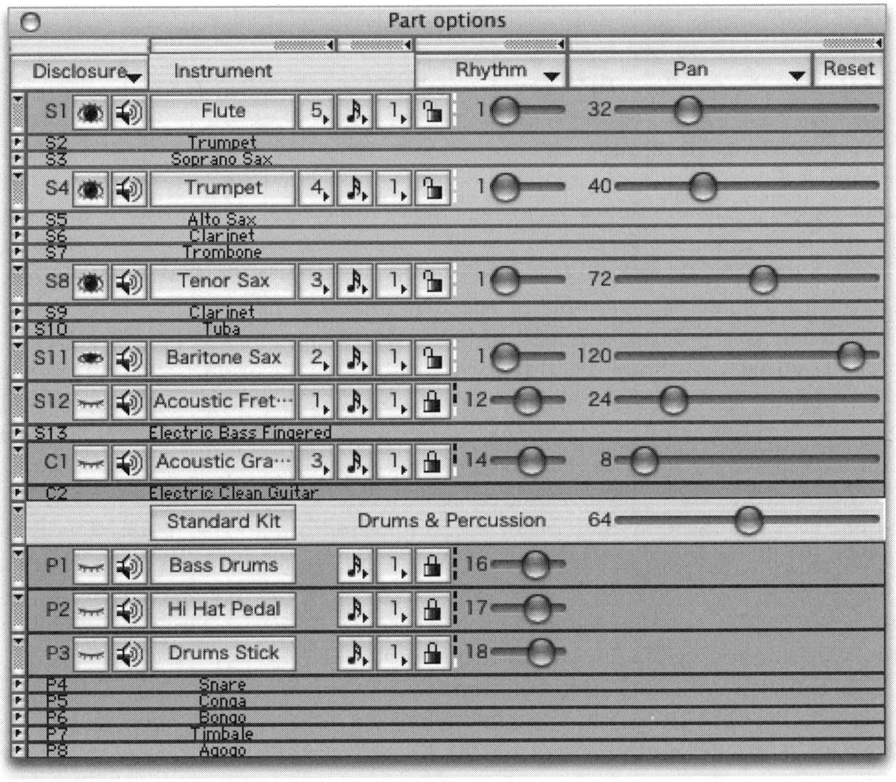

Fig. 12.8. Part option dialog of SBEAT3.

allocated for each part is for setting the correspondence between musical parts and genotypical parts. The buttons with the lock icon are for indicating protection. These operations are applied to one of three chromosomes indicated by the pull-down menu at the top row of these sliders and buttons.

It is possible for the user to indicate protection of arbitrary parts of genotype corresponds to functional or physical part of phenotype at any time he/she wants. To reduce the number of operations for pressing arbitrary number of buttons at once, we implemented a method to choose them by the *press-drag-release* operation of mouse. The buttons in the rectangular area indicated by mouse operation act as being clicked. It makes it easy to revise any parts again and again by breeding independently until any acceptable solution is found.

This method was invented through an application for music, but it will be useful for another domain where the solution candidates are complex but well-structured [21]. However, it is difficult to apply this method to SBART, because the user hardly understands which part of genotype affects which feature of phenotype.

12.7 Direct Genome Operation

Breeding is a good method for producing novelty, but it is mostly redundant when we know what type of direct modification brings a better result. The genome editor was designed to answer this requirement by all owing the user to edit chromosomes directly.

The user is allowed to edit the genome of any individual on the field. Figure 12.9 shows an example of the windows of genome editor in SBART. As shown in the right window of Fig. 12.9, the user selects a node from tree structure of genome to cut, copy, paste, and swap with the subtree in the copy buffer, and to replace it with another symbol. The new function symbol, variable, and constant can be indicated using the left dialog window of Fig. 12.9.

Figure 12.10 shows an example of the windows of genome editor in SBEAT. It has two windows, a score of an individual and an editing panel. The user selects a part to be edited using a pop-up menu,** and then operates buttons allocated to each beat of each chromosome. The button of each beat has different type of function among chromosomes because the data types of allele are different among the types of chromosomes.

In the case of SBART, this function of direct editing is not so useful because it is usually difficult for the user to understand the concrete correspondence between genotype and phenotype. But in the case of SBEAT, it is relatively clear which loci affect which feature and part in phenotype even though loci and features do not always have a one-to-one correspondence. It can play a

---

** "Pop-up menu" is a term in MacOS that is called "option menu" in Motif.

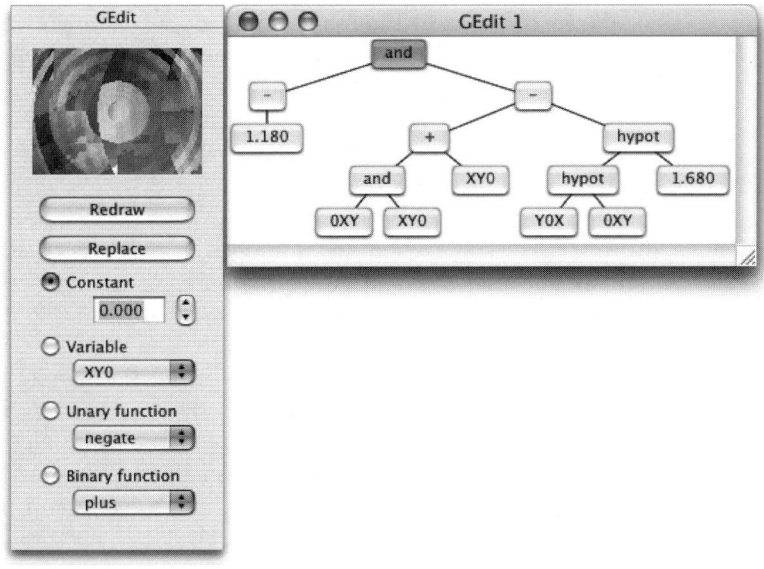

Fig. 12.9. Genome editor of SBART.

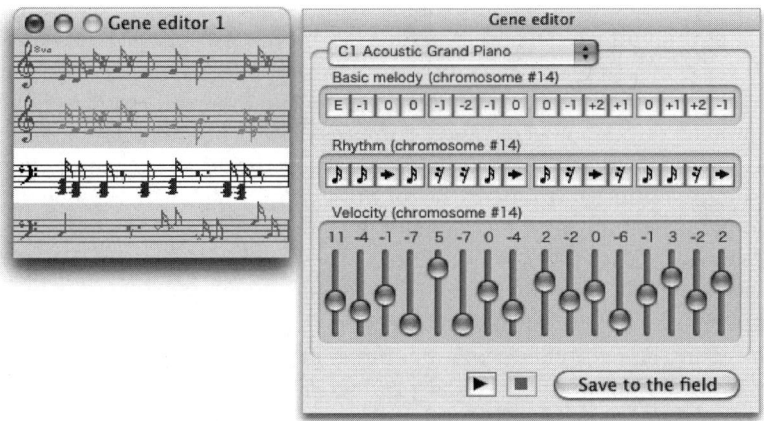

Fig. 12.10. Genome editor of SBEAT.

different role that allows the user to input the score already known if possible.*** Collection of the mutant of a known melody can be useful to make an arrangement of tune.

12.8 Production Samples

The readers have already seen some examples of images produced with SBART in Fig. 12.3, but to understand the potential possibility of this system this section shows other examples produced using augmented functions to embed an external video data.

T. Kamei, a VJ in Tokyo, suggested that it would be nice if SBART could import a movie file to embed and to deform it, similarly to importing image files to make a collage. It needs a fast and sophisticated smoothing algorithm among related pixels in video frames that wastes much of computation resources. It seemed to be impossible to process it within reasonable time by the personal computer some years ago. But now GHz CPU and hundreds MB memory on board are available at reasonable prices. The newest version of SBART includes this feature, and we are investigating some technical issues and developing new algorithms and user interfaces for achieving feasible usability [23].

Two new nonterminals were added to realize this functionality. One is named "movief" that extracts pixels' HSB color values from one frame of time t at the position indexed by referring to the first and second elements of the argument vector as x- and y-coordinates. The other one, named "moviec," similarly extracts color values, but it assumes the movie data as the three-dimensional volume and picks a boxel up by referring to three elements.

The upper sequence of movie frames in Fig. 12.11 is external movie data in half size of NTSC DV format, 320×240 pixels of frame size, 14.98 frames per second, and 30 seconds' duration. It includes $14.98 \times 30 = 449$ frames, then totally $320 \times 240 \times 449 = 34,483,200$ boxels. It was taken by a handy camcorder in the campus during a campus festival in the fall of 2003.

Figure 12.12 shows two typical productions using the boxel method. The genotype of the left side drawing has the function moviec at the root of the tree structure. This makes nonlinear transformation of the shape of original pattern. The time axis was expanded along the horizontal axis. Some vertical lines included in the resultant image indicate rapid reaction of automatic exposure adjustment by the camcorder. Small vertical vibration along the horizontal axis means it was difficult to keep the handy gadget steady in the operator's hand.

The right one has a more complex genotype that includes "moviec" at the intermediate nodes. It produces not only deformation of the shape but

---

*** In the current implementation of SBEAT, some types of score cannot be mapped backward to genotype due to the algorithm of morphology.

a. Original external movie.

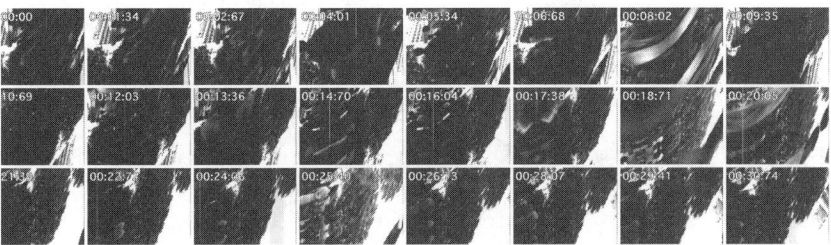

b. movief(hypot(0.648, XTY) + XTY + YXT)

c. −0.203 + (0.648 + YXT + movief(XYT))

Fig. 12.11. Sample frame sequences produced with *frame image method*.

also modification of colors. As shown in both drawings, the boxel method brings us a new effect to produce more complicated and unpredictable results from some types of external movies by inheriting the complexity of three-dimensional pattern involved in the movie data.

The middle and lower frame sequences in Fig. 12.11 are sample movies produced from genotypes that includes "movief." The middle one includes the function at the root, and the lower one includes it at just above a leaf of variable XYT. The former one produces shape deformation, and the latter one produces color modification, similarly to the two examples for boxel method.

We also examined another film taken at a concert of a student big band. It can produce a very interesting and effective movie clip that seems useful to create a music video or so on.

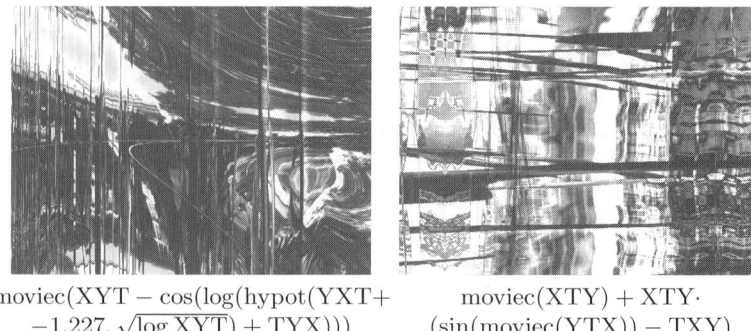

moviec(XYT − cos(log(hypot(YXT+ −1.227, $\sqrt{\log \text{XYT}}$) + TYX)))

moviec(XTY) + XTY· (sin(moviec(YTX)) − TXY)

Fig. 12.12. Sample images produced from the external movie in Fig. 12.11 by boxel method.

Figure 12.13 is a score of example production bred using SBEAT that consists of six parts. The target of breeding in SBEAT is a bar of 16 beats and 23 parts as described before. This tune was composed by integration of nine bars each of which restricted only five solo parts and one chord part. A set of sample tunes composed by the author in both SMF and MP3 format is available from the web page of SBEAT.

12.9 Future Works

Of course, there are many types of further works to be tried in the future concerning the simulated breeding method. From the viewpoint of engineering, it would be important to examine various types of alternative methods usable for similar purpose and to compare them to each other in several aspects such as efficiency, usability, flexibility, and so on. For the technical evaluation, it must be important to execute experiments on the human-machine interface employing a number of subjects as typical users. One feature that should be examined is the method of artificial selection. In some application domain or for some types of users, stochastic selection by fitness-value rating might be essential to obtain satisfactory results efficiently.

Our project of SBEAT is now still less than four years old. Some researchers are struggling to build similar systems using their original ideas of musical application of IEC technique such as [15, 16]. Including the previous pioneers' approaches including sound filtering [8] and sound generation [2], it may be fruitful to combine several different ideas to build up more practical integrated system to support human activities of music composition.

SBEAT was designed under assumption of off-line composition, that is, the processes of composition and performance are separated. But it is also potentially usable for live performance on time. The system needs some extension to have two separated channels for sound output for a breeder and listeners, because mutation may sometimes spawn less interesting sounds.

Fig. 12.13. Sample score composed with SBEAT.

The combination of SBART and SBEAT should be considered as an integrated system to make a computer graphics animation with music. The variety of result products should be enhanced to realize this plan because the products from current systems seem unsuitable to combine each other. Using a video editing tool on the personal computer currently available, it is possible to combine the products of SBART and SBEAT. But, interactive breeding between these two systems seems important to improve the final results.

12.10 Conclusion

The framework of simulated breeding has been described. Through the experience with SBART and SBEAT, we may expect future expansion of application of these systems and their framework. In addition to the basic framework of IEC, multifield user interface, partial breeding, and direct genome editing extend efficiency and usefulness of breeding.

Simulated breeding provides not only an alternative method to support humans' design activity, but also quite a new style of production based on cooperation between human and machine. The only one thing the user has to do is selection according to his/her preference. The user needs to know a little about the operation of breeding, but does not need to know how the target system can be built up. Though more than 18 years have passed since the original idea of *Blind Watchmaker*, and some artists have employed this idea for their productions, such as W. Latham [14] and S. Rooke [10], it is still not popular enough comparing with the potential power.

These ideas may contribute to create a type of new culture in the near future.

Acknowledgments

The author appreciate those who concern our two projects, SBART and SBEAT. Masafumi Nishikawa, Shinichi Sakata, Takanori Yanagisawa, Eiichi Nakada, Manabu Senda, Nobuyuki Mizuno, Megumi Soda, Kayoko Mizuno, and Seiji Takaki contributed to these projects as graduate and undergraduate students at Soka University. Harley Davis suggested that the author introduce new functions "and" and "mix" to SBART in 1993. These functions are implemented in the current version of SBART. Karl Sims, who developed the original breeding system of 2D Computer Graphics, gave the author permission to distribute the source and binary code of SBART through the Internet in 1993. Taro Kamei, a VJ in Tokyo, introduced SBART in his article of a magazine as a tool to make stuff for a video clip in 2000.

References

1. Biles JA (1994) GenJam: A Genetic Algorithm for Generating Jazz Solos. In: em Proceedings of International Computer Music Conference. International Computer Music Association, San Francisco, CA, pp 131–137.
2. Dahlstedt P (2001) Creating and exploring huge parameter spaces: Interactive evolution as a tool for sound generation. In: Proceedings of International Computer Music Conference, Instituto Cubano de la Musica and International Computer Music Association, Havana, pp 235–242.
3. Dawkins R (1986) Blind Watchmaker, Longman, Essex, UK.
4. Goldberg DE (1989) Genetic Algorithms in Search, Optimization and Machine Learning. Addison-Wesley.
5. Koza JR (1992) Genetic Programming: on The Programming of Computers by Means of Natural Selection, MIT Press.
6. Nelson GL (1993) Sonomorphs: An Application of Genetic Algorithms to Growth and Development of Musical Organisms. In: Proceedings of the Fourth Biennial Art & Technology Symposium, Connecticut College, pp 155–169.
7. Nelson GL (1995) Further Adventures of the Sonomorphs. In: Proceedings of the Fifth Biennial Art & Technology Symposium, Connecticut College, pp 51–64.
8. Ohsaki M, Takagi H (1998) Improvement of Presenting Interface by Predicting the Evaluation Order to Reduce the Burden of Human Interactive EC Operators. In: Proc. IEEE Conference on Systems, Man and Cybernetics, San Diego, CA, pp 1284–1289.
9. Pettey CB, Leuze MR, Grefenstette JJ (1987) A Parallel Genetic Algorithm. In: Proceedings of the Second International Conference on Genetic Algorithms, LEA, pp 155–161.
10. Rooke S (1999) Artist Talk. In: Dorin A and McCormack J (eds.) Proceedings of First Iteration, CD-ROM. Melbourne, Victoria, Australia.
11. Sims K (1991) Artificial Evolution for Computer Graphics. Computer Graphics 25:319–328.
12. Smith JR (1991) Designing Biomorphs with an Interactive Genetic Algorithm. Proceedings of the Fourth International Conference on Genetic Algorithms, San Diego, CA, pp 535–538.
13. Takagi H (2001) Interactive Evolutionary Computation: Fusion of the Capacities of EC Optimization and Human Evaluation. Proceedings of the IEEE 89:1275–1296.
14. Todd S, Latham W (1992) Evolutionary Art and Computers. Academic Press.
15. Tokui N, Iba H (2000) Music Composition with Interactive Evolutionary Computation. Proceedings of the Third International Conference on Generative Art, Milan, Italy.
16. Unehara M and Onisawa T Composition of Music Using Human Evaluation, Proceedings of 2001 IEEE International Conference on Fuzzy Systems. Melbourne, Victoria, Australia.
17. Unemi T A Design of Multi-Field User Interface for Simulated Breeding. Proceedings of the third Asian Fuzzy Systems Symposium. Masan, Korea, pp 489–494.
18. Unemi T, Nakada E (2001) A Tool for Composing Short Music Pieces by Means of Breeding. Proceedings of the IEEE Conference on Systems, Man and Cybernetics 2001. Tucson, AZ, pp 3458–3463.

19. Unemi T, Senda M (2001) A New Musical Tool for Composition and Play Based on Simulated Breeding. In: Dorin A (ed), Proceedings of Second Iteration. Melbourne, Victoria, Australia, pp 100–109.
20. Unemi T (2002) SBART 2.4: An IEC Tool for Creating Two-Dimensional Images, Movies and Collages. Leonardo 35:189–191.
21. Unemi T (2002) Partial Breeding - a Method of IEC for Well-structured Large Scale Target Domains. Proceedings of the IEEE Conference on Systems, Man and Cybernetics 2002, CD-ROM Proceedings, TP1D, Hammamet, Tunisia.
22. Unemi T (2002) A Tool for Multi-part Music Composition by Simulated Breeding. Proceedings of the Eighth International Conference on Artificial Life, Sydney, Australia, pp 410–413.
23. Unemi T (2004) Embedding Movie into SBART – Breeding Deformed Movies. Proceedings of the IEEE Conference on Systems, Man and Cybernetics 2004, The Hague, Netherlands.

13

Enriching Aesthetics with Artificial Life

Alan Dorin

Perhaps one day our machines will be able to take us beyond environments that look more and more familiar as we traverse them, into spaces that continue to surprise us as we explore. Can our engineered artifacts ever rival the intricacy of nature?

13.1 Introduction

Artificial life is studied largely as a means of furthering our understanding of biology and of complex adaptive systems in general. While it has demonstrated potential in a number of fields, in particular as a means of solving engineering problems, Artificial life techniques have also been applied by some in the art community. The field promises to continue to enrich artistic practice and our approach to contemporary aesthetics, even as its initial flash of popularity wanes. It is this continued application to aesthetics which the present chapter begins to address.

The techniques of art based in artificial life form a subset of *generative art*. This is an artistic practice that adopts an aesthetic of *process*. This means that although the final outcome of a work may depend for its appeal on the aesthetics of an image, sound, sculpture, or other form, the process that generates it is also significant. The generative artist is responsible for setting up initial conditions and a process to act upon them. The work that unfolds is the result of this series of changes. This is analogous to a biological phenotype (usually an organism and its behavior) being the result of the physical and chemical interactions that govern its development from a genotype (its genetic material as stored in DNA). Hence, there are conceptual connections between generative art and artificial life as well as practical ones.

Generative/process-based art is no longer treated as a fresh field for aesthetic exploration. Fascination with its possibilities seemed to fade sometime after its heyday in the late 1960s. This of course was the time of the *Cybernetic Serendipity* exhibition in London, Jack Burnham's text *Beyond Modern*

Sculpture, and much other activity linking art and computer technology in innovative ways. Recently artists involved in artificial life have retrodden some of the ground cleared by their predecessors in cybernetic art and have cleared some new space for themselves. Now that artificial life is also unfashionable, perhaps a serious assessment of its past and future contributions can be made while side-stepping the hype that initially accompanied the field.

The first section below begins by discussing the sense of wonder people often feel while contemplating nature or simple physical systems. This is then related to the tradition of the *sublime* in aesthetics. The chapter then discusses means of employing artificial life techniques to explore the *computational sublime* such that a computational system emulating the physical world's capability to generate complexity and novelty might be devised.

13.2 Wonder and the Sublime in Art and Nature

People stare contemplating the ocean as it swells and crashes on a rocky shore. They gaze fixedly into a fire until the sting of smoke raises their awareness. People may lie on their backs and follow passing clouds, or marvel at the glittering of stars. There are many things that fascinate us, that mesmerize us, that cause us to forget ourselves and our situation as we become lost in a timeless appreciation of nature.

There are also circumstances under which we may have an experience that reminds or forces us to consider our insignificance: the feeling that accompanies the vastness of spaces such as the ocean, a desert plain, or an endless mountain range, or the feeling of insignificance when contemplating the age of the universe or the years over which a trickle of water has eroded a canyon, for example. These expanses can nevertheless be made subject to reason. We are mentally equipped to discuss the concept of infinity, even if we are unable to quite fathom it intuitively. This paradoxical experience Kant has labeled the *mathematical sublime* [8].

Likewise Kant introduces the *dynamically sublime* as relating to encounters with the ferocity of nature and the sense of vulnerability this entails, coupled with the triumph of reason over fear. In his own writings on the sublime, Edmund Burke takes the view that the sensation of incomprehensibility, the fear of hopelessness or of danger, coupled with the knowledge that one *is* able to reason about something beyond one's senses, or one is not inadequate or in danger, causes a kind of delight through internal conflict — a sublime experience [11]. That is to say there is an element of the sublime, perhaps not an artistic element, in resisting the urge to flee as a tiger roars behind bars. One's body responds with fear to the situation, but reason easily overcomes this and forces the body to stand its ground — generating a sense of delight tinged with terror. In the case of a painting, the viewer's separation from a wild scene of stormy seas or a vast desert is not enforced by iron bars, but by the picture plane. This is coupled with the knowledge "it is only a picture."

How can a work of art, specifically a work of computer-based, generative software, approach the sublime? While there is a vast amount of literature on the sublime in art dating back as far as Longinus [15], the focus of this chapter is a little more narrow. A recent publication [5,17] outlines the *computational sublime*. This arises from viewing the computer in terms of its capability to perform logical operations at a rate and on a scale vastly outside our own abilities in this area. Due to its speed, the computer is able to mediate between our human perceptual apparatus and (practically) infinite computationally defined spaces. Yet, since we are the makers and programmers of these machines, our power of reason is not only able to overcome, but also to *define* these very spaces that our senses are unable to grasp fully.

Before discussing computer-based art in more detail, some much simpler artifacts, possibly just for a moment, rival natural wonders in the fascination they hold. How does this relate to the sublime? It seems that there are a number of methods by which the sensation may be encouraged and that some of these have been recreated in artifacts specifically for this purpose. They are categorized below for convenience.

Marking Time

Maybe the simplest examples of our mesmerizing creations include a stream of liquid running from a water-clock or fountain, the shifting sands of the hour glass, and the oscillating pendulum. Each of these marks time in its own manner: one a continuous stream; the next a finely particulate flow; and the last in clear, discrete stages. The eternal flow, the innumerable sand particles, the never-ceasing oscillations confront us with the infinite through this visible marking of time. Although these natural processes were utilized in desk ornaments to amuse the bored office worker of the 1980s, even in "serious" art, simple processes like this may give a sense of the sublime.

Exposing Spaces

The wire-suspended *mobiles* of Calder successfully employ mechanical processes in a manner accepted within the art world [21]. Calder's playful pieces are captivating and elegant for all their simplicity. Their workings are laid plainly before the viewer, all that they are is apparent at a glance — and yet this is not so, for their movement brings a vitality and opens a space the static sculpture does not possess. The universe a mobile sweeps out is contained within its wires, rods, and solid forms, so in one sense they may be held in (and created from) the palm of a hand. Yet as they are touched by invisible air currents their inner complexity is exposed.

Intricacy

Many a visitor has been fascinated by the button-driven clockwork and gearing of exhibits in traditional science museums. Here a sense of wonder at the machine in its entirety arises, but also a fascination with the intricacy of the mechanism. Each gear meshes with another, each component is configured "just so," and together the pistons and wheels turn in harmony to produce a composite that might drive a clock, crush a quartz boulder, pump water, or power a vehicle. This is not the beauty of a crashing ocean or a sunset, but the charm of peering into an ant's nest or through a microscope at a drop of pond water. There is something in these systems that causes one to marvel at a complexity that is just beyond grasp.

Defying the Natural Order

There is still another wonder to be described here, that of somehow defying the natural order of things. It appears wonderful that a huge boulder might come to be balanced on a slender rock column; that a gyroscopic top remains on its tip despite interference; that a bird or a massive airplane can remain suspended in the air, or a colossal steel ship can float; that a magnet can push another away without touching it. These things, of course, are dealt with to some extent by simple science. Sadly, only children may wonder at these things. Yet implicitly these interactions remain in need of continual re-explanation since each instills apprehension through not being quite "right." That boulder or spinning top might topple at any moment. That bird should fall from the sky and the ship ought to take on water. The magnets are behaving unnaturally. All of these systems cause one to ponder, "How can this be?" even if one can reason about the answer through science.

Curiosity

Related to all of the above phenomena, in particular the previous one, attention can also be held by riddles and intellectual pursuits. Included in this are mind games such as chess, paradoxes, and mathematical puzzles, but also scientific enquiry. These all captivate us through our drive to learn why something behaves as it does, especially if it seems to defy the natural order of things. Of the algorithmic art exhibition at Xerox PARC in 1994, Bern writes, "The appearance of algorithmic visual art should raise the temporal questions of 'How is this made?' and 'Can this be extended?' " [2].

While the use of the term *should* is of questionable accuracy, nevertheless there is something of relevance in the idea that algorithmic art may invite a question and arouse curiosity as much as it satisfies visual aesthetic criteria associated with traditional media.

Any of the preceding devices (and no doubt many besides) may be used to convey a sense of the sublime. All of them expose us to our own limitations in terms of comprehension, experience, or endurance, while simultaneously presenting us with the power to reason about or to encapsulate a phenomenon in a word or representation, or the opportunity to walk away unharmed. Of course, the context in which the preceding occurrences and objects are encountered will have much to say about the extent to which the sensation derived relates to art. However, the potential to employ any of these basic devices for artistic purposes in search of the sublime experience is present.

13.3 Sublime Software

Now we return to the issue at hand — writing artificial life software for artistic purposes. There are, of course, infinitely many reasons why an artist might wish to do this. Let us suppose in this instance that the goal was software that surprised, not only a viewer, but also the artist who fashioned the work. This is in keeping with a proposal made elsewhere by the author [6]. The surprise required might not be a trivial one-off shock, but a genuine and continuing fascination with the novelty of the outcome generated, combined with a sense of being lost in a complex world beyond one's grasp. The work requires an aesthetic quality that exhibits the character listed above as *intricacy* and also at the level listed as *curiosity*.

It so happens of course, that the techniques of artificial life are well suited to this application, Conway's *Game of Life* cellular automata (CA) being a case in point [9]. CAs are fascinating for their ability to (practically, if not theoretically) produce ever-fresh patterns. Like clockwork automata or Calder's mobiles, the patterns produced may fall well within a limited domain, often even a cycle. However, especially in a large-scale configuration, there is always some aspect of the system that remains to be discovered in the vast universe these interactions define.

The innovative design pair, the Eames, understood this aspect of a complex visual field. They used their understanding effectively in the 1964 New York, World Fair exhibit for IBM to build a multiscreen cinema. The screens displayed related material simultaneously in such a way as to make it impossible to view all of the footage in detail. Viewers could watch the spectacle as a whole and see it as a multiscreen montage, or they could pick and choose elements to observe in detail — much as one examines a complex clockwork machine, a microscopic world, or a beehive — piecemeal.

On a related topic, Tufte indicates the benefits for presenting information in parts grouped carefully together, "Panorama, vista and prospect deliver to viewers the freedom of choice that derives from an overview, a capacity to compare and sort through detail" [25]. Such considerations also assist painters in creating worlds that reward careful study of their detail. For example, Hieronymous Bosch's *Garden of Delights* (c. 1500) portrays a world over which the eye may wander at will as it takes in relationships between couples, groups of people, sections of garden, and so on. Of course, where the object under study is static, a viewer may take the time to examine and re-examine the various parts of a display and avoid missing anything of importance (as Tufte would prefer). When the object is constantly changing, as with multiscreen cinema or a *Game of Life* run, an investigation of one element results in irrevocably missed information about another. Under these circumstances, no matter where a viewers' attention is focused, she is left with the impression that an abundance of chances was missed. Her faculties are fundamentally unable to absorb all that is before her.

While one of the attractions of the *Game of Life* occurs at the visual level, the software is also an attractive subject for philosophical discussions concerning emergence and complex systems [3]. It contains a vast number of possibilities within the bounds of its simple virtual-physics. While its transition rules may be considered in terms of biological analogy (overcrowding and mutual support of living cells, for instance), the result is still an intrinsically digital system. Cells are in one of exactly two states, and their behavior is completely deterministic. Yet from this emerges a milieu of flickering forms that somehow *suggest* life, without mimicking it.

The question "How does it work?" is implied by any given run of the *Game of Life* in which it is recognized that the output is not at all random, but highly organized and structured according to its own internal rules. Even once the viewer know these rules, that they are capable of creating such a bewildering outcome remains a source of fascination to the artificial life researcher and to the newly informed student alike.

13.4 The Betrayal of Points and Lines

Having briefly discussed the concepts of wonder and the sublime, this section now addresses the representational schemes that may be used to bring the digital realm to the realm of sublime experience. Of particular interest is the way in which points of light may be used to give the bounded computer screen the appearance of *intricacy* and an ability to expose *unbounded* space (see the earlier categorization of methods for approaching the sublime). This has already been touched upon while discussing the *Game of Life* in the previous section.

Taking the lead of Kandinsky, the discussion begins with the geometric point, an invisible thing too perfect to exist [13]. An artist may approximate it by instigating a collision between a sharp tool and a flat plane. The artist's point has character. It is not one of Plato's Ideal Forms, but it is beautiful for all its imperfection.

The point may also be displayed on a CRT or LCD monitor. The size and shape of the smallest displayable shape are dictated by the display technology. Beyond a single pixel the character of the point may also be altered, albeit with less potential for variation than in the analog world.

Anyone familiar with Islamic or Roman mosaics, medieval tapestry, Pointillist painting, the television screen, or a computer monitor is aware that in vast numbers, the point may vanish in an ocean of its kind. Here it becomes simply one atom in a larger texture — mobs of points are not as honest as individuals.

If the draftsman drags a pen across the page, another form results, a line. Like the point, the line seems unpretentious, especially if it is straight and completely surrounded by white space. However, place a few straight lines together and important transformations may take place. For example, the *triangle* is born of three lines and is eventful for its ability to enclose space on the plane and thereby define a boundary, and with it, an object. The second transformation of relevance here is the apparent shift into three dimensions brought about by the *Cartesian axes*. This is also born of three lines and is eventful for its ability to *suggest* space that extends beyond the plane in which the lines are drawn.

Under some circumstances the three lines that represent Cartesian space may appear simple and flat; under others, however, the third dimension "pops" out of the plane at the viewer. It is outside the scope of this chapter to discuss how this second transformation occurs; the interested reader is referred to [12]. For now it is sufficient if it be acknowledged that at least in some cases, three Cartesian axes suggest a volume where there is none, this being (of course) the principle that underlies Renaissance painting and a host of styles up to and, of relevance to this discussion, including modern computer graphics. Using only lines one may build a two-dimensional representation of a solid object in unbounded three-dimensional space.

To return at this stage to the *Game of Life*, the system is typically displayed as, strangely enough, a grid of points. The choice of the point as the basic element of the simulation excludes the misleading suggestions of line drawings. Still, even within this limited visual space, the CA is successful at its evocation of life and with it *intricacy*. How can similar systems expose or suggest spaces that are infinitely large *and* intricate?

13.5 Moving Beyond Two Dimensions

The *Game of Life* and CA-based generative art such as *IMA Traveler* [7] work in the domain of points and suggestion, as outlined earlier. With a computer monitor it is easy to represent lines and surfaces using a multitude of similarly lit pixels.

IMA Traveler, while working with points in a plane, recursively sub-divides these, giving the viewer the sensation of a bottomless plummet. This is an interesting perceptual phenomenon when it is considered that by continuously zooming in on a two-dimensional image (the points aren't modeled in three-dimensional space) one can instill the sensation of motion through a continuous and infinitely detailed universe. The fractal zooms of the 1980s are perhaps the most familiar and overused form of this same trick. In their work *Powers of Ten* (1968), the Eames also utilized rapid scale shifts to produce a film of great effect.

The CA and its artistic derivatives draw attention for evoking natural phenomena and for prompting the viewer to determine the underlying principles by which they operate. Not all artificial life software is of this type, even if it is important to the research field for other reasons. One may propose a full range of works of which the CA-based software falls near the center. This spectrum runs from abstract systems such as Ray's *Tierra* [20], to clearly representational systems such as Sims' *Virtual Creatures* [23].

Ray's work emphasizes the principles of selection and evolution through rapid reproduction, and has itself proved a useful model and a starting point for other researchers such as Pargellis [18] (discussed ahead) to further the study of evolutionary systems. However, Ray's work does not have the visceral appeal that visual cellular automata may have. *Tierra*'s space of machine code instructions is abstract and not typically represented in such a way as to be comprehended by the eye. A fascination with *Tierra* arises through careful study and is predicated upon an understanding of the core workings of the system and the way in which the instructions interact and occupy memory. This contrasts with the CA, in which the rules need not be known to understand the system at one level. It is this first level of visceral comprehension that prompts theorizing about what underlies the behavior of the CA cells.

At the opposite end of the spectrum, Sims' *Virtual Creatures* fascinate researcher and layperson alike. His jumping, swimming, running and limping creations are so full of character that one easily takes a leap of faith by referring to them as "creatures," even though their bodies are clearly rendered cuboids. This leap erases any chance of a viewer posing the question, "How does it work?" because it is implied by the visualization that these *are* creatures! While a graphics researcher or software engineer may see Sims' video and wonder at the means of producing such marvelous results, this question is not implied by the creatures' visualization as it is by the CA. The virtual creatures do not operate according to unknown rules; we are tricked into believing that they operate according to the rules all creatures obey. There is seemingly nothing here to discover.

This aspect of Sims' creatures is largely due to the way in which they are visualized — the representations of three-dimensional space, of solids and their surfaces, of friction and other forces are all customary. In this case the visualization is prescriptive, rather than evocative. McCormack's *Eden*, which was constructed as an artwork (see article in this issue and [16]), similarly represents organisms and their real-world behaviors. But it displays them using iconic forms on a two-dimensional grid (mapped to an "X" in three-dimensional space) and in a world nevertheless governed by rules of survival, energy, mating, and space, based on those of the real world. In contrast with Sims' work, this underlying link to the physical world is not prescribed and takes some experience to decipher if a viewer is able to decipher it at all. Although the system is still considerably more representational than the *Game of Life*, what remains is an aesthetic visual experience akin to viewing an intricate CA, coupled with the implicit question, "How does it work?"

This discussion of Ray's, Sims', and McCormack's work is in no way intended as an evaluation of their worth. These examples only serve to illustrate the various ways in which a viewer may contemplate a generative process and its outcome, and therefore the various ways in which the devices may be employed for artistic purposes. The next section takes current generative artworks and artificial life software as a starting point. It explores areas into which artists might move to further expand the sense of wonder their works inspire.

13.6 Spaces That Build Themselves

An artist aiming to produce a system capable of sustaining a continuous increase in complexity shares a goal with many artificial life researchers [1]. Why would an artist wish to do such a thing? To return to the ideas discussed earlier, the artist searching for the computational sublime would find it, perhaps in its ultimate form, by generating an experience of open-ended complexity governed by processes instantiated on a computer. The loss of control would be complete — the system would build its own structures and define its own universe. It would do this according to human-engineered rules, yet in a way that defies humans to anticipate its outcome.

This system would be following the code a programmer laid down and run on a machine an engineer designed. Would this device behave in a way about which we could easily reason? In this conflict between control and riot lies the sublime. Mary Shelley knew this well — her friends and contemporaries were much interested in the sublime — when she vividly penned *Frankenstein* and his monster run amok [22]. For a historical overview of theories of the sublime in this period, see [11].

How *does* one write code that will produce the hierarchically organized composite structures associated with life and ever-increasing complexity? If we consider the cells of a CA grid as analogous to molecules, and higher-level emergent structures such as gliders as analogous to organelles (a far stretch when one considers the complexity of interactions a physical molecule or an organelle may undergo, and the feeble interactions between neighboring cellular automata), can we code the system so that still larger-scale groupings of structure occur? Can it produce structures at the level of single cells, a multicellular organism, or an ecosystem?

In theory, even gliders, spinners, and other structures of the *Game of Life* may be carefully arranged into larger-scale units (such as a self-reproducing machine incorporating a universal Turing machine, if one has the patience to arrange its 10^{13} cells [3]). The question remains though, is it possible that such a higher-level structure will appear of its own accord? If software could be arranged to facilitate this, the structures that arose would do so on their own terms and *might* therefore behave in ways the creator did not envisage.

This *might* provide an effective source of complexity to assist an artist in his search for the computational sublime.

If theories about the process of natural increase in complexity (such as those extensively discussed by Kauffman, for example [14]) hold true in virtual systems, then the elements in the virtual space might self-assemble into simple stable structures. Perhaps, if the virtual physics and chemistry of the world allowed it, simple reactions might occur, possibly some in auto- and cross-catalytic sets such as those described by Dorin [4]. These might form the basis of a recognizable topology with the bare bones of a metabolism. What next?

As natural evolution demonstrates, one way to achieve an increase in complexity beyond this is to have the structures engage in a reproductive battle against one another for resources (see [24]). Pargellis' system *Amoeba* manages to initiate reproduction randomly. It establishes conditions in which practical CPU and memory resources are sufficient for a replicator to appear spontaneously from the prebiotic soup [18]. In a *Tierra* run such an event is much less likely than in *Amoeba*. Hence Ray initially seeded *Tierra*'s population with a replicator to allow evolution to commence. The problem of coding a simulation that can make the leap from self-organization to spontaneous evolution of structure seems (as far as this author is aware) unmade by any researcher.

Setting aside the leap from self-organization to evolution, even though systems solely employing artificial evolution are readily implemented, getting these to mimic natural evolution's progression from molecules to organelles to cells and on to multicellular creatures and ecosystems has proved a stumbling block. Although worlds such as *SOCA* give rise to auto- and cross-catalytic sets, *Amoeba* may randomly give rise to replicators, and *Polyworld* [28] gives rise to simple communities, there has been limited success (arguably no success) in writing software that encompasses more than one of these important level shifts without resorting to abstractions so high that the simulations they are contained within become trivial.

The reasons for this difficulty are not yet clear. In part, current computational resources may be to blame. However, this is quite likely only a part of the story, and maybe only a small part at that. Rasmussen, for instance, has suggested that the bottom level of our simulations are not complex enough to give rise to the kind of multilayered outcomes we desire. He proposes that only by adding complexity to the bottom-level elements of a simulation can we expect to gain extra levels of organized structure on top of any earlier ones [19]. This claim seems to contradict the "complex systems dogma" that explicitly treats complex phenomena as emergent from simple interactions. Since in Rasmussen's paper notions of "complexity" and "adding complexity" are only loosely defined, it is not clear exactly how and to what extent this might be the case. This is discussed in detail elsewhere [5].

Rasmussen supports his view with a claim about a model he has constructed. Gross and McMullin [10] argue that this model does *not*, in fact, demonstrate the emergence of multiple levels, and that a similar outcome can be obtained without adding complexity at the base layer.

It is outside the scope of this chapter to become too deeply embroiled in this battle. Rasmussen's suggestion may in some sense prove true. Either way, further questions need to be addressed simultaneously. Might there be a limit to all this "complexity adding"? How much added complexity is necessary to move from one level to the next? Questions like these remain open and continue to be debated.

Besides issues raised above, there may be fundamental problems with current approaches to solving the problem. It is possible that simulations on current computer architectures and employing computer programs as they are currently understood will turn out to be practically limited in their ability to produce the kind of truly open-ended complexity increase required. Issues of available resource consumption are an obvious reason why infinite increase is impossible; however, are there reasons why *any* interesting string of increases in complexity may be impossible with current programming and computer technology? These questions remain a topic for a further chapter and, in one sense (counter to the claims of the Renaissance writer Vasari about artists surpassing nature [27]), the hope of one day creating a virtual space as multi-faceted as nature remains faint.

13.7 Conclusion

Although the limitations of our abilities to code multiple-level hierarchies are apparent, clearly this does not imply that our art is similarly constrained. The element of the sublime in a Caspar David Friedrich canvas does not arise from the intricacy of its mechanism, but from contemplating nature and our place in it from behind the safety of a picture plane. Even more apparent is the irrelevance of intricacy and nature (taken literally) to postmodern interpretations of the sublime such as those discussed by Jean-François Lyotard [26]. Hence works such as the dark canvasses produced in Mark Rothko's later years may be discussed in terms of their contribution to the *postmodern sublime*. The sublime does not lie *in* a work, rather the work may act to trigger a sublime experience in a viewer. In the case of Lyotard's ideas, this relates to a sense of formlessness and therefore of things that may be better left unpresented.

Since our machines are faster at mathematics than we are they will always maintain the ability to play the role of mediator between us and the vast computational spaces outside our direct experience. Perhaps one day these same machines will be able to take us beyond spaces that look more and more familiar as we travel through them, into spaces that increase in complexity and continue to surprise us. Here the sublime experience of nature's vastness and ferocity may be rivaled through a sense of the computational sublime. We will be sensing a space rendered maybe with points on a plane and computed on-the-fly by our fastest machines, and it will seem to us as terrible and delightful as standing on an icy summit surveying all the world.

References

1. Bedau MA, McCaskill JS, Packard NH, Rasmussen S, Adami C, Green DG, Harvey I, Ikegami T, Kaneko K, Ray TS (2000) Open Problems in Artificial Life. In: Artificial Life 6, Bedau and Taylor (eds.). MIT Press, pp 363–376.
2. Bern M (1999) Art Shows at PARC. In: Art and Innovation, Harris (ed). The MIT Press, pp 259–277.
3. Dennett DC (1991) Real Patterns. Journal of Philosophy 88:27–51.
4. Dorin A (2000) Creating a Physically-based, Virtual-Metabolism with Solid Cellular Automata. In: Proceedings Artificial Life 7, Bedau et al (eds.). MIT Press, pp 13–20.
5. Dorin A, McCormack J (2002) Self-Assembling Dynamical Hierarchies. In: Proceedings of Artificial Life 8, Standish et al (eds.). MIT Press, pp 423–428.
6. Dorin A (2004) The Virtual Ecosystem as Generative Electronic Art. In: Proceedings of 2nd European Workshop on Evolutionary Music and Art, Applications of Evolutionary Computing: EvoWorkshops 2004, Coimbra, Portugal, April 5-7, Günther RR, Cagnoni S, Branke J et al. (eds.), Springer-Verlag Heidelberg, pp 467–470.
7. Driessens E and Verstappen M (2001) Keynote presentation in Proceedings of Second Iteration, second international conference on generative systems in the electronic arts, Dorin (ed.), CEMA, Melbourne, Australia, pp 12–13.
8. Feagin SL (1995) Sublime. In: The Cambridge Dictionary of Philosophy, Audi (ed.), Cambridge University Press, p 774.
9. Gardner M (1970) The Fantastic Combinations of John Conway's New Solitaire Game, "Life". Scientific American 223:120–123.
10. Gross D, McMullin B (2001) Is It the Right Ansatz? In: Artificial Life 7, Bedau and Taylor (eds.). MIT Press, pp 355–365.
11. Hipple WJ (1957) The Beautiful, the Sublime, and the Picturesque in Eighteenth-Century British Aesthetic Theory. Southern Illinois University Press.
12. Hoffman DD (2000) Visual Intelligence: How We Create What We See. Norton.
13. Kandinsky W (1979) Point and Line to Plane, Dover Publications, New York (first published 1926).
14. Kauffman SA (1993) The Origins of Order. Oxford University Press.
15. Longinus (1963) On the Sublime. Translated by Havell. In: Aristotle's Poetics, Demetritus on Style, Longinus on the Sublime, Everyman's Library, Dutton New York, pp 133–202 (first written c 250 AD).
16. McCormack J (2001) Eden: An Evolutionary Sonic Ecosystem. In: Advances in Artificial Life, 6th European Conference, Kelemen and Sosik (eds.). Springer, pp 133–142.
17. McCormack J, Dorin A (2001) Art, Emergence, and the Computational Sublime. In: Proceedings of Second Iteration, Second international conference on generative systems in the electronic arts, Dorin (ed.), CEMA, Melbourne, Australia, pp 67–81.

18. Pargellis AN (2001) Digital Life Behaviour in the Amoeba World, Artificial Life 7, Bedau and Taylor (eds.). MIT Press, pp 63–75.
19. Rasmussen S, Baas NA, Mayer B, Nilsson M, Olesen MW (2001) Ansatz for Dynamical Hierarchies, Artificial Life 7, Bedau and Taylor (eds.). MIT Press, pp 329–353.
20. Ray TS (1991) An Approach to the Synthesis of Life. In: Artificial Life II, Langton, Taylor, Farmer, Rasmussen (eds.). Addison-Wesley, pp 371–408.
21. Rower ASC (1998) Calder Sculpture, National Gallery of Art, Washington DC, Universe.
22. Shelley M (1989) Frankenstein, the Modern Prometheus, first published 1818, reprint, Joseph, M.K. (ed.). Oxford Univeristy Press.
23. Sims K (1994) Evolving Virtual Creatures. In: Proceedings of SIGRRAPH 1994, ACM Press, pp 15–34.
24. Taylor T (2002) Creativity in Evolution: Individuals, Interactions and Environments. In: Creative Evolutionary Systems, Bentley and Corne (eds.). Academic Press, pp 79–108.
25. Tufte ER (1990) Envisioning Information. Graphics Press.
26. van de Vall R (1995) Silent Visions, Lyotard on the Sublime. In: The Contemporary Sublime, Sensibilities of Transcendence and Shock, Hodges (ed.). Art and Design. VCH Publishers, pp 69–75.
27. Vasari G (1976) The Lives of the Artists, first published 1568, translated by Bull G. Reprint Penguin Books.
28. Yaeger L (1994) Computational Genetics, Physiology, Metabolism, Neural Systems, Learning, Vision and Behavior or Polyworld: Life in a New Context. In: Proceedings, Artificial Life III, SFI Studies in the Sciences of Complexity, Langton (ed.). Addison-Wesley, pp 263–298.

A

Appendix: Artificial Life Software

Related chapter, software name and license type	Description	Web site (http://), availability, requirements
1. Avida. Free and open source (GPL).	A digital world in which simple computer programs mutate and evolve. Avida can be used to study questions and perform experiments in evolutionary dynamics and theoretical biology.	dllab.caltech.edu/avida/ Linux, Unix, MacOS X, MS Windows
2. Framsticks GUI. Free for educational and research use, otherwise shareware.	A powerful graphical user interface (GUI) for the Framsticks simulator of 3D life forms.	www.frams.alife.pl MS Windows
2. Framsticks Theater. Free for educational and research use, otherwise shareware.	Easy-to-use application that illustrates basic phenomena like genes and genetics, mutation, evolution, user-driven evolution and artificial selection, etc. Recommended for education (e.g., biology, evolution, optimization, simulation, robotics), illustration, entertainment, screen-saving mode, etc.	www.frams.alife.pl Linux, Unix, IRIX, MS Windows and more
2. Framsticks simulator CLI, server, clients, editor (FRED), viewer. Free. Clients and FRED are open source.	CLI is a command-line interface for the Framsticks simulator. Network server and clients are used to separate simulation engine and user interfaces. FRED is a user-friendly graphical editor of creatures. Viewer visualizes 3D creatures grown from genotypes.	www.frams.alife.pl FRED and network clients: all platforms (Java required) Other programs: Linux, Unix, MS Windows, and more

A Appendix: Artificial Life Software

3. Nerve Garden. Free, Java sources available (GPL).	A work in progress designed to provide a compelling experience of a virtual terrarium that exhibits properties of growth, decay, and energy transfer reminiscent of a simple ecosystem. The project combines a number of methods and technologies, including L-systems, Java, cellular automata, and VRML.	`www.biota.org/nervegarden/` All platforms that provide Java 1.1 and VRML97 within a web browser (including MS Windows, MacOS, Linux)
4. GenePool. Free for educational use.	An animated artificial life simulation demonstrating evolution of swimming skill via autonomous mating among hundreds of physically based organisms. Mate choice affects the evolution of morphology and motor control. Various interactive controls allow exploration of the simulation while it is running.	`www.ventrella.com/GenePool/gene_pool.html` MS Windows
5. Sodarace. Free to use and develop.	The online olympics pitting human creativity against machine learning in a competition to design robots that race over 2D terrains using the Sodaconstructor virtual construction kit.	`www.sodarace.net` All platforms (Java plug-in required)
6. Recursive Porous Agent Simulation Toolkit (Repast). Free and open source (BSD).	An advanced agent-based modeling toolkit. Repast supports the development of extremely flexible models of living social agents, but is not limited to modeling living social entities alone.	`repast.sourceforge.net` Repast for Java and Repast for Python Scripting: all platforms (requires JRE to run models and JDK to create models) Repast.Net: Windows 2000/XP (requires a .Net framework to run models and .Net compiler to create models)

Related chapter, software name and license type	Description	Web site (`http://`), availability, requirements
7. EINSTein. Freely available; source code will be released.	Multiagent-based simulation of land combat; includes agent personalities, weapons behaviors, intelligent targeting, and terrain effects.	`www.cna.org/isaac/` MS Windows
8. StarLogo. Free for educational and research use.	A programmable complex systems modeling environment for students and teachers.	`education.mit.edu/starlogo` All platforms (Java plug-in required)
9. Eden. Copyrighted, personal edition available on CD-ROM.	An interactive evolutionary system where creatures evolve different strategies using sound. Individual creatures use a classifier-based learning system. Over time, they learn to adapt and survive in their environment. In many instances this involves using sound, so as the system evolves users hear the musical compositions of the creatures.	`www.csse.monash.edu.au/~jonmc/projects/eden.html` MacOS X. OpenGL and stereo speakers required
10. Mirek's Cellebration (MCell and MJCell). Free and open source (GPL).	A feature-rich cellular automata explorer. Its main purpose is enjoying existing and creating new rules and patterns of Conway's Game of Life and other cellular automata. The program supports 15 different CA families and is equipped with 300+ rules and over 1000 pattern files.	`www.mirekw.com/ca/` MCell: MS Windows. MJCell: all platforms (Java plug-in required)

11. Discrete Dynamics Lab (DDLab). Free for personal use. License required for commercial or institutional use. Source code may be available on request.	Interactive graphics software for studying multivalue discrete dynamical networks including cellular automata and random Boolean networks. Unique in its ability to generate basins of attraction. Space-time patterns can be generated in 1D, 2D (square or hex), or 3D. Many tools and functions are available for creating the network (its rules and wiring), setting the initial state, analyzing the dynamics, and amending parameters on-the-fly.	www.ddlab.org Linux, Unix, MacOS X, DOS, IRIX or MS Windows command line
12. SBART. Free.	A design support tool to create an abstract 2D computer graphics image based on artificial selection, which was originally proposed as Artificial Evolution by Karl Sims.	www.intlab.soka.ac.jp/~unemi/sbart/ Ver. 1: Unix (Linux, FreeBSD, Solaris, HP-UX, IRIX), requires Motif 1.2 (or LessTif) and jpeg6 library Ver. 2: MacOS 8, 9, requires QuickTime 3 or later Ver. 3: MacOS X 10.1 or later, requires QuickTime 5 or later, G4 or better recommended
12. SBEAT. Free.	A composition support tool to create short musical phrases and rhythms based on artificial selection. Includes utility mechanisms to build up a complete tune.	www.intlab.soka.ac.jp/~unemi/sbeat/ MacOS 8, 9, X. Requires CarbonLib 1.3 or later for MacOS 8 and 9, and QuickTime 5 or later

Index

actuator 218
aesthetic selection 63, 81, 225
agent personality 153
agent-based modeling 117, 145
Amoeba 332
artifact 325
artificial life 116, 211, 323
autopoiesis 158
avatar 76
Avida 6, 338

battlefield 152
Biota 73
Boolean networks 263
Braitenberg's vehicles 147

cell 17, 45
CelLab 235
Cellsprings 235
Cellular 235
cellular automata 147, 233, 263, 327
cellular automata, binary 237
cellular automata, cyclic 238
cellular automata, totalistic 237, 273
cellular automata, voting 245
cellular automata, WireWorld 250
chemostat 30
chemotaxis 135
Chojo 78
Collidoscope 235
combat models 144
Connection Machine 195
Core War 5
cybernetics 212

Darwin Pond 81
Discrete Dynamics Lab, DDLab 235, 263, 341
dynamics, global 268
dynamics, local 268

Echo 213
ecosystem 30, 60
Eden 213, 340
edge of chaos 264
effector 42
EINSTein 147, 340
embryology 95

Flatland 89
Framsticks 37, 95, 338

Game of Life 69, 233, 242, 249, 327
Game of Life, weighted 247
garden-of-Eden 269
gene 45, 168
GenePool 81, 339
genetic algorithm 50, 82, 168
genome 5, 11, 43, 221
genotype 16, 43, 94, 101, 305, 323
Germinator 69

hypercycle 130

Interactive Evolutionary Computing 303
ISAAC 147

L-systems 68

Lanchester equations 143
Lanchesterian combat 159
land combat 145
Life32 235
LifeDrop 95
Living Melodies 213
Lotka–Volterra 61, 144

mathematical sublime 324
MCell 233, 340
mutations 15, 44

Nerve Garden 67, 339
neuron 41

phenotype 16, 44, 94, 221, 226, 306, 323
polymorphism 92
polyvore 75
Polyworld 332
predator–prey model 60, 144, 206

receptor 42
Repast 115, 339

SARCASim 235
SBART 302, 304, 341
SBEAT 302, 306, 341
scheduling 17
self-organized criticality 161
sensor 42, 217
Sims 77, 82, 330
Sodaconstructor 97
SodaPlay 95
Sodarace 97, 339
Sonomorph 306
sound 222
StarLogo 187, 235, 340
sugarscape 132
swarming 163
swimbot 81

Telegarden 69
Tierra 5, 69, 82, 332
tropism 79

virtual machine 9